AF361450

Lee Kuan Yew:
The Beliefs Behind the Man

Lee Kuan Yew: The Beliefs Behind the Man

Michael D. Barr

GEORGETOWN UNIVERSITY PRESS / WASHINGTON, D.C.

Georgetown University Press, Washington, D.C. 20007
© Michael D. Barr 2000
Typesetting by the Nordic Institute of Asian Studies
Printed and bound in Great Britain

Library of Congress Cataloging-in-Publication Data

Barr, Michael D.
    Lee Kuan Yew, the beliefs behind the man / Michael D. Barr.
        p. cm.
    Includes bibliographical references and index.
    ISBN 0-87840-816-9 (cloth)
        1. Lee, Kuan Yew, 1923– 2. Singapore - Politics and government.
    3. Prime ministers–Singapore–Biography. I. Title.

DS610.73.L45 B37 2000
959.5705'092–dc21
[B]   00-039327
                                                                      CIP

Contents

Acknowledgements

In the several years I devoted to researching and writing this book, I have accumulated many debts of gratitude, both large and small. The book is a slightly updated and modified version of my PhD thesis of the same name, which I undertook in the Department of History at the University of Queensland. My primary debts are to the History Department itself, and to those associated with this phase of the work.

First, I need to thank my main supervisor, Professor Martin Stuart-Fox. He challenged me to extend my analysis well beyond my comfort zone and I can see clearly that the finished product is a much deeper and more rounded work as a result of his advice. I also owe a particular debt of gratitude to Fr James Minchin and Dr Robert Cribb. Fr Minchin is an Anglican priest and the author of *No Man Is an Island: A Study of Singapore's Lee Kuan Yew.* Although he has had no official role in my work, I have been the beneficiary of both his academic and personal generosity. Not only did he make several decisive interventions that affected the course of my research, but despite his heavy duties as a parish priest, he has read and commented upon my entire manuscript. Dr Cribb was my supervisor for the first year of my research until he accepted an appointment to the Nordic Institute of Asian Studies in Copenhagen. Even after he shifted to the other side of the world, he continued to read some of my work and offered timely advice. Notwithstanding my debts to Prof. Stuart-Fox, Fr Minchin and Dr Cribb, my conclusions and any errors are my own.

I am grateful also to a number of people in Singapore, England, Malaysia and Australia who responded generously to my appeals for help even though I was a complete stranger. This includes the many people listed in my bibliography who allowed me to interview them or engage them in correspondence, but there were also many others who assisted me in less public ways. First in this list are my friends at Bukit Timah, who offered me hospitality and friendship during my research trip to Singapore. I do not know how I would have managed without their generosity. Many others gave me advice, introductions and often much-welcome meals and company. I take nothing for granted and wish to thank them all.

I also received some assistance from institutions. The Ministry of Education, Singapore, for instance, was kind enough to give me permission to inspect the Raffles Institution Archives, and the Singapore Press Holdings Library gave me uninhibited access to its microfilm files on Lee. The National University of Singapore Library and the Institute of Southeast Asian Studies each allowed me to use their resources. I am grateful to all of these bodies.

It would be remiss of me not to thank also those who have assisted and advised me in the process of turning my thesis into a book. This includes my thesis examiners and the anonymous peer reviewers who offered valuable criticism and advice, the Queensland University of Technology, which offered me a Fellowship to see the book through its final stages, and Gerald Jackson, editor-in-chief at the Nordic Institute of Asian Studies, who has nursed me through the traumas of publication.

I should also mention that a version of Chapter 6 appeared in the *Journal of Contemporary Asia*, vol. 29, no. 2, (1999). I am grateful to JCA for permission to re-use this material.

On a more personal level, I am particularly grateful to my parents who have been a constant source of stability and support.

MDB

Introduction

My good friend, Fr James Minchin (author of *No Man Is an Island: A Study of Singapore's Lee Kuan Yew*), has told me that I am lucky because I have managed to write a critical study of Lee Kuan Yew without becoming emotionally involved in my subject. I have never met Lee, and so have not been overwhelmed by his formidable person. None of my friends or acquaintances has suffered at his hands. Furthermore, I have no political agenda demanding that I demonise him, or paint him as an unblemished hero. Yet for all of my emotional dispassion about my subject, I found that he engaged me completely as I tried to untangle the skein of his life and his political thought for my PhD thesis in the University of Queensland History Department. It has left me feeling as though I should have a personal relationship with this man, and it is only by a peculiar oversight that I do not.

Of course, none of this means that I do not have strong opinions about Lee, or that I came to my research without preconceptions or a plan. I am content to leave the book to speak for my current opinions, but perhaps I should say something about my objectives and my preconceptions.

At the outset I should warn the reader that I did not set out to write a biography, and I do not believe that I have done so, despite the presence of strong biographical elements. This book is an exploration of the development of Lee Kuan Yew's political thought, taking the trail back as far as I could, seeking both the emotional and intellectual sources of his worldview. Hence the book places great emphasis on Lee's childhood and young adulthood when his character, preconceptions and reactive impulses were being forged amidst daily experience. It also places great stock on his early public life, when he was learning how to relate his preconceptions and personality to leadership and politics in colonial and post-colonial Singapore. This emphasis has led to a telescoping of my picture of Lee's life, with the later period – especially the

1980s and 1990s – being considered more for the light they throw on his early formation than as periods of interest in their own right. Although I had no deliberate plan to treat the later period so cavalierly, it must be admitted that it has made it much easier to retain the book's focus on the development of Lee's thinking. This luxury would not have been possible if my approach had been strictly biographical.

If my academic approach was slightly unusual, so were my preconceptions about Lee. Unlike most Western academics, I came to study him as a fairly uncritical admirer, and I approached my subject with a strong, though somewhat misplaced sense of identification. In retrospect, the basis of my perceived affinity was rather slim: anti-communism, a rejection of Western libertarianism, and a predisposition towards admiring strong, effective government. I had just come from writing an Honours thesis that covered the period of Lee's heroic struggle against the communists in the late 1950s and early 1960s, and I was full of admiration for his courage, intelligence and leadership ability. I still stand in awe of these characteristics, and I am still an admirer, though I am rather more critical these days. Nevertheless, in the course of my research I inevitably improved my understanding of Lee, and came to realise that the areas of commonality were more coincidence than any natural points of affinity, and that at heart our respective worldviews were poles apart – he full of 'isms' (progressivism, elitism, social evolutionism, Chinese suprematism), and I the conservative, social democratic, Australian Catholic.

Yet perhaps my preconceptions served me well enough. Fr Minchin has suggested that because of my unusual perspective I asked questions that others did not, and recognised something that others have missed. I hope he is right.

Abbreviations

There has been minimal use of abbreviations, but the following glossary may, nevertheless, prove useful.

AMP   Association of Muslim Professionals
AWARE   Association of Women for Action and Research
BS   Barisan Sosialis (Socialist Front)
CCC   Citizens' Consultative Committee
CDAC   Chinese Development Assistance Council
CEC   Central Executive Committee (of a political party)
CPF   Central Provident Fund
EA   Eurasian Association
GRC   Group Representative Constituency (a multi-member electorate)
HDB   Housing and Development Board
ISD   Internal Security Department (successor of the colonial Special Branch)
LF   Labour Front
MC   Management Committee (of a Community Centre)
MCA   Malayan Chinese Association (after 1964, Malaysian Chinese Association)
MCP   Malayan Communist Party (later Communist Party of Malaya)
MENDAKI   Council for the Development of the Malay-Muslim Community (before 1989, Council for the Development of Muslim Children)
MIC   Malayan Indian Congress (after 1964 Malaysian Indian Congress)
NCMP   Non-Constituency Member of Parliament
NMP   Nominated Member of Parliament
NSS   Nature Society of Singapore

NTUC   National Trades Union Congress
NUS   National University of Singapore
PA   People's Association
PAP   People's Action Party
PP   Progressive Party
PUB   Public Utilities Board
RC   Residents' Committee
RI   Raffles Institution
SAF   Singapore Armed Forces
SAP   Special Assistance Plan (for elite Chinese-language schools)
SDP   Singapore Democratic Party
SINDA   Singapore Indian Development Association
SLP   Singapore Labour Party (forerunner of the Labour Front)
SPA   Singapore People's Association
SPP   Singapore People's Party
TC   Town Council
UMNO   United Malays' National Organisation
WP   Workers' Party

Note on Transliteration of Chinese

Chinese names and words have been given a single, consistent spelling
and rendered in Pinyin, regardless of the style used in the original quota-
tions. The exception to this rule is the bibliography where original spelling
has been retained.

· 1 ·

Singapore's Lee Kuan Yew

The question is often asked whether Lee Kuan Yew was influenced by the writings of a particular thinker or philosopher. Was he influenced by the writings of Confucius or Mao Zedong? Is he today, subconsciously perhaps, following a pattern of thought set during his formative years in schools and colleges in Singapore, in Cambridge? What forms the basis of his thinking?

Alex Josey, *Lee Kuan Yew: The Struggle for Singapore*, Singapore: Angus & Robertson, 1974, pp. 31–32.

In 1968 a professional Asia-watcher called Willard Hanna wrote that 'Lee Kuan Yew ... deliberately, perversely and quite successfully makes an enigma of himself. ... The mystery is: ... what is his vision of his own and of Singapore's future?'[1] Thirty years later we are still grappling with these questions, and the emerging answers differ drastically from anything anyone could have guessed in the 1960s. Lee Kuan Yew, or Harry Lee, as he was known before he entered politics, has always been something of an enigma. He has earned immense domestic and international respect for the economic and political achievements he has won for Singapore, but there are many aspects of his life and career that have provided entertainment for a generation of political scientists and the occasional historian. Lee, for instance, was a socialist who transformed Singapore into a successful capitalist economy. He was a nationalist who opposed independence and a democrat who locked up his opponents. He was the anti-communist 'hard man' of Southeast Asia who in recent times has devoted himself to legitimising Communist Party rule in China and Hong Kong. He is also a multiracialist who, at the end of his career, has come out of the closet as a Chinese supremacist.

Yet interest in Lee is not based primarily on the apparent inconsistencies of his political postures. He is, after all, a politician and

1

inconsistencies in politicians are fairly commonplace. So why should Lee Kuan Yew be worthy of attention beyond the confines of Singapore and outside the halls of academia? The answer to this question is the fact that although Singapore rates barely a footnote in world politics or economics, Lee himself is a figure of international stature. He is credited not only with Singapore's economic miracle, but with being a leader of economic development throughout Asia. He is also a leading figure in the contemporary revival of Confucianism throughout the Chinese world and was the principal architect of the 'Asian values' campaign of the 1990s, which maintains – broadly speaking and at the risk of parodying the position – that democracy and human rights are culturally anathema to Asians, who are more interested in strong families, strong government, and economic prosperity. In short, Lee is at the forefront of both practical and theoretical efforts to reconcile undemocratic, illiberal elitism with the requirements of a prosperous capitalist state operating in the global economy.

The dimensions of Lee's international standing can be seen in many features of his life, not least being the four pages of solicited tributes reproduced at the beginning of the first volume of his memoirs.[2] In these pages, the current British Prime Minister competes with former American Presidents and Secretaries of State, and former British, European, Asian and Australian Prime Ministers to heap praise on to Lee. Most of these tributes are effusive, with only a handful showing signs of being an act of politeness. Yet perhaps the standing of the man can best be seen, not in the tributes of his admirers, but in those of his detractors. Such a tribute came from Lee's outspoken opponent in the 'Asian values' debate: the last Governor of Hong Kong, Chris Patten. In his highly polemical book, *East and West*, Patten treated Lee as his principal combatant and described him as 'the most intellectually rigorous of the exponents of ['Asian values'], its high priest if not its most obvious exemplar'.[3] Despite the fact that Lee had no direct connection with Hong Kong, he appears more frequently in Patten's book than anyone else except Patten himself.

...

It is difficult to overestimate the insignificance of Singapore without Lee. At 647.5 square kilometres it is a mere full stop at the end of the Malayan Peninsula. Its highest peak, Bukit Timah [Malay for 'Tin Hill'], could be walked without raising a sweat except for the incredibly oppressive humidity that overwhelms everyone on the island a few seconds after they step out of air-conditioning. Fortunately, almost everything in Lee Kuan Yew's Singapore is air-conditioned, at least for the swollen middle class. As one of the people I interviewed for this book explained to me: 'The humidity isn't so bad. You wake up in your air-con home, go to your air-con office in your air-con car and you hardly notice it'. And that just about typifies Lee's Singapore in two sentences. Everything works – except democracy. Everything is clean – except the red-light district where the foreign guest workers spend their evenings. Nearly everything is controlled and predictable and every creature comfort and opportunity is available to those with money, intelligence and energy – providing they follow the rules.

In many ways Singapore is as much an enigma as Lee himself. It was founded by Sir Stamford Raffles in virtual defiance of his superiors in the East India Company, and then only because the Dutch beat him to the islands of Sumatra's Riau Archipelago. Raffles secured the island as a trading post in 1819, and paid rent to the traditional Malay rulers for the privilege until Britain secured sovereignty in 1824. In 1826 Singapore was joined to the British settlements of Penang and Malacca to become the Straits Settlements, an arrangement which lasted, with only slight amendment, until the British created separate colonies of Malaya and Singapore after the Second World War. Raffles was not directly involved in Singapore for very long. Like an errant father, he was there at the start and then went off to pursue other dreams. Yet he did much to determine the character of the island. He recognised that Singapore's deep harbour and her strategic position at the junction of the Pacific and Indian Oceans were her only natural assets and determined to use them to the fullest. He made Singapore a free port, geared for entrepôt trade: a shop window linking India, China and Britain. He also determined that Singapore would be open to anyone of any race who wanted to work, thus opening the door to a flood of Chinese and Indian sojourners, many of whom stayed to make Singapore their home. By the time Lee Kuan Yew's great-grandfather, Lee Bok Boon, arrived in 1863, Singapore's population had grown from a few hundred to 80,000 of whom 62 per cent were Chinese, 16 per cent Indians and nearly 14 per cent Malays.[4] By the time of the 1947 Census, the population had grown to 945,000, of whom 79 per cent were Chinese, 7 per cent Indian and 10 per cent Malay;[5] proportions that did not vary drastically over the next fifty years, during which time the population grew to around 3 million. Although Singapore has always been open to workers of all races, Raffles determined from the start that each race would live in its own designated section of the city. Thus even today, Singapore still has Little India, Chinatown, and the last remnants of an Arab Quarter.

If Singapore rates no more than one footnote in history, that note must surely be its honour as the site of the end of the British Empire, when Fortress Singapore was captured by a bicycle-borne army of 'Asiatics' who had just swept their way down the Malayan Peninsula with frightening ease. Lee Kuan Yew was a young student at Raffles College when Singapore fell to the Japanese, and the effect on him was electric. Until this moment he had held the British in awe, and his highest aspiration was to imitate them. This cataclysm ended the world he knew and the world in which he expected to make his way as an English-educated 'King's Chinese'. The journey from being a 'Brown Englishman' to the leader of a Confucian revival movement is full of paradoxes. Some of these quandaries have become slightly less mysterious in recent years because Lee has become more openly reflective about his life as he approaches its end. His journey from being a Fabian socialist to a self-proclaimed 'economic liberal'[6] was canvassed frankly in his 1998 authorised biography, as was the development of his Chinese suprematism and his growing disenchantment with democracy.[7] Yet, despite his openness with his biographers, there is something dissatisfying about accepting at face value a person's own account of his career and his life. Even the most honest and uncomplicated person would be unlikely to have a comprehensive understanding of his or her actions and motivations, and Lee, as an active politician who has 'deliberately, perversely and quite successfully' made an enigma of himself, could hardly be described as uncomplicated.

Lee's complexity is reflected in the developing character of the present book. It began as a modest attempt to improve our understanding of the development of Lee Kuan Yew's political thought from a purely ideological perspective: an examination of the predominantly Western ideas which influenced his thinking as an adult. It soon became apparent, however, that this task could not be accomplished satisfactorily without examining the personal influences in Lee's life and his childhood to find the underlying, possibly unconscious premises of his worldview. This led to the realisation that the Sinic perspective could not be ignored: how have Lee's Chinese ethnicity and culture, however defined, influenced his worldview, his ideology and the development of his political thought? Thus, this book is biographical, but is not a biography. It presents a tightly argued thesis that attempts to explain – without explaining away – Lee Kuan Yew.

The methodology of research was very simple: the author relied primarily upon Lee's own words to identify his key ideas and the life experiences that helped to form them. These accounts were supplemented, put in context and sometimes challenged by secondary and other primary sources, but Lee's own words remained the central reference point throughout the project. There can be no doubt that the most significant established source was the official collection of Lee's speeches.[8] On their own, however, the established sources would have been a rather weak base from which to launch a project as ambitious as this one. The author regards himself as fortunate that he was able to make contact with a substantial number of people who have known Lee at various stages of his life, and that in nearly all cases they agreed to assist in the research. Some of these people, such as Goh Keng Swee, Lim Kim San, E.W. Barker and Maurice Baker, are already well established in the national history of Singapore. Others are unknown outside their own circles, and whatever their own achievements in life – and the list includes a retired permanent secretary, a senior business manager, four academics, an English judge, a doctor – they appear in this text only because they have personal memories of Lee, and were willing to share them. The input of these people has been complemented by a small collection of interviews with people who were contemporaries or near-contemporaries of Lee at school or university, but who did not know him personally. These people not only gave useful background: in each case they were able to convey some piece of information which made a significant, or at least an interesting contribution to the overall thesis.

The argument advocated in this book has several distinct components. Chapter 2 supplies a biographical sketch of Lee. Using new material, both published and unpublished, it takes a fresh look at Lee's life and character, and opens some of the questions that will be explored later in the book. Chapter 3 begins the argument proper. It contends that progressivism – a belief in human progress that verges on a secular faith – forms one of the most basic elements of Lee's worldview and his ideology. Some of the schoolboy origins and the later formative influences on Lee's faith in progress are uncovered and examined. Chapter 4 examines Lee's elitism. It characterises the logic by which he has justified and applied elitism as his system of government and as the structure of Singapore society. It examines the family and cultural influences that led him to see the world as a social 'pyramid' in which members of an almost pre-ordained elite rule by virtue of their superior talent.[9] His geneticist ideas of inherited talent and intelligence are also explored. Chapter 5 looks at Lee's theory of cultural evolutionism, whereby he reduced culture to not much more than a transient and ephemeral entity: a tool to be wielded from above by a progressive elite. It follows the gradual shift of his thinking from this premise towards the final phase of his thought, where he elevates Chinese culture to a central place in his political thinking and his personal affection. Chapter 6 looks at Lee's views on race, and how they relate to the other elements of his ideological thinking: his progressivism, elitism, cultural evolutionism and geneticism. Chapter 7 moves on from considering Lee's ideology, and tries to deconstruct Lee's political technique into its essential elements. It studies the relationship between Lee's ideology and his record in government. This chapter also takes the opportunity to consider Lee's career in the light of traditional Chinese political thought. Chapter 8 is an assessment of the character of Lee's creation: what has been the practical effect of Lee and his ideas on the development of Singapore. Chapter 9 concludes with an assessment not of Lee's success and achievements, but of the reasonableness of his worldview.

NOTES

1. Tommy T.B. Koh, 'A world statesman', in *Trends*, a publication of the Institute of Southeast Asian Studies, issued in *The Straits Times*, 27 December 1990, p. 1.

2. Lee Kuan Yew, *The Singapore Story: Memoirs of Lee Kuan Yew*, Singapore; New York; London; Toronto; Sydney; Mexico City: Prentice Hall, 1998, before the title page.

3. Chris Patten, *East and West*, London: Macmillan, 1998, p. 93.

4. Ministry of Information and the Arts, *Singapore 1996*, Singapore: Ministry of Information and the Arts, 1996, p. 20.

5. Goh Keng Swee, *Urban Incomes and Housing: A Report on the Social Survey of Singapore. 1953–54*, Singapore: Government Printing Office, 1958, p. 20.

6. Han Fook Kwang, Warren Fernandez and Sumiko Tan, *Lee Kuan Yew: The Man and His Ideas*, Singapore: Times Editions and Singapore Press Holdings, 1998, p. 130.

7. *Ibid.*, pp. 127–151.

8. Lee Kuan Yew, *Prime Minister's Speeches, Press Conferences, Interviews, Statements, etc.*, Singapore: Prime Minister's Office, 1959–90, and Lee Kuan Yew, *Senior Minister's Speeches, Press Conferences, Interviews, Statements, etc.*, Singapore: Prime Minister's Office, 1991–95.

9. Lee Kuan Yew, *New Bearings in Our Education System*, Singapore: Ministry of Culture, [1966–67], p. 13.

· 2 ·

Father of the Nation

I do not know whether I could be altogether happy myself if I were to live in a placid society.

Lee's address to the Malaysian Students' Association, Sydney, 20 March 1965, in Lee Kuan Yew, *Prime Minister's Speeches, Press Conferences, Interviews, Statements, etc.*, Singapore: Prime Minister's Office, 1959–90.

Despite his outward confidence, Lee Kuan Yew was sure only of some things all of the time, and of all things only some of the time.

Dennis Bloodworth, *The Tiger and the Trojan Horse*, Singapore: Times Books International, 1986, p. 148.

Lee Kuan Yew's authorised biography, *Lee Kuan Yew: The Man and His Ideas*, is an elegant vehicle for conveying his ideas and his vision.[1] The book was published in a coffee-table format, with lots of pictures, and was written by three senior Singaporean journalists who pointedly refrained from giving any critique of Lee's views or his career. The authors nevertheless gave the reader considerable insight, not only into his vision of the world, but also into his self-image. Chapter 1, for instance, has a section entitled 'Beginnings', which follows Lee's tradition of tracing his ancestry back to Lee Bok Boon, one of his great-grandfathers.[2] Bok Boon was a Hakka from Guangdong province who arrived in Singapore at the age of sixteen, made his fortune and in his old age returned 'home' to China to die.[3] The significant feature of this genealogy is that it accepts unquestioningly the Chinese practice of tracing ancestors exclusively through the male line. Hence the Lee line is followed from father to son: Bok Boon to Hoon Leong to Chin Koon to Kuan Yew.[4] Lee's maternal ancestors appear in the family tree only as wives and mothers of various generations of Lees.[5] This patrilineal genealogy provides the premise by which Lee justifies his self-image as a 'rugged' Hakka, descended from the hardy stock of northern China. Hakkas, Lee told his biographers, consider themselves 'very special' and are over-represented in the Singapore Cabinet because they are 'harder-working, tougher and therefore higher achievers'.[6] Lee's traditional Chinese approach to genealogy and clan foreshadows two of the enigmas in Lee Kuan Yew's life. First, his traditional Sinic outlook is enigmatic in one who had an Anglo-centric upbringing and who learnt to speak Chinese only as an adult. Second, his traditional emphasis on the male line is striking in a eugenicist who has spent the later decades of his life emphasising the importance of the female contribution to the gene pool. These two enigmas are superficial manifestations of questions that go to the heart of Lee's political thought. As a preliminary step in studying the development of his thinking, this chapter will present a biographical sketch of Lee Kuan Yew. It will not, however, provide either a comprehensive picture of Lee's life or career, or a detailed analysis of his thinking. It will aim simply to give the reader sufficient background knowledge to navigate a passage through the intricacies of Lee's developing ideas as they unfold throughout the rest of the book.

Despite Lee's fascination with his ancestry, our survey of his life can begin satisfactorily at the time of his birth. Lee's parents, Lee Chin Koon and Chua Jim Neo, were very young when they married, and were twenty and sixteen respectively when their first child, Harry Kuan Yew, was born on 16 September 1923.[7] Each came from a wealthy *baba* family that had lived in British Singapore for generations. The *baba* culture is indigenous to the Straits of Malacca, and is the direct result of early intermarriage between Chinese men and Malay women. The culture is quite distinct from other strands of Chinese tradition, being a fascinating blend of Malay and Chinese culture entwined under the protective umbrella of British colonial rule.[8] The *baba*s were a significant minority in pre-war Singapore and stood apart from the dialect-speaking Chinese who were usually first- or second-generation migrants. Like most *baba* families, the Lees spoke little Chinese and conversed with each other in English and Malay.[9] Kuan Yew's father, Lee Chin Koon, was a man of modest ambition who assumed that his father's money would carry him through life.[10] When his father lost his fortune in the Depression, Chin Koon became a storekeeper and then a middle-manager for the Shell Company.[11] Despite Lee Kuan Yew's emphasis on Confucian values and familial respect, he has rarely spoken a kind word about his father, and attributes the success of his family exclusively to his mother, Chua Jim Neo.[12] Chin Koon was eclipsed by his wife and his father, Hoon Leong, in the rearing of his children,[13] and between them these two strong characters appear to have instilled in Kuan Yew a strong sense of self-importance and self-confidence, along with a distinct contempt for failure which probably reflected their contempt for Chin Koon.[14] Jim Neo decided that Harry, as Lee Kuan Yew was and is called by his family, should receive an English-language education so that he could succeed in colonial Singapore, as had Hoon Leong and Bok Boon before him. Harry entered Telok Kurau English School at the age of six, and continually topped his class with effortless ease.[15] Given his natural ability and his grandparents' money, both life and school were easy for Harry.

Soon after his entry to Telok Kurau English School, however, both of Lee's grandfathers lost their wealth in the Depression.[16] Although Lee's family was far from destitute, seeing relatives and presumably the parents of school friends lose their houses, properties and jobs must have had a profound impact on young Harry. Looking at the character of the adult Lee, it is reasonable to assume that the Depression taught Lee that life is neither fair nor easy. Like many other Depression children around the world, Lee surely acquired a new resoluteness of character in this period. Lee himself has attributed two features of his life directly to the Depression. First, he cites this experience as the basis of his propensity to plan for worst-case scenarios, and never to assume that the good times will last.[17] Second, when Lee's parents pointed out that the people who were doing well despite the Depression were the doctors and the lawyers, he made a conscious decision to pursue a career in law.[18]

In 1936 Lee entered Raffles Institution (RI), which accepted only the top ten boys from each English-language primary school in Singapore.[19] In RI Lee found a completely different environment to Telok Kurau English School: a highly competitive, streamed education system, in which his academic supremacy could not be taken for granted.[20] Lee worked hard at RI and after three years of coming second in his form, he finally topped the Cambridge Senior Exams, not only in Raffles Institution, but throughout the whole of Malaya. Yet Lee did not concentrate on his academic work to the exclusion of all else. He played some sport, was a member of the school debating team and generally threw himself into the school's extra-curricular activities.[21] Although Lee did not decide to enter politics until after the Japanese Occupation, by his final year at RI he had already developed an interest in politics, which, extraordinary as it sounds, appears to have been cultivated by his teachers. The 1937 RI *Syllabus of Instruction* reveals that the school deliberately set out to develop in the boys 'an intelligently critical attitude towards public affairs', and encouraged a sense of public spirit towards the broader community.[22] This objective was to be achieved primarily through the study of Empire history, which, according to the *Syllabus*,

> contributes to an understanding of circumstances governing constitutional changes; it imparts some knowledge of the difficulties inherent in administration, of problems to be overcome by administrators in removing abuses and instituting reforms, sometimes in the face of strong popular opposition; it explains the manner of achieving a measure of agreement or working compromise between peoples of different race, religion, ideals, ways of thought, for the communal development of the resources of a country.[23]

The school magazine, *The Rafflesian*, reveals evidence of a surprising volume of mild political discourse in the school. Editorials and articles in *The Rafflesian* canvassed topics as diverse as the Abyssinian War[24] and the character of 'modernity'.[25] The Principal, D.W. McLeod, used his position to invoke mild social commentary, which was almost Fabian in character.[26] The effect of such commentaries on young Harry was probably very slight, but they appear to have planted the seeds of political interest. In Lee's final year at RI, each of the boys in the form was asked to write an essay on the future of the world. When McLeod was handing back the essays, he observed to Lee's class that 'out of this class one of you will be Prime Minister of this country'.[27] No one had any doubt that McLeod was speaking of Harry Lee.

Lee matriculated from RI in 1940. Jim Neo had planned to use her savings to send Harry straight to England to enrol in an English university, but this ambition was frustrated by the outbreak of war.[28] Instead he entered Raffles College on the Sir John Anderson Scholarship.[29] At College, Lee studied English literature, economics and mathematics.[30] At the end of his first year, he chose mathematics as his area of specialisation.[31] Lee's study at Raffles College was cut short by the Japanese Occupation in February 1942, and since he did not re-enrol after the British returned, he studied there for less than a year and a half. Lee himself attributes little significance to his time at Raffles College, crediting it merely with giving him a background in economics.[32] Although the College encouraged a 'slightly utopian outlook upon the world',[33] it did not stimulate any significant political discussion beyond general discontent with the inferior status of the Asians in Malaya,[34] and some expression of sympathy for a group of workers on the Malayan Peninsula who had been striking over poor conditions.[35] Lee's interests appear to have been primarily academic and social,[36] though he still found time to throw himself into the debating society.[37] Beyond these general observations, Maurice Baker has recounted one incident from Raffles College which is worthy of note because it demonstrates that Lee's intolerance of inefficiency and his ruthlessness in dealing with incompetence was by then well developed, and must therefore be regarded as a deep-seated trait which influenced his political style, rather than a trait which he learned as a result of his political experience. The story is told best in Baker's own words:

> We had a picnic organised by the [students'] union. And [Lee] was very unhappy at the way it was organised, and in the following week or two he summoned an extraordinary general meeting of the students and he gave the Secretary of the Union a hell of a time. In fact the poor chap burst into tears. He disliked the idea of anybody undertaking a job and not doing it well. And that is a characteristic all through life. Any minister, anyone who did not come up to the mark, sort of disappeared – was asked quietly to go. Likewise the civil servants with whom he was not happy, once the PAP took over, were asked to retire in the interests of the State, even if they were in their forties. That is a characteristic you might be interested in: the desire for efficiency, and the lack of tolerance for any weakness in doing a job of anybody who had undertaken to do a job and not come up to expectation.[38]

This characteristic in Lee's personality has had an obvious impact on the style of his rule of Singapore, which hardly needs further elaboration. Of less obvious significance is the fact that this trait made Lee fundamentally ill-equipped to deal with the Malay leadership of Malaysia during the period of Singapore's membership of Malaysia, for whom loyalty to friends, efficient or not, was a paramount virtue.

In early 1942, the Japanese Occupation of Singapore shattered Lee's world and ended his term at Raffles College. In 1965, Lee described his reactions to an Australian audience:

> [T]he Japanese armies overran Singapore and some 90,000 Commonwealth troops, British, Indians and Australians tramped into captivity. I saw them tramping along the road in front of my house for three solid days – an endless stream of bewildered men who did not know what had happened, why it happened, and what they were doing there in Singapore in any case.

> I was bewildered too. We were all unprepared for this. We thought Singapore was an impregnable fortress and the British Navy was supreme. No one expected the Japanese to march down Southeast Asia and capture us. Nobody had warned us of this.[39]

The shock of seeing the British humiliated by Asians destroyed all of the assumptions on which the young Lee had planned his life. Survival became the only priority, and Lee proved to be a survivor. In the first days of the Occupation, Lee was subjected to bullying and beatings by Japanese soldiers on two occasions, and narrowly escaped being rounded up for summary execution on a third.[40] Nevertheless, Lee and his family survived the Occupation with less hardship than many Singaporeans. During this period Lee decided that it would be prudent to learn some Chinese characters to enable him to understand Japanese notices.[41] Subsequently he enrolled in a Japanese school, learnt Japanese properly, and worked as a clerk in two Japanese companies.[42] Then, late in 1943, he began working as a transcriber in the Japanese Propaganda Department.[43] It was not a very heroic role for the future father of the nation, but it had the virtue of paying a wage:

> My job – and I needed a job to make a living – was to do a kind of crossword puzzle. They [the Japanese] intercepted ... all the Allied news agencies during the war. And because reception was never very good especially during daylight hours, there would be blanks in the transcription. And my job was to guess what the words were. And then classify them into eastern front, western front, Pacific front and so on.[44]

While Lee's role during the Occupation was not ignoble, he has become retrospectively dissatisfied with his own complicity during Japanese rule. Twenty-one years after the return of the British, Lee spoke of this period:

> Those who made themselves submissive and meek and self-effacing survived after a fashion when the British were the Master, or during the Japanese occupation when the Japanese pushed out and replaced the British; but they survived without the every [*sic*] important quality of self-respect.[45]

The use of the third person when speaking of those who were 'submissive and meek and self-effacing' to the Japanese is significant, considering Lee learnt Japanese and worked in the Propaganda Department.

Lee has since marked the Japanese Occupation as the catalyst that gave birth to his anti-colonialism:

> [The Japanese] made me and a whole generation like me determined to fight for freedom – freedom from servitude and foreign domination. I did not enter politics. They brought politics upon me. From that time onwards, I decided that our lives should be ours to decide. That we should not be pawns and playthings of foreign powers.[46]

Speaking of the Occupation, Lee told Trevor Kennedy in 1988: 'It wasn't just being smacked or brutalized by the Japanese. It's the outrage, the sense of hopelessness that your life is being run by other people. You suddenly found a whole community just captive'.[47] While these accounts served Lee well during his political career, he was more circumspect in his memoirs, where he described the Occupation as merely the beginning of a long period over which his outlook changed.[48] E.W. Barker is adamant that the Occupation was not enough to make Lee or anyone go into politics: 'It opened many people's eyes that the white man is not invincible. That's all'.[49] It seems more likely that it was the return of the British after the Occupation, rather than the Occupation itself, which really gave birth to Lee's nationalism. He resented the British presumption that they could return after the defeat of the Japanese and resume their colonial rule as if nothing had happened. He no longer regarded the British as superior, and detested their assumption that they enjoyed a continued right to rule over his people. Maurice Baker reflected on the change he saw in his friend after the war:

> I remember the Chinese Swimming Club was having a big party at which they announced that it would be exclusive to Chinese, and an uncle of Kuan Yew's was the President. I remember that he decided that he wanted to go and I was with him. And we went up to the club and we went in and found that no one would be admitted except Chinese, but when he went in he found a few Europeans who had been invited.

> He came out very angry and told me: 'I am going to get you in no matter what it takes'. I said: 'I don't like this confrontation. Let's forget it and go elsewhere'. He said: 'No, no, no'. He went in there. He confronted his uncle and got me admitted. This was 1946 or 1947.[50] It was alright if it was exclusively Chinese, but then there were a few Englishmen who had been admitted.

> He would not tolerate discrimination of this sort. You can understand the bitterness. Even his own community treated the Europeans as a special class, and he resented this.[51]

Before the war Lee accepted British superiority as a natural part of the social landscape. 'There was no question of any resentment', he wrote in his memoirs:

> The superior status of the British in government and society was simply a fact of life. After all, they were the greatest people in the world. They had the biggest empire that history had ever known, stretching over all time zones, across all four oceans and five continents. We learnt that in history lessons at school.[52]

But after the war, Lee came to resent bitterly the special treatment received by the British in Singapore, and was particularly embittered by the sense of betrayal. Baker continued:

> The fundamental thing that made him go into politics was the fact that the Japanese defeated the British in thirty days or so, and we all

believed that Britain could never be beaten. We had done English history. We knew that they may lose a battle or two but they always win in the end. We felt fully protected. ... We were very confident until the *Prince of Wales* and the *Repulse* were sunk, and then we knew that was it. We felt very let down.

I remember him saying: 'We must not let this happen again. We must defend ourselves and look after ourselves. Let us get control of the country and run it ourselves. We must be able to look after our own affairs and not be subject to someone else'. This was 1946, 1947. We all thought the same way.[53]

It should be noted that while Baker's account superficially gives credence to Lee's descriptions of the politicising effect of the Occupation, the basis for this part of his assessment is simply that they 'felt let down' by the British. Although Baker was Lee's companion at the time of the fall, Lee's assertion that 'we must be able to look after our own affairs' was made in 1946, not in 1942. The Occupation disillusioned Lee and his generation about the British, but the genesis of his anti-colonialism is not found in the Occupation itself. 'In the Occupation, we had too many troubles [to think about politics]', retorted E.W. Barker.[54] Maurice Baker's evidence shows that it was the return of the British after the war, and the resumption of their privileged pre-war position in society that prompted the beginnings of Lee's nationalism, which at the time was expressed by his attraction to the anti-colonialist Malayan Democratic Union.[55]

After the Japanese surrender on 15 August 1945, Lee still hoped to study in England, but this seemed little more than an elusive dream. He was already twenty-two years old, and had not received even a Raffles College diploma. Further, there seemed only a remote hope of completing his college studies. Many of the Raffles College staff had been interned or died during the Occupation.[56] The Japanese military had used Raffles College as its headquarters and there was little optimism that the library collection had survived, or that there remained any records of degrees and enrolments, let alone the grades of 'current' students.[57] Although these fears proved largely unfounded,[58] at that stage no one knew when the college would re-open or under what conditions. How Lee was to continue his studies was far from clear. There is no reason to doubt that his focus at this stage was still on study in England. He displayed his commitment to further study in a general way by approaching Lim Tay Boh, one of his former teachers at RI and his former tutor at Raffles College, to conduct seminars on economics which were held in Lee's family home.[59] Lee also applied for and was accepted into one of the London Inns of Court, membership of which was a prerequisite for legal studies in England.[60] In late 1946 Lee's efforts were rewarded and he left for England on a British troopship, having used his letter of acceptance to Middle Temple to secure his berth.[61]

Lee enrolled at London University upon his arrival in England, but London proved to be a disappointment. He lived a lonely life, living and eating alone, commuting to and from classes through a city devastated by the Blitz, and which was burdened by rationing and shortages of everything that made life comfortable.[62] Although he was dissatisfied with London and with the standing of the law degree that he would receive,[63] Lee did find his political home in London: it was here that he became a Fabian socialist.[64] Lee nevertheless decided that he would attempt to transfer to the Cambridge University Law School after the first semester. Achieving this goal was no mean feat. Cambridge was overflowing with ex-servicemen who received priority over other Britons, let alone over colonial students. As a consequence the law tutorials had been expanded from the normal four students to ten, which was considered to be excessively large.[65] Half the academic year had already passed and he would need to convince the authorities that he could catch up. Furthermore, entry to Cambridge depended upon securing a place in a college, and all of the colleges bar one were residential and fully occupied. Lee did not have a letter of introduction, nor did he know any of the officials or academics at Cambridge. Lee's goal appeared impossible, but despite the odds, he succeeded in gaining entry at his first attempt.[66] He asked Cecil Wong, a Singaporean who was studying at Fitzwilliam House, to help him.[67] Fitzwilliam House was the newest and least prestigious college at Cambridge, but was the only one that was non-residential.[68] Wong introduced Lee to William S. Thatcher,[69] who was Censor at Fitzwilliam House and who was widely known to have a great deal of sympathy for colonial and dominion students.[70] Thatcher admitted Lee to Fitzwilliam, thereby giving him entry to the Cambridge Law School and beginning a lifelong friendship between the two men.

Lee found Cambridge more congenial than London in every respect. His flat was more comfortable, his meals were prepared for him,[71] and the company was more to his taste, especially after his future wife, Kwa Geok Choo, arrived at Girton College. Initially he travelled around Cambridge by bicycle, but he later bought a motorcycle and travelled throughout Britain and Europe, enjoying the life of the undergraduate at play.[72] His friend Michael Lever remembers

> crashing Harry's motorcycle into a beautiful bed of flowers outside a
> smart hotel. Rather unusually for those days when men outnumbered

women by 20 to 1 at Cambridge, [Lee] actually had a girlfriend in residence, whom he later married. So *la vita* was pretty *dolce*.[73]

Lee as an undergraduate travelled, smoked heavily[74] and imbibed his share of English 'bitters',[75] but always made time for study. He approached his study like a campaign. Minchin reports stories of Lee keeping his fellow students up late at night, carousing and talking, and then when they had gone to bed, beginning the night's study, surviving on only a few hours' sleep.[76] Lee used even the lack of tutors at Fitzwilliam House[77] to his advantage. Since he had to find tutors from other colleges, he sought out the best. 'He chose them. Somehow he knew who were the good tutors', reported E.W. Barker.[78]

Lee succeeded in combining an active social life with spectacular academic success, which is as much attributable to his innate intelligence as to his dedication. Michael Lever recalls:

[Lee] was never a serious sort of man, in the sense of being a heavy intellectual. What he *did* have was the most dazzling and electric intelligence of any man I'd ever met. In more than 40 years in the law I have met some very, very clever men, but I would rate him with Gerald Gardiner and Hartley Shawcross as the best *legal* brain I have ever encountered. He loved every minute of it, and I have no doubt that at that stage, most of his serious thinking was about law, pure and simple. He walked away with every prize on offer, and one particular memory I have was of him in our Finals strolling out paper after paper, after about an hour of the allotted three, for a leisurely cigarette in the sunshine, whilst he waited for the *hoi polloi* like myself to struggle on. Of course, he got a starred First.[79]

Lee also settled into his new political home at Cambridge. He became involved with the left wing of the British Labour Party and with the Fabians, completing the transformation of Lee the anti-colonialist into Lee the democratic socialist. More will be said on this in Chapter 3.

Lee finished his three-year law degree in two and a half years, winning a Star for distinction, while Kwa, whom he had married secretly in December 1947, gained her law degree, with first-class honours, in two years. Their return to Singapore, however, was delayed until late 1950, since they needed to sit for their Bar examinations in London.[80] During this hiatus, Lee was able to associate more regularly with other politically conscious Malayans through a London-based group called the Malayan Forum. The Malayan Forum was an informal group of students from Malaya and Singapore, which had been started in 1949 by Maurice Baker, Tun Razak and Goh Keng Swee.[81] Lee Kuan Yew had been able to attend only occasional meetings of the Malayan Forum until he graduated and moved to London, and even then Maurice

Baker does not remember him being very active.[82] Nevertheless, the Malayan Forum is significant in our study of Lee Kuan Yew because it provided the venue for Lee, at the age of twenty-seven, to expound his programme of political action in a speech called 'The Returned Student'. Below is a précis of Lee's speech:

The British in colonial Malaya form the ruling caste. The upper caste among the Asians of Malaya are those who, through their English-language education, and preferably through study in England itself, have adopted British mores and either possess wealth, or have made themselves useful to the colonial government. We returned students will return to Malaya to assume our place in this hierarchy, but only for so long as Malaya remains under British rule. British rule, however, cannot continue indefinitely, since Malaya is almost the last vestige of colonialism in Asia.

Independence is inevitable, but the problems caused by Malaya's racial mix have allowed Britain to delay her withdrawal. It is possible that the British might try to hang on to Malaya for an indefinite time. While returned students have usually replaced their former colonial rulers after a country gains independence, the delay has created an unusual situation: the nationalists have not even begun to organise, but the Communist Party has already built a powerful organisation. This leaves doubt about who will succeed the British as the new elite. Although the end of colonialism is inevitable, the returned students can assist themselves and their country by working for an orderly hand-over of power to themselves. Because the alternative is the Communist Party, this is more than a matter of preference: it is a matter of survival. The threat from communism also means that a redistribution of wealth and the creation of a more egalitarian society must accompany independence in order to blunt the appeal of the communists.

Despite the fact that the communists are more organised than we are, the returned students have the advantage of being the group most acceptable to the British. The returned students have also the best chance of finding a solution to Malaya's racial problems and of forming a united nationalist political front strong enough to achieve decolonisation without resorting to force. Besides these advantages, the common man in Malaya regards us as superior anyway, so we are the natural leaders of the new movement. Yet the dangers should not be understated. While Malay nationalism is well developed, and Malayan Chinese nationalism is starting to develop, these movements could just as easily be a source of division as a source of unity.

While the actual steps we take when we return to Malaya cannot be foreseen, our duty is clear: to help bring about social cohesion, and to convince the British that their position in Malaya is untenable.[83]

The basic argument contained in Lee's speech was simultaneously brilliant and hopelessly erroneous. As might be expected from one as immersed in British culture and politics as Lee, he demonstrated a superb understanding of the nature and limits of colonial rule and the thinking of the British, but showed little grasp of the nature of Malayan and Singaporean society. It is true that the English-educated had been well regarded by the Chinese-educated before the war, but that did not mean that this situation would continue after the Occupation. The Chinese-educated communists were the heroes of the Occupation, and almost as he spoke, were being given additional standing by the communist victory in China. The Chinese-educated were able to look to their own for leadership. The peninsular Malays, both before and after the war, looked to their traditional, aristocratic leaders, and it was only of incidental significance that most of these were English-educated. Lee appears to have had little inkling as to the nature of either of these bonds of ethnic loyalty. He learnt the error of his assessment regarding the Chinese-educated soon after his return to Singapore, but it took the trauma of Singapore's brief membership of Malaysia for him to begin to understand the thinking of the Malays. It should be noted also that Lee's political programme included only the most innocuous vision of a socialist Malaya.

Lee returned to Singapore late in 1950, prepared for a career in the law, but determined to build a career in politics. Before we can begin to follow Lee's next steps towards the prime ministership, however, it is necessary to divert briefly our study from Lee himself, and consider the broader political and social milieu of Singapore. Lee returned to a Singapore that had been separated administratively and politically from the Peninsula. Singapore was by then a crown colony ruled directly by the British, but recently given a partially elected legislature as part of a slow progression towards self-government.[84] By far the numerically strongest communal group in post-war Singapore was the Chinese, outnumbering the combined Malay, Indian, Eurasian and other communities by four to one.[85] Although most of these people were disenfranchised 'aliens', by the beginning of the 1950s it was obvious that both China-born and local-born Chinese were going to be given citizenship in the near future.[86] Any party that hoped to govern Singapore later in the decade would need to appeal to this constituency, which, in the early 1950s was dominated by the illegal Malayan Communist Party (MCP). The strength of the MCP among the Chinese was established in the immediate post-war period. During the war the British had helped the MCP to build a formidable organisation to fight the Japanese in Malaya. After the war the Party was not only the most organised force in Singapore, but also its leaders were heroes. Some were even decorated by the Supreme Commander of the Allied Forces,

Admiral Lord Louis Mountbatten, with full pomp and ceremony. The MCP had no significant political base outside the Chinese community, but it made full use of the assets that it did possess. The Party turned its organisational talents to the Chinese trade unions and in 1946 was able to call a political strike to which 150,000 workers responded, bringing Singapore to a standstill for two days.[87] The successful communist revolution in China intensified the MCP's hegemony over the Chinese, particularly among the young. On 10 October 1949, ten days after Mao's declaration of the People's Republic, about one hundred Chinese associations and middle schools welcomed the 'birth of a new China', and celebrated Mao's victory in the presence of two huge communist flags.[88] The communists represented hope and pride to the impoverished Chinese masses living in the stench of overcrowded slums. Throughout the 1950s and the first half of the 1960s, all Singaporean politics can be seen against the backdrop of MCP hegemony over the Chinese masses.

In contrast to the seething energy of the Malayan Communist Party, the approach of the legal political parties was sedate and gentlemanly. The major legal party of the early 1950s was the Progressive Party (PP), which was founded in 1947 by leaders of the Straits Chinese British Association and the Singapore Association to protect the political and business interests of British subjects in Singapore. The Progressive Party represented the small, elite group of English-educated Europeans and Chinese.[89] Its three founders, John Laycock, C.C. Tan and N.A. Mallal were all London-trained solicitors, and all three were monolinguistic anglophones. It is not surprising, therefore, that they viewed with disdain efforts to give the vote to nearly 300,000 Chinese 'aliens', none of whom was likely to identify with C.C. Tan and his associates.[90] The PP advocated a slow, cautious creep towards self-government, which would leave it as the dominant political party in a nearly powerless Legislative Council.[91] The only significant rival to the PP in the early 1950s was the Singapore Labour Party (SLP).[92] The SLP was founded in 1948 by three Indian trade union leaders who wanted to capitalise on what they perceived as the higher political consciousness of the Indian community. The SLP consciously modelled itself on the British Labour Party but, unlike its role model, it never achieved any depth of membership, organisation, cohesion or ideology. Despite being a party of the left, in most respects it was even less advanced than the Progressive Party in adapting to the demands of mass politics. The Labour Party managed to establish several branches that functioned intermittently, but which were systematically closed down by the General Council as a result of factional disputes.[93] The Labour Party had no office, no proper membership records and no well-managed system for collecting subscriptions.[94] The SLP had some success in having candidates elected to the City Council and the Legislative Council, but it suffered a fatal split in 1952, leaving both the SLP and the break-away Singapore Socialist Party as token representatives of the left.

Singapore did not, therefore, offer a very hospitable landscape to an English-educated, left-wing solicitor who wanted to lead his country to independence without handing it over the communists. It should not be surprising that Lee Kuan Yew's early political efforts lacked direction and finesse. He secured a position with John Laycock's law firm and dabbled initially in the conservative politics of the Progressive Party.[95] He came quickly to the conclusion, however, that there was no future in existing political parties, if only because they would all be swept aside by more aggressive anti-colonialist forces. After his flirtation with the Progressive Party, Lee attempted, without much success, to interest his old Malayan Forum friends in politics.[96] Then, in early 1952, his fortunes changed when he was offered the chance to represent the postal workers in a major industrial dispute.[97] Lee proved to be an extremely effective negotiator, advocate, adviser and press officer, and he led the postal workers to a decisive victory. This was the breakthrough Lee needed, for it gave him a public profile, at least in the English-language press, and access to the political capital of the English-speaking trade unions, which to date had been the fiefdom of the Progressive Party and the Labour Party. After his spectacular success with the postal workers, other English-speaking unions sought his services until he had, in the words of Dennis Bloodworth, 'thread[ed] trade unions onto his list of legal clients like satay on a stick'.[98] By 1953, Lee had already met most of the people who were to form the anti-communist nucleus of the People's Action Party: Goh Keng Swee, Toh Chin Chye, K.M. (Kenny) Byrne, and S. (Sinnathamby) Rajaratnam. He had also met and had various legal or trade union dealings with a disparate group of English-educated communists and fellow-travellers: Sandra Woodhull, James Puthucheary, Jamit Singh, C.V. Devan Nair and Samad Ismail.[99] With his trade union base growing steadily, Lee tried to forge an anti-colonialist united front between the two groups. Under Lee's tutelage, though not precisely under his leadership, this group began meeting in the basement of his home in 1953 with a view to forming a new political party.[100] Yet this was an extremely flimsy base for political action, since the group still lacked a mass following. Years later, Lee described the situation in the mid-1950s thus:

> Our primary concern was how to muster a mass following. How did a group of English-educated nationalists – graduates of British universities – with no experience of the hurley burley of politics or the conspiracies of revolution, move people whose many languages they did not speak and whose problems and hardships they shared only intellectually?[101]

The solution presented itself in May 1954, when the Chinese Middle School students demonstrated against National Service and forty-eight students were arrested. Chinese-educated tertiary students then took up their cause through the University of Malaya Socialist Club, and eight of them were arrested in turn. The students were having difficulty finding legal representation,[102] and so they turned to the now-prominent trade union advocate, Lee Kuan Yew. Lee and his close colleagues saw the students' approach as a major political opportunity. Goh Keng Swee has testified, 'We thought we could tap these people. It was a major breakthrough. If we formed a new political party and could get the Chinese-educated Chinese on our side, we would have a winning combination'.[103] Despite the political gift the students represented, however, Lee always regarded them as manipulated pawns and as 'brats' and 'bobby-soxers' who should be doing their study instead of engaging in politics.[104] He was more interested in meeting the adult communists who were manipulating the children and students. After securing a spectacular victory for the students in court, he passed word into Chinese trade union circles that he wished to meet Chinese representatives of the Party.[105] After some weeks, Lim Chin Siong and Fong Swee Suan, two of the most powerful Chinese communist trade union leaders on the island, cautiously joined the circle in Lee Kuan Yew's basement. Lee and Lim then entered into a tenuous dialogue, which led eventually to the formation of a united front with the communists.[106] Lee was to boast years later, 'We were riding a tiger, and we knew it'.[107] Goh Keng Swee, on the other hand, has confessed:

> It was an act of reckless folly. ... We totally misread the situation. ... We did not understand that the mass base was firmly in the grip of the communists, ably led by the underground Singapore Town Committee of the Malayan Communist Party. The People's Action Party was immediately captured by the Town Committee and we were their prisoner. We were like innocent virgins roaming a brothel area.[108]

The People's Action Party was formed in November 1954 as an uneasy marriage between three groups: Chinese-educated communists such as Fong Swee Suan and Chan Chiaw Thor; English-educated communists and left-wingers such as Devan Nair and James Puthucheary; and English-educated anti-communists such as Lee Kuan Yew and Toh Chin Chye.[109]

Lee spent the next few years pursuing a series of high-risk Machiavellian strategies that took him into office in spectacular fashion. His first electoral test was the 1955 elections for Singapore's first Legislative Assembly. Lee wanted to gain a voice in the Assembly but did not wish to risk becoming the dominant group, both because the new Rendel Constitution left most executive power in the hands of colonial officials, and because his own party was dominated by the MCP.[110] To this end he formed a de facto electoral alliance with David Marshall's Labour Front[111] (successor of the Labour Party) whereby he ensured that the PAP gained a small presence in the new Legislative Assembly without taking on the responsibility of real power. Then, when Marshall formed a coalition government, he attacked it ferociously for administering 'colonialism in disguise'.[112] He condemned Marshall for retaining the Emergency Regulations (with their provision for detention without trial),[113] but when he was in London he ensured that detention without trial would continue to be the centrepiece of Singapore's ongoing security regulations.[114] He protested whenever Special Branch detained the communists in the PAP, but relied upon such detentions to remove his opponents and enable him to retain control.[115] He was one of the fiercest anti-colonialist politicians on the island, but when in London for constitutional talks, he successfully charmed and impressed the British authorities and so became their favoured candidate for the prime ministership.[116] Over 1957–59 he almost simultaneously conducted secret communications with Richard Corridon of Special Branch,[117] Devan Nair (a pro-communist member of the PAP who was considering changing sides),[118] Fang Chuang Pi (head of the Singapore Town Committee of the MCP)[119] and Sir William Goode (Governor of Singapore).[120] This was quite an impressive achievement for someone who could barely keep control of his own party. In truth, however, there was very little forward planning on Lee's part and hardly any of these liaisons occurred at his initiative. Lee's great political gift at this stage of his career was in having the perspicacity and courage to seize opportunities when they presented themselves. In fact, despite his 'special relationship' with Special Branch and the Governor, Lee was very close to being detained himself and was saved from this martyrdom only by the principled intervention of his parliamentary *bête noire*, David Marshall.[121]

The events of 1954–59 culminated in the PAP contesting and winning the 1959 elections for Singapore's second Legislative Assembly. By this stage Lee had manoeuvred his communist allies into a relatively weak position. When Fang Chuang Pi of the MCP's Singapore Town Committee tried to open secret negotiations with Lee in 1958, Fang thought he was in a strong position because the MCP had been fostering a rival to the PAP, namely David Marshall's new creation, the Workers' Party (WP). At the outset of his negotiations, however, Lee insisted successfully that the MCP withdraw its members from the Workers' Party, thus destroying the WP's campaign in the City Council elections and effectively removing the PAP's only rival for communist support. Having convinced the MCP to burn its bridges, Lee then refused to make Fang any promises, and would not even guarantee that the PAP would contest the 1959 elections.[122] Lee's strategy distressed the Party for three reasons. First, since the MCP had just destroyed the Workers' Party as a viable political force, the only alternative to the PAP was a conservative government over which it would have no influence, and which would continue the policy of mass detentions. Second, the party was relying on a PAP victory to ensure the release of its most effective open front leaders from prison.[123] Third, the stakes were much higher in these elections than they had been in 1955. The previous Constitution had been designed as a temporary expedient that gave little power to the locals. The Constitution of 1959, on the other hand, gave Singaporeans effective self-government and was likely to last for as long as Britain wished to retain her naval base on the island. Whoever won these elections would probably be running Singapore into the foreseeable future. For this reason, the communists wanted to contest the elections at almost any cost. After Lee had secured more concessions from the left, the PAP did contest the 1959 elections and won office with 53 per cent of the vote, and forty-three out of fifty-one seats.[124] Lee maintained scrupulously the facade of unity with his communist allies throughout the late 1950s and into the early 1960s, but in one remarkable speech just before polling day he gave notice to his allies that he would break the united front when it suited him. As he told a PAP election rally,

> [i]n this fight the ultimate contestants will be the PAP and the MCP – the PAP for a democratic non-communist Malaya, and the MCP for a Soviet Republic of Malaya. It is a battle that cannot be won by just bayonets and bullets. It is a battle of ideals and ideas.[125]

Then, in a line that was to foreshadow a dominant theme of his rule, he added, 'and the side that recruits more ability and talent will be the side that wins'.[126]

The PAP won a spectacular victory at the 1959 elections, and Lee became Singapore's first Prime Minister. Yet despite Lee's victory over the communists in the pre-election brinkmanship, Lee's group was in a highly vulnerable situation in the aftermath of winning office. Lee and his close associates spent the first two years of government preparing desperately and inadequately for the day when they and the communists would be open enemies. Lee needed to build a new support base, which required that the government deliver tangible economic and social achievements. Progress was, however, extremely modest. Unemployment was one of the most pressing public concerns, and although Finance Minister Goh Keng Swee approached the problem with a vengeance, he did not succeed in making obvious headway for some years. Except for some outstanding achievements in housing development[127] and a few more modest successes in fields such as health care,[128] Lee's group had, in fact, achieved remarkably little by the time the split with the communists came in 1961. To make matters worse, Lee's group had been totally impotent in their efforts to cleanse the PAP organisation of communists and to build new structures to rival the organisational strength of the MCP. Fong Sip Chee was a PAP cadre at the time, and his account of the PAP split that created Barisan Sosialis [Socialist Front] shows how pitifully Lee's group had prepared for the day:

> The Party Branch organisations were near breaking down. Many of them were virtually collapsed. Of the 51 Branches, 35 went Barisan. Branches lost their premises, furniture, sewing machines, bank deposits and all, while those which survived were left with only empty premises with their belongings emerging later with symbols erased or replaced, at the new Barisan branches; many had the premises padlocked when the entire core of office-bearers simply disappeared, and Party HQ staff, under Robin Sim had to break them open so that activities could continue with new batches of cadres. These cases were not too bad, however. Others suffered [an] even worse fate when the Branches were lost – lock, stock and barrel. The Barisan signboard simply replaced ours. Party Branches were near annihilation. Paid secretaries ... surfaced as ring leaders who directed the 'operation defection and robbery'. 19 of the 23 paid secretaries rebelled.[129]

The impotency of Lee's efforts to develop alternative political structures to the PAP and the MCP was demonstrated by the developments in the community centres at the time of the split. The community centres were developed under the charge of the government-sponsored People's Association, which was chaired by Lee himself. They were designed specifically to provide a social, organisational and propaganda structure to rival the communist open-front organisations, including the PAP branches,[130] but instead became new targets of communist infiltration. After the PAP–Barisan split in 1961, the centres became a significant outlet for Barisan activity. There were fifty-two community centres in 1961, and Lee Kuan Yew found it necessary to dismiss twenty-four staff because they had gone over to Barisan.[131] Neither Lee Kuan Yew nor Goh Keng Swee was prepared for the onslaught from the left in 1961, and according to Goh it was only Toh Chin Chye's courageous example that kept the leadership group from falling apart in those catastrophic weeks.[132] Considering how ill-prepared Lee was at the time of the split, it is remarkable that his government survived a month, let alone into the next century.

Lee's group in the PAP had only one source of hope during those dark days. In May 1961, when Lee's problems were escalating to dangerous proportions, Tunku Abdul Rahman, who was by then the Prime Minister of the Federation of Malaya, threw Lee a lifeline by declaring his support for a merger between Singapore and Malaya. With the benefit of hindsight we now know that this merger was not the panacea that Lee's group thought it would be, but at the time it appeared to be an answer to a prayer. Lee's political career had been built upon the premise that Singapore was historically and economically part of Malaya and that Britain's separation of Singapore and Malaya was unjust and unnatural. By 1959, Lee had lifted this rhetoric to the centrepiece of his strategic planning. Under the terms of the Constitution agreed upon in London in 1957, internal security in the self-governing colony of Singapore was to be jointly in the hands of the Singaporean, British and Malayan governments.[133] While this arrangement stood, there would always be an external whip-hand to deal with Singapore's communists. If Singapore became independent, however, this external check would disappear, since an independent nation could hardly have two foreign powers controlling its internal security. Since Lee regarded the external check as a vital restraint on communist insurgency, this led to the odd situation whereby Lee, one of the island's leading anti-colonialists, had every reason to oppose independence. He solved his political dilemma by insisting that Singapore must shake off the last vestiges of colonialism by merging with Malaya rather than by becoming independent.[134] In this way, the external whip-hand would still be in place (in Kuala Lumpur) and the communists would always be vulnerable. We may presume also that Lee foresaw the day when he would be Prime Minister of Singapore and that he was reluctant to take the personal responsibility of ordering detentions and security measures. It is a credit to Lee's powers of negotiation that he pressured the communist and extreme left leadership to commit themselves in writing to preferring merger to independence – a position that was contrary to their own political and personal interests.[135] As well as these security and political reasons for wanting a merger with Malaya, there were also powerful economic imperatives. After coming to power, the PAP government received advice from Dr Albert Winsemius of the World Bank to press for an economic federation with Malaya so that Singapore's manufacturers would have a substantial domestic market on which to base production.[136] The advice was warmly received but hardly necessary, since Goh Keng Swee had made the same call in the PAP's 1959 election manifesto.[137]

Lee spent the first eighteen months of his prime ministership trying to convince the Tunku that it was in Malaya's interests to accept Singapore into the Federation, but believed that he was making little progress.[138] Then, on 27 May 1961, the Tunku suddenly reversed his stance and began canvassing support for a new Federation of Malaysia, which would encompass not only Singapore, but also the North Borneo states of Sarawak, Brunei and British North Borneo (now Sabah).[139] It is not clear – even to the British diplomats who had been working for merger – what prompted the Tunku to reverse his position so suddenly.[140] Lee believes that the PAP's spectacular by-election loss of the seat of Hong Lim made the Tunku realise how vulnerable the Singapore situation was, and that this was the final catalyst which drove the Tunku to bring Singapore under Kuala Lumpur's wing.[141] Regardless of his motivation, the Tunku's switch drove the left to break from the PAP.[142] Now that the distant prospect of merger had become an immediate threat, they could no longer continue to support a stance that was bound to end in their arrest.

After the formation of Barisan Sosialis Lee took the game of brinkmanship to new heights. In a series of radio broadcasts Lee revealed his secret negotiations with Fang Chuang Pi of the Singapore Town Committee of the MCP, and released copies of the hitherto confidential letter in which the leadership of the left in the PAP committed itself to merger ahead of independence.[143] These broadcasts marked the beginning of a campaign that had two aims: to reduce Barisan's electoral base down to a pro-communist rump; and, to make the PAP the only credible alternative for anyone who had any anti-communist tendencies. Lee's campaign for merger over 1961–63 contained three critical elements that were to remain part of his basic approach to politics for decades. First and most prominent was his use of argument and reason. Reading *The Straits Times* of the period, one is struck not so much by the propaganda and rhetoric of the government's campaign, but by the forensic approach that Lee took to exposing errors in the opposition's arguments. Reading those newspaper accounts even decades later, one cringes with embarrassment for Lee's opponents as he dissects their rhetoric to reveal every inconsistency and false syllogism. Second, Lee used the machinery of the state as his personal political vehicle. State radio and television, community centres, the Ministry of Culture and the nightly meetings of assemblymen with their constituents were used unapologetically as arms of the PAP in the merger campaign. As one minister of the time noted, 'In many ways, the PAP and the government machinery have become one and the same'.[144] Third, the observer must be struck by Lee's brilliant use of theatrics and chicanery to achieve a political result. The key feature of the merger campaign was the referendum of September 1962. The referendum campaign was a piece of high drama designed to polarise the electorate and isolate Barisan Sosialis, but the actual vote was almost meaningless. Decades later, Toh Chin Chye described the referendum thus:

> The ballot paper was crafted by Lee Kuan Yew. Whichever way you voted, you voted for merger. There were three choices: A, B, or C. But frankly, they were all votes for merger. And we moved in the Referendum Bill that spoilt votes will be counted as votes for merger.
>
> Few understood the ballot paper. ... How do you choose? Which way do you vote? But we got away with it. ... It was a win–win situation for the government.[145]

Over the decades, Lee was to perfect the practice of placing the government in 'win–win' situations, usually with the accompanying theatrics of Parliamentary Privileges Committees or courtroom settings.

The government won 75 per cent of the vote in the referendum and scored a stunning victory. With his political authority thus buoyed, Lee continued his negotiations with the Malayan government to determine the terms of merger. There was, however, an odd characteristic about Lee's conduct during these negotiations. Lee was an experienced advocate and negotiator, and from his track record in representing the unions and dealing with the left in the PAP, he could have been expected to protect his interests during these talks competently. Yet on the surface, this does not seem to have been the case. He seemed to be incapable of identifying his own interests unless his colleagues pointed them out to him. Goh Keng Swee was concerned about financial arrangements, Singapore's free port status and the common market, and so Lee fought valiantly but unsuccessfully for guarantees and compromises in these areas.[146] Toh Chin Chye objected to Singapore giving Kuala Lumpur control of education, and so Lee secured Singapore's continued control of education.[147] Apart from these matters, the only issues on which Lee took a stance were on the questions of citizenship rights,[148] and control of labour and the electronic media.[149] The rest of the 'negotiations' would be better characterised as a series of uncontested capitulations. To Toh Chin Chye's dismay, Lee gave Kuala Lumpur control of every other aspect of government, which reduced the island to little more than an administrative unit of the central government.[150] Lee accepted a humiliatingly small representation for Singapore in the federal Parliament and even acquiesced to the introduction of Malay special rights in Singapore which, as Toh later complained, was contrary to everything in which the PAP believed.[151] Even on the central question of internal security, Lee must have been disappointed with the result. A major purpose in pursuing merger was to ensure that an outside party would be in charge of security because he did not believe that a Singaporean government could weather the political storm of detaining popular local leaders.[152] It must have been frustrating, therefore, when the Tunku insisted that Lee engage in a major security sweep before merger and before the 1963 Singaporean elections, so that Lee was forced, after all his efforts, to accept a major portion of the responsibility for mass detentions.[153] The final pre-merger humiliation came for Lee when the Tunku told him unilaterally not to enter the PAP in elections on the Peninsula. 'You stay in Singapore', he said.[154] Lee put the best face he could on the Tunku's fiat. He initially announced the PAP's decision not to contest the elections as a unilateral act of goodwill towards the Tunku,[155] and later described it as a 'gentleman's understanding' with the Tunku, whereby each of the Prime Ministers gave mutual undertakings to 'stay out of each other's backyard'.[156] Goh Keng Swee has made it clear, however, that the Tunku's words were a straightforward instruction, to which Lee acquiesced grudgingly.[157]

We will probably never be completely sure why Lee approached the merger negotiations in such an unprofessional manner, but several lines of thought suggest themselves. There is merit in Toh Chin Chye's suggestion that Lee was 'in a hurry',[158] but this is hardly an adequate explanation. It is also likely that after years of living with the tension of pursuing high-risk strategies, Lee had lost some of his emotional equilibrium and had probably already begun the slide into the stress-related instability that drove him to the point of collapse in August 1965.[159] It should also be realised that Lee was in an extremely weak position in the negotiations. As Lee wrote in his memoirs:

> My handicap in dealing with the Tunku was that while I wanted merger, he did not. I had listed the weaknesses of Singapore without it in order to persuade our people to accept it. He took that to be the total truth and became extremely difficult, since he felt we had everything to gain and he was taking on a multitude of problems. The result was an unequal bargaining position.[160]

He was desperate to be part of Malaysia, but the Tunku was accepting Singapore into Malaysia only reluctantly. As late as June 1963 the Tunku was able to threaten to form Malaysia without Singapore, and the threat was treated as being completely credible.[161]

Yet there was another problem in Lee's approach to the negotiations and to Malaysia which perhaps goes close to the heart of the matter: he and the Tunku had fundamentally different concepts of the prospective nation and they were talking largely at cross-purposes. The Malay leaders regarded Malaysia as a vehicle for Malay aspirations and for the retention of Malay cultural, linguistic and political domination under the *bumiputera* [sons of the soil] policy. To this end, the Tunku forged a political system in the late 1950s in which each ethnic community was represented by a communally based party, which then coalesced as the Alliance Party.[162] The United Malays' National Organisation (UMNO) not only was the representative of the Malays, and the senior partner in the Alliance government, but it also assumed the right to appoint the leadership of its Alliance partners, the Malayan Chinese Association (MCA) and the Malayan Indian Congress (MIC).[163] UMNO's programme of dominance was tempered by the practice of a Malay-centred multi-racialism, but no UMNO leader considered that the *bumiputera* policy could be modified until the Malays had reached a position of economic parity with the Chinese community. Despite his conversion to the cause of Malaysia in early 1961, the Tunku was still fundamentally a Malay nationalist and he would not willingly allow a Chinese-dominated state or party to exercise critical political power. The Singapore leaders, on the other hand, regarded the new country as a modern state which would aim to deliver economic prosperity to the population, while moving inexorably towards the ideal of equality of status and opportunity for all of the population regardless of race.[164] Lee's vision had been moulded by the political and ideological formation that he had received in England. His vision was forward-looking, fundamentally critical of traditional culture *per se*, and particularly critical of Malay culture, which he regarded as primitive and 'soft'.[165] Goh Keng Swee believes that Lee did not understand the thinking of the Malay leadership and that he 'totally misread UMNO'.[166] Lee was, according to Goh, genuine in his acceptance of the political supremacy of UMNO and was 'totally prepared to accept a Malay Prime Minister in his generation',[167] but he assumed that the PAP could enjoy full democratic rights in the new Malaysia. He assumed, for instance, that the PAP had the intrinsic right to challenge the MCA for leadership of the Chinese on the Peninsula[168] and passed word to the Tunku to this effect.[169] From his Western perspective, Lee's expectations were completely reasonable, but UMNO regarded them as a challenge to its hegemony[170] and therefore a challenge to the nature of the Malay state. As Lee wrote in his memoirs:

> I thought I understood them. In fact, I did not. I did not understand that their objection was basic; they did not want the Chinese to be represented by a vigorous leadership that propounded a non-communal or a multiracial approach to politics and would not confine its appeal only to the Chinese.[171]

In fact, there is a near-universal consensus that Lee was singularly ill-equipped to conduct the merger negotiations. Philip Moore, the British Deputy Commissioner in Singapore, noted how poorly Lee dealt with the Malay leadership and encouraged him to be more diplomatic.[172] Malayan-born Toh Chin Chye has expressed his conviction that Lee had no understanding of Malay culture because he did not grow up in the Malay-dominated culture of the Peninsula.[173] Lee's Malayan-born friend, Maurice Baker, has gone further and has provided firm evidence that Lee did not understand the 'subtleties of Malay conversation', and was capable of totally misunderstanding the meaning of the Tunku's words. Baker's evidence for his assertion is a conversation he had with Lee during 1964. The PAP had recently defied the Tunku's instructions and had contested some seats on the Peninsula with little success. Baker asked Lee why he had done this:

> He said: 'Well, I talked to the Tunku, and I asked him, "Tunku, do you mind if we contest these seats and try our luck to see if we will succeed?" And the Tunku said, "Well, if that's the way you feel, go ahead." So I went ahead'.

> I said: 'You know this is the Malay way. If they hesitate … They will not say "no" to it. They will say, "I'll think about it."' When I was High Commissioner to Malaysia, I would see Razak. He would never tell me, 'No'. He would say, 'I'll think about it, and let you know', which means, 'Don't bring this subject up again because I can't do anything about it'. The subtleties of Malay conversation, Kuan Yew never understood.[174]

If Lee was able to misunderstand the Tunku's ordinary conversation in such a fundamental way, it is not surprising that he did not understand the Tunku's unspoken assumptions during the negotiations. In his memoirs, Lee claims to have become belatedly aware of his ignorance of 'the Malay mind'[175] and 'the nuances of Malay talk',[176] and yet even now he seems to be genuinely ignorant of the offensive character of many of his speeches. For instance he still denies UMNO accusations that he described the Tunku as being 'not a politician of high calibre' during a speech in Malacca, and appears to be blissfully unaware that the accusation refers to an occasion when he spoke in highly disparaging terms of the 'quality and direction of the [UMNO–MCA] political leadership' of Malacca.[177] Since the Tunku was the de facto patron of the Malacca government, he could not but take Lee's statement as a personal attack upon himself.

Lee thought he was entering a new era of progress and prosperity when he took Singapore into Malaysia, but it turned out to be two years of frustration and disappointment. The common market recommended by Winsemius and sought so desperately by Goh Keng Swee never eventuated, and in fact Goh felt that Kuala Lumpur was acting in 'utter bad faith', treating Singapore as an economic rival to be crushed, rather than as a constituent state of Malaysia.[178] The Tunku treated the PAP with suspicion, and Lee personally was treated as an enemy by critical elements in the UMNO leadership, including Deputy Prime Minister Tun Abdul Razak.[179] The more Lee tried to heal the growing rift, whether by conciliation, compromise or confrontation, the worse it became. The stress of this period took its toll on Lee in highly visible and destructive ways. Lee even found it difficult to exercise self-control in front of a microphone, and he developed a pattern of making outrageous and inflammatory speeches, which Toh Chin Chye later characterised as anti-Malay.[180] When Lim Kim San, a key Cabinet minister during the period, was asked by Melanie Chew whether he counselled Lee to tone down his speeches, he replied: 'Oh yes! We did! But once he got onto the podium in front of the crowd, *paah*, everything would come out. Exactly what we told him not to say, he would say!'[181] Lee's habitual self-control slipped badly during this period and after separation his level of frustration was so high that he had to take a six-week break at the government barracks at Changi to recover his equilibrium.[182] More will be said of the Malaysia period in Chapter 3, but for the moment it is sufficient to note that in mid-July Goh Keng Swee opened negotiations with the leadership of UMNO to separate Singapore from Malaysia.[183] A fortnight after that, Singapore was 'expelled' from Malaysia and faced the world as an independent republic.

Lee and Singapore were never quite the same after Singapore's 'expulsion' from Malaysia on 9 August 1965.[184] Lee found himself the Prime Minister of a city-state without resources or natural markets. He summed up Singapore's new situation in an important speech to civil servants soon after separation:

> Before if the batsman missed the ball there was the wicket keeper. If the wicket keeper missed the ball, there was the long stop. And if it goes to the boundary, you throw the ball back and start all over again, with one batsman out.

But now we are sovereign and independent. There is no long stop. There is no British army and, much as the Malaysians think that they can step in, I think they will find that this is a real hornet's nest if they do step in. If this place goes wrong and goes communist, that is the end of the works. Before, you could always reshuffle the pack of cards and deal out a new hand. Every time you reshuffle the cards, they get more dirty and crumpled. But you could reshuffle. Now, you can't.[185]

In the spirit of this speech, the 'survival' motif became a prominent part of Lee Kuan Yew's rhetoric and dominated political discourse for the next few years.[186] The dimensions of the post-independence crises needed little exaggeration. Economically, the country had lost its hinterland and faced collapse. Socially, the country faced the challenges of racial unrest between Chinese and Malays and related religious tension between mainly-Chinese Christians and mainly-Malay Muslims.[187] Internationally, Singapore was a Chinese city surrounded by two predominantly Malay–Muslim countries.[188] Politically, the communists were a formidable force and at this stage they still had the capacity to make a parliamentary comeback through Barisan Sosialis. Faced with such a range of challenges, the PAP government was able to justify imposing draconian measures on Singapore to ensure economic prosperity and social harmony. Lee set out to build a hard-working, 'rugged'[189] community that would survive against the odds. Trade union leaders, newspaper editors, religious leaders and Chinese clan and cultural leaders were convinced, cajoled or pressured to co-operate with the government's plans. Private and communal interests were put to one side as the government transformed Singapore into an industrial city. Singapore swung solidly behind the PAP during this period of crisis. Opposition parties were consequently ignored by the electorate in the first decade after independence, and failed to capture a single seat in the Singapore Parliament until 1981. Lee used this new-found consensus to try to build a new status for the PAP as a national movement in the mould of Indonesia's Golkar, rather than as a mere political party.[190]

Lee Kuan Yew and Singapore went from strength to strength throughout the 1970s. Lee's unique contribution during this period was to provide the political and social stability upon which economic development depended. In very difficult circumstances Lee built a strong, competent government team, backed by a highly competent cival service, both of which were virtually free of corruption. He created a political system that was stable enough to satisfy the most nervous foreign investor without abandoning democracy completely. He curtailed Chinese triumphalism while dispersing the Malay kampongs so that there would be little opportunity or cause for communal violence.

Singapore became the post-colonial success in a world littered with post-colonial disasters. Lee had to abandon the last vestiges of socialism to achieve his end, but he succeeded beyond the expectations of most observers.

By the end of the 1970s, Singapore was beginning to look like a developed Western country in the making. It was, in short, becoming a prosperous, avaricious, secular, English-speaking, middle-class society. Even the peculiarity of having no opposition MPs in a more-or-less democratically elected Parliament[191] seemed to be a short-term aberration, since opposition candidates were gradually increasing their share of the vote. Lee also saw the trend towards Westernisation, but unlike many of his admirers and detractors in the West, he reacted with horror and announced that he had no intention of allowing Singapore to become a permissive, atomistic Western society.

In 1978 Lee turned to the native cultures and languages of Singapore's communities, with a heavy emphasis on the Chinese language, as an antidote for this latest example of 'yellow culture'.[192] Lee set out ostensibly to build a Singaporean 'Asian culture', but it increasingly began to resemble a modernised Chinese culture with its heavy emphasis on Mandarin and Confucianism. In the late 1970s and early 1980s Lee engaged in a series of moves that gradually placed Chinese culture and language at the centre-stage of Singaporean life and made the non-Chinese communities uncomfortable.[193] Even Lee's eugenics programme, which he launched in 1983, began to display an overtly pro-Chinese bias when its logic was used as a justification for increasing Chinese immigration.[194]

Apart from the Chinese aspects of Lee's programme, one feature has struck most observers as being particularly self-serving: his use of 'Asian values' and 'Confucianism' as a rationale for the high degree of political and social control that the government continues to maintain over its people. In the first decade after independence, when the country's problems were glaringly obvious, Lee was able to maintain a very broad domestic and international consensus that the government needed extraordinary freedom of action to achieve results. By the late 1970s, however, the crises had mostly passed and the basis of this consensus was fading with them. While the PAP still had widespread support, as a competent government should, the twin assumptions that Singaporeans had a duty to support the PAP, and that it was necessary for the government to intervene in most aspects of life, were breaking down. The consensus collapsed finally in 1981 when J.B. Jeyaretnam was elected to Parliament on the Workers' Party ticket. Lee, however, was not ready to let the power he had accumulated during the post-independence years slip away. As he was to show during his eugenics campaign, he intended to increase the level of government intervention in the private lives of Singaporeans rather than decrease it. By reference firstly to Confucianism and later to 'Asian values', he attempted to justify Singapore's highly conformist, illiberal culture as being a normal state of affairs, rather than as an extraordinary measure to meet the crises of the 1960s and 1970s. Asians have no tradition of democracy and no concept of individual rights, he said. Lee argued that Asian cultures differ fundamentally from Western cultures because Asians have very strong traditions of placing the needs of the community ahead of the needs of the individual, and that this was the basis of East Asia's new-found economic success. Western liberal values therefore cannot and should not be used to judge Asia.[195] Lee's powerful advocacy of 'Asian values' has been one of the factors that have given him a world and Asian stature far beyond that of the tiny country he led.

The sudden creation of a small parliamentary opposition in the early 1980s was a significant factor that prompted the development of Lee's 'Asian values' campaign. Restricting dissent, however, required more immediate and practical measures. Lee was by this stage a consummate master of the art of exercising power, and he deployed both the iron fist and the velvet glove against the nascent dissent. The velvet glove was innovative and took the form of government efforts to channel grievances in directions harmless to itself. These devices included the introduction of a government-appointed opposition to blunt the widespread desire for an elected opposition, and the creation of a 'Feedback Unit', which enabled people to register their concerns about government actions without having to resort to the ballot-box.[196] The iron fist, on the other hand, was a more traditional exercise of power. Lee had a long-established practice of using the full armoury of state power as his personal political weapons, but in the late 1970s and early 1980s he had refined his technique, and for the first time chose a target who was not remotely associated with the communists or communalists: Workers' Party leader, J.B. Jeyaretnam. Jeyaretnam was elected as Singapore's sole opposition MP in 1981, but was expelled from Parliament in 1986 and subsequently disbarred from practising as an advocate and solicitor. The basis of both actions was that Jeyaretnam had been found guilty in the High Court of Singapore on three counts of having dishonestly or fraudulently removed Workers' Party money in order to avoid paying the party's creditors, and one count of making a false declaration receivable in evidence.[197] This was merely one of a number of instances of Lee Kuan Yew's pursuit of Jeyaretnam through the courts. In 1979 and again in 1989 Lee sued Jeyaretnam for libel and was awarded S$130,000 on the first occasion and S$230,000 on the second.[198] In 1997 Jeyaretnam was sued successfully by Lee and ten other PAP MPs, and was again taken before the Law Society.[199]

The cases against Jeyaretnam are of particular interest because of the light they shed on the role of the judiciary. Independent bodies of high standing have studied two of the four major cases against Jeyaretnam. The Privy Council in London, which at the time was the highest court in the Singaporean legal system, subjected the 1980s disbarment of Jeyaretnam to a blistering condemnation. Their Lordships of the Privy Council described aspects of the proceedings as 'erroneous', 'unfortunate', and 'unacceptable'. They found that the Chief Justice of the High Court should have disqualified himself because of a conflict of interest, and that the prosecution held evidence that would have exonerated Jeyaretnam of one of the charges, but chose not to present it. The court's judgment was 'wholly unconvincing' and involved 'a serious error of law'. Jeyaretnam and his co-accused, said their Lordships, had suffered

> a grievous injustice. They had been fined, imprisoned and publicly disgraced for offences of which they were not guilty. The appellant [Jeyaretnam], in addition, had been deprived of his seat in Parliament and disqualified for a year from practising his profession.[200]

Despite the success of Jeyaretnam's appeal in reversing his disbarment, the Privy Council was unable to restore either his seat in Parliament or his eligibility to contest the forthcoming elections. The government responded to the judgment by restricting the right of Singapore citizens to appeal to the Privy Council.[201] The 1997 libel action, on the other hand, was the subject of a report published by the International Commission of Jurists (ICJ), which was equally cutting, though expressed in more circumspect language. In this instance Lee and his prime ministerial successor, Goh Chok Tong, were two of eleven plaintiffs who successfully sued Jeyaretnam for defamation of character. The ICJ observer, Stuart Littlemore, QC, noted that the judge asked questions at the end of the trial which betrayed 'an almost total ignorance of the technicalities of this specialist area of law', and that 'the significance of appointing to such a sensitive case a judge patently unfamiliar with defamation law escaped few of the lawyers present'.[202] Apart from this detraction from the credibility of the trial, Littlemore found two 'causes for concern' in the decision itself. First, he argued:

> The most troubling aspect of the decision is the judge's undue deference to the plaintiff [Goh Chok Tong]. He came to the court as an ordinary citizen, not as the Prime Minister, but it is impossible to escape the impression that [the judge] treated him as a litigant of a higher status than he was entitled to.
>
> That attitude informed not just the award of aggravated damages, but findings of fact on issues (notably reputation and injury to it) where no evidence was adduced.[203]

Littlemore also expressed concern that the judge found Jeyaretnam guilty on grounds different to that argued in the court – a 'lesser meaning' – and against which Jeyaretnam had not had the opportunity to argue a defence. He described this as a denial of natural justice[204] and concluded his critique with a savage piece of understatement:

> It would be unfortunate indeed if the judge's articulation of a lesser meaning were irregular within the Singapore judicial system – because it would strongly suggest that the Prime Minister had been given specially favourable treatment to avoid the embarrassment of losing his case.[205]

In the event, the trial judge's initial award of damages and costs against Jeyaretnam – S$20,000 damages for PM Goh alone and 60 per cent of the costs – did not satisfy the Prime Minister. Upon appeal his damages were increased five-fold to S$100,000 and he was awarded full costs.[206]

Yet for all the brutality of the PAP's treatment of Jeyaretnam, Lee actually has a deft touch in choosing his enemies. The treatment meted out to Jeyaretnam is reserved for opposition politicians who challenge the basic tenets of the Singapore ideology or who question the competence or honesty of the PAP government.[207] Opposition MPs who avoid these 'errors' have received much milder treatment. Chiam See Tong is the best example of such an opposition MP. After losing a blistering exchange with Lee Kuan Yew in Parliament in 1985, soon after being elected, Chiam learnt to restrict his statements on national issues to narrow parameters, while focusing mainly on municipal matters. Chiam has since gone to great lengths to stay within acceptable opposition parameters. When Chee Soon Juan began using Chiam's Social Democratic Party (SDP) as a base for more forceful attacks on the government, Chiam responded by leaving the SDP and joining the Singapore People's Party.[208] Chiam then successfully sued Chee and eleven other members of the SDP Central Executive Committee for libel and was awarded S$120,000 in damages.[209] As a result of his efforts and his circumspection, Chiam has become the PAP's favourite opposition figure, and Lee Kuan Yew has even described him as an 'asset' to Parliament.[210]

Lee retired from the prime ministership at the end of 1990. He had spent four years as Prime Minister of the Colony of Singapore, two years as Prime Minister of the Malaysian State of Singapore, and twenty-five years as Prime Minister of the Republic of Singapore. The dimensions of his achievements in these thirty-one years are staggering. Albert Winsemius recalls the climate in Singapore when he first arrived in 1960 on his World Bank mission to advise the government on economic policy:

> It was bewildering. There were strikes about nothing. There were communist-inspired riots almost every day and everywhere. ... After a couple of months the pessimism within our commission reached appalling heights. We saw how a country can be demolished by unreal antithesis. The general opinion was: Singapore is going down the drain, it is a poor little market in a dark corner of Asia.[211]

The contrast between Winsemius's recollection and the prosperous, sophisticated, orderly Singapore of the 1990s could not be starker. Yet even in 'retirement', Lee's work has not finished. As he told the 1988 National Day Rally, 'Even from my sick bed, even if you are going to lower me into the grave and I feel something is going wrong, I will get up'.[212] He also pointed out that he did not need to retain any official positions in government to 'have a very strong last word on policy'.[213] In fact Lee did retain an official position in government. Having spent nearly twenty years recruiting and grooming his 'second generation' of leaders, he 'retired' to the position of Senior Minister in the Prime Minister's Office – a non-executive Cabinet position originally created for S. Rajaratnam upon his semi-retirement. From this position Lee has continued to influence events in a variety of ways. His opinions still carry weight with the public and in Cabinet, and he still wields power in his own right, partly because he maintains unfettered access to information about everything and everyone in Singapore.[214] His direct interventions in domestic and regional affairs are often spectacular, though not always positive. His suggestion that Singapore and Malaysia may re-merge, for instance, provoked a new note of discord in relations with Malaysia,[215] which was exacerbated by his later statement that the Malaysian State of Johor was 'notorious for shootings, mugging and car-jacking'.[216]

Despite his ongoing interest in domestic and regional affairs, and despite two operations to clear blocked arteries in 1996, Lee has used his 'retirement' to travel the world as a roving consultant, guest speaker and advocate of Singaporean business. It is a mark of his standing that the former Prime Minister of an insignificant city-state receives such a warm welcome from world leaders. Nowhere, however, is his welcome warmer than in Beijing, where he has been a frequent visitor. It is not difficult to understand Beijing's interest in Lee and Singapore. Not only is Singapore a source of capital and technical expertise to fuel China's economic development, but as the architect of the 'Asian values' campaign, Lee has provided Beijing with a shield of respectability against accusations of human rights abuses. He has also been an ardent defender of Beijing's undemocratic rule of Hong Kong.[217] Lee's regular visits to China have ostensibly been to build *guanxi* [networking][218] on behalf of Singaporean businessmen, but his fascination with China appears to go well beyond business needs. One of the purposes of this book is to make some sense of Lee's sinicisation, of which his fascination with China is only a part.

Lee had lived several lifetimes' worth of experiences by the time he was fifty. By his own standards of judging a person's worth according to their achievements, he has lived a life of unqualified success. His chosen vocation was politics – the exercise of power over people – and he mastered his craft like an artisan. Richard Nixon once described Lee as one of the ablest leaders he had met, placing him ahead of Jawaharlal Nehru, Indira Gandhi and Sukarno.[219] Certainly in terms of building achievements for his country, and exercising power, Lee Kuan Yew is in a much higher class than any of these three, although he never achieved their status as idols of their people. But a quick overview of Lee's life and career, such has been given in this chapter, brings us no closer to understanding Lee and his worldview. Mere biography is insufficient for this task. These questions require a thematic analysis of his intellectual development: one that identifies the central planks of his ideology, and then explores them back towards their origins and forward to their consequences. This is the task of the next four chapters, which explore Lee's progressivism, elitism, cultural evolutionism, and his geneticism and racial views. Although they are discussed in turn, these ideological pillars are closely inter-related, and, like the nave of an ancient cathedral, each pillar depends upon the others to help it support the entire construction.

NOTES

1.   Han Fook Kwang, Warren Fernandez and Sumiko Tan, *Lee Kuan Yew: The Man and His Ideas*, Singapore: Times Editions and Singapore Press Holdings, 1998.

2.   *Ibid.*, p. 23; Lee's interview with Gerald Stone of the ABC, 7 July 1972, in Lee Kuan Yew, *Prime Minister's Speeches, Press Conferences, Interviews, Statements, etc.*, Singapore: Prime Minister's Office, 1959–90.

3.   Han, Fernandez, Tan, *Lee Kuan Yew: The Man and His Ideas*, p. 23.

4.   *Ibid.*

5.   Alex Josey, *Lee Kuan Yew: The Crucial Years*, Singapore; Kuala Lumpur: Times Books International, 1980, p. 39.

6.   Lee in Han, Fernandez, Tan, *Lee Kuan Yew: The Man and His Ideas*, p. 173.

7.   The best accounts of Lee's early life are in Lee Kuan Yew, *The Singapore Story: Memoirs of Lee Kuan Yew*, Singapore; New York; London; Toronto; Sydney; Mexico City: Prentice Hall, 1998, pp. 25–43; and Han, Fernandez, Tan, *Lee Kuan Yew: The Man and His Ideas*, pp. 23–27. For a more critical account, see James Minchin, *No Man Is an Island: A Portrait of Singapore's Lee Kuan Yew*, Sydney: Allen & Unwin, 1990, especially pp. 308–312.

8.   See Felix Chia, *The Babas Revisited*. Singapore: Heinemann Asia, 1994; and G. William Skinner, 'Creolized Chinese societies in Southeast Asia', in Anthony Reid (ed.; assisted by Kristina Alilunas Rodgers), *Sojourners and Settlers: Histories of Southeast Asia and the Chinese*, Sydney: Asian Studies Association of Australia and Allen & Unwin, 1996, pp. 51–93.

9.   Lee, *The Singapore Story*, p. 35.

10.   *Ibid.*, p. 27.

11.   Lee in Han, Fernandez, Tan, *Lee Kuan Yew: The Man and His Ideas*, p. 27.

12.   *Ibid.*, p. 25.

13.   *Ibid.*, pp. 23, 25, and; Lee, *The Singapore Story*, pp. 28–29.

14.   Lee, *The Singapore Story*, p. 34.

15.   Lee in Han, Fernandez, Tan, *Lee Kuan Yew: The Man and His Ideas*, p. 26.

16.   *Ibid.*, p. 27.

17.   Lee Kuan Yew's National Day Rally speech, 19 August 1984, *Productivity Digest*, vol. 3, no. 8, 1984, p. 12.

18.   Lee in Han, Fernandez, Tan, *Lee Kuan Yew: The Man and His Ideas*, p. 27; Lee, *The Singapore Story*, p. 38, and; Interview with Teo Kah Leong, 29 October 1996. Teo was Lee's classmate at RI.

19.   Interview with Lim Chin Aik, 21 October 1996. Lim was in Lee's form at RI.

20.   Lee in Han, Fernandez, Tan, *Lee Kuan Yew: The Man and His Ideas*, p. 26.

21.   Interview with Lim Chin Aik, 21 October 1996. Lim regularly joined Lee in the school debating team.

22.   *Raffles Institution, Singapore, Syllabus of Instruction, 1937*, p. 107.

23.   *Ibid.*

24.   *The Rafflesian*, vol. XI, no. 2, November 1935, pp. 24–26.

25.   *Ibid.*, vol. XII, no. 2, August 1936, pp. 1–2.

26.   *Ibid.*, pp. 4–8.

27.   Letter from Erik Goonetilleke to the author, 4 December 1996; and, interview with Teo Kah Leong, 29 October 1996.

28.   Josey, *Lee Kuan Yew: The Crucial Years*, p. 40; Minchin, *No Man Is an Island*, p. 33.

29.   Eugene Wijeysingha, *The Eagle Breeds a Gryphon: The Story of Raffles Institution 1823–1985*, Singapore: Pioneer Book Centre, 1989, p. 160.

30.   Lee, *The Singapore Story*, p. 39.

31.   *Ibid.*

32. Josey, *Lee Kuan Yew*, p. 5.

33. Interview with Teo Kah Leong, 29 October 1996.

34. Interviews with Maurice Baker, 25 October 1996, and Kiang Ai Kim, 14 October 1996. Letter from Lim Kim San to the author, 27 October 1996.

35. Interview with Maurice Baker, 25 October 1996.

36. *Ibid.* In contrast to his life at Raffles Institution, Lee threw himself into the social life at Raffles College and made many friends.

37. Minchin, *No Man Is an Island*, p. 33.

38. Interview with Maurice Baker, 25 October 1996. According to Lee's memoirs, this clash occurred over the organisation of a college students' union dinner, rather than over a picnic. See Lee, *The Singapore Story*, p. 42.

39. Lee interviewed on the ABC's 'Guest of Honour' programme, 23 March 1965 in Lee, *Prime Minister's Speeches, etc.*

40. Lee, *The Singapore Story*, pp. 53–57.

41. Lee's in Raj Vasil, *Governing Singapore*, Singapore: Eastern Universities Press, 1984, pp. 172–173.

42. Lee, *The Singapore Story*, pp. 62–63.

43. Han, Fernandez, Tan, *Lee Kuan Yew: The Man and His Ideas*, p. 29.

44. Lee in *The New Paper*, 7 June 1989.

45. Lee's address at the Annual Review and Display of the Boys' Brigade, Singapore Battalion, 28 August 1966, in *The Mirror*, vol. 2, no. 36, 5 September 1966, p. 1.

46. Lee's speech to a Mass Rally at Padang, 25 August 1963, in Lee, *Prime Minister's Speeches, etc.*

47. Lee in Trevor Kennedy, *Top Guns: Seventeen World Leaders in Politics, Media and Business Tell How They Made it to the Top – and Stayed There*, Melbourne and Sydney: Macmillan, 1988, p. 268.

48. Lee, *The Singapore Story*, p. 113.

49. Interview with E.W. Barker, 16 October 1996.

50. In fact this incident must have occurred in 1946, because by 1947 Lee had already left Singapore for England.

51. Interview with Maurice Baker, 25 October 1996.

52. Lee, *The Singapore Story*, p. 51.

53. Interview with Maurice Baker, 25 October 1996.

54. Interview with E.W. Barker, 16 October 1996.

55. Minchin, *No Man Is an Island*, p. 40.

56. Thomas Silcock, *A History of Economics Teaching and Graduates in Singapore*, Singapore: Department of Economics and Statistics, National University of Singapore, 1985, p. 84.

57. *Ibid.*, p. 86.

58. *Ibid.*, p. 88.

59. *Ibid.*, pp. 39–40.

60. Reply by Lee to the Chamberlain's Address at the Presentation of the Honorary Freedom of the City, 15 July 1982, in Lee, *Prime Minister's Speeches, etc.*

61. Lee at the Presentation of the Honorary Freedom of the City, 15 July 1982, in *ibid.*

62. Reply by Lee to the Chamberlain's Address at the Presentation of the Honorary Freedom of the City, 15 July 1982, in *ibid.*

63. Lee in Vasil, *Governing Singapore*, p. 179.

64. Lee, *The Singapore Story*, pp. 105–107.

65. Interview with David Allan, 10 May 1996. Allan was a fellow student and casual friend of Lee's in the Cambridge Law School.

66. Interview with Maurice Baker, 25 October 1996.

67. *Ibid.*

68. *Ibid.* and interview with George Dixon, 11 July 1996. Dixon was a student at Fitzwilliam House in 1948 and 1949. Dixon, an Australian ex-serviceman, was enrolled in the English tripos and did not know Lee.

69. Interview with Maurice Baker, 25 October 1996.

70. Interview with George Dixon, 11 July 1996.

71. Reply by Lee to the Chamberlain's address at the presentation of the Honorary Freedom of the City, 15 July 1982, in Lee, *Prime Minister's Speeches, etc.*

72. Interview with E.W. Barker, 16 October 1996; Letter from Michael Lever to the author, undated, (received 5 June 1996); *The Straits Times*, 22 December 1995. Barker was also a student at Cambridge at the time and Lever was a fellow law student and a friend of Lee.

73. Letter from Michael Lever to the author, received 5 June 1996.

74. Lee's interview with Kenneth Liang, 16 January 1987, in Lee, *Prime Minister's Speeches, etc.*

75. Lee, *The Singapore Story*, p. 123.

76. *Ibid.*

77. Interview with David Allan, 10 May 1996.

78. Interview with E.W. Barker, 16 October 1996.

79. Letter from Michael Lever to the author, received 5 June 1996.

80. Minchin, *No Man Is an Island*, p. 44.

81. Interview with Maurice Baker, 25 October 1996.

82. *Ibid.*

83. The full text of 'The Returned Student' was published for the first time in Han, Fernandez, Tan, *Lee Kuan Yew: The Man and His Ideas*, pp. 256–262.

84. See Yeo Kim Wah, *Political Development in Singapore, 1945–55*, Singapore: Singapore University Press, 1973, pp. 52–58, for a description of the political development of Singapore during the late 1940s and early 1950s.

85. Goh Keng Swee, *Urban Incomes and Housing A Report on the Social Survey of Singapore, 1953–54*, Singapore: Government Printing Office, 1958, p. 20.

86. *The Straits Times*, 6 January 1951; John Drysdale, *Singapore: Struggle for Success*, Sydney and London: George Allen & Unwin; Singapore: Times Books International, 1984, pp. 38–39.

87. Drysdale, *Singapore: Struggle for Success*, pp. 10–21.

88. *The Straits Times*, 11 October 1949.

89. Yeo Kim Wah, *Political Development in Singapore 1945–1955*, pp. 99–100. There were also English-educated Indians and Malays in Singapore, but the Progressive Party did not reach into these communities very effectively.

90. *Ibid.*, p. 100. Also see *The Straits Times*, 6 January 1951, for an example of agitation for the enfranchisement of 'alien' Chinese.

91. In the 1951 election, only 48,155 people were registered to vote. Of these, only half actually voted in the general elections of that year. As late as September 1952, the PP was advocating seven years' residency for eligibility to stand in the City Council elections. See *The Straits Times*, 11 April 1951, 24 September 1952.

92. The United Malays' National Organisation (UMNO) and the Malayan Chinese Association (MCA) were rivals of the PP, but were narrowly based, sectional parties. They were never likely to be major players in Singapore politics.

93. *The Straits Times*, 24 September 1952, reported that the SLP had no branches operating at that time.

94. Yeo Kim Wah, *Political Development in Singapore, 1945–1955*, p. 110.

95. Minchin, *No Man Is an Island*, p. 60.

96. Lee's speech at the valedictory dinner for ministers and MPs who stepped down or retired as part of self-renewal, *Petir*, March 1982, p. 5.

97. Lee in Han, Fernandez, Tan, *Lee Kuan Yew: The Man and His Ideas*, p. 35.

98. Dennis Bloodworth, *The Tiger and the Trojan Horse*, Singapore: Times Books International, 1986, p. 85.

99. Singh, Nair and Ismail were MCP cadres, but Woodhull and Puthucheary had a more ambiguous relationship with the MCP. Nair eventually switched sides and became one of Lee's most faithful supporters until their falling out in the mid-1980s.

100. Bloodworth, *The Tiger and the Trojan Horse*, pp. 49–51.

101. Lee in People's Action Party, *People's Action Party 1954–1979. Petir, 25th Anniversary Issue*, Singapore: Central Executive Committee, People's Action Party, 1979, p. 31.

102. The students originally sought the legal services of David Marshall, later to become Singapore's first Chief Minister as leader of the Labour Front, to represent them in court. Marshall, however, rejected their request and denounced them as distributors of 'venomous communist propaganda'. Drysdale, *Singapore: Struggle for Success*, p. 95.

103. Goh Keng Swee in Bloodworth, *The Tiger and the Trojan Horse*, p. 66.

104. See Kwa Geok Chew and Lee Kuan Yew in *ibid.*, pp. 85, 132; and Lee Kuan Yew in Singapore Legislative Assembly, *Debates: Official Report*, 16 May 1955, column 224.

105. Lim Chin Siong in Melanie Chew (ed.), *Leaders of Singapore*, Singapore: Resource Press, 1996, p. 115.

106. See Kwa Geok Chew in Bloodworth, *The Tiger and the Trojan Horse*, p. 85.

107. Lee in People's Action Party, *Petir, 25th Anniversary Issue*, p. 31.

108. Goh Keng Swee, (Linda Low [ed.]) *Wealth of East Asian Nations, Speeches and Writings by Goh Keng Swee*, Singapore; Kuala Lumpur; Hong Kong: Federal Publications, 1995, p. 145.

109. *The Straits Times*, 22 November 1954. The English-educated communists and the Chinese-educated communists can be considered different entities because they answered to different controllers in the MCP. See Bloodworth, *The Tiger and the Trojan Horse*, p. 86.

110. The Rendel Constitution was inaugurated on 1 April 1955. Named after its substantive author, and drafted after consultation with local political groups, it was designed as a significant but limited step towards self-government. See Yeo Kim Wah, *Political Development in Singapore, 1945–1955*, pp. 58–61, 267. Also see S. Rajaratnam in S. Rajaratnam, (Ang Hwee Suan [ed.]), *Dialogues with S. Rajaratnam, Former Senior Minister in the Prime Minister's Office*, Singapore: Shin Min Daily News, 1991, pp. 9–10.

111. Drysdale, *Singapore: Struggle for Success*, pp. 97–98.

112. *Legislative Assembly*, 26 April 1955, column 22.

113. *The Straits Times*, 28 April 1955.

114. *Legislative Assembly*, 4 March 1959, columns 2164–2165; and Lee, *The Singapore Story*, pp. 229, 256–259.

115. Bloodworth, *The Tiger and the Trojan Horse*, pp. 142–149; Drysdale, *Singapore: Struggle for Success*, pp. 176–185.

116. See Drysdale's interviews with Governor Robert Black and Secretary of State Alan Lennox-Boyd in Drysdale, *Singapore: Struggle for Success*, pp. 169, 198–199.

117. Bloodworth, *The Tiger and the Trojan Horse*, p. 182.

118. *Ibid.*

119. *Ibid.*, pp. 174–175, 180–182.

120. *Ibid.*, p. 181.

121. Drysdale, *Singapore: Struggle for Success*, pp. 206–207.

122. These events are described in Lee Kuan Yew, *The Battle for Merger*, Singapore: Government Printing Office, [n.d., c. 1961], pp. 26–29.

123. *Ibid.*, p. 203; Bloodworth, *The Tiger and the Trojan Horse*, pp. 180–189. Each of these books contains highly detailed accounts of the events leading to the PAP's electoral victory in 1959.

124. Minchin, *No Man Is an Island*, p. 101.

125. *The Straits Times*, 26 May 1959.

126. *Ibid.*

127. In its first term the PAP government built more public flats than the colonial administration had built in the previous thirty-two years: 29,635 flats and shops from 1961 to the general elections in 1963. See Goh Keng Swee, *Decade of Achievement (1970 Budget Speech)*, Singapore: Ministry of Culture, 1970, pp. 6–7; Thomas Bellows, *The People's Action Party of Singapore: Emergence of a Dominant Party System*, New Haven: Yale University Southeast Asian Studies, Monograph Series no. 14, 1970, pp. 50–51.

128. Indications of steady but unspectacular achievement in the building of new hospitals, outpatient dispensaries, maternity and child health clinics are contained in Kernial Singh Sandhu and Paul Wheatley (eds), *Management of Success: The Moulding of Modern Singapore*, Singapore: Institute of Southeast Asian Studies, 1989, pp. 173–174.

129. See Fong Sip Chee, *The PAP Story: The Pioneering Years (November 1954–April 1968) A Diary of Events of the People's Action Party: Reminiscences of an Old Comrade*, [Singapore]: Times Periodicals, [1979], p. 105.

130. Seah Chee Meow, *Community Centres in Singapore: Their Political Involvement*, Singapore: Singapore University Press, 1973, p. 18.

131. *Ibid.*, p. 22; *The Straits Times*, 9 October 1961.

132. Lee quoting Goh Keng Swee in Lee's speech at valedictory dinner, pp. 5–6.

133. Drysdale, *Singapore: Struggle for Success*, pp. 165–169.

134. See, for instance, Lee in the *Legislative Assembly*, 5 March 1957, column 1467.

135. See the statement by Sandra Woodhull, Fong Swee Suan, Lim Chin Siong, C.V. Devan Nair and Chan Chiaw Thor in Lee, *The Battle for Merger*, pp. 184–189. Also see Lee's account of these events in Han, Fernandez, Tan, *Lee Kuan Yew: The Man and His Ideas*, p. 70. The fact that these men were in prison strengthened Lee's hand in his negotiations.

136. Kees Tamboer, 'Albert Winsemius: "founding father" of Singapore', *IIAS [International Institute of Asian Studies] Newsletter*, vol. 9, 1996, p. 29.

137. People's Action Party, *The Tasks Ahead, P.A.P.'s Five-Year Plan, Part 1*, Singapore: Central Executive Committee, People's Action Party, 1959, p. 21.

138. On 11 May 1961 Lee reported to Fang Chuang Pi of the MCP's Singapore Town Committee that there was 'no immediate likelihood' of merger, but that he was 'hoping for common market arrangements with the Federation'. See Lee, *The Battle for Merger*, p. 36.

139. See the Tunku's speech in *ibid.*, pp. 119–123.

140. Lee, *The Singapore Story*, p. 366.

141. Lee in Han, Fernandez, Tan, *Lee Kuan Yew: The Man and His Ideas*, p. 71.

142. *The Straits Times*, 22 July 1961. After abandoning the PAP during the Anson by-election, the left abstained from voting on a confidence motion in the Legislative Assembly. Thirteen assemblymen abstained, including some who were not part of the communist group, but who, for various reasons, aligned themselves with the dissidents.

143. The text of these broadcasts, with supporting documentation, was published in English, Malay, Tamil and Chinese under the title, *The Battle for Merger*.

144. Bellows, *The People's Action Party of Singapore*, p. 48.

145. Toh Chin Chye in Chew, *Leaders of Singapore*, p. 92.

146. See, for instance, *The Straits Times*, 2–14 March, 14–19 April, 29–30 April, 22–26 June, 6–10 July 1963.

147. Toh Chin Chye in Chew, *Leaders of Singapore*, pp. 93–94.

148. See *The Straits Times*, 16 August 1962.

149. *The Straits Times*, 24 July, 5 August 1963.

150. Toh Chin Chye in Chew, *Leaders of Singapore*, p. 93.

151. *Ibid.*, p. 94.

152. Lee, *The Singapore Story*, p. 393.

153. See *The Straits Times*, 4, 5 February 1963, and Milton Osborne's eyewitness account of these events in Milton E. Osborne, *Singapore and Malaysia*, Ithaca: Cornell University Southeast Asian Program, 1964, p. 31. Since Lee not only survived, but profited politically from these detentions, we may presume that

this episode contributed to his confidence in using selective detentions as an ongoing tool of government.

154. Interview with Goh Keng Swee, 1 October 1996.

155. *The Straits Times*, 10 September 1963.

156. Lee's speech at valedictory dinner, p. 7.

157. Interview with Goh Keng Swee, 1 October 1996.

158. Toh Chin Chye in Chew, *Leaders of Singapore*, p. 94.

159. See *ibid.*, pp. 97, 98 for Lee's breakdown. See Minchin, *No Man Is an Island*, p. 156; and Willard Hanna, *Success and Sobriety, Part IV: The Privacy of the Prime Minister*, New York: American Universities Field Staff Reports, 1968, p. 23, for references to Lee's reliance upon prescription stimulants and sedatives during this period.

160. Lee, *The Singapore Story*, p. 475.

161. *The Straits Times*, 21 June 1963.

162. The system of communal politics in Malaya and Malaysia is explained and analysed in James P. Ongkilli, *Nation-Building in Malaysia, 1946–1974*, Singapore; Oxford; New York: Oxford University Press, 1985, pp. 75–136.

163. The story of how UMNO came to exercise an overriding influence within the Malayan Chinese Association, is told in Raj Vasil, *Politics in a Plural Society: A Study of Non-Communal Parties in West Malaysia*, Kuala Lumpur; Singapore; London; New York: Oxford University Press for the Australian Institute of International Affairs, 1971, pp. 15–31; and Heng Pek Koon, *Chinese Politics in Malaysia: A History of the Malaysian Chinese Association*, Singapore; London; New York: Oxford University Press, 1988, pp. 256–258.

164. This stance was spelt out in an embryonic form in Lee Kuan Yew's earliest political speech, which was delivered at the Malayan Forum in London, in 1950. See Han, Fernandez, Tan, *Lee Kuan Yew: The Man and His Ideas*, pp. 256–262. It was stated clearly in the earliest PAP manifesto. *The Straits Times*, 22 November 1954. It was the basis of the PAP's entire political strategy from the time it took office in 1959 until Malaysia was created in 1963. People's Action Party, *The Tasks Ahead, PAP's Five Year Plan 1959–1964, Part 1 and Part 2*, Singapore: People's Action Party, 1959.

165. The theme of Lee's ideological position and his attitude to culture is explored in detail in Chapters 3, 5 and 6.

166. Interview with Goh Keng Swee, 1 October 1996.

167. *Ibid.*

168. *Ibid.*

169. Lee, *The Singapore Story*, p. 519. Also see *The Straits Times*, 19 May 1963 for unconfirmed reports of Lee canvassing the Tunku for the right to supplant the MCA in the Alliance government.

170. Interview with Goh Keng Swee, 1 October 1996.

171. Lee, *The Singapore Story*, p. 542.

172. *Ibid.*, pp. 509–510.

173. Toh Chin Chye in Chew, *Leaders of Singapore*, pp. 93–94; and, Maurice Baker's interview with the author, 25 October 1996.

174. Interview with Maurice Baker, 25 October 1996.

175. Lee, *The Singapore Story*, p. 662.

176. *Ibid.*, p. 515.

177. *Ibid.*, p. 546; Lee Kuan Yew, *The Winds of Change*, Singapore: Ministry of Culture, 1964, p. 39.

178. Part of Goh Keng Swee's account can be read in Lee, *The Singapore Story*, pp. 600–601.

179. In July 1964 Razak gave Goh Keng Swee de facto confirmation that he was in overall charge of the anti-Lee campaign that was currently raging in UMNO's newspaper, *Utusan Melayu*, along with the anti-Chinese riots that had recently swept Singapore. See Goh's accounts in *ibid.*, pp. 568–569.

180. Interview with Maurice Baker, 25 October 1996, p. 95.

181. Lim Kim San in Chew, *Leaders of Singapore*, p. 167.

182. Toh Chin Chye in *ibid.*, p. 98.

183. Goh Keng Swee in *ibid.*, p. 147, and; Lee, *The Singapore Story*, pp. 629–631.

184. The circumstances of Singapore's 'expulsion' from Malaysia are discussed in Chapter 3.

185. Lee's address to civil servants, 30 September 1965, in 'The Prime Minister speaks to civil servants', *Bakti*, vol. 3, no. 2, December 1965, p. 4.

186. See Lee's press conferences immediately after separation from Malaysia (9–14 August 1965), in Lee, *Prime Minister's Speeches, etc.* Also see Lee's addresses to civil servants, 30 September 1965 and 15 October 1965, in 'The Prime Minister speaks to civil servants', pp. 1–8; Lee's address at the Convent of the Holy Infant Jesus, Serangoon Gardens, 11 December 1965; Lee's 1966 New Year's Day Message, 1 January 1966, in Lee, *Prime Minister's Speeches, etc.*; Lee's speech to Political Study Centre, 13 July 1966 in 'Discipline for survival', *The Mirror*, vol. 2, no. 30, 25 July 1966; Lee's address at the Annual Review of the Boys' Brigade, Singapore Battalion, 28 August 1966, in *The Mirror*, vol. 2, no. 36, 5 September 1966, p. 1; Lee's address to school principals, 29 August 1966, in *New Bearings in Our Education System*, Singapore: Ministry of Culture, [1966–67]; Lee Kuan Yew, *We Want to Be Ourselves: Speech by Mr Lee Kuan Yew Prime Minister of Singapore at Seminar on 'International Relations' on October 9 1966 at the University of Singapore* [Singapore: Ministry of Culture, 1967]; Lee's radio broadcast, 22 March 1968, in 'The Crucial Years', in Lee, *Prime Minister's Speeches, etc.* Also see Chan Heng Chee, *Singapore: The Politics of Survival 1965–1967*, Singapore and Kuala Lumpur: Oxford University Press, 1971.

187. See, for instance, Lee's address to religious representatives and members of the Inter-Religious Council, 30 September 1965, in *The Mirror*, vol. 1, no. 32, 9 October 1965, p. 1.

188. Kawin Wilairat, *Singapore's Foreign Policy: The First Decade*, Singapore: Institute of Southeast Asian Studies, 1975, p. 47.

189. For references to building a 'rugged society' see Lee's speech at Tanjong Pagar Community Centre, 30 October 1965, Lee, *Prime Minister's Speeches, etc.*; Lee's speech to the Political Study Centre, 13 July 1966, in *The Mirror*, vol. 2, no. 30, 25 July 1966, p. 1; Lee's Broadcast on Eve of National Day, 8 August 1966, in *The Mirror*, vol. 2, no. 33, 15 August 1966, p. 1; Lee's speech to Queenstown

Community Centre, in *The Mirror*, vol. 2, no. 34, 22 August 1966, p. 1; Lee's Opening Address to National Trades Union Congress (NTUC) Seminar on 'Modernization of the labour movement', 16 November 1970, in NTUC, *Why Labour Must Go Modern*, Singapore: NTUC, 1970, p. 19.

190. See, for instance, Lee's speech at valedictory dinner, p. 4, where Lee said, 'The PAP is at the heart of this nation ... I make no apologies that the PAP is the government and the government is the PAP'.

191. The limitations on the working of democracy in Singapore are considered in Chapter 4.

192. See, for example, *The Straits Times*, 12 February, 14 February, 21 April 1978; and *New Nation*, 21 April and 1 June 1978.

193. This phase is explored thoroughly in Chapter 5.

194. The eugenics campaigns and Lee's racial logic are explored in Chapters 5 and 6. Though the explicit racial bias of Lee's eugenics campaign did not become manifest until 1989, a more subtle racial bias was arguably present from the very beginning of the eugenics campaign. See Geraldine Heng and Janadas Devan, 'State fatherhood: the politics of nationalism, sexuality and race in Singapore', in Andrew Parker; Mary Russo, Doris Sommer and Patricia Yaeger (eds), *Nationalisms and Sexualities*, New York and London: Routledge, 1992, p. 345.

195. For an exceptionally well-argued exposition of Lee's views on the place of democracy and human rights in Asia, see Lee's address at the Asahi Shimbun Symposium, Tokyo, 9 May 1991, in *Ministerial Speeches*, vol. 15, no. 3, May–June 1991, pp. 12–24.

196. See Jon S.T. Quah and Stella R. Quah, 'The limits of government intervention', in Sandhu and Wheatley, *Management of Success*, p. 119.

197. *JB Jeyaretnam v Law Society of Singapore* [1988] 3 Malayan Law Journal 425, at p. 425.

198. International Commission of Jurists [S. Littlemore], *Report to the International Commission of Jurists, Geneva, Switzerland, on a defamation trial in the High Court of Singapore, Goh Chok Tong vs J.B. Jeyaretnam, August 18–22, 1997*, (cited on Young PAP, http://ypn.youngpap.org.sg, 15 October 1997), p. 2. It should be noted that Lee does not gain a pecuniary reward from winning libel actions, since much of his winnings goes towards paying his solicitors and he habitually donates the rest to charity.

199. See *The Straits Times Weekly Edition*, 15 March and 10 May 1997.

200. See *JB Jeyaretnam v Law Society of Singapore*, at pp. 430–434.

201. See *Far Eastern Economic Review*, 26 January and 2 February 1989.

202. ICJ, *Report to the International Commission of Jurists, 1997*, p. 9.

203. *Ibid.*, p. 14.

204. *Ibid.*

205. *Ibid.*, pp. 14–15.

206. *The Straits Times Weekly Edition*, 18 July 1998.

207. Direct political and judicial action against opposition candidates and MPs is only the most spectacular aspect of Lee's and the PAP's means of intimidating and restricting the activities of the opposition. Some other aspects are examined in Chapter 4.

208. Chee Soon Juan has received rough justice for his efforts. After standing as an opposition candidate in the 1992 general elections, university lecturer Chee was accused by his superior, who was also a PAP MP, of misusing S$220 of his research funds. He was dismissed from his lecturing position at the National University of Singapore. When Chee said his dismissal was politically motivated, his former superior sued him and was awarded S$210,000 in damages while the Dean of the Arts Faculty was awarded a further S$75,000. See Chua Beng Huat, 'Beyond formal strictures: democratisation in Singapore', *Asian Studies Review*, vol. 17, no. 1, July 1993, p. 105, note 17, and *The Straits Times Weekly Edition*, 10 May 1997. Just before the 1997 general elections, Chee's character was thoroughly assassinated by a parliamentary committee after he failed to correct an error of fact in a hastily prepared submission to an official inquiry. He is now described as a 'liar and a cheat as a matter of common parlance', leaving him with little public credibility. See James Minchin on 'Asia Focus', 13 June 1997, ABC Radio Australia, International Service. Chee and all of his Singapore Democratic Party colleagues were roundly defeated in the 1997 elections. See *The Straits Times Weekly Edition*, 4 January 1997.

209. See Diane K. Mauzy, 'Singapore's dilemma: coping with the paradoxes of success', *Southeast Asian Affairs 1997*, Singapore: Institute of Southeast Asian Studies, 1997, p. 268.

210. *The Straits Times Weekly Edition*, 8 February 1997.

211. Tamboer, 'Albert Winsemius: "founding father" of Singapore', p. 29.

212. *The Straits Times*, 15 August 1988.

213. *Ibid.*

214. Lee's command of information is legendary. He once told journalists that he had information about an opposition politician that 'could have exploded a bomb on him', and that he had considered passing it on to people who would make use of it. See *The Straits Times*, 24 December 1984. It is generally assumed that Lee's relations with the Internal Security Division (ISD) are such that even in his 'retirement', he can still draw upon its resources at will.

215. *Asia Week*, 21 June 1996.

216. *The Straits Times Weekly Edition*, 22 March 1997.

217. See the collection of interviews published as: Lee Kuan Yew, (Lianhe Zaobao [ed.]), *Lee Kuan Yew on China and Hongkong after Tienanmen*, Singapore: Lianhe Zaobao, 1991.

218. 'Guanxi' can be loosely defined as 'networking', though Lee quoted a more precise definition: 'the asset value of personal relationships built up from family, village schoolmates and so on'. See Lee's address, 'Developing a global *guanxi*', at the 2nd World Chinese Entrepreneurs Convention, Hong Kong, 22 November 1993, *Ministerial Speeches*, vol. 17, no. 6, November–December 1993, p. 36. A more detailed explanation of *guanxi* is found in Tu Wei-Ming (ed.), *The Triadic Chord: Confucian Ethics, Industrial East Asia and Max Weber, Proceedings of the 1987 Singapore Conference on Confucian Ethics and the Modernisation of Industrial East Asia*, Singapore: The Institute of East Asian Philosophies, 1991, pp. 236–238.

219. *The Straits Times*, 12 October 1982.

$$\cdot\ 3\ \cdot$$

The Challenge of Progress:
Hope, Fear and Praxis

We must not go against what is historically inevitable. This does not mean that we passively wait for history to unfold itself. We must actively strive to accelerate the process of history.

Lee Kuan Yew, 6 November 1960, in Lee Kuan Yew, *Prime Minister's Speeches, Press Conferences, Interviews, Statements, etc.*, Singapore: Prime Minister's Office, 1959–90.

A dominant characteristic of Lee Kuan Yew's personality came to the fore at Cambridge: his impatience. 'Lee Kuan Yew was always a man in a hurry. This is what struck me', reported fellow student David Allan. 'He would burst in waving papers and say, "I am supposed to get these off and can anyone tell me about this?" Or "I have to see so and so." He might have a quick drink, and before anyone knew what had happened, he had gone'.[1] This personal characteristic of being 'a man in a hurry' is a consistent strain in the make-up of Lee Kuan Yew. William S. Thatcher, the censor at Fitzwilliam House, described him as 'impatient' and 'in a hurry' in June 1949.[2] E.W. Barker made a similar observation of the Harry Lee he knew at Raffles Institution, saying 'he always seemed to be in a hurry'.[3] In 1955, Singapore's first Chief Minister, David Marshall, described Opposition Leader Lee as 'a young man in a hurry',[4] while Malaysian Prime Minister Tunku Abdul Rahman used almost the same words in a thinly veiled attack on Lee in 1965.[5] Lee's precipitation seems to be a natural part of his temperament, and was exaggerated by his and his family's perception that he was destined for greatness. The wasted war years, and the consequent fact that he did not gain a tertiary qualification until he was in his mid-twenties undoubtedly heightened Lee's appreciation of the preciousness of time.

It would, however, be an error to dismiss this as a mere personality trait. Lee's consciousness of time is a result also of the pessimistic character of his progressivism, whereby his faith in the ongoing progress of mankind is matched only by his fear that he and Singapore will be left behind.

The future is a foreboding reality for Lee Kuan Yew. 'I am not interested in the next election', he told an audience in 1966. 'I am interested in the next 100 years'.[6] Singaporeans are by now used to Lee outlining the country's prospects for ten, twenty or thirty years hence, and he links this need for forward planning directly to his views on progress. In 1962, Lee spoke to a meeting of Malayan students in London on his ideas of progress, albeit tailored to relate to the young audience he was addressing:

> If we lose, fritter away the next decade that we have and not make preparations for our take-off into the industrial age, then we may well live to regret it. ...
>
> When I was a student here you could tell a Malayan from a West Indian student or an Indian student by the amount of money he has got to spend. He is better clothed, he is better shod and he has got a better girlfriend because he can take them out to the better places. ...
>
> We have got to make sure that the capital we have accumulated is put to good use, that in ten years we take one stride forward, in twenty years we enter the industrial age and thirty years definitely, we are an emerged nation, not an emerging one. Because definitely in thirty years, we are going to have an emerged China and either there is also an emerged India, or there will be a submerged Asia, and if these two emerge and we don't, well, then I say Malayan students who come to London will find that the Indian boys and girls are better clothed and shod and probably have better girlfriends to take to better places. And that is the meaning of planning for progress.[7]

This speech reveals a number of characteristics of Lee's thinking which have been dominant throughout his adult life. Lee was not urging the students in his audience to plan for progress primarily so that their lives would improve, but so that their standard of living would not deteriorate relative to their neighbours. 'One of these days', he warned, 'we will look over our shoulders and suddenly find that our neighbours have got on in the world and we haven't'.[8] His certainty of progress was based not only on his reading of current trends, but it reflected the worldview that was instilled in Lee in his school-days and reinforced by his subsequent education and experience. He had no doubt that progress would occur. The only question was whether Malaya would be part of that progress, or whether it would be left behind. It is this facet of Lee's progressivism which is distinctive, and which has been crucial to much of his success. It is a common characteristic of progressivist thinking to assume that progress will be general and will include either the whole of humanity, or at least one's own society. Hence there is a tendency to take an inherently optimistic view of the world, to plan for the best, and then be disappointed. Because Lee's progressivism makes no assumption that his own society would benefit from the general progress of humanity, his progressivism is inherently pessimistic. He plans for the worst and is quietly satisfied when the worst-case scenario does not eventuate. 'And that', as Lee told his London audience, in 1962, 'is the meaning of planning for progress'.

The seed of Lee Kuan Yew's faith in the idea of progress was planted during his adolescence, while he was studying at Raffles Institution (RI). It has been noted in Chapter 2 that Lee's political consciousness began developing while he was at RI. It is now appropriate to begin exploring the nature of those ideas insofar as they can be discerned. We can assert with relative certainty that Lee's political thought did not contain much in the way of welfarism, socialism, anti-colonialism or nationalism. As late as the immediate pre-war years such ideas were not discussed in English-speaking political circles or among the students at Raffles College, so it stretches credulity to believe that they had made an impression on Lee while he was in high school.[9] Yet people such as D.W. McLeod may have succeeded in instilling in Lee a more general sense of social justice, or at least resentment at social injustice, since he had no aversion to speaking his mind on such matters. His Principal's Address at the 1936 Speech Day, for instance, called for 'a more equitable distribution of the world's goods', and condemned the practice of offering 'a well-educated boy a lower rate of wage than is expected by the meanest unskilled labour' as an 'injustice' and 'a foolhardy braking of the social machine'.[10] To move beyond these superficial statements, however, we must search for clues to Lee's later political thought in the syllabus that he studied.

The young Lee regarded the British as his natural superiors, and the benefactors of mankind.[11] English literature was one of his strongest subjects at Raffles Institution and so Lee learnt to appreciate the high culture of the British.[12] The history course was explicitly a study of the history of the British Empire, using textbooks with titles like *The Cambridge History of the British Empire*, *The Development of the British Empire*, and *The History of British Civilisation*.[13] The British Empire was presented by his teachers as the natural vehicle for the progress of mankind, and the assumption of British superiority was explicit and all-pervasive.[14] All but one of RI's pre-war syllabuses have been lost, but we are fortunate that the one that survives covers the period of Lee's studies.[15] The syllabus confirms the general orientation of the curriculum towards Britain and the British Empire in the English, geography and history courses. Of most significance is the orientation that the syllabus reveals about the history course. As recently as 1934 the history course had been basically English history, with Empire history being taught only in the senior years. By 1937, English history in the lower grades had been replaced by Empire history. In the senior grades, Empire history had been transformed into a constitutional history of the Empire, and was focused implicitly upon the gradual devolution of power to the colonies, dominions and commonwealths throughout the Empire.[16] Although the revised 'History Scheme' introduced in 1937 was a direct response to changes in the Cambridge Syllabus, the RI syllabus was unique. The 'History Scheme' had been developed through a series of group meetings of RI teachers over the previous year, and so reflected to some extent the values and worldview of the teachers in the school.[17] The new emphasis tried to reconcile the concept of the Empire as a glorious, permanent institution bringing benefits to all its subjects, with the reality that while Britain ruled the waves, already she did not rule in several parts of the Empire, and would rule less and less as colonies attained varying degrees of self-government. According to the Syllabus, it was designed also to prepare the boys to take their place as leaders in this society: 'Empire History goes some way towards developing an intelligently critical attitude towards public affairs, so that a boy on leaving school … may contribute his mite towards the improvement of the conditions under which he and his fellows live'.[18]

The history of the Empire was presented as part of the history of mankind's progress. Due emphasis was placed on the errors that led to the loss of the American colonies, which was juxtaposed to the constitutional and political evolution of Canada, Australia, New Zealand and South Africa under the Union Jack.[19] Hence, the course focused upon the nature of the differing constitutional arrangements for mandates, protectorates, crown colonies and self-governing dominions.[20] Britain had a special role in the world of this history course because of the moral virtue it displayed in building its Empire, while the Empire itself was an important vehicle for bringing about the progress of mankind. Whereas Britain's 'new' nineteenth-century Empire grew 'naturally', Britain's European rivals 'snatched up' unclaimed islands and territories that were 'too backward to defend or control themselves'.[21] The subordinate place of Malaya and the Straits Settlements was also firmly established in the minds of the students. Whereas the self-governing dominions are bound to Great Britain largely by 'the racial bond and the common cultural heritage',[22] the crown colonies 'are inhabited, for the most part, by backward populations or have been taken from other empires, and would, therefore, not be considered capable of governing themselves according to British standards'.[23] Common to all of Britain's 'daughter nations' – especially the white dominions and commonwealths – was a 'profound love of liberty, in the time-honoured British sense of liberties', a love that stood even the fiery test of the Labour Party winning power in Australia and New Zealand early in the twentieth century![24] Although culture in the colonies and dominions had not developed 'to even its normal extent amongst peoples of European stock',[25] the continuing evolution of British civilisation 'as expressed in a free Commonwealth of Nations' may be critical to the 'fairest hopes of mankind'. Only thus can we hope to develop patriotism 'purged of every selfish and ignoble taint'.[26] It is no wonder that the students at Raffles Institution considered Britain to be a 'superior nation'.[27]

The notion of the near-inevitability of mankind's progress was overt and obvious. Lim Chin Aik remembers: 'We were made always to understand that there was progress all the time. That things would be quite bleak if it were not for the British'.[28] The 1937 syllabus told RI's history teachers:

> If we accept history as 'a process of human development', frequent references – in addition to regular 'book history' events like the League of Nations Conferences, the Anglo-German Naval Treaty, the refortification of the Dardanelles – should be made to such notable human achievements as the construction of the Sydney Bridge; the building of the Queen Mary, with allusions to the changed Atlantic traffic conditions which necessitated the building of such a ship, the question of government subsidy, etc., etc., the opening of vast irrigation works in the Punjab.[29]

It may be thought that this instruction to teach a progressivist view of history could have been taken casually by teachers and be of dubious significance to a study of Lee Kuan Yew. There is, however, firm evidence that this instruction was followed to the letter. Lim Chin Aik recalled:

> In those days the Sydney Bridge was something phenomenal and the *Queen Mary* seemed impossible. These things were highlighted. We thought if they could do that they can do anything. The notion that man is always moving forward was very strong, very overt.[30]

Teo Kah Leong was in the same class as Lee all through RI, and he also recalled the *Queen Mary* and the 'Sydney Bridge' being used as examples to demonstrate the continuing progress of mankind and the great achievements of the British.[31] The progressivist culture at RI was reinforced by one of the more idiosyncratic texts in the history course: H.G. Wells's *The Work, Wealth and Happiness of Mankind*.[32] This book is an overtly progressivist social history of mankind. Wells looked forward to a nearly utopian future based upon the foundations of 'world controls', scientific planning and education.[33] While in Wells's scenario progress is not assured, nevertheless 'hope and courage are inevitable' and the potentiality of mankind is without 'conclusive limitations'.[34]

The Raffles Institution ethos of near-blind faith in scientific development and its role in mankind's progress perhaps accounts for the naïve faith that the adult Lee shows regularly in the latest scientific theory which he has read in some academic journal, whether on hereditary intelligence,[35] health,[36] or brain functions in the learning of a new language.[37] The apparent surety of natural science, and the perception that this was a vehicle for seemingly inevitable progress held a strong emotional appeal for Lee, and possibly accounts for his love of mathematics, which is indeed a science of absolute certainty. Even the most casual student of Lee Kuan Yew is struck by his frequent use of statistics, and the regular inclusion of tables and charts in his speeches. Many of his more idiosyncratic initiatives, such as his eugenics programmes, have been justified in the first instance by the use of statistics, which gives his arguments a positivist aura of authority. S. Rajaratnam has testified that Lee enjoys playing with figures and statistics.[38] This characteristic dates back to RI, where mathematics, along with English, was Lee's strongest subject.[39] Sadly Lee has never distinguished clearly between the certitude of pure mathematics, the qualified knowledge offered by the natural sciences, and the conjectural interpretation of statistics.

At this point, we are able to draw some inferences about the world-view that lay behind Lee's early political thought, if not about the content of his political beliefs.[40] Lee was inculcated with an Anglo-centric positivism that viewed the evolving world society as the product of the development of technology and of social evolution. This social evolution was not morally neutral, but was inherently positive, moving naturally towards higher and higher goals. Britain and her Empire were the highest examples of this social evolution. Lee did not necessarily see progress as inevitable, but he was taught to see a trend in history that regarded progress as natural. In this worldview, backward colonies such as Malaya and the Straits Settlements would aspire to self-government only after a long period of social development. During that time they would be taught to look after their own affairs, and would come to appreciate the superior virtue of the British concepts of liberty, justice and responsible government. Lee's vision probably included a harmonious world order facilitated by a body such as the League of Nations, with the British Empire setting an example for the rest of the world. Such was the heady cocktail of ideas that Harry Lee took with him from Raffles Institution. Impractical idealism and naïve progressivism flowed freely through his worldview. As Lee told an audience of students in 1966:

> When you are young, from about 15 or 16 until you are about 25 or perhaps even 30, it is an age of idealism when you believe nothing is beyond fulfilment. And you are motivated not by selfish, greedy desires of wanting to advance yourselves at the expense of your fellow-human beings, but by a desire to try and bring about a better world. And that is an asset to any community.
>
> I became what I am in those crucial years of my life and so it has been with many of my colleagues.[41]

While Lee's faith in Britain was to suffer terminal injury in the years following the fall of Singapore in 1942, his underlying faith in the generally progressive nature of technology, society and human rationality appears to have survived more or less intact to this day. As recently as 1992, for example, Lee declared that 'Mankind's progress has been achieved chiefly because of progress in science and mathematics',[42] while in his 1998 memoirs he still speaks of 'human evolution' as a progressive and ongoing phenomenon.[43] These statements suggest that even today Lee has retained the essential core of the progressivism he learnt in his adolescence.

Yet even by the end of the Occupation, Lee Kuan Yew was a very different man from the boy who wrote his essay on the future of the world for D.W. McLeod.[44] He was by then in his early twenties and had seen an era come to an end, along with the cosy future for which he and his family had planned. The certainty of the Union Jack had been replaced by an age of revolution, and he was driven by his experience to regard the British presence in Singapore with disdain. His youthful admiration and endorsement of the British Empire were washed away by a nascent nationalism and anti-colonialism which consumed Lee in common with most members of his generation. Yet in other ways, Lee was still the captive of the ideas and the worldview he had absorbed while he was at Raffles Institution. Although the British were no longer his idol, he retained the progressivist worldview that had been cultivated in him by his teachers at RI. Indeed, this progressivism had been reinforced to some extent by his perception of the futility of Britain's return to Singapore and Malaya:

> I learnt that no country or society can ever go back to *status quo ante*, to what it was before.

The British who came back were different people. Even the old hands who had departed as the Japanese came down the Peninsula, had changed their outlook and attitudes. They had lost respect because they ran away. The British could not re-establish their authority.[45]

This retrospective account suggests that at this point bitter experience began to personalise Lee's progressivist worldview, which he had absorbed at RI, transforming it into a more overtly political view of the world and society. He had assumed that society would move forward with the British, but now he saw with his own eyes that attempts to return to that British past were fruitless. His ideas were as yet unrefined, but there was time to explore them. Further study in England awaited him, where he would find his place in the world of social revolutions.

Lee Kuan Yew arrived at Cambridge University in 1947, armed with his intelligence, his dedication to work and play, and the energy of a twenty-three year old. Cambridge proved to be critically important to the development of Lee's view of society, culture and politics. He left Singapore in 1946 with ill-formed notions of anti-colonialism and pro-gressivism. He returned to Singapore in 1950 with an ideological worldview that was based loosely upon Fabian socialism, but was essentially a highly sophisticated version of the progressivism he had learnt at Raffles Institution. He returned also with a fiancée whom he had already married in secret,[46] a first-class law degree, political ambition, an incipient political programme, and the beginnings of a network of associates who were to form the nucleus of the People's Action Party. Lee was a chrysalid in Cambridge and he was looking for a fresh vision of the world. Some of his university tutors became Lee's lifelong friends and powerfully influenced his outlook: men such as William S. Thatcher and 'Tel' Ellis Lewis. The account of Ellis Lewis and Lee Kuan Yew given by David Allan is worth recounting in full because it demonstrates the spirit of rebellion which was present in Lee, not just in terms of politics, but in his attitude to life and the old social order:

> Lee Kuan Yew had a very close relationship with Ellis Lewis. Lee Kuan Yew was very fond of him. Ellis Lewis had been his supervisor in I don't know how many subjects and whenever Lee Kuan Yew was in England, he always made a point of visiting Tel. He was a great supporter of Tel. It was a very close relationship. He was not the best lecturer. His influence was outside lectures. His tutorials were social occasions and one could always drop into his rooms for a beer.
>
> After he was retired I visited him once and he said to me: 'What are you doing while you are here?' I said: 'Well, tomorrow night I am going to exercise my rights as a member of the college and I am going to dine at High Table'. Tel said he would take me and would pick me up at seven

o'clock. At six thirty there was a knock at the door. There was Tel with his hat and walking stick. He said: 'We're not going to have dinner with that lot. Come on. We're going to the pub'. He was that sort of character.

Ellis Lewis spoke his mind. He was a free-thinker. He had no time for pomposity, rules, conventions that he thought didn't have any purpose and he'd kick them over. Now either you related to that or you didn't. Lee Kuan Yew certainly did. There was a responsive streak in Lee Kuan Yew to that sort of thing.[47]

After his return to Singapore, Lee Kuan Yew ensured that his old friend was never short of Chivas Regal, and Allan is sure that Lee was one of the group of former students who organised and financed the purchase of a house in Cambridge for Lewis's retirement. The strength of the bond between them is indicated by the fact that in the mid-1980s, Lee rushed to England upon being told by Allan that Lewis was near death.[48] While the bond between Lee and Lewis is touching, the significance for this study is that Lee sought out and formed such a strong bond with Lewis, who was defiantly unconventional and rebellious, although this rebelliousness did not manifest itself politically.

In some ways Lewis's spirit of defiance was similar to that displayed by William S. Thatcher, another law don who was to become a lifetime friend of Lee's. Thatcher was a conservative both politically and personally, yet Lee was not deterred by political differences between himself and his idols. It may be the case that he found assurance in their 'old values' even as he was inspired by their recalcitrance. Lee's friend, Leslie Wayper, made the following telling remark:

> It is always difficult to say how much influence people have on each other, but it is I believe revealing that the people [Lee] thought most highly of and felt most indebted to were the least doctrinaire of men and were indeed conservatively inclined. One was W.S. Thatcher, the Censor or Head of Fitzwilliam House who admitted him.[49]

Like Lee, George Dixon was also an overseas student admitted to Fitzwilliam House by Thatcher. Dixon recalls that Thatcher gave the appearance of being conservative, blunt, remote and unapproachable. Yet he had a great sympathy for dominion and overseas students and was 'very much the leader. A sort of pedagogue. He was easy to admire'.[50] Thatcher was all the more admirable because he suffered badly from having been gassed in the First World War, and Josey reported that Lee admired the way that he bore his pain stoically, never asking for special favours and never allowing it to break his spirit.[51] Despite being a conservative, Thatcher displayed a spirit of unpretentious defiance, expressed through his refusal to allow his poor health to stop him teaching, by his obvious self-assurance in his dealings with people, and his unconventionally strong sympathy for 'colonials'.

By the time Lee began his study at Cambridge, he felt let down, excluded and betrayed by his adopted British culture. Now approaching his mid-twenties, he found himself lacking a cultural home, and was almost certainly having difficulty coming to grips with the transitory nature of social and political realities which he had presumed to be permanent. Hence, Lee's mind was open to ideas that would help him to understand and rationalise the revolutions that had disrupted his world. In the event, the reformism, that permeated both the political environment of post-war Britain and the intellectual climate of the Cambridge University Law School provided Lee with a worldview based upon constant change and improvement. In the process of rationalising his life, Lee adopted a clinically utilitarian view of the role of culture, which stayed with him at least until he discovered his Chinese roots in the 1970s. Lee attended Cambridge during a time of great political and social change. The Labour government was building the welfare state, and reforming education, health and the processes of the law. In 1967 Lee told a British Labour Party rally, 'Half the members of the Singapore Cabinet of ten were students in a Labour Britain immediately after the last war. We imbibed the values and ideals that moved Britain towards a more just and equal society'.[52] Lee did not just witness the transformation of British society. He immersed himself in it. After the shock of seeing his adopted British culture swept aside so easily by the Japanese, he was looking both for reassurance and for new ideas. It is understandable but ironic that he turned to the latest phase of that same British culture to find inspiration.

The lessons of reformism and social reconstruction being taught by the Labour Party were reinforced in the law course, where Lee learnt to regard culture and society as transient and malleable. The dominant political and social philosophy of the law tripos was one to which the culturally bereft Lee could relate easily and whose lessons he learnt well: the use of the law to reconstruct society.[53] Reformism was strongly advocated by a number of the lecturers and dons of the Law School and was the dominant intellectual and political force among the students.[54] One of the reformist lecturers was Herscht Lauterpacht, who lectured in International Law and was heavily involved in the construction of the United Nations during the period.[55] Historical Introduction to the English Legal System was taught by R.M. Jackson, another of the leading reformers among the teaching staff, and was substantially devoted to reconstruction and reform.[56] David Allan had trouble conveying to the author the excitement that this course caused among the students.[57] Some of that excitement was, however, captured in the Preface to the 1953 edition of Jackson's book, which explained that this edition was very different to the 1939 edition because most of the reforms advocated in the earlier edition had been implemented in the late 1940s.[58] That is to say that Lee, Allan and their fellow students were able to read about the implementation of reforms in the newspapers as they were studying the proposal of those reforms in their textbooks and in the classroom. Jackson, too, shared much of Ellis Lewis' contempt for hubris and pointless conventions. Jackson's *The Machinery of Justice in England* contains a particularly scathing critique of the 'closed guild' of English divorce court judges, which maintained and justified their positions by having 'rules that were obscure and self-contradictory'.[59] 'Common law judges', wrote Jackson in a passage laced with poisonous sarcasm,

> may interpret the law so that men are hanged or imprisoned or set free, trade unions may be crippled or exalted, the whole range of civil liberty may grow greater or lesser through precedent upon precedent, but 'discretion' in divorce is too important for the public welfare for it to be entrusted to such unreliable judges. The grotesque edifice ... might come toppling down if vulgar hands were to touch their work. The Lord Chief Justice has said that: 'Perhaps it is not vouchsafed to everybody, whether in Holy Orders or out of them, to appreciate the full sublimity and beauty of the doctrine that if one of the two married persons is guilty of misconduct there may properly be divorce, while if both are guilty, they must continue to abide in the holy estate of matrimony'.[60]

While Jackson paraded his iconoclasm in many passages of his book, the chapter on 'The Personnel of the Law' is more subtle, but of greater significance to our study of Lee Kuan Yew. Jackson observed that the similarity of training and experience in men who become judges produces a 'certain measure of uniformity in ... outlook', which 'enables us to talk about judges almost as we do about the Cabinet, tacitly postulating a body of men whose varying inclinations will appear homogenous'.[61] This tendency, combined with the fact that judges are universally educated and trained in the common law, has led to clashes between the ideas of judges and modern social tendencies:

> If a layman studies a statute aimed at slum clearance he would come to the conclusion that Parliament meant what it said, and that the core of the matter was an explicit intention to interfere with property rights. ... In fact, it is generally taken for granted that social legislation is meant to interfere or control. ... Yet when one of these statutes comes before the courts the process is this: 'The common law upholds freedom of contract and rights of property; we presume that Parliament meant to legislate in accordance with existing law; therefore we will start by

assuming that Parliament did not intend to alter freedom of contract or rights of property'. It is not surprising that with such an assumption the courts often succeed in wrecking a statute.[62]

Jackson came to the conclusion that 'the courts are in effect applying a political philosophy of individualism or *laissez-faire* in a society that has abandoned that philosophy over half a century'. In this passage Jackson argued that there is no single philosophy of law which is appropriate at all times and in all societies, and that it is perfectly proper, and indeed necessary, for the judiciary to adjust its philosophy of law to accommodate society's expectations and aspirations, as expressed through the legislature. The law is a tool that can hinder or facilitate social reform. This reformist, utilitarian attitude to the law appears to have dominated the ethos of the Law School. Lee's formal studies gave him more than just a utilitarian concept of the law. Taken in the context of the dominant ethos of the Law School, they taught Lee to regard culture as malleable and impermanent. The very essence of R.M. Jackson's arguments is that no principle of law or society is valid for all time, and that the social ethos of one age may be destructive in another. According to David Allan, there was a prevalent view among staff and students at the Cambridge Law School that

> there was not really anything that was fundamentally law – that you can make the law, you can adapt it. You can define what ends you want the law to achieve and you can model the law. The whole post-war spirit was: 'Let's make a new system that suits us'. I think possibly we went too far to that extreme.[63]

This view and the direct influence of Jackson can be seen in Lee Kuan Yew's address to the University of Singapore Law Society in 1962:

> There is a gulf between the principles of the rule of law, distilled to its quintessence in the background of peaceful 19th-century England, and its actual practice in contemporary Britain. The gulf is even wider between the principles and its practical application in the hard realities of the social and economic conditions of Malaya. You will have to build a bridge between the ideal principles and its practice in our given sociological and economic milieu.
>
> … the acid test of any legal system is not the greatness or the grandeur of its ideal concepts, but whether in fact it is able to produce order and justice in the relationships between man and man and between man and the State.[64]

These lessons were emphasised in Lee's mind by his experience at the Bar in colonial Singapore:

> The British colonial system was a pragmatic one. Its legal system used the trappings and some of the forms of Westminster, but its content was

adapted to meet local circumstances. The skill of the colonial legal and judicial system rested not in the straightforward application of the forms and rules spelt out in the Courts of Justice at Westminster and in the Inns of Court, but in ensuring that these rules were adapted to ensure the maintenance of good Government with the largest practical measure of individual freedom.[65]

In this speech Lee was concerned mainly with defending his Government's de facto continuation of the Emergency Laws by the Preservation of Public Security Ordinance, but the principles enunciated here have since permeated the PAP regime's philosophy of law and politics, and its relationship with the judiciary. The law is a tool for bringing about progress and cultural change. It is not a sacrosanct set of principles, but is one of the means by which society transforms itself, defines itself and evolves. The Singapore judiciary, therefore, should not be regarded as subservient to the government, despite the apparent ease with which the government and its ministers seem to win in the courts. Indeed, institutionally it would be difficult to argue that the Singapore judiciary – which enjoys security of tenure and remuneration and probably the highest salaries of judges anywhere in the world – is subservient to the government. Rather the courts are merely acting in accord with the needs and wishes of society and following well-established precedent and case law. If the judiciary were to adopt an alternative course, it would be expressing an unacceptable and unreasonable alternative philosophy of law and society – just as were those English judges criticised by Jackson. According to this logic, such a course of action would be tantamount to usurping the legislative role of Parliament. The conservatism that is built into the system is further buttressed by the fact that English case law, especially on issues like defamation, tends to favour the state rather than the individual.

The reformist philosophy dominating the Law School coloured much of the conversation and private reading of the students as they searched for ideas in lectures, political societies and books. Lee read 'a lot of Nehru', and identified with his *cri de coeur*: 'I cry when I think that I cannot speak my mother tongue as well as I can speak the English language'.[66] Jawaharlal Nehru was, of course, a major figure on the Asian and the world stage in the late 1940s. India had received her independence just prior to Lee's departure for London, and Nehru was seen by many as the radical leader of a new world movement of anti-colonialism. Volumes of his writing were being published at regular intervals during and just prior to Lee's time in Cambridge.[67] Although it would be foolish to exaggerate the amount of common ground between Lee and Nehru, the broad similarities between the thinking of

Nehru and that of the early Lee Kuan Yew are striking. Nehru believed that an underdeveloped country needed to develop through science, technology and state-directed and state-owned industrialisation.[68] He bemoaned the regressive impact of many aspects of tradition, describing them as a 'prison' and a 'chain ... clinging to us when we want to move on'.[69] Although he believed in a much more ideological version of socialism than Lee ever did, Nehru was, like Lee, primarily a nationalist. As Nehru wrote in a volume published in 1936:

> I am convinced that the only key to the solution of the world's problems and India's problems lies in Socialism, and when I use this word I do so not in a vague humanitarian way but in the scientific, economic sense. ... I work for Indian independence because the nationalist in me cannot tolerate alien domination, I work for it even more because for me it is the inevitable step to social and economic change.[70]

Like Lee, he took an expansive view of world history, and harboured a conviction that man is progressing. 'A study of history should teach us how the world has slowly but surely progressed', wrote Nehru to his daughter in 1931.[71] Yet there was a twist to Nehru's progressivist thinking which is of particular interest to our study of Lee Kuan Yew, for Nehru held his progressivist worldview despite being frankly aware of the dark side of history and human nature. 'History is not pleasant', wrote Nehru:

> Man, in spite of his great and vaunted progress, is still a very unpleasant and selfish animal. And yet perhaps it is possible to see the silver lining of progress right through the long and dismal record of selfishness and quarrelsomeness and inhumanity of man.[72]

Nehru's consciousness of the 'black heart' of humanity was probably both part of the basis of Nehru's appeal to Lee Kuan Yew, and a stimulant to Lee's dim view of human nature.

Although many similarities can be discerned between Nehru's ideas and those of Lee Kuan Yew in the 1950s, perhaps the most overt result of Lee's fascination with Nehru was not the import of his ideas at all, but a negative lesson that Lee drew from reading Nehru. A dominant aspect of Nehru's pre-independence career was his record of multiple detentions by the British authorities. Nehru became a martyr and a national hero, but while he was in prison he lost almost all of his capacity to influence events. In 1930, for example, Nehru and Gandhi contrived to be arrested as part of the Civil Disobedience campaign, and spent most of the next year in prison. Although their arrest provided a focus for the Civil Disobedience movement, it deprived Nehru of most of his influence in the continuing campaign. While not drawing a lesson of the futility of incarceration himself, Nehru wrote in his diary of the other members of the Working Committee who 'were outside and were still carrying on an active struggle against the Government'.[73] When Nehru decided that a 'No Tax' campaign was needed to take the Civil Disobedience campaign to the rural areas, it was only during a brief period of freedom that he could act.[74] This aspect of Nehru's early career is surely not unrelated to Lee's conviction, expressed to E.W. Barker while they were at Cambridge, that 'we should strive for independence but in the process we mustn't be put in gaol'. 'Once you are in gaol', Lee said, 'there is nothing much you can do. You will be a martyr and a big hero, but you will be useless'.[75] Lee walked a fine line between freedom and detention until Singapore's separation from Malaysia in 1965, but as Barker observed, 'He did that well. Many times, we were nearly put in gaol, but somehow he was never detained'.[76] There can be little doubt that Nehru's example was a major factor in the strategic basis of Lee Kuan Yew's aversion to detention, though a more personal reason may be found in Nehru's depressing descriptions of life in a colonial prison.

Nehru's influence on Lee can be seen also in Lee's decision to identify the PAP with the Non-Aligned Movement, though this development was not to come until years after Lee left Cambridge. During the heady days of the 1950s his identification with Nehru was the key to the rationalisation of his united front with the Malayan Communist Party. 'Like Mr Nehru', he said, 'I say that Colonialism is infinitely worse than Communism'.[77] 'At present I follow Nehru's line of neutralism'.[78] Although Nehru provided Lee with a convenient formula whereby he could avoid offending the communists, he in fact was strongly anti-communist, and had been afraid of the ruthlessness and cruelty of the communists ever since he saw and heard their execution squads at work after the Japanese surrender in 1945.[79]

Of greater significance than Nehru to this study of Lee Kuan Yew was Arnold Toynbee's *A Study of History*, which was one of the more commonly read extra-curricular texts during Lee's time in the Law School. 'We all had our own copy. Everybody was interested in it and everybody was talking about it', said David Allan as he showed me his old copy of Somervell's abridgement, which he purchased while studying at Cambridge.[80] There are many aspects of Toynbee's thesis which are relevant to a study of Lee Kuan Yew: the progressivism which lurks behind Toynbee's cyclical view of history; the malleable nature of culture; and the role of the 'creative minority' as the dynamic leadership of the passive or 'uncreative' majority.[81] For the moment, however, it is sufficient to note that Toynbee maintained that civilisations are created and then continually evolve in response to a series of internal and external challenges.[82] 'Civilisations are not static conditions', wrote Toynbee, 'but dynamic movements of an evolutionary kind. They cannot stand still, but they cannot reverse direction without breaking their own law of motion'.[83] The nature of the challenges to a people or a civilisation, and their subsequent response to these challenges, determine the dominant characteristics of a society. An integral part of the Toynbeean worldview is the transient nature of civilisations, society and culture. That Lee Kuan Yew was a devotee of Toynbee from his earliest days in politics is beyond doubt since Goh Keng Swee has confirmed that Lee regularly quoted Toynbee's 'Challenge and Response' thesis in Cabinet meetings from the time the PAP first came to office in 1959.[84] As a devotee of Toynbee, Lee adopted an evolutionary and utilitarian view of culture, regarding it as something that is fluid and malleable, both reflecting and driving social changes. In one sense the evolutionary reformism in the Law School went further than Toynbee. 'For the most part', said Allan,

> I think there was this feeling that you could look back on history and – there was this historical cast to the syllabus – and you could see the pattern of evolution emerging, but we were very much at the point where we could say that we could control that. That it is not something that we just sit back and let happen.[85]

To some extent, the climate of Cambridge as a whole was influenced by a strongly utopian urge for reform and change. This was not restricted to the Law School, or just to the political left. Boris Christa was a student in the modern languages tripos during Lee's time, and described himself as a liberal. Nevertheless, he was conscious of

> a quite distinct utopian flavour about our thinking. Perhaps we had some disagreements about how, but the notion of a new Britain being built as a land fit for heroes, that was really quite a living ideal. We really did believe that things would go that way and we could help to swing it that way.[86]

In Christa's post-war idealism, society was 'always moving forward. That seemed to us almost axiomatic that in this way we could move forward and would achieve greater justice, a better world'.[87] Cambridge in the late 1940s was a cauldron of ideas. Bertrand Russell and G.M. Trevelyan were both on campus and their lectures were the regular diet of many students who were not even enrolled in their subjects.[88] The Cambridge Union attracted national and international speakers from all shades of the political spectrum.[89] Julian Huxley and Arnold Toynbee's ideas were well known and actively discussed.[90] Communism was a strong force, particularly among the colonial students. In the background was the reality that the spirit of reform and reconstruction had become so pervasive that the radical reforms recommended in the Beveridge Report had been broadly endorsed by both the Conservative and the Labour parties, and indeed the previous Conservative government had moved to implement many of its recommendations.[91] Nevertheless, Labour was the party most strongly identified with the Report and the one to which reformers were most naturally drawn.[92]

After perusing the diversity of political ideas in Cambridge, Lee found his home in the democratic left, which appeared to be the dynamic force behind British reformism and Britain's efforts to divest herself of her empire. Yet as with most elements of Lee's life, it would be over-simplistic to think that he merely became a socialist. According to his friend, Michael Lever, Lee's views were thoroughly non-doctrinaire.[93] The development of his political thought at this stage of his life almost eludes categorisation. This is reflected in the diverse and superficially conflicting accounts of Lee's politics given by his friends and associates at Cambridge. One fascinating feature of Lee's mentality does, however, emerge: the compartmentalisation of different aspects of his life. At Cambridge his study, his social life and his political life were kept almost separate, which meant that Lee showed a different face to each group of friends and associates. Michael Lever believes that 'most of his serious thinking was about law, pure and simple', and reports that

> if he had any serious coherent political philosophy at the time, he certainly didn't talk about it. ... In my view he was not a real socialist, but some-one who would obviously look upon as allies, socialists who were by defini-tion, against colonialism. ... He was, to my mind, a complete pragmatist.[94]

> The Labour administration's ... mind set was instinctively with the poor against the rich, with the workers against the bosses, and with the oppressed (e.g. colonial peoples) against the oppressors (e.g. imperialists). So of course, Lee was more than willing to march in step with them. In a phrase, they were useful allies to help him achieve his political objective, which was to achieve freedom for Malaysia in general and Singapore in parti-cular. That had nothing to do with socialism.[95]

Yet another Cambridge friend, Leslie Wayper, reports:

> My impression is that Lee was a socialist before he came to Cambridge. Lee was then often thought of as being a communist. He often said that if he had to choose between Colonialism and Communism he would prefer Communism. He made bitter references then to British Colonialism but nothing he said suggested he had any illusions about Communism. It was obvious that he was a strong Socialist: Colonialism and Com-munism were both evils he wanted to avoid.[96]

David Allan believes that Lee 'would have been a socialist only in the sense that he thought society had to be remodelled',[97] and all he could recall of Lee's anti-colonialist views at the time is 'a vague recollection of a conversation when Lee was holding forth about colonialism over a pint of beer or something late one night'.[98] While these accounts are not in conflict and each carries its own insight into the early development of Lee's political thought, clearly Lever, Wayper and Allan did not see the side of Lee which E.W. Barker observed. When asked how heavily Lee was involved in the Labour Party and the Labour Club at Cambridge, Barker replied:

> Oh, very much so. He had a lot of friends in the Labour Party. ... Lee became interested in politics while he was at Cambridge – while he was a student. He mixed up with these chaps in the Labour Party. ... His English friends were mostly Labour. ... The Labour Party was part of his inspiration.[99]

Unbeknownst to some of his friends, Lee was, in fact, heavily involved in the Cambridge University Labour Club, and in the Labour Party, and in 1950 he even campaigned in a by-election on behalf of a Labour Party candidate in Devon.[100] Lee was also closely associated with the Fabian Society, and maintained that association until the 1970s.[101] Yet his friends' multi-faceted perception of Lee's politics gives a better clue to the Cambridge phase of Lee's developing political thought than does his more overtly political involvement in the Labour Party. It is not that Lee's flirtation with British Labour was feigned. Speaking in the 1990s of Britain's post-war Labour government, Lee could still capture some of the excitement of the period and at the same time indicate the utilitarian aspect of his own attraction to socialism:

> They were going to create a just society for the British workers – the beginning of a welfare state, cheap council housing, free medicine and dental treatment, free spectacles, generous unemployment benefits. Of course, for students from the colonies, like Singapore and Malaya, it was a great attraction *as the alternative to communism*.[102]

Lee had already been courted by the communists at London University, and had rejected their overtures.[103] He was emotionally repelled both by the savagery he saw in the communist execution squads after the Japanese Occupation, and by the injustices of capitalism.[104] Democratic socialism was certainly a palatable alternative for an anti-colonialist who craved change but who had rejected communism. Yet if we are to give Lee's youthful socialism any credence, this is an insufficient explanation. Likewise Michael Lever's explanation of Lee adopting the British Labour Party as a mere ally of convenience in his anti-colonialist crusade seems to trivialise Lee's socialism, although the tenor of Lee's campaign speech in Devon suggests that there were elements of truth in Lever's assessment.[105] It is just conceivable that Lee's 'socialism' was never more than posturing, but it stretches credulity to accept such a simple scenario. It is more likely that Lee's socialism was both genuine and convenient: an attractive and fashionable vehicle through which he could express his deeply held ideological notions of progress and social evolution, while furthering his political programme of anti-colonialism and social reform. Lever goes some way towards supporting this view of Lee, though he sees the influence of progressivist ideology as incidental, rather than central:

> All the 'colonial' students at Cambridge knew, of course, which way the wind was blowing, and it was in their favour. Their political 'philosophy' was simple. Number one, in capital letters: INDEPENDENCE. Number two, unstated but assumed (and accurate as it turned out in many cases) that they themselves would be the new leaders of their countries. ...
>
> Their natural mentors were what you call progressivists – Shaw, Wells, the Fabians – and their natural allies the socialists, or to be more specific the British Labour leadership of my generation. ...
>
> There is a phrase in an essay by Shaw, I think, that describes the Harry I knew perfectly. I cannot put my finger on the quotation precisely, but in describing a particular historical hero of his, he said that he was essentially a man who would have suited the modern world, because like modern man he wanted to move fast, and he who wants to move fast, travels light, unencumbered by the heavy luggage of doctrine, whether political or religious.[106]

Yet there is reason to believe that Lee's freedom from 'the heavy luggage of doctrine' was true only within the context of his progressivist worldview. We have already seen that the progressivism that Lee absorbed at Raffles Institution was reinforced by the return of the British after the Occupation and given a new level of sophistication by the intellectual and political climate in the law tripos and Cambridge as a whole. If we think of Lee's attraction to the company and the ideas of iconoclasts such as Ellis Lewis and R.M. Jackson, along with the influence of Nehru and Arnold Toynbee,[107] it is not difficult to see a deeper set of values at work than merely political ideas. He was yearning for a new way to view the world and himself which would explain the fundamental changes which had rocked the foundations of his Anglo-centric world and his anticipated place within it. The 'doctrine' he chose was one with which he was already familiar: progressivism. This proved not to be 'heavy luggage', but a fast and highly manoeuvrable vehicle which would have served Michael Lever's 'modern man' very well. Apart from socialists being natural allies of non-communist anti-colonialists, socialism was attractive to Lee primarily because it was a political theory of social progress. It was, however, only a theory, and years later Lee was to feel no compunction about modifying and eventually abandoning socialism while retaining the essence of the worldview upon which, in his mind, the theory rested.

We have already considered the origins of Lee's worldview at Raffles Institution and most of the immediate post-war influences on the development of his ideological progressivism. To proceed further, we need now to consider the details of a major source of inspiration for Lee's progressivist ideology, Arnold Toynbee's *A Study of History*.[108] First, however, it is necessary to look briefly at the characteristics of progressivist thought *per se*. Progressivism, or 'a belief in progress', is described by Sidney Pollard as implying that

> things will in some sense get better in the future, but it has never been limited to this simple idea of melioration. It is, to begin with, never a belief in a religious sense, as a dogma, nor is it based on the hope of a conjunction of favourable accidents. It is, instead, always in the nature of a scientific prediction, based on the reading of history, or at least of recent history, and the operation of laws of social development. Thus a belief in progress implies the assumption that a pattern of change exists in the history of mankind, that this pattern is known, that it consists of irreversible changes in one general direction only, and that this direction is towards improvement from a less to a more desirable state of affairs.[109]

Progressivist thought has been dominant in Western thinking to some degree since the Renaissance, though its strength has ebbed and flowed with the degree of optimism in the Western world. The horror and futility of the First World War, for instance, shattered the exuberant optimism of the pre-war years and the last quarter of the nineteenth century. The hopes that many people pinned on inter-war developments, including the creation of the League of Nations, went some way towards restoring hope, but blind faith in progress was lost for a generation. On the other hand, the Allied victory against the Axis Powers in the Second World War ushered in a short period of credulous optimism in Western Europe and the United States, which was directly associated with a re-surgence of progressivist thought. In Britain this phase of progressivism took the form of faith in a better world through social reform, de-colonisation and international co-operation. Lee Kuan Yew's progressivist worldview germinated in the mildly optimistic milieu of the inter-war years. His progressivism developed into a sophisticated worldview in the rosy period immediately after the Second World War. It was in this environment that Toynbee's 'Challenge and Response' thesis made such a big impression on Lee Kuan Yew. In 1996 the following exchange took place in an interview with Goh Keng Swee:

MDB: Lee seems to have been driven by the need for improvement, whether of society, whether it is himself...

Goh: Oh yes. Of course. Everybody had.

MDB: Even down to the people. I am thinking here of the married graduates programme.

Goh: Correct. He was influenced by that British writer, Toynbee. He used to quote examples of Toynbee at Cabinet meetings. The gist of Toynbee's view is this: The society must be faced with a challenge, and that challenge must be powerful, but not too powerful, so they can organise themselves to overcome.

MDB: How early did you become aware of Toynbee's influence?

Goh: During Cabinet meetings straight after we formed the government.[110]

Goh Keng Swee's testimony goes further than merely confirming the influence of Toynbee on Lee. His interview confirmed that the drive for improvement was endemic in the milieu of his generation of Malayans, and he was surprised that this fact needed to be stated. Toynbee's influence followed that of the seminal contribution of Raffles Institution. It coincided with Lee's reading of Nehru and the influence of the contagious reformism of the British Labour Party and the law tripos at Cambridge University. Yet among all of the progressivist ideas which influenced Lee as a young adult, it was Toynbee whose effect was the most overt and lasting. Lee read into *Study* a progressivist theory of history beyond anything intended by Toynbee himself. Lee took Toynbee's concept of 'universal states', which Toynbee argued was one of the last stages of a civilisation's decay,[111] and twisted it into a stage of a civilisation's advance: 'Man gropes forward towards progress. One thing I do know: That it is universal states and universal religions – as Toynbee has analysed – that really bring the whole of mankind forward'.[112]

Toynbee claimed not to be writing a progressivist view of history, yet *Study* meets most of the criteria of progressivism outlined by Pollard. The early volumes of *Study* identified a pattern of history that was, to use Pollard's words, 'in the nature of a scientific prediction, based on the reading of history ... and the operation of the laws of social development'. Strictly speaking, Toynbee postulated that there is a cyclical, rather than a progressive pattern in history. He identified the factors that lead to the creation of a civilisation, the stages in its development, and finally the basis of its nearly inevitable collapse.[113] From this collapse, a new civilisation might be born, thus beginning the cycle again. Toynbee conceived of and planned the argument for *Study* immediately after the First World War,[114] when Victorian optimism was lying dead on the battlefields of France. He argued that he had found a pattern of history that explained the great trauma into which Europe had been senselessly plunged. Yet Toynbee had been educated and lived his life thus far in the positivist milieu of the Victorian era, when belief in progress and rationality was firm and unquestioned and he retained many of the tenets of a progressive worldview. Underlying his cyclical view of history was an assumption that development was progressive up to the onset of the 'times of trouble' which presaged the civilisation's fall.[115] Toynbee judged a civilisation as successful only if there was continuous improvement[116] and a society where there was no improvement was dismissed as an 'arrested civilisation' whose contribution to the future development of mankind was marginal.[117] On the other hand, a successful civilisation's breakdown contained the seeds for the formation of one or more successor civilisations.[118] While Toynbee technically argued that the successor civilisations need not be morally or socially superior to their predecessor, the whole language of *Study* assumed that this would, in fact, be the case. As Toynbee himself admitted:

> The metaphor of the wheel [used in the cyclical conception of history] offers an illustration of recurrence being concurrent with progress. The movement of the wheel is admittedly repetitive in relation to the wheel's own axis, but the wheel has only been made and fitted to its axle in order to give mobility to a vehicle.[119]

The fundamentally progressivist assumptions of *Study* were established in the first volume. As Toynbee wrote:

> Mankind could not have become human except in a social environment; and this mutation of sub-Man into Man ... was a more profound change, a greater step in growth, than any progress which Man has yet achieved under the aegis of civilizations.[120]

In Toynbee's world, the advent of humanity was itself the result of social progress among sub-humans. Since then, humanity has continued to progress as social development has continued. The progressivist conception of development was reinforced by the use of an analogy whereby civilisations trying to advance were likened to mountain climbers trying to conquer a sheer cliff face. Those who are, at the moment, resting on a ledge have climbed to that level, and may or may not continue their quest, while those above them are climbing to the next ledge, although they have no idea how far above them that may be, nor how difficult the climb will be.[121] In Toynbee's and Lee Kuan Yew's conception, this analysis is appropriate because civilisations have predetermined but unknown levels of development through which they must pass if they are to continue their ever-upward climb.[122] 'Some [societies] may eventually come to rest', Toynbee opined, 'by attaining ... the goal of human endeavours: the mutation of Man into Superman',[123] while arrested civilisations, using the imagery of the mountain climbers, 'have been brought up short and can go neither backward nor forward'.[124] The progressivist conception of history is the essential milieu that sustains the logic of *Study*, and without it, the entire edifice collapses.

It is axiomatic that in the world of Toynbee, progress means change in a civilisation's culture and in its very essence. Indeed, 'as soon as a civilization has ceased to grow, the charm of its culture evaporates'.[125] According to both Toynbee and Lee Kuan Yew, healthy civilisations are never static, but are dynamic and evolutionary movements.[126] Toynbee offered a number of historical examples of such fundamental social changes, including the impact of industrialism on slavery, the impact of democracy and industrialism on the state, and the impact of religion on caste.[127] Toynbee saw progress as being driven by challenges to which a society must respond successfully. A successful response brings social development and progress, while an inadequate or erroneous response spells temporary or permanent stagnation, or even the death of the civilisation. Further, it is not sufficient to respond merely effectively to a challenge. According to Toynbee,

> Growth is achieved when an individual or a minority or a whole society replies to a challenge by a response which not only answers that challenge but also exposes the respondent to a fresh challenge which demands a further response on his part.[128]

Although Goh Keng Swee's testimony confirms that Lee cited Toynbee regularly from 1959 onwards, the direct influence of the 'Challenge and Response' thesis on Lee's thinking was not obvious in the decade following his return to Singapore. Rather, Lee's progressivism was subsumed into the anti-colonialist and democratic socialist rhetoric of the PAP and into his and Rajaratnam's cultural evolutionary programme.[129] With the benefit of our knowledge of Lee's ideological development, however, it is possible to reconstruct with reasonable certainty some of Lee's motivation for his rapid transformation of Singapore's society and its economy in the first, frantic decade of government. When Lee began his political career, he purported to be a socialist in the mould of the British Labour Party. There is an almost unbroken line of continuity between his attraction to democratic socialism at Cambridge, and his election to government as the leader of a socialist party in 1959.[130] It was argued earlier in this chapter that Lee was attracted to socialist ideas at Cambridge because the socialists made ideal allies in the anti-colonialist struggle, and because the socialist worldview accorded roughly with his own progressivism. An examination of Lee's record in government up to 1965 allows us to be more precise in our characterisation of the nature of Lee's socialism. Lee did identify with Fabianism's general desire for social progress, but more significantly, he regarded democratic socialism as an economic and social system which would 'pitchfork' Malaya into the modern world.[131] Lee took a strictly linear view of progress, whereby societies that were 'behind' had their path substantially mapped out for them by the 'leaders'. Lee consequently regarded the social, economic and technological progress of Europe as the benchmark of progress in the world. If we apply Toynbee's analogy of the cliff face, we might say that Europe had reached and moved past several ledges, including that of colonialism and industrialisation. There was no doubt in Lee's mind that the capital accumulated as a result of Europe's colonialist history was a critical factor in its success. Lee said in 1962:

> No historian of economic history has attempted to deny that the Industrial Revolution of the Western countries was in large measure due to the capital accumulation made possible by the large surpluses drawn from their colonial possessions. Even America, a country at present with the world's highest standard of living, owes its wealth to the tremendous human sacrifices which the Negro slaves taken out from Africa laboured to produce for the Americans of European descent.[132]

But Malaya had to industrialise without the benefit of exploiting colonies. In much the same way that Mao set out to use socialism to by-pass Marx and Lenin's theoretical stages of dialectical materialism, Lee set out to use socialism to by-pass some of the Toynbeean 'ledges' in the history of Europe's progress to industrialisation.

Lee entered politics espousing fairly conventional Fabian socialist views, believing that 'for the first time in the history of man, he is trying to establish an egalitarian society', and that 'the process towards such a view is inevitable'.[133] Yet from the beginning there were notable discrepancies between his position and that of British and European socialists. In 1955 Lee indicated that he regarded 'state planning and control' as central to the concept of socialism: 'I have always thought that a Socialist is one who believes that state planning and control would bring about the greatest benefit to the community as a whole'.[134] While Lee's description of socialism is accurate insofar as it goes, Lee deliberately avoided acknowledging that widespread state ownership is normally considered to be a feature of a socialist state and that it was one of the tenets of both Nehru's socialism[135] and that of the British Labour Party. It is reasonable to surmise that Lee was choosing his words carefully because he did not wish to be held to a programme of nationalisation which would be difficult, if not impossible, to implement in Singapore. If, however, Lee was choosing his words with such care, we may also conclude that he was serious in his attraction to 'state planning and control', and that his vision of socialism was based substantially upon the utility of a strong, centralised state as a tool for achieving national goals. Indeed, Lee's subsequent career has demonstrated that this paternalistic centralism was more deep-seated in his psyche than any theory of socialism. In 1957 he revealed that his vision of socialism was directed primarily to achieving economic development:

> In our desire ... to expand industrially and rapidly, we have to attempt all kinds of not quite orthodox socialist schemes to try to do in ten or twenty years what European nations have taken about a hundred years to do.[136]

Lee regarded the strong paternalistic state as a useful tool to accumulate and deploy capital to achieve unnaturally rapid economic development. Because state control was a more substantial part of Lee's socialism than state ownership, he had no hesitation in curtailing plans for nationalisation of enterprises. In 1959 Lee told a mass rally that despite the theory of socialism, 'the continuance and development of the entrepôt economy means that private enterprise and capital must be allowed to further develop trade and commerce, and to break new ground in building up manufacturing industries'.[137]

To Lee, socialism was primarily a means of organising society to industrialise and so bring prosperity in the shortest possible time. The key feature of Lee's socialism, and the feature which is common at all stages of its development, is the concept of catching up to the developed world: 'to do in ten or twenty years what European nations have taken about a hundred years to do'. In this spirit, Lee told the Socialist International Congress in September 1965:

> The democratic socialist has to organise to get the people to put in more effort after independence. He has to demonstrate that the sensation of improved living standards can give encouragement and enthusiasm to people in their effort, so speeding up capital accumulation and the acquisition of higher technical skills which can bring about a better life.[138]

Earlier in the same year he told the Asian Socialists' Conference that democratic socialists must 'mobilise human resources, to pitchfork our countries and backward economies into the industrial and technological era'.[139] The element of making progress and 'catching up' dominated Lee's socialism as early as 1957 and was still the primary feature of his rhetoric in 1965. After separation from Malaysia, Lee was to prove that this was more than just polemic as he, with Goh Keng Swee and other colleagues, led Singapore on an enviable march of economic development in which Singapore did 'catch up' with most of the West by the 1990s. We know from Goh Keng Swee's testimony that Lee regularly quoted Toynbee's 'Challenge and Response' thesis during this period and that he regarded the task of 'catching up' with the West economically as a major challenge facing Malaya. In the absence of more conclusive evidence, we may surmise that he saw this challenge in Toynbeean terms, and that he regarded the adoption of modern ideas and social changes, most notably those that would facilitate industrialisation, as the correct response to the Toynbeean challenge. At this stage of Lee's life, a centralised, paternalistic socialist state appeared to be most credible mechanism for responding adequately to this challenge.

In the first decade of Lee Kuan Yew's political career his chosen role was that of a socialist and an anti-colonialist leader, and an intrinsic component of his rhetoric and programme was his advocacy of merger with Malaya. Lee saw merger partly as the answer to the problems created by Singapore's small size and lack of resources. Lee put this argument succinctly in a political radio broadcast in 1961:

> [Malaya] is the hinterland which produces the rubber and tin that kept our shop-window economy going. ... Without this economic base Singapore would not survive.

> Without merger, without a reunification of our two governments and an integration of our two economies, our economic position will slowly and steadily get worse.[140]

By 1965, Singapore had joined Malaysia, and Lee was fighting a losing battle to make the new Federation a success. In this period the latent pessimism in Lee's progressivist thinking became a dominant feature of his personality and his worldview. Gone was the comforting Fabian notion of inevitable worldwide progress. He told a socialist conference in 1965:

> There was a time not so long ago ... when people expected the whole world to go socialist. Throughout the world there seemed to be a inevitable trend towards a more egalitarian society. ...

> Today, two decades later, we have a much more sober realization, that automatic progress towards an equal and just world is not something that can be taken for granted.[141]

A sense of desperation took such a powerful grip on his mind that it had a serious effect on the character of his leadership. The failure of socialist governments in Britain and in the developing countries undermined Lee's general faith in socialism,[142] but his concern was focused primarily on the immediate situation in Malaysia. Relations between the PAP and Kuala Lumpur were already strained when racial tensions spilled into the streets less than a year after Malaysia's formation. In July 1964, four people were killed and 178 were injured in race riots between Singapore's Chinese and Malay communities.[143] Lee's frustration with Kuala Lumpur, which was already high, reached a new peak when the enormity of the amount of power he had handed over to the central government dawned upon him. Whereas before merger, Special Branch and the police had reported to the Singapore government, they now reported to and took their orders from the Federal Minister for Home Affairs, Tun Abdul Razak. As a consequence, the PAP had no warning of the riots and was totally unprepared.[144] To add insult to injury, during another set of riots, Lee Kuan Yew, Toh Chin Chye, Goh Keng Swee and S. Rajaratnam were so helpless that all they could do was lodge a formal complaint at a police station, and try to telephone Razak in Kuala Lumpur. Razak could not be found because he was 'probably on the golf course'.[145]

Chapter 2 has mentioned how the stress of the Malaysia period affected Lee's emotional balance. He developed a pattern of making inflammatory anti-Malay speeches,[146] and continued to make them even after his colleagues counselled him to tone them down, and he nominally agreed.[147] After separation Lee had a minor breakdown and he needed six-weeks' rest to recover.[148] There were many reasons for Lee's instability during this period apart from the intense pressure under which he was placed by the contending forces.[149] These include a reliance on sedatives, tranquillizers and 'pep pills', to help him sleep, to wake him up and to get him through the day.[150] There was, however, another reason for his conduct which has a direct bearing on our current study of Lee's pro-gressivist ideology: his fear that China and perhaps India would emerge so successfully over the next few decades that Southeast Asia would be swamped by the new giants. We have already considered Lee's 1962 statement to the Malayan students in London:

> If we lose, fritter away the next decade that we have and not make preparations for our take-off into the industrial age, then we may well live to regret it. ...

> We have got to make sure that the capital we have accumulated is put to good use, that in ten years we take one stride forward, in twenty years we enter the industrial age and in thirty years definitely, we are an emerged nation, not an emerging one. Because, definitely in thirty years, we are going to have an emerged China.[151]

This statement's significance to our assessment of the pessimistic nature of Lee's progressivism is particularly strong when it is considered that this speech was made a year *before* the creation of Malaysia, when

Lee was still optimistic about the future. This is, however, merely one example of several speeches echoing his fear of being left behind. In August 1964, when Lee had good reason to be fearful for Malaysia's future, he was more explicit in articulating his fear:

> One day, God forbid, not too soon, in [Indonesia] ... some order will be restored in place of chaos, and they will begin to move forward. Any time now, it is estimated that the Chinese government can explode a nuclear device. Any time now, the Indians are going to set up jet fighter factories. But in two or three decades, we must accept the position that if we have not by then congealed the three main component parts of Malaysia [the Malay, Chinese and Indian communities] into one nation ... with a national identity of its own, then it must break. The moment one of these countries outstrips Malaysia in the human material comforts of life ... the parts [of Malaysia] must go asunder.[152]

A month later he gave basically the same message to a meeting of Malaysian students in London:

> One day, I don't know when – 10, 15, 20 years – one of these three countries will overtake us in terms of material wealth and power; either Indonesia or China, or India. And if before then, we have not yet welded the three communities into a new national identity, then I say it must come unscrambled ...
>
> ... Time is not on our side, as far as this crucial issue is concerned.[153]

It would be tempting to dismiss these statements a mere consequence of the pressure upon Lee except for the fact that Lee had expressed the same sentiments, albeit in less apocalyptic terms, in his speech to Malayan students in London in 1962. The seeds of his pessimism were already inherent in his thinking and character, but his experiences in Malaysia magnified them and made them a persistent feature of his worldview.

Lee's fear of the consequences of being overtaken by China and India may strike the reader as slightly paranoid. Even granting the strong elements of validity in Lee's analysis, this scenario, which in the event proved substantially erroneous, does not account for the extremities of his reactions to the problems in Malaysia. His instability indicates the presence of much deeper forces at work in Lee's psyche than is suggested merely by his argument: forces that drove him to the point where his doctor felt the need to place him on a liberal regime of drugs. The key to understanding the extremity of his reactions during this period is found in Lee's conviction that life has no point without progress and that without progress and achievement, we are little better than animals. In a press conference in March 1965, Lee made an extraordinary statement:

> You have got to believe in something. You are not just building houses in order that people can procreate and fill these houses up because there is no point in that. You do these things because you believe that in the end you create a happy and a healthy nation, a society in which man finds fulfilment and you have got to have the ideological basis. ... If you treat human beings just like animals you just feed them, keep them sleek, well-exercised, healthy like dogs or cats. I don't think it will work. Nations have gone through tremendous privations and hardships in order to achieve specific goals which have inspired and fired their imagination.[154]

To Lee it was anathema for people to live and work merely for their families. There must be a 'higher' ideological purpose, otherwise they are 'just like animals'. Whereas it may be commonly thought that society and nation are tools that serve people, Lee reversed this order: the purpose of people is to build a healthy nation and society. With this ideological position firmly and deeply entrenched in Lee's mind, it should not be surprising that he came to regard people as mere 'digits' in his calculations.[155] Decades later, Devan Nair belatedly realised the dehumanising character of Lee's logic: 'First principles were stood on their heads. Economic growth and social progress did not serve human beings. On the contrary, the primary function of citizens was to fuel economic growth – a weird reversal of roles'.[156] Lee's passion for progress and achievement was by this stage the *raison d'être* for his political and probably his personal life. In March 1965 he told a Malaysian audience in Sydney: 'I do not know whether I could be altogether happy myself if I were to live in a placid society'.[157] Decades later, Lee was still totally baffled by the notion that anyone could be satisfied with a life that was not a constant struggle to achieve. The younger generation of Singaporeans 'don't see the point of striving and achieving any more. They're just comfortable and they're happy', he warned a university audience in 1988.[158]

Lee's worldview put him fundamentally at odds with Malays, whose Islamic faith and kampong lifestyle gave them a sense of fulfilment without any need to resort to an ideology of struggle. While they wanted and expected economic development to improve their living standards, they saw no reason to disrupt their centuries-old way of life, and were highly defensive of their traditions. In Lee's mind, however, their traditions were those of '*orang hutan*' [Malay for 'jungle people'].[159] 'All these antiquated ideas', he said, 'cannot stand the fresh air of the twentieth century. It is not possible'.[160] Malaysia, he said, 'was a conservative, static society wanting to keep what was in the past, wanting to reinforce the forces that kept the society where it was', while Singapore 'was an innovating society, prepared to reach for the stars, prepared to try and experiment, pick the best that would suit us'.[161] Trying to retain the traditional Malay social hierarchy, with its sultans, aristocracy and village elders was, to Lee, a derisively futile exercise in trying to return to the past:

> History is on our side. We cannot lose. Show me one country in Asia, in Africa, in any part of the world where time moved backwards, not forwards. You know, when after chasing out British imperialists, colonialists, chasing out the French and so on, you go back to the tribal society, and the chiefs become bigger chiefs ... You know, in Africa, they have African chiefs all with gold stools, and they sit down ... Whoever has the gold stool, he is the boss man. Modern chiefs now: Kwame Nkrumah, Osagayfo of Ghana – and he is not superstitious. He hasn't got a golden stool. He has got a big chair in Parliament House, and he sits down there with lancers blowing trumpets. So, time must move forward.[162]

Despite the incoherence of this passage, which was delivered at the height of Lee's troubles with Malaysia, its meaning is clear, and more honestly expresses his derisory attitude towards Malay culture than his more considered speeches.

The trauma of the Malaysia period left Lee Kuan Yew drained physically, emotionally and mentally. He had little optimism about Singapore's future as an independent state,[163] and he feared that Singaporeans would be forced to 'crawl' on their 'hands and knees' to Kuala Lumpur, begging to be readmitted on any terms.[164] During his six week retreat, Lee began forging a new political language to meet the challenges facing Singapore. Lee has since reported that around this time he returned to reading Toynbee's *A Study of History*.[165] 'I took comfort', he said, 'from the fact, that according to [Toynbee] ... without the challenge, man does not climb up higher the face of the cliff to reach a higher level of life, a higher quality of civilisation'.[166] After separation, Lee set out to build a 'rugged' and 'tightly knit' society capable of ensuring the country's survival.[167] The 'survival' motif became all-pervasive in his rhetoric, used as a vehicle for implementing a profound set of changes in Singapore's culture. Chan Heng Chee explains:

> The most striking feature of PAP thinking after separation ... is the party's unshaken belief that the survival of Singapore will depend on the willingness and ability of the Singapore citizen to adopt a new set of attitudes, a new set of values, and new set of perspectives; in short, on the creation of a new man.[168]

The nature and the import of the cultural revolution which Lee imposed upon Singapore will be studied in Chapter 5, but for the moment I want to examine how Lee used the concept of 'Challenge and Response' as part of his political technique.

It is the hallmark of an ideological approach to politics for a leader to make conscious use of problems and crises to drive the political situation towards an ideologically preferred end. In the most serious political crisis of Lee's career, namely Singapore's separation from Malaysia, it was to Toynbee's notions of 'Challenge and Response' that Lee turned. Lee was well positioned to make use of the 'politics of survival' in the late 1960s, largely because the plight of the country was genuinely desperate and nearly hopeless, as Lee himself admitted years later.[169] Singapore–Kuala Lumpur relations had been in difficulties since Lee Kuan Yew decided to contest the March 1964 federal elections on the Peninsula against Tunku Abdul Rahman's wishes.[170] Soon afterwards the Tunku and Lee began trying to find a tension-easing formula which would allow more freedom for Singapore while keeping her within the Federation.[171] Britain however was not ready to see the end of the Malaysian experiment. Anthony Head, the British High Commissioner to Malaysia, successfully frustrated the attempted disengagement between Singapore and Kuala Lumpur and instead pressured the Tunku to include the PAP in the federal government – to no avail.[172] By April 1965, Lee was desperate to find a compromise and regarded the June Prime Ministers' Conference in London as the last opportunity to convince the Tunku to allow a political truce between Singapore and Kuala Lumpur. The alternative, he considered, was racial violence, the bloody fragmentation of Malaysia,[173] and the detention of the Singapore Cabinet by federal authorities.[174] Lee prevailed upon the Australian Prime Minister, Robert Menzies, to intervene personally with the Tunku on Singapore's behalf. 'There is probably no person', wrote Lee to Menzies, 'who can play the role of friend and counsellor to him better than you. I know you command his respect and, even more important, his confidence'.[175] Sadly, the Prime Ministers' Conference passed without finding a resolution to Malaysia's problems.

A few weeks after the Prime Ministers' Conference, Goh Keng Swee approached Lee Kuan Yew with a proposal to open negotiations with Kuala Lumpur to secure Singapore's secession from Malaysia. Lee approved[176] and so, without further reference to his Cabinet or PAP colleagues,[177] Goh met Tun Razak and Dr Ismail from the central government on 20 and 26 July 1965 and negotiated the terms of Singapore's secession from Malaysia.[178] E.W. Barker was flown to Kuala Lumpur on 6 August to draft the final agreement.[179] At this point, the deception being perpetrated by Lee and Goh began in earnest. That night Lee Kuan Yew, who had been in Kuala Lumpur all day, telephoned S. Rajaratnam and Deputy Prime Minister Toh Chin Chye, who were the most ardent advocates of Malaysia in Cabinet. He asked each of them to come directly to Kuala Lumpur without telling either of them the purpose of the trip, nor that the other had been summoned, thus giving them no chance jointly to speculate on the purpose of the meeting, or to co-ordinate their responses.[180] The weeks of negotiations were kept secret from Toh and Rajaratnam, and instead Lee told them that the Tunku had unilaterally decided that Singapore must leave Malaysia and they had been summoned to decide on Singapore's response. Lee perpetuated the charade by presiding over a pointless two days of brooding and analysis, and he even allowed Toh to write to the Tunku pleading for a reprieve from his supposedly unilateral decision. The Tunku replied that his decision was final.[181] This account became the official version of events and formed the basis of Lee Kuan Yew's immediate post-Malaysia political strategy.[182]

Lee and Goh have now revealed that a prime purpose of acting swiftly and in secret was to circumvent opposition from Toh, Rajaratnam, and the British.[183] The British, of course, had the power to stop separation 'cold', while Toh and Rajaratnam made up half the inner circle of PAP leaders and would have caused difficulties for Lee and Goh's plans.[184] These were ample reasons to account for the secrecy surrounding the move, but they do not sufficiently account for the concoction of the story of Singapore's 'expulsion'. Except for the Malays, the population of Singapore was delighted that separation had come, and greeted the news with 'a thunderous explosion of firecrackers' in the streets.[185] There were, therefore, few immediate political reasons for hiding the truth. It is true that the deception, which was maintained for thirty-one years, enabled Lee to avoid opposition from Toh and Rajaratnam. The story also minimised Lee's personal embarrassment over his reversal. Yet more importantly, the deception served Lee well by preparing the ground for the 'politics of survival', whereby Lee could present Singapore's very existence as a challenge of the highest order. On the basis of this story, he was able to build an *esprit de corps* among both the country's leadership and among the population as a whole so that they reluctantly accepted draconian restrictions and drastic changes in their lives, including a wholesale rethinking of the basis of wage and salary scales and the curtailing of trade union activity. While there would have been no problem of logic with initiating separation and then claiming that the situation was desperate, the case was much easier to 'sell' and was much more powerful if the very creation of an independent Singapore were seen as a challenge foisted upon the country from outside. Without a story such as this, it would have been much more difficult, for instance, for Lee to lecture trade unionists in the following tone:

> [T]he touchstone of our policies is survival. There are people who believe – and this is the reason they booted us out – that by booting us out, they would have the squeeze on us.
>
> … Meanwhile, this is a lesson of survival. Forget all about bonuses and this, that and the other for the next two years. We have really got to pull ourselves up by the boot straps. …
>
> … It means that until you break through, you can't have your labour running around doing foolish things.[186]

On this occasion, the main object lessons were the need to put aside normal industrial action and pay demands, to co-operate with foreign capital in order to create jobs, and to maintain impeccable standards of workmanship. While the lessons could have been taught without the need to refer to Singapore being 'booted out' of Malaysia, this reference enabled Lee to base the 'survival' motif on an external challenge: the threat of being 'squeezed'. The emotional power of such a message converted a mere lesson in economics into a nation-building challenge. Lee was able to use the situation as an orchestrated Toynbeean exercise whereby a challenge purportedly threatened the country's survival and required an effective response. The response in turn hailed the implementation of a cultural shift.

The development of the 'survival' motif proved to be too important in Lee's plans to believe that it was not a consideration during the negotiations for separation. In 1980, while addressing a PAP conference, Lee looked back on the turmoil and the racial tension of the Malaysia period and dated the seeds of the post-separation cultural shift as being planted in 1964:

> Perhaps in 10, 20 years' time, PhD students will pick up my remark and build their treatise on this one climacteric which triggered off a Singaporean entity. It started with the riots in 1964 when the police were out of our control and the army was not at our disposition; when we realised how vulnerable we were. So we learned to be patient but to be firm on gut issues – issues involving race, language, religion, culture.
>
> It is necessary to remind our young that when we started, in 1954 and when we formed government in 1959, we did not have the basic elements to be a nation. The attributes of nationhood were missing: a common ethnic identity … a common language.[187]

The significance of this passage is not whether 'this one climacteric' did 'trigger off a Singaporean identity', but Lee's perception that this was so. Earlier in the speech Lee opined that if the British had given Singapore its independence without the colony having 'first joined Malaysia and learned the sharp lessons of the politics of communal intimidation', then 'we would not have made it'.[188] The Chinese community would have

> stayed mesmerised, trapped by Marxist slogans and Chinese chauvinist chants. They would never have come down to earth to face reality, or if they did, they would have been shocked by the sheer colossalness [*sic*] of the problem of becoming a nation on our own. ... The bitterness at racial domination, [however] transformed people's attitudes. Hence we, the government, were able to mobilise strong support; we checked reckless and stupid politicking aimed at the prejudices of different races, languages, religions and cultures. So after separation, we succeeded despite the overwhelming odds against us.[189]

There is a certain amount of hindsight in Lee's 1980 speech, but given the traumatic effect of the turmoil and racial violence of 1964, it is safe to assume that these events did have a profound effect on him, and that by the end of the Malaysia period, when Lee was turning his mind to a post-Malaysia future, he saw the potential for nation-building in these catastrophes.

Lee's analysis was almost dialectical in character, but it would be more accurate to describe it as a derivation of Toynbee's 'Challenge and Response' thesis. Except that he was dealing with a tiny country instead of a civilisation, all of the elements of 'Challenge and Response' were present. The challenge of going straight from a colony to a nation would have been too great and would have ended in disaster, but the challenge of coping successfully with communalism 'transformed people's attitudes'. Meeting this challenge was within the capacity of the society, which began building the basic 'attributes of nationhood', enabling the society to face the next challenge and begin climbing towards the next stage of development. In the Toynbeean world, the ideal response will provoke a new challenge, thus providing the catalyst for continual improvement and progress. In this instance, the new challenge was independent nationhood, which was a struggle for survival and required further and continuing changes to the culture. Both in contemporary speeches and in retrospective accounts, Lee has described the post-Malaysia period in a way strongly resonant of Toynbee's analysis. In late 1966, he told a trade union dinner:

> Civilizations emerge because human societies in a given condition, respond to the challenge. Where the challenge is just about right ... the human being flourishes. And without that challenge, in a hot, humid climate like Singapore, we will all go down the drain.[190]

A week later he told another trade union meeting:

> Human beings always respond to a challenge. Where there is no challenge, there is very seldom more than ordinary performance. It is true that sometimes, where the challenge is too intense, too sustaining, too enervating, the response can never be equal to the challenge. But the

situation in which we have found ourselves and the response that there has been from the people in the past year shows first, a lively appreciation of the hazards which lie along the road we want to travel and also the capacity to surmount these problems.[191]

In 1985, he observed of this period:

> [W]e altered the relationship between workers and management by the Employer Act. We put an end to hostile confrontational trade unionism. We got people to accept National Service to defend what we set out to build. We rid ourselves of the give-me social security approach to life. *Each change was a conscious exercise of will to respond to and overcome a new challenge.*[192]

Lee was able to use this challenge, as he has used others, to forge a consensus in society. Crises were an essential part of Lee's political technique during the post-separation period, because they were needed to galvanise the population to accept changes that would have been unacceptable in a placid political environment. In Toynbeean terms, this was the path towards building a healthy society that was advancing to a 'higher level of civilisation'.

That Lee saw the post-Malaysia situation in Toynbeean terms is beyond serious doubt. How early Lee began consciously thinking in these terms, however, is not so obvious. Did he consciously set out to concoct his separation story in July 1965 with the 'Challenge and Response' model of progress in mind? Did he begin to think consciously of 'Challenge and Response' only during his six-week retreat, or even over the following year or so? We cannot be certain of the answers to these questions, but we can take this analysis at least to the point of saying that in July 1965, Lee was conscious of the value of crises in fostering dramatic changes in society, and that he believed that further dramatic changes would be needed if Singapore were to survive. The 'Challenge and Response' theory had been part of his thinking since at least 1959, if not from 1949, and this theory of praxis suited his achievement-driven personality and his crisis-driven political style. While he may have refreshed his theoretical conviction in the value of 'Challenge and Response' only during his rest at Changi, or even afterwards, his personality, his theoretical background, and his political experience and style all urged him in the same direction as political expediency: to interpret the new situation as a set of unambiguous challenges which could be used to spur the country down the road of progress and economic development.

Although this methodology had lost much of its effectiveness by the end of the 1970s, when most of the obvious crises facing Singapore had been successfully met, Lee has continued to use his model of crisis-driven development down the next three decades, and the model has served him well. The announcement of the premature closure of the British bases in 1968 was a crisis that needed no exaggeration.[193] Meanwhile Lee declared that Singapore needed a defence force not for the ordinary reasons a country needs a defence force, but because Singapore was 'an Israel in a Malay–Muslim sea'.[194] In 1969 Lee declared his fear that dysgenic fertility trends threatened to turn Singapore into an 'anaemic' society, necessitating the Abortion and Sterilisation Bills of that year.[195] The challenge of Chinese chauvinism, communist infiltration and 'black operations' justified strict controls on the press in 1971.[196] The 1974 oil crisis was followed by the fall of Vietnam in 1975. 1976 saw more communist 'black operations' uncovered in Singapore.[197] In 1978 the bilingual education system was deemed a failure which placed the future of the country at risk.[198] In 1979 the trade union empire of Phey Yew Kok had to be dismantled because it was becoming too powerful and threatened the well-being of Singapore.[199] Throughout 1980 trade unionists were told that they faced a leadership crisis which threatened their special relationship with the PAP and therefore endangered the stability and prosperity of Singapore.[200] In 1982 an all-pervasive campaign was initiated to introduce Confucian ethics into schools and most aspects of public and private life as an antidote to the threat posed by Western values.[201] In 1983 Singaporeans were reminded that they risked their economic prosperity if the poorly educated kept having more children than the well educated.[202] In 1984, when a tiny opposition had been elected to Parliament, Lee mooted the idea of an Elected President with reserve powers to protect the country from the possibility of an irresponsible government emerging in the future.[203]

The above survey of the crisis-driven nature of the post-Malaysia political landscape is far from complete, but it is sufficient to convey the picture that Singapore seems to suffer from more than its fair share of crises, many of which served the interests of the government very well. Some of these crises, such as the oil crisis of the 1970s, were genuine, while others are merely ordinary political or policy developments contrived to appear as crises. As recently as 1997 Lee Kuan Yew felt the need to declare another crisis, when opposition candidate Tang Liang Hong purportedly resurrected Chinese chauvinism during the general election campaign.[204] As if this threat to the stability of the country were not enough, Lee went further and without producing any evidence, raised the spectre of Tang being 'underwritten by someone or some agency' who wished to damage Singapore.[205] The 'crisis' theme is not the only current remnant of Lee's post-Malaysia political style. The 'survival' motif also surfaces at regular intervals, one of the more recent being in his address to a National Day dinner in 1995: 'We are responsible for our own survival. If that survival is jeopardised, we can expect no Santa Claus, no Lone Ranger to come to the rescue'.[206] Only a few days earlier, Lee gave Singapore a 20 per cent chance of collapsing beyond restoration at some stage in the future.[207] Behind Lee's propensity for declaring a crisis at every turn is not only the obvious Machiavellian cynicism of a consummate politician, but also a conviction that crises, or challenges, are necessary to mould a progressive society. This feature, combined with Lee's genuine pessimism, has given Singaporean politics a neurotic character, leaving Singaporeans, according to John Clammer, with 'the feeling that there is a permanent sense of crisis':

> [P]olitically Singapore is threatened with subversion from within and without; economically the situation is always precarious; the education system is changed constantly at all levels; expensive projects are begun and ... rendered obsolete two years hence ... [C]hange, construction, urgency are the keywords. But why? What is the ultimate purpose of all this activity, all this energy spent changing what has just been finished? Nobody quite knows, for the system seems to require that today's solution is tomorrow's problem.[208]

If the citizens of Singapore took to heart every crisis that was presented to them by their leaders, and particularly by Lee, it is doubtful whether the society would be able to function. Albert Winsemius, Lee's friend and economic adviser, made a similar observation, though in much kinder terms:

> I don't know if you've ever noticed that Singapore and its government often behave like adolescents in a one-sided way, over-stressing a thing and forgetting the rest; then dropping the subject and focusing, once more one sided, on the next thing.[209]

Despite its limitations and its tendency to distort his perception of events, Lee has continued to use the 'Challenge and Response' thesis to the present day. As recently as 1994 he implicitly used the theory to analyse the problems of Canada and Australia, and postulated that unlike East Asia, these countries had too many natural advantages and insufficient challenges:

> They are both vast resource-rich countries with small populations that will never be able to consume their cornucopia of national resources for a thousand years. This immense wealth has created a resource-rich syndrome, the opposite of East Asia – a relaxed, not an intense society.
>
> ... The newly industrialised economies and Japan, Korea, Taiwan, Hong Kong, Singapore, Vietnam and China are the opposite – they have had to gear themselves culturally for a very hard driving way of life.[210]

While Lee has retained his ideas about 'Challenge and Response', he has not been able to maintain successfully the intensity of the crisis-ridden atmosphere of the 1960s, largely because of the success of his own policies and leadership. Thus over the decades he has had to vary the techniques by which he has achieved results, a process that will be considered later in this book.

Thus far our analysis of Lee Kuan Yew's political thought has been restricted to a consideration of Lee's progressivism up to the early 1970s, with only a cursory perusal of developments since then. Before proceeding with a chronological analysis of the development of Lee's political thought it is necessary to pay attention to the development of other aspects of his thinking during the 1950s and 1960s, since the various strains of his ideology have become increasingly intertwined over the decades. Already a study of Lee's progressivism has led directly to a consideration of his pessimism, and this study has thus far tried to account for the personal, political and theoretical origins of each.

While much of Lee's pessimism may seem, with the benefit of hind-sight, to have been misplaced, the truth is that the situation was at times so desperate that most people would have walked away. And if his ideas of progress appear to have been rather simplistic, we should remember that Lee is a man of action and, as one Cambridge friend put it, 'never a serious sort of man, in the sense of being a heavy intellectual'.[211] Lee himself stated his attitude to ideas and theories very clearly in 1966:

> I am not interested in ideas as ideas themselves, however much of an esoteric thrill these can give you by way of intellectual stimulation. I am interested in ideas insofar as they can galvanise ... our society.[212]

Lee was fundamentally interested in praxis, and the overriding significance of the 'Challenge and Response' thesis to this study is that Toynbee's theory helped Lee to link his instinctive and deep-seated progressivism to the task of leadership in a critical period of Singapore's history. If 'Challenge and Response' had not provided Lee with this bridge between theory and practice, it is doubtful whether he would have given it any serious consideration at all.

Notes

1. Interview with David Allan, 10 May 1996.
2. Lee Kuan Yew, *The Singapore Story: Memoirs of Lee Kuan Yew*, Singapore; New York; London; Toronto; Sydney; Mexico City: Prentice Hall, 1998, p. 119.
3. Interview with E.W. Barker, 16 October 1996.
4. *The Straits Times*, 7 May 1955.

5.   *Ibid.*, 8 March 1965.

6.   Lee's speech at Commonwealth Drive Car Park, 1 January 1966, in Lee Kuan Yew, *Prime Minister's Speeches, Press Conferences, Interviews, Statements, etc.*, Singapore: Prime Minister's Office, 1959–90.

7.   Speech to Malayan students in London, 14 September 1962, in *ibid.*

8.   *Ibid.*

9.   Letter to the author from Lim Kim San, 27 September 1996; and interviews with Goh Keng Swee, 1 October 1996, and Maurice Baker, 25 October 1996.

10.   *The Rafflesian*, vol. XII, no. 2, August 1936, pp. 6–7.

11.   Lee's interview with Alan Ashbolt in ABC studios in Canberra, 24 March 1965, in Lee, *Prime Minister's Speeches, etc.*

12.   Interview with Teo Kah Leong, 29 October 1996.

13.   Raffles Institution, Singapore, *Syllabus of Instruction, 1937*, pp. 106–115; J. Holland Rose, A.P. Newton, E.A. Benians (eds), *The Cambridge History of the British Empire, Volume I, The Old Empire from the Beginnings to 1783*, Cambridge: Cambridge University Press, 1929; Howard Robinson, *The Development of the British Empire*, Boston; New York; Chicago; San Francisco: Houghton Mifflin, [n.d., c. 1922]; Esmi Wingfield-Stratford, *The History of British Civilisation*, New York: Hartfield Brace & Company, 1932.

14.   Letter from fellow student Eric Goonetilleke to the author, 4 December 1996; interviews with Lim Chin Aik, 21 October 1996; Teo Kah Leong, 29 October 1996; and Velauthar Ambiavagar, 15 October 1996. Lim and Teo were fellow students with Lee. Ambiavagar was a history teacher at RI, though he did not teach Lee Kuan Yew.

15.   *Raffles Institution Syllabus, 1937.*

16.   *Ibid.*, and; interviews with Kiang Ai Kim, 14 October 1996; and Velauthar Ambiavagar, 15 October 1996. The description of the earlier history course is based on the accounts of Kiang Ai Kim and Velauthar Ambiavagar. Kiang was a student from 1930 to 1934, while Ambiavagar had been a history teacher at RI up to about 1935. Both men were surprised by the extent of the shift in emphasis revealed by the 1937 syllabus.

17.   *Raffles Institution Syllabus, 1937*, p. 106.

18.   *Ibid.*, p. 107.

19.   *Ibid.*, pp. 112–114.

20.   *Ibid.*, p. 115.

21.   Robinson, *The Development of the British Empire*, p. 431.

22.   *Ibid.*, p. 436.

23.   *Ibid.*, p. 438.

24.   Wingfield-Stratford, *The History of British Civilization*, pp. 1188–1189.

25.   *Ibid.*, p. 1189.

26.   *Ibid.*, p. 1284.

27.   Letter from Eric Goonetilleke to the author, 4 December 1996.

28.   Interview with Lim Chin Aik, 21 October 1996.

29. *Raffles Institution Syllabus, 1937*, p. 107.

30. Interview with Lim Chin Aik, 21 October 1996.

31. Interview with Teo Kah Leong, 29 October 1996.

32. H.G. Wells, *The Work, Wealth and Happiness of Mankind*, London: William Heinemann [n.d., c. 1932].

33. *Ibid.*, pp. 666, 807–813.

34. *Ibid.*, pp. 808–809, 811, 813.

35. See, for example, Lee's speech to Parliament on the Abortion Bill, 29 December 1969, where he cited Professor Richard Lynne's article in *New Scientist* of 20 March 1969 on hereditary intelligence. Lee, *Prime Minister's Speeches, etc.*

36. See Lee's address to the 5th Asian-Pacific Congress of Cardiology Delegates' Dinner, Singapore, 13 October 1972, in *ibid.* Also see S. Rajaratnam in *The Straits Times*, 27 November 1990. In this interview Rajaratnam said that Lee reads a lot about health matters: 'I think he even instructs doctors how to diagnose him – that's true'.

37. See, for example, Lee's address on 'The Joint Campus: The Importance and the Limits of Bilingualism' organised by the Joint Campus Students' Association, 5 January 1979, in Lee, *Prime Minister's Speeches, etc.* In this speech Lee lectured with self-assumed authority on the 'current state of research' on the functions of different parts of the brain, particularly the left lobe. Garry Rodan has noted Lee's blind faith in science to the point of characterising it as an ideology of 'scientism'. Rodan regarded 'scientism' as primarily a means of rationalising the class divisions which emerged in Lee's technocratic society. Garry Rodan, *The Political Economy of Singapore's Industrialization: National State and International Capital*, Kuala Lumpur: Forum, 1991, pp. 89–90. Rodan's class analysis, however, takes insufficient account of the personal influences in Lee's early life which have been the major influences on his worldview.

38. *The Straits Times*, 27 November 1990.

39. Interview with Teo Kah Leong, 29 October 1996.

40. It should be noted that even after the publication of Lee's memoirs we are still unable to proceed further than inferences. Lee covered his time at Raffles Institution in three pages, and gave no hint of being aware of any worldview being communicated beyond a simple pro-British bias. See Lee, *The Singapore Story*, pp. 36–38.

41. Lee's speech to students at the Singapore Polytechnic, 12 October 1966, in Lee, *Prime Minister's Speeches, etc.*

42. Lee at the Special Academic Awards 1992 Presentation Ceremony, 20 August 1992, in Lee Kuan Yew, *Senior Minister's Speeches, Press Conferences, Interviews, Statements, etc.*, Singapore: Prime Minister's Office, 1991–95.

43. Lee, *The Singapore Story*, p. 129.

44. See Chapter 2.

45. Lee in *The Straits Times Weekly Edition*, 25 September 1993.

46. Lee, *The Singapore Story*, p. 115.

47. Interview with David Allan, 10 May 1996.

48. *Ibid.*

49. Letter from Leslie Wayper to the author, 13 June 1996. Wayper was a friend of Lee's in Fitzwilliam House, but was not studying in the law tripos.

50. Interview with George Dixon, 11 July 1996.

51. Alex Josey, *Lee Kuan Yew: The Struggle for Singapore*, Sydney: Angus & Robertson, 1974, pp. 31–32.

52. Lee Kuan Yew, *Social Revolution in Singapore*, Singapore: Government Printing Office, [n.d., c. 1966–67], p. 1.

53. Interview with David Allan, 10 May 1996.

54. *Ibid.*

55. Interview with David Allan 13 February 1997. Also see *Supplement to the Handbook of the Cambridge Law School 1946–1947*.

56. Interview with David Allan, 10 May 1996 and *Supplement to the Handbook of the Cambridge Law School 1946–1947*.

57. Interview with David Allan, 10 May 1996.

58. R.M. Jackson, *The Machinery of Justice in England, Second Edition*, Cambridge: Cambridge University Press, 1953, p. vii.

59. R.M. Jackson, *The Machinery of Justice in England*, Cambridge: Cambridge University Press, 1939, p. 50.

60. *Ibid.*, p. 51.

61. *Ibid.*, p. 212.

62. *Ibid.*, p. 214.

63. Interview with David Allan, 3 June 1996.

64. Lee's address to the University of Singapore Law Society Annual Dinner, 18 January 1962, in Lee, *Prime Minister's Speeches, etc.*

65. *Ibid.*

66. Lee Kuan Yew in Singapore Legislative Assembly, *Debates: Official Report*, 12 April 1956, column 1919. Lee was probably referring to Nehru's letter to his daughter of 14 January 1931, reproduced in Jawaharlal Nehru, *Glimpses of World History: being further letters to his daughter, written in prison, and containing a rambling account of history for young people*, London: Lindsay Drummond, 1949, p. 23.

67. As well as *Glimpses of History*, see Jawaharlal Nehru, *Jawaharlal Nehru: An Autobiography, with Musings on Recent Events in India*, Bombay; New Delhi; Calcutta; Madras: Allied Publishers, 1962, originally published as *Jawaharlal Nehru: An Autobiography*, by John Lane of London in 1945; and Jawaharlal Nehru, *Discovery of India*, New York: The John Day Company, 1946.

68. Jawaharlal Nehru (K.T. Narasimha Char [ed.]), *The Quintessence of Nehru*, London: George Allen & Unwin, 1961, pp. 123–139.

69. See, for instance, Nehru, *The Discovery of India*, p. 520, where Nehru wrote, 'India must break with much of her past and not allow it to dominate the present. Our lives are encumbered with the dead wood of this past'. Nehru, however, never advocated a complete break with the past, but just with those aspects that were an obstacle to progress. See *ibid.*, p. 526. Also see Nehru, *Glimpses of World History*, p. 21.

70. Jawaharlal Nehru, *India and the World: Essays*, London: George Allen & Unwin, 1936, p. 82.

71. Nehru, *Glimpses of World History*, p. 6.

72. *Ibid.*, p. 476.

73. Nehru, *An Autobiography*, p. 228. It is most likely that Lee was dismayed at the sheer size of the volumes that Nehru wrote while in prison, rather than by any particular reference in Nehru's books. *Glimpses of World History* contained nearly 200 letters and filled a volume of nearly 1,000 pages. *The Discovery of India* contained nearly 600 pages. The thought of this great leader and activist reduced to the role of amateur history teacher must have rankled Lee considerably.

74. *Ibid.*, pp. 226–234.

75. Interview with E.W. Barker, 16 October 1996.

76. *Ibid.*

77. *The Straits Times*, 6 May 1955.

78. *Chung Shing Jit Pao*, (Editorial), 7 May 1955, cited in Colony of Singapore, *Weekly Digest of the Non-English Press 1954–59*, Singapore: Colony of Singapore, 1954–59.

79. Lee in Han Fook Kwang, Warren Fernandez and Sumiko Tan, *Lee Kuan Yew: The Man and His Ideas*, Singapore: Times Editions and Singapore Press Holdings, 1998, p. 41.

80. Interview with David Allan, 10 May 1996. Arnold Toynbee, *A Study of History, Abridgement of Volumes I–VI* by D.C. Somervell, London: Oxford University Press, 1948.

81. *Ibid.*

82. See especially, Arnold Toynbee, *A Study of History, Volumes I* and *II*, London; New York; Toronto: Oxford University Press, 1935.

83. Toynbee, *A Study of History, I*, p. 176.

84. Interview with Goh Keng Swee, 1 October 1996.

85. Interview with David Allan, 3 June 1996.

86. Interview with Boris Christa, 27 May 1996.

87. *Ibid.*

88. Interview with David Allan, 10 May 1996, and with Boris Christa, 27 May 1996, and George Dixon, 11 July 1996.

89. Interview with Boris Christa, 27 May 1996. Lee attended Cambridge Union debates. See Lee Kuan Yew, 'The Singapore experience and its relevance to Africa', *Ministerial Speeches*, vol. 17, no. 6, November–December 1993, p. 12.

90. Interview with David Allan, 10 May 1996, and with Boris Christa, 27 May 1996, and George Dixon, 11 July 1996.

91. Derek Fraser, *The Evolution of the British Welfare State: A History of Social Policy since the Industrial Revolution*, (2nd edn), London: Macmillan, 1984, pp. 219–223.

92. *Ibid.*

93. Letter from Michael Lever to the author, undated, received 5 June 1996.

94. *Ibid.*

95. Letter from Michael Lever to the author, 1 August 1997.

96. Letter from Leslie Wayper to the author, 24 May 1996.

97. Interview with David Allan, 10 May 1996.

98. Interview with David Allan, 3 June 1996.

99. Interview with E.W. Barker, 16 October 1996.

100. The text of his speech is contained in Han, Fernandez, Tan, *Lee Kuan Yew: The Man and His Ideas*, pp. 253–255.

101. Interview with Goh Keng Swee, 1 October 1996 and Lee, *The Singapore Story*, p. 107.

102. *The Straits Times Weekly Edition*, 25 September 1993. Italics added.

103. Lee in Raj Vasil, *Governing Singapore*, Singapore: Eastern Universities Press, 1984, p. 181.

104. Lee in Han, Fernandez, Tan, *Lee Kuan Yew: The Man and His Ideas*, p. 129.

105. Lee in *ibid.*, pp. 253–255.

106. Letter from Michael Lever to the author, undated, received 5 June 1996.

107. Apart from Goh Keng Swee's evidence that Lee regularly cited Toynbee in Cabinet meetings from 1959 onwards, the influence of Arnold Toynbee on Lee since the mid-1960s is well documented in speeches and interviews. Lee first *publicly* cited Toynbee on 10 April 1967 in his address at the East Asian Christian Conference. See Lee Kuan Yew, *Leadership in Asian Countries*, [Singapore: Ministry of Culture, 1967], p. 7.

108. Arnold Toynbee, *A Study of History*, London; New York; Toronto: Oxford University Press: Volumes I, II and II published in 1935; Volumes IV, V and VI published in 1939; Volumes VII, VIII, IX and X published in 1954. Also see Arnold Toynbee, *A Study of History, Abridgement of Volumes I–VI* by D.C. Somervell, London: Oxford University Press, 1948 and Arnold Toynbee, *A Study of History, Abridgement of Volumes VII–X* by D.C. Somervell, London: Oxford University Press, 1961. According to David Allan in his interview of 10 May 1996, the *Abridgement* was more commonly read than the original volumes at Cambridge in the late 1940s.

109. Sidney Pollard, *The Idea of Progress: History and Society*, New York: Basic Books, 1968, p. v.

110. Interview with Goh Keng Swee, 1 October 1996.

111. Toynbee, *A Study of History*, *IV*, p. 2.

112. Lee, *Leadership in Asian Countries*, p. 7.

113. In Volume IX of *A Study of History*, Toynbee speculated on the possibility that Western civilisation might be able to avoid the pitfalls that led to the collapse of other civilisations, but these books were published only after the period of Lee's life that is currently under consideration.

114. Arnold Toynbee in M.F. Ashley Montagu (ed.), *Toynbee and History: Critical Essays and Reviews*, Boston: Porter Sargent, 1956, p. 8.

115. Toynbee, *Study, Abridgement of Volumes I–VI*, p. 12.

116. Toynbee, *A Study of History*, *I*, p. 176.

117. Toynbee, *Study, Abridgement of Volumes I–VI.*, pp. 164–186.

118. *Ibid.*, pp. 265–266.

119. *Ibid.*, p. 253.

120. Toynbee, *A Study of History, I*, p. 192.

121. *Ibid.*, pp. 192–193. Also see Toynbee, *Study, Abridgement of Volumes I–VI*, pp. 49–50.

122. Lee used the 'cliff' analogy, citing 'a British historian', in an address to Representatives of Leading Organisations of German Industry and Commerce, Bonn, 28 September 1970, in Lee, *Prime Minister's Speeches, etc.*

123. Toynbee, *A Study of History, I*, p. 194.

124. Toynbee, *Study, Abridgement of Volumes I–VI*, p. 165.

125. *Ibid.*, p. 405.

126. Toynbee, *A Study of History, I*, p. 176; There are many examples of Lee Kuan Yew echoing Toynbee's views of the inherently dynamic nature of society. In 1972, for instance, Lee said, 'We either move forward, or fall backwards. It is not possible to stand still'. See Lee's address to the Princess Elizabeth Estate Community Centre's 8th Anniversary Celebrations, 25 June 1972, in Lee, *Prime Minister's Speeches, etc.*

127. Toynbee, *Study, Abridgement of Volumes I–VI*, pp. 580–581.

128. *Ibid.*, p. 241.

129. Although Lee's cultural evolutionary views did stem substantially from his progressivism and the influence of Toynbee, they will be studied separately in Chapter 5.

130. There is one point of aberration in this line of continuity. Upon his return to Singapore in 1950, Lee campaigned for the conservative Progressive Party (PP) in the 1951 City Council elections, and became secretary of its sister organisation, the Straits Chinese British Association (SCBA). It is unlikely, however, that these political adventures represented any fundamental aberration in his thinking. Lee had been away for four years, and apart from watching the early growth of the abortive Malayan Democratic Union, he had never seen political activity in Singapore. His old Malayan Forum friends were proving a disappointment, and he was not welcome in many of their homes. See Lee's speech at the valedictory dinner for ministers and MPs who stepped down or retired as part of self-renewal, *Petir*, March 1982, p. 5. It should not be surprising that he dabbled in established political parties to explore the territory. Considering these factors, and also the fact that Lee's employers and his new brother-in-law were heavily involved in the Progressive Party, his actions hardly need elaborate explanation or rationalisation. See James Minchin, *No Man Is an Island: A Portrait of Singapore's Lee Kuan Yew*. Sydney: Allen & Unwin, 1990, p. 60.

131. Lee Kuan Yew, *Socialist Solution for Asia, A Report on the 1965 Asian Socialists' Conference in Bombay*, Singapore: Ministry of Culture, 1965, p. 6.

132. Lee in the Legislative Assembly Debate on West Irian, 23 January 1962, in Lee, *Prime Minister's Speeches, etc.*

133. *Legislative Assembly*, 4 October 1956, column 401.

134. *Ibid.*, 25 November 1955, column 1540.

135. Jawaharlal Nehru, *Glimpses of World History*, p. 543.

136. *Legislative Assembly*, 9 January 1957, column 1239.

137. Lee Kuan Yew in PAP, *The Tasks Ahead, Part 2*, p. 24.

138. Lee Kuan Yew, *One Hundred Years of Socialism*, Singapore: Ministry of Culture, 1964, p. 31.

139. Lee, *Socialist Solution for Asia*, p. 6.

140. Lee Kuan Yew, *The Battle for Merger*, Singapore: Ministry of Culture, [n.d., c. 1961], p. 5.

141. Lee, *Socialist Solution for Asia*, p. 1.

142. *Ibid.*

143. *The Straits Times*, 22 July 1964. Josey reports the casualties as totalling twenty-two dead and 461 injured. Alex Josey, *Lee Kuan Yew: The Crucial Years*, Singapore; Kuala Lumpur: Times Books International, 1980, p. 211.

144. Toh Chin Chye in Chew, *Leaders of Singapore*, p. 94.

145. *Ibid.*.

146. *Ibid.*, p. 95.

147. Lim Kim San in *ibid.*, p. 167.

148. Toh Chin Chye in Chew, *Leaders of Singapore*, p. 98. Although Lee spent this period recuperating, and was unable to perform his regular duties, he still attended weekly Cabinet meetings in the city. Interview with E.W. Barker, 16 October 1996.

149. For Lee's personal account of this period, see Lee, *The Singapore Story*, especially pp. 13–25 and 511–663.

150. Minchin, *No Man Is an Island*, p. 156 and Willard Hanna, *Success and Sobriety, Part IV: The Privacy of the Prime Minister*, New York: American Universities Field Staff Reports, 1968, p. 23.

151. Lee's speech to Malayan students, London, 14 September 1962, in Lee, *Prime Minister's Speeches, etc.*

152. Lee to a symposium organised by the Historical Society of the University of Malaya, 28 August 1964 in Lee Kuan Yew, *Some Problems in Malaysia*, Singapore: Ministry of Culture, 1965, pp. 6–7.

153. Lee to Malaysian students in London, 10 September 1964, in Lee, *One Hundred Years of Socialism*, pp. 37–38.

154. Lee's press conference at TV Singapura studios, 5 March 1965, in Lee, *Prime Minister's Speeches, etc.*

155. For examples of Lee's characterisation of people as 'digits', see Lee Kuan Yew, *New Bearings in Our Education System*, Singapore: Ministry of Culture, [1966–67], p. 19; Lee in 'Questions and Answers after Prime Minister's address on "University autonomy and social responsibility" at the Historical Society Meeting at the University of Singapore', 24 November 1966, in Lee, *Prime Minister's Speeches, etc.*; Lee Kuan Yew, 'Change is the essence of life in the world today', *The Mirror*, vol. 3, no. 19, 8 May 1967, p. 6; Lee's address to University of Singapore Matriculation Ceremony, 5 September 1969, *University of Singapore Students' Union*, [n.d., c. 1970], p. 87; Lee's speech at the University of Dar-Es-Salaam, 6 September 1970, in Lee, *Prime Minister's Speeches, etc.*

156. Devan Nair in Francis T. Seow, *To Catch a Tartar: A Dissident in Lee Kuan Yew's Prison*, New Haven: Yale Center for International and Area Studies, 1994, p. xii.

157. Lee's address to the Malaysian Students' Association, Sydney, 20 March 1965, in Lee, *Prime Minister's Speeches, etc.*

158. Lee's speech to National University of Singapore and Nanyang Technological Institute students, 22 August 1988, in Han, Fernandez, Tan, *Lee Kuan Yew: The Man and His Ideas*, p. 188.

159. Lee's speech at Commonwealth Drive Car Park, 1 January 1966, in Lee, *Prime Minister's Speeches, etc.*

160. Lee's interview with Fred Emery, of *The Times* of London, 13 August 1965, in *ibid.*

161. Lee's speech to the Medical Society, Singapore, 26 February 1965, in Lee Kuan Yew, *Are There Enough Malaysians to Save Malaysia?*, Singapore: Ministry of Culture, 1965, p. 2.

162. Lee's address to a lunch-time rally at Fullerton Square, 2 July 1965, in Lee, *Prime Minister's Speeches, etc.* This is a full transcript of this section of the speech. Most of the speech attacked UMNO and the Malays.

163. Lee in *The Straits Times*, 16 April 1986.

164. Lee Kuan Yew, 'Mass politics and parliamentary politics' (speech to Parliament), *Petir*, July 1978, p. 11.

165. Lee's speech at the dinner given by President Julius Nyerere of Tanzania in Dar-Es-Salaam, 5 September 1970, in Lee, *Prime Minister's Speeches, etc.*

166. Ibid.

167. There are many examples of Lee speaking of 'a rugged society', a 'tight-knit society', or using similar terms. One of the earliest is Lee's speech at the Tanjong Pagar Community Centre, 30 October 1965, in *ibid.*

168. Chan Heng Chee, *Singapore: The Politics of Survival 1965–1967*, Singapore and Kuala Lumpur: Oxford University Press, 1971, p. 49. This monograph provides a comprehensive account of the use of the 'survival' motif in the immediate post-Malaysia period.

169. Report on Lee's reply to John Howard, *The Straits Times*, 16 April 1986.

170. Interviews with Maurice Baker, 25 October 1996; and Goh Keng Swee, 1 October 1996. See Chapter 2 and Michael D. Barr, 'Lee Kuan Yew in Malaysia: a reappraisal of Lee Kuan Yew's role in the separation of Singapore from Malaysia', *Asian Studies Review*, vol. 21, no. 1, pp. 1–17, for more details.

171. Lee, *The Singapore Story*, pp. 581–92; and Goh Keng Swee in Chew, *Leaders of Singapore*, p. 147.

172. Lee, *The Singapore Story*, pp. 581–592; and letter from Lee Kuan Yew to Australian Prime Minister Robert Menzies, 20 April 1965.

173. *Ibid.*

174. Interview with E.W. Barker, 16 October 1996.

175. Letter from Lee Kuan Yew to Robert Menzies, 20 April 1965.

176. Lee, *The Singapore Story*, pp. 628–631.

177. Toh Chin Chye was ignorant of these negotiations until Melanie Chew asked him about them during his interview for *Leaders of Singapore*. See Chew, *Leaders of Singapore*, p. 97.

178. Goh in *ibid.*, p. 147.

179. Interview with E.W. Barker, 16 October 1996.

180. Toh in Chew, *Leaders of Singapore*, p. 97.

181. Tunku Abdul Rahman took public responsibility for the decision. See *The Straits Times*, 10 August 1965.

182. The false story of these events was told in a series of emotional press conferences and television interviews given by Lee Kuan Yew over the next few days. See the transcripts of seven press conferences and interviews held by Lee Kuan Yew from 9 to 14 August 1965, all cited in Lee, *Prime Minister's Speeches, etc.*

183. Lee, *The Singapore Story*, pp. 630, 639–641; and Goh in Chew, *Leaders of Singapore*, p. 147.

184. The other half of the inner circle of leaders was Lee Kuan Yew and Goh Keng Swee.

185. *The Straits Times*, 10 August 1965.

186. Lee's speech at the 15th anniversary celebrations of the Singapore Printing Employees' Union, 17 October 1965, in Lee, *Prime Minister's Speeches, etc.*

187. Lee Kuan Yew, 'History is not made the way it is written', *Petir*, March 1980, p. 7.

188. *Ibid.*, p. 6.

189. *Ibid.*

190. Lee to a VIP dinner organised by the National Trades Union Congress to launch the Devan Nair Research and Training Endowment Fund, 24 September 1966, in Lee, *Prime Minister's Speeches, etc.*

191. Lee's speech at the Delegates' Conference of the National Trades Union Congress, 2 October 1966, in *ibid.*

192. Lee's National Day Message, 9 August 1985, in *Singapore Business Yearbook, 1985*, p. 84. Italics added.

193. See, for instance, Lee's interview on the BBC, 12 January 1968, in Lee, *Prime Minister's Speeches, etc.*

194. Kawin Wilairat, *Singapore's Foreign Policy: The First Decade*, Singapore: Institute of Southeast Asian Studies, 1975, p. 47. Goh Keng Swee, who was Singapore's Minister of Defence during this period, said years later that he always believed that the image of Singapore as the Israel of Southeast Asia was 'a far-fetched analogy'. C.M. Turnbull, *A History of Singapore: 1819–1975*, Kuala Lumpur; London; New York; Melbourne: Oxford University Press, 1977, p. 330.

195. Lee's speech in the abortion debate in Parliament, 29 December 1969, in Lee, *Prime Minister's Speeches, etc.*

196. See *The Straits Times*, throughout May and June 1971. Also see Lee's press conference after the results of the general elections had been announced, 3 September 1972, and Lee's speech at the Press Club Dinner, Hilton Hotel, 15 November 1972, in Lee, *Prime Minister's Speeches, etc.* 'Black operations' are, in Lee Kuan Yew's vocabulary, surreptitious foreign intervention in domestic politics. Lee accused American 'intelligence' and Chinese communist agents from Hong Kong of running separate 'black operations' through Singapore's press. See *The Straits Times*, 12 May and 11 June 1971.

197. Jon S.T. Quah, 'Singapore: towards a national identity', *Southeast Asian Affairs 1977*, Singapore: Institute of Southeast Asian Studies, 1977, p. 212.

198. Lee Kuan Yew, *Bilingualism in Our Society*, Singapore: Ministry of Culture, 1978; and, reports in *New Nation*, 21 April and 1 June 1978.

199. Garry Rodan, *The Political Economy of Singapore's Industrialization*, pp. 156–161.

200. The campaign to reform the trade union movement and its leadership was partly a response to Phey Yew Kok's new power base. The campaign to introduce the reforms began in earnest with Lee's speech to the National Trades Union Congress Seminar, 'Progress into the '80s'. See Lee's address to the National Trades Union Congress May Day campfire at the National Youth Leadership Training Institute, 30 April 1980, in *Singapore Investment News*, August 1980, p. 3.

201. The mechanics and motivation of the Confucian phase of Lee's leadership is discussed in Chapter 5.

202. Lee's speech at National Day Cultural Show and Rally, 13 August 1983, in Lee Kuan Yew, 'The education of women and patterns of procreation', *RIHED bulletin*, vol. 10, no. 3, July–September 1983, pp. 1, 4–7.

203. See Linda Low and Toh Mun Heng, *The Elected Presidency as a Safeguard for Official Reserves: What Is at Stake?*, Singapore: Times Academic Press for Institute of Policy Studies, 1989; and C.T. Ernest Chew and Edwin Lee (eds), *A History of Singapore*, Singapore; New York: Oxford University Press, 1991, pp. 396–398.

204. *The Straits Times Weekly Edition*, 4 and 11 January 1997.

205. *Ibid.*, 3 May 1997.

206. Lee's address to the Tanjong Pagar Group Representative Constituency National Day Dinner, 12 August 1995 in Lee, *Senior Minister's Speeches, etc.*

207. Lee's interview with Henry Kamm of the *New York Times*, 3 August 1995 in *ibid.*

208. John Clammer, *Singapore: Ideology, Society and Culture*, Singapore: Chopmen Publishers, 1985, p. 27.

209. *The Sunday Times*, 27 January 1985.

210. Lee's speech to the Australian National Press Club, Canberra, in *The Australian*, 19 April 1994.

211. Letter from Michael Lever to the author, undated, received 5 June 1996.

212. Lee's address to a dinner of the Law Society of the University of Singapore, 7 October 1966, in Lee, *Prime Minister's Speeches, etc.*

· 4 ·

Elitism and the Search for Talent

In any given society, of the one thousand babies born, there are so many percent near geniuses, so many percent average, so many percent morons.

I am sorry if I am constantly preoccupied with what the near-geniuses and the above average are going to do. But I am convinced that it is they who ultimately decide the shape of things to come. It is the above-average in any society who sets the pace.

Lee Kuan Yew, 27 August 1966, in Lee Kuan Yew, *Prime Minister's Speeches, Press Conferences, Interviews, Statements, etc.*, Singapore: Prime Minister's Office, 1959–90.

Grand visions of progress are useful rhetorical and inspirational tools for political leaders, but they are insufficient in themselves to meet the needs of practical politicians seeking tight political control of a movement or a country. Leaders need to supplement rhetoric with a mechanism that delivers effective power. When Toh Chin Chye, as Chairman of the PAP's Central Executive Committee (CEC), was faced in 1957 with an effective and well-organised communist challenge, he looked to the Communist Party of the Soviet Union (CPSU) and to the Catholic Church for inspiration.[1] The CPSU offered the example of the Leninist party, in which a self-appointed elite assumes to itself the legitimacy of the whole movement, and theoretically resolves all differences within its own conceptual and organisational boundaries. The Leninist party rules absolutely and perpetuates itself by the mechanism of democratic centralism, whereby the next generation of leaders is selected by the ruling elite from a pool of talent which is imbued with its values and is trained to exercise power. This concept was not new. The Roman emperors attempted to rule through such a self-perpetuating elite, though it was hampered by, among other serious limitations, the largely hereditary nature of power in the imperial system. The Catholic Church copied and arguably

97

perfected this model through the creation of a celibate episcopacy and the College of Cardinals, thus exorcising the hereditary aspects of the Roman imperial system.

In 1957, when Toh Chin Chye successfully changed the PAP constitution to create a new class of 'cadre' members, he consciously emulated the Leninist and Catholic models. The CEC appointed the cadre members, whose main function was to elect the CEC, thus creating a self-perpetuating circle of power. The expedient of converting the PAP into a Leninist party satisfied the immediate demands of political necessity, but it did nothing to provide an ideological framework legitimising the ruling group. Lee Kuan Yew has since corrected this shortcoming. He has taken Singapore beyond the Leninist model by expounding a sophisticated theory of elitism that reduces the party to a merely convenient and ultimately dispensable vehicle through which the 'talented' members of society rule, supposedly for the benefit of all.[2] Lee has refined his concept of 'the elite' over the years, though there is no evidence to suggest that he has amended his fundamental assumptions. Rather, he has merely adapted his ideas to the changing political and social conditions in Singapore.

Lee began his political life by applying the term 'elite' to the political leadership, but during the 1950s he gradually expanded the concept to include the civil service and the legal profession. When Singaporean society developed to the point of producing cohorts of local-born, university-educated managers and professionals, Lee again expanded his definition to encompass virtually the entire upper echelon of society, though the apex of the elite was always restricted to the decision-makers, primarily the managers of resources and people. In the 1980s, Lee publicly and unequivocally linked his idea of the elite to his ideas of genetics, inherited intelligence and innate talent. This chapter explores the development and some of the implications of Lee's elitist vision of society and government. It argues that Lee's elitism is based substantially on his perception of himself, and has been one of the most fundamental tenets of his worldview since childhood.

If one were to identify the common features of most of the 'great men' of history, self-confidence would have to be high on the list. Without self-confidence, whether based on an accident of birth, on an inflated ego, or on a critical assessment of one's ability and achievements, the ambition needed to achieve 'greatness' is likely to be absent. For better or for worse, Lee Kuan Yew has never lacked self-confidence:

> That I was better than most of my peers I knew, I suppose, from the
> time I was about 12 because I was always among the top few in the class

and that continued right through school and into college. ... Yes, I knew that quite early on.[3]

From his teen years his mother encouraged him to think of himself, not just as the eldest son in a Chinese family, but as the de facto head of his family.[4] As a young man he even courted his future wife with the line that 'I [am] not likely to find another girl who [is] my equal'.[5] Lee grew up knowing that he was one of the best, to the point where fellow classmates at Raffles Institution (RI) considered him 'cocky'.[6] 'He struck me right from the beginning as a very ambitious, forceful character', recalled classmate Teo Kah Leong. 'He was also a bit arrogant, but not to the extent of being hateful. His head was always held high in the air'.[7] Lee's 'arrogance' was not affected and he claims not to have been aware that he was perceived in this manner.[8] He had few friends from his own age group, however,[9] and tended to associate with younger boys whom he could dominate.[10] His attitude was a natural product of his upbringing, his already proven academic ability, and his character.

Lee maintains that he became an elitist only in the 1960s after witnessing the failure of egalitarianism in Singapore, Britain and Europe.[11] While this assertion may be true of the political dimension of his elitism, there is ample evidence that Lee was, by nature and upbringing, an elitist from childhood. From an early age Lee Kuan Yew was given the clear message by his family that he was an exceptional child of whom great achievements were expected. The very accidents of his birth fostered this self-perception of being better than most people. Lee was the first-born child of a *baba* family, which in the Singapore of the pre-war years gave him two social advantages. First, he was given the preference traditionally accorded a first-born son in a Chinese family. The significance of this detail should not be overlooked because Lee himself is on record as regarding it as a basis for determining status. He told a university audience in 1966:

> I think one of the facts of life is that no two things are ever equal either in smallness or in bigness. Living things are never equal. Even in the case of identical twins, one comes out before the other and takes precedence over the other! So it is with human beings; so it is with tribes and so it is with nations.[12]

Second, in the 1920s and 1930s the *baba*s were the elite among the Chinese communities of Singapore. Because of their proficiency in English, those who went into business could cater to wealthy markets, while those with less entrepreneurial flair usually entered the medical or legal professions, or gained employment in the service of the colonial government or British companies. According to Kiang Ai Kim, who was a *peranakan* [Malay for 'Straits-born Chinese'] but not a *baba*, the *baba*s were so well respected by the other Chinese communities in the pre-war years that he always took it as a compliment when he was mistaken for being a *baba*.[13]

The pampering of Lee's ego, however, went much further than these observations suggest. Lee's father was a great disappointment to his and his wife's families, who regarded him as 'something of a dropout' because of his gambling, philandering and modest ambition.[14] The focus of their attentions moved to Harry, who was, for both families, the first-born male of the next generation.[15] Lee's paternal grandfather, Lee Hoon Leong, regarded the Englishman as the 'model of perfection', and decided that Harry, his first-born grandson, would grow up to be the 'equal of any Englishman'.[16] Lee was groomed for worldly success, as he confirmed in late 1965:

> In my father's generation they thought that the acme of success was to be a successful professional man. Then, you made a lot of money, you bought a lot of houses, you had a lot of cars, and that was the symbol of success. I was trained to meet that situation, and to be successful in that kind of situation.[17]

With his future planned by his family, Lee entered Telok Kurau English School, which was one of the top English-language primary schools on the island.[18]

The whole family planned their lives around the educational needs of Harry. His mother, Jim Neo, earned extra money and saved for Harry's future education[19] by teaching *baba*-style *Nonya* cooking, taking in boarders and, during her husband's many work-related absences, offering hospitality to Tan Chong Chew. Tan was a wealthy Harbour Board contractor who was to become Jim Neo's 'special friend' until the end of the Japanese Occupation.[20] As a schoolboy his mother showed Harry extraordinary favouritism. He was free to absent himself from family life and to withdraw into his own ambitious world of study and achievement, punctuated by episodes of aggression and childish rebellion for which he received infrequent and ineffectual punishments.[21] Minchin recounts the following story which 'came from a family source':

> The eleven-year-old Harry asked an uncle for one of his canaries. The uncle refused and thought no more about it until he discovered the bird dead: the boy had pulled all its feathers out. 'If he could not have it, no one else would'. 'Lee would hit anybody' was the testimony of another old family friend.[22]

If Lee acted as if rules did not apply to him, it was probably because he was treated as if he was, indeed, above the rules. Jim Neo had compromised herself and made extraordinary sacrifices, substantially to provide for Harry's education in England, and even when the family of five children lived in a two-bedroom bungalow, she insisted that Harry should have room for quiet, undisturbed study.[23] It is little wonder that Lee was confident and arrogant. Sadly Lee blamed his father completely for his family's hardships,[24] and there can be little doubt that part of his driving ambition stems from a determined rejection of Chin Koon as a role model. In retrospect, Jim Neo seems to have stepped into a role familiar to the biographers of 'great men': that of the self-sacrificing, domineering mother who pushed her son to greatness. Typically, such women operated most successfully when the direct influence of the boy's father was weak either because of his absence, or because he offered an inadequate role model. Pinky MacArthur and Hannah Nixon are two examples of such women, who are best known through the achievements of their sons, Douglas and Richard.

After receiving the head start of enrolling at Telok Kurau, Lee largely made his own opportunities. Lee's first ambition was to gain entry to Raffles Institution (RI), which could be achieved exclusively by academic excellence. Rivalled only by St Joseph's Institution, RI was the elite boys' school in Singapore. Upon his entry to RI, Lee and the boys of his year sat for an examination that determined their academic ranking. Lee had already been marked as an exceptional student and was expected to top his year. His teachers and probably Lee himself were therefore surprised when he was beaten by Teo Kah Leong, who continued to surpass Lee academically until their final year.[25] The rivalry between Teo and Lee was a dominant feature of Lee's years at RI, with his teachers sometimes taking bets on which of them would top the exams.[26] Even at this age, Lee does not appear to have been comfortable in the company of a serious rival for attention or achievement. Teo believes that the rivalry between the two boys stopped a friendship developing between them, both in their school years and later in life. Lee later developed a propensity to seek out the services of old associates for special jobs. E.W. Barker, Maurice Baker and Hon Sui Sen are three examples of such people. Teo became a Permanent Secretary in the civil service by his own merit, yet despite both the old association between Lee and Teo, and Teo's proven intelligence and talent, Teo neither enjoyed the privileges nor suffered the onerous burdens of being pressed by Lee to assist him in his cause. Teo reports that despite the full observance of the forms of politeness whenever Lee had professional dealings with him later in life, there was 'a little bit of cold ice' between them.[27] Teo does not believe it was conscious, just as Lee's 'arrogance' at RI was not conscious, but 'it was just one of those things'.[28] Lee was never comfortable with anyone surpassing him. Richard Nixon once said to Lee's wife, Kwa Geok Choo, that he understood that she beat her future husband in their law exams at Cambridge. In a response laced with both truth and wit, Kwa replied, 'Mr President, do you think he would have married me if that were the case?'[29]

Raffles Institution proved to be of great importance in the making of Lee Kuan Yew. Although it is difficult to conceive of a more elitist inspiration for a model of democratic politics than that of the relationship between teacher and student, Lee has consciously adopted this model. In 1966 he gave an address to an assembly of school principals:

> In my experience – both as a pupil in school and in universities, and subsequently in trying to teach people at large simple political ideas – the most important person is the man who is in charge of the boy. ... For effective teaching – such as explaining to an ignorant audience the simple A.B.C. of currency or reserves backing, and why our currency could be sound if we do this or that – one really has to give of oneself. The process demands effort and nervous energy.[30]

He continued: 'To me, the school was the beginning and an end of life, with the teachers who were in charge of me'.[31] The significance of the teacher–student relationship in Lee's mind should not be underestimated. 'Some of my experiences during those years [at RI] became points of reference for the rest of my life', he wrote in 1993.[32] He once told a seminar of teachers that he 'can think of no closer an association than that of teacher and pupil',[33] thereby placing this relationship above that of parents and their children.

One of the most prominent of Lee's role models at RI was the principal, D.W. McLeod. When McLeod spoke, Lee listened carefully, which Lee believes helped him gain his fluency in English, since expatriate teachers were the only native English-speakers with whom the boy had contact.[34] Lee has said that McLeod introduced the practice of Monday morning school assemblies as a means of building a feeling of belonging, and a spirit of loyalty to the school.[35] In fact school historian Eugene Wijeysingha reports that McLeod 'brought the boys to the hall as much as three times a week, simply to talk to them, to spur them on, to make them feel that they were wanted by the school and that being a Rafflesian should be their greatest pride'.[36] Elements of the McLeod methodology can be discerned in Lee's subsequent record as Prime Minister, as he applied himself to the task of nation-building in Singapore.

Lee's admiration for McLeod and a number of other teachers was expressed indirectly, yet eloquently in 1966:

> Many years ago, as a young man, I saw a film about English schools and school masters. I never went to an English public school. But I thought that that was what a school master should be. It was called 'Goodbye Mr Chips'.
>
> At the end of the day, when you have left your school and you feel that you have left a friend and mentor behind, then that man whom you felt so much for and who must have felt for you to have given of himself, that man deserves a gold medal.[37]

Lee's choice of role model is interesting because McLeod was a flawed hero and no great intellectual. The 1930s was a time when the Colonial Office imposed a strict racial barrier and pay differentials between Asian and expatriate teachers. The Office also forbade marriage between expatriate teachers and Asian women, though it was happy to turn a blind eye to less formal liaisons. McLeod had no compunction about enforcing these rules. He dismissed one expatriate teacher who protested against this regime by eating in the Asian teachers' staffroom, and had another transferred to an insignificant school in Malacca after he announced that he planned to marry a Eurasian woman whom he had originally mistaken for being English.[38] While these incidents show McLeod's limitations as a role model, it would be a mistake to read much significance into them, since such attitudes were a largely unquestioned part of the social landscape in colonial Singapore. Fellow teacher Velauthar Ambiavagar in fact describes McLeod as possessing the racist attitudes typical of his class and era, but who was exceptional in that he recognised the fallacies of his prejudices and struggled to overcome them.[39]

Lee could not have been more than dimly aware of such details of the man's character or career, but regarded McLeod as special simply because 'he cared'. Like Lee himself in his later career, no matter was so small that it was beneath the notice of this headmaster. He 'flitted in and out of classrooms', taking over classes, assisting or correcting teachers, stretching the boys' minds with probing questions, praising a particular boy or class or sporting team, or just standing and watching and listening.[40] Kiang Ai Kim remembers one of these occasions when McLeod asked him whether a cow lowers itself to the ground forelegs or hind legs first.[41] The habits of cows were not part of any curriculum but McLeod wanted the boys to make observation and critical thought a natural part of their lives. McLeod was very much the father-figure that Lee lacked at home. His severity was more apparent than real and he assisted and encouraged his teachers and students much more than he admonished or punished them. He was easily admired and earned the respect of everyone under his benevolent rule.[42] These were the characteristics that Lee admired in McLeod. In 1960 Lee was almost certainly thinking of McLeod when he observed that although RI had to follow the Colonial Office syllabus, the teachers went beyond this. In language reminiscent of Lee's later advocacy of the need to build a 'rugged society',[43] he said that these teachers produced people 'sufficiently resilient to adjust and meet the challenge of the changed world which emerged after the Second World War'. They imparted 'the will to work and learn and face and overcome difficulties'.[44] It is difficult to avoid seeing parallels between Lee's perception of McLeod as teacher and Lee's perception of himself as Prime Minister.

When considering the impact of Lee's years at RI, one specific incident is worthy of mention since it probably marks the genesis of his mistrust of the democratic process. Upon his arrival at RI, Lee quickly gained for himself a reputation as a formidable debater. He modelled his debating style after that of Gerald d'Cruz, an older boy who was later to become a prominent communist.[45] As well as honing the techniques of oratory, Lee was exceptional in that he thoroughly researched his cases and prepared his arguments. Lee was always the first speaker representing the school in debates and Lim Chin Aik was usually the second speaker. Lim remembers this time:

> No matter what subject it was, [Lee] would take pains to delve into the subject and go to the library. He would pick things up and he would quote this person and that person who said this and that. And history has shown that this would happen.[46]

With his record of thoroughness, no one was surprised when, in a mock-election for the 'Mayor of Singapore', Lee expounded in great detail upon the statutes and laws he would amend and the reforms he would introduce. Lee's election speech greatly impressed Lim, who, as Lee's opponent in the 'election', had done no preparation at all, and did not know what he was going to say until he stood up to speak. Nevertheless Lim's electoral instincts proved more sound than Lee's. Lim promised his electorate of fourteen-year-old boys that he would introduce co-education, twenty-four hour cabarets, and lower water and electricity charges. The resultant landslide for Lim appalled the teacher, who berated the class for being swayed by emotive, opportunistic and uncosted arguments, which were designed to appeal purely to self-interest.[47] The themes raised by the teacher proved to be an enduring motif in Lee Kuan Yew's rhetoric and actions as a politician. Fear of the rise of an irresponsible opportunist who might squander his government's achievements was the explicit basis for the proposal of an Elected President with reserve powers in 1984.[48] It was also a large part of the reason why Lee made Members of Parliament substantially responsible for the administration of housing estates in their electorates. If opposition MPs have the capacity to diminish their constituents' standard of living either by design, neglect or incompetence, then those constituents are less likely to support such 'opportunists' and more likely to stand by the experienced technocrats offered by the PAP.[49] It would be foolish to think that Lee's experiences as a fourteen-year-old scarred him for life and that they account for the decisions taken much later, but it may well be that this incident laid the seeds of his fear of opportunists.

At the end of Lee's time at RI, he finally managed to establish his pre-eminence among his peers by topping the Senior Cambridge Exams throughout Malaya and winning the Sir John Anderson Scholarship for obtaining the best school certificate results of those entering Raffles College.[50] His long-time rival, Teo Kah Leong, remembers Lee, perhaps generously, as being 'gentlemanly' in victory, simply saying to Teo, 'At last I have beaten you'.[51] Lee's plans to study in England immediately after matriculating from RI were thwarted by the war. The next seven years of his life were spent studying, working and surviving in Singapore. As we have seen in Chapter 2, these years were of critical importance in the making of Lee Kuan Yew as a man and a politician, but they have limited significance in terms of his elitism. At the end of the Occupation, he did, however, dramatically revise one critical aspect of his elitism: he no longer assumed that the British were his betters, or that they would always be his superiors. 'We believed, or were led to believe, that the British were there because they were superior', Lee told Alan Ashbolt of the ABC in 1965, but 'in about two weeks of fighting ... we discovered that his superiority was really the capacity to use guns and to frighten the other chap':

> Three-quarters of the technique of colonial governments is the spell you cast over subject peoples. You make the slave not only behave like a slave by force, but you are supreme and the slave thinks he is a slave – you know, that he is inferior, that he ought to serve.[52]

This development of Lee's thinking was crucial to his future and the future of Singapore, but hardly requires further elaboration.

Cambridge University marked the next significant step in the development of Lee's elitism. By the time he arrived at Fitzwilliam House, he was already twenty-four years old and it must be presumed that his character was already substantially formed. The critical point for this study is that he had lived his life thus far on the assumption that he was a cut above everyone else. Of course this attitude did not have to translate into an elitist political ideology, but it is not difficult to discern the influences at Cambridge which confirmed and developed the ideas that were to become a central part of his ideology. Lee was living and studying in one of the most prestigious and exclusive centres of learning in the world. It shared with Oxford the cream of the English public school system and of Britain's wartime armed forces, and was producing the political leaders and academics for the dying Empire. Two former students of that period have described in interviews the sense of being 'set apart' from the rest of society at Cambridge. George Dixon, an Australian ex-serviceman who studied in the English tripos, reported that they were 'treated like princes', routinely welcomed into the best homes and sometimes presented to royalty.[53] Indeed, W.S. Thatcher had once told Lee, 'When you come up to Cambridge, you are joining something special, like joining the Life Guards and not just joining the army. You have to stand that extra inch taller'.[54] Boris Christa made the same point to the author using a slightly different analogy. He was a former captain in the British army, and confessed in an interview:

> I suppose, if the truth was known, we were all fairly elitist and we did think of ourselves as being genetically favoured, that an elite would have to lead and guide [in the post-war world]. That seemed to us almost part of the air we were breathing. ...

> Cambridge appeared elitist from the outside, but when you were there, it was like an officers' mess in the army. Although you have the colonel, the old man who was the boss, unequivocally, nevertheless within the mess the officers also have a lot of democratic society because they were all officers and gentlemen and therefore there was a certain feeling of brotherhood. And that is also part of the tradition of Cambridge.[55]

It is surely not a coincidence that Lee later perceived the *esprit de corps* of the elite in similar terms to Christa's description of Cambridge. As he told a Law Society dinner in 1966:

> That is one of the qualities which any elite assiduously cultivates: a sense of calculated importance. They take themselves seriously because they know, from the performance of past generations of students from a particular institution, that they have been in the top echelon of leadership in their society.[56]

Even if one wanted to dismiss this statement as coincidence, there can be no doubt that Lee was thinking of his experiences and his acquaintances at Cambridge when he made the following statement in the same period:

> It is essential to rear a generation at the very top of society that has all the qualities needed to lead and give the people the inspiration and the drive to make it succeed. In short, the elite. ...

> Every society tries to produce this type. The British have special schools
> for them: the gifted and talented are sent to Eton and Harrow and a
> few very exclusive private schools which they call 'public schools'; after
> that they go to Oxford and Cambridge. And they have legends which
> say that the Battle of Waterloo was won on the playing fields of Eton.[57]

In this speech Lee also directly linked his elitism and his progressivism:

> True, not every boy is equal in his endowments in either physical stamina
> or mental capacity or character. But all those with the potential to
> blossom forth must do so. That is the spearhead in the society, on whom
> depends the pace of our progress.[58]

Lee's elite are the cadres of progress.

Beyond these general observations of the social environment and
example of Cambridge, there was also a powerful elitist influence which
was specific to the Law School, and which has already been considered
at length in Chapter 3: the ethos of reformism which proclaimed the use
of the law as a tool to transform society. Let there be no mistake. The
assumption behind this ethos was that they, the future solicitors, barristers
and judges, would use the law to change society from above. As an
expression of self-conscious elitism, this self-perception must rank just
behind Lee's model of the politician as a teacher. The reformism of the
Law School provides the key to understanding a minor paradox in the
development of Lee's political thought: if Lee was instinctively an elitist
at Cambridge, how could he have been genuine in his belief in Fabian
socialism, an ideology which purported to be egalitarian? The two faces
of Lee are easily reconcilable if we acknowledge that Lee wanted to
introduce an egalitarian society from above, whereby the elite rules as
a benevolent leadership and identifies its interests with those of the
poor and marginalised in society. This is not an extraordinary proposition.
After all, many an elitist has successfully gained power and ruled with
this specific intention. This argument is supported by Lee's insistence
that egalitarianism meant equality of opportunity, particularly in education, rather than equality of outcome.[59] If equality of opportunity is
viewed as a mechanism whereby the 'genetically favoured', to use Boris
Christa's term, rise to the top and take their place in the elite, then
egalitarianism becomes the means for building an elite which will in
turn foster egalitarianism. This is a very tidy rationale for reconciling the
apparent contradictions in Lee's thinking during his 'socialist' phase,
which lasted until 1965.

Even before Lee Kuan Yew arrived at Cambridge he was instinctively
an elitist, but at Cambridge this tendency was confirmed and began developing into an ideological position. In 'The Returned Student' speech

of 1950, Lee displayed a distinct sense of comfort with the notion of a clear dichotomy between leaders and followers. 'There can be no leaders without a body to lead. There can be no body to lead without cohesion', he told the Malayan Forum.[60] His concept of leadership appears to have been extremely simple, though the earlier part of his speech demonstrated a more comprehensive understanding of the nature of power and the role of elites in the exercise of that power.[61] By the time of his election to the Legislative Assembly in 1955, however, Lee had developed his concept of leadership to a new level of sophistication. By this stage, Lee had come to see national leadership as comprising more than merely the political leadership offered by a party or a government. The non-political elite, comprising the university-educated intelligentsia, formed in his mind an implicit partnership with the political leadership without which the latter was impotent. In one of his early speeches to the Legislative Assembly, opposition leader Lee indicated his holistic conception of national leadership by expressing concern for the special place of the educated elite in society. In 1955 he warned that

> the 'elite' in the University of Malaya should not be antagonised ... There is your intellectual corps. There is your final battle, not for mass support. Masses can be swayed by emotions. But there is your group of workers, of brains, of intellect, of men who will do things out of conviction.[62]

A year later, Lee repeated his message even more forcefully:

> This government will find that there will be, as there was in China and in Indo-China, a flight of the intellectuals away from them. And intellectuals do matter. They may have only one vote and may not matter from the point of view of that one vote. But from the point of view of organising the masses and influencing them, their desertion will make the result catastrophic.[63]

In 1957, he revealed that the reason the intellectuals and university students 'do matter' is that 'they are the administrators, the D.O.'s, the magistrates, and the future political leaders of Malaya'.[64] Lee's credulous faith in the inherent rationality of the intelligentsia, along with his perception of their pivotal role in society, suggests that from the beginning Lee was an atypical democrat. The concept of rule by an alliance between an elite which dominates the political, administrative and legal professions is not necessarily incompatible with democracy, and is arguably merely a description of how successful democracies work in practice, but it does not sit well with the common perception of Lee Kuan Yew in the 1950s as a left-wing democratic politician. Yet despite suggestions that Lee has betrayed his early democratic convictions, he has never hidden his reservations about democracy. Even during his early phase as a 'democrat', he believed that the competence of the political and administrative elites was more important than the system under which they operated. During a Legislative Assembly debate in 1957, he declared:

> I prefer to see the Indian [democratic] experiment work itself out to its logical conclusion. Let us face facts. If a people have lost faith completely in their democratic institutions, because they cannot find men of calibre to run them, then, however good that system, it perishes. Ultimately it is the men who run the system who make it come to life.[65]

A decade later, Lee confirmed that in his mind, the 'calibre of the men who run the system' was still more important than the system itself when he argued that democratic socialism will not necessarily produce the best results in all societies because talent is not available equally in all societies.[66] By the time Lee came to power in 1959, the administrative elite had assumed a central role in his plans, and one of his first actions after being appointed Prime Minister was to create the Civil Service Study Centre, one purpose of which was to win Singapore's civil servants over to the PAP cause.[67] In the 1950s and the early 1960s, Lee's concept of the elite was still very narrowly based. In 1956 Lee gave an *ad hoc* definition of 'an elite' as 'a person who was groomed to govern'.[68] His concept of the elite was restricted primarily to those people who were trained to take an active role in the government. In the 1960s such people were found mainly in politics, the civil service and the legal profession, since at this stage of Singapore's development there was no significant body of highly educated local people outside these arenas.

Many of the early experiential factors in the development of Lee's elitism have been considered already, but the focus on the civil service warrants closer attention. It is apparent that Lee was influenced heavily by the advice of Goh Keng Swee and K.M. Byrne, two members of the PAP's inner group of leaders who were senior civil servants. At the opening of the Civil Service Study Centre in August 1959, Lee himself highlighted the role of these two men in influencing his thinking:

> For several years, two of your Ministers and I have been discussing the problems which a democratic socialist party ... will have to face when it assumes power in Singapore. And one of these problems is the civil service through which we have to translate our policies. These two Ministers were then your colleagues. They know the civil service as well as any of you, for no one can accuse Dr Goh Keng Swee or Mr K.M. Byrne of not knowing the civil service, in which they have spent the greater part of their lives.[69]

Lee was frank about the results of his discussions with Goh and Byrne. The civil service must be brought to 'see through the placid surface of constitutional change in Singapore to the revolutionary forces that are contending for supremacy beneath the constitutional facade', so that the civil service will become 'as anxious as we are to bring about a more equal and just society'.[70] The PAP was 'not interested in the theory of the separation of powers and the purpose and function of a politically neutral public service', but in having 'an administration more sensitive and responsive to the needs and moods of the people'.[71] The messages coming from Goh and Byrne were reinforced by Lee's own observation and study of the newly independent countries of Asia and Africa. In December 1956, months before Lee said that he 'preferred to see the Indian experiment work itself out', Lee quoted at length from a recent work by K.M. Pannikkar, an Indian historian and a member of India's diplomatic corps, on the nature of power in colonial India.[72] Pannikkar's study focused upon Britain's successful, albeit racist rule through the civil service. Lee condemned the racism of the colonial system and then proceeded to draw upon India's experience to highlight the critical importance of the civil service to the Malaya's future. He argued the need to have not only efficient administrators in the civil service, but people who were filled with zeal for the national purpose. Lee told the Assembly: 'If we have a lot of weak-kneed, flabby and feeble types who are more concerned with their personal welfare than the welfare of the people ... the whole fabric of government will collapse.'[73]

From the mid-1950s until Singapore's separation from Malaysia in 1965, Lee kept his attention fixed primarily on the political and administrative elite. After separation, however, Lee broadened and intensified his public focus on the elite when he introduced the concept of the social 'pyramid' and the concept of the state controlling the politicians. The social 'pyramid', said Lee, consisted of 'top leaders' at the apex, 'good executives' in the middle, and a 'highly civic-conscious broad mass' at the base.[74] The role of each of these social strata was distinct, requiring 'qualities of leadership at the top, and qualities of cohesion on the ground'.[75] Lee supplemented his imagery of the pyramid with that of a military organisation,[76] and argued that after the leaders come the 'middle strata of good executives', because 'the best general or the best prime minister in the world will be stymied if he does not have high-quality executives to help him carry out his ideas, thinking and planning'.[77] Finally comes 'the broad base' or the 'privates'.[78] They must be 'imbued not only with self but also social discipline, so that they can respect the community and do not spit all over the place'.[79]

With this speech, Lee's articulation of his elitism changed fundamentally in character. It is appropriate, therefore, to consider whether he changed his political ideas about the elite, or whether he merely began speaking his mind more openly. There is a strong case to say that Lee did change his thinking just before this period, in that he came to regard the elite not just as a means to an end, but as the central feature of his political programme. Singapore had just emerged from the tumultuous period of its membership of Malaysia and Lee had approached independent statehood with much trepidation. There can be no doubt that Lee faced the future with a new sense of desperation that would, in itself, prompt revision of any leader's priorities and assumptions. Lee himself has presented the desperation of the post-separation challenges as a reason for his abandonment of socialism.[80] Yet in our consideration of the development of Lee's elitism, there is reason to believe that the trauma of the two years' membership of Malaysia may have had a more fundamental impact on his ideas of the elite than the challenge of independence. Lee is on record on at least two occasions in the immediate aftermath of separation as deprecating the intolerable collapse of the standard of government services and departments while Singapore was under Malaysian rule. Three days after separation, he told an Australian journalist of the 'semi-gauleiters, who came down [from Kuala Lumpur] and squatted on people here; letters unanswered; Singapore departments which became Federal departments and became sluggish ... '[81] Then, at the end of September, he told civil servants of several recent occasions on which he encountered poor standards. He dealt with an 'impertinent' and 'jacksadaisical' [*sic*] telephone operator, a work brigade that was 'slacking', and a button in a government building that did not work. He did not even know what the button was supposed to do, but 'when you have a button, there must be a purpose', and he announced that he would not tolerate this sloppiness.[82] Lee had no difficulty in explaining the cause of this deterioration in standards: 'Two years in the Federal Department and she was just impertinent on the telephone. ... It is less than two years and the thing has happened like that', he complained.[83] Significantly, Lee took it upon himself to redress personally the problems as he came across them. Lee called the hapless telephonist and her supervisor into his office to explain that 'this is not the way'.[84] He took charge of giving the work brigade 'one big douche of cold water',[85] and of course he made sure that the notorious button worked the next day:

> I want to make sure that every button works. And even if you are using it only once in a while, please make sure every morning that it works. And if it doesn't when I happen to be around, then somebody is going to be in for a rough time because I do not want sloppiness.[86]

More than three decades later, it is rare to find a button in Singapore that does not work. Lee was appalled at the deterioration in efficiency when the elite was not in charge, as, in his mind, was the case during the Malaysia period. 'Sluggishness' at the top translates directly into a 'jacksadaisical' attitude at the base.

Apart from giving the civil service a 'douche of cold water', Lee determined to transform it into an elitist organisation:

> I want those who believe that joining the government service means automatically you are going up the ladder to forget it. Not with this government. Those who have got the vitality and the grit and the drive and can climb up that rope, well, he goes up. Those who are sluggish ... I say forget it. Because the rules are going to be changed. ... He can be dispensed with.[87]

The future of Singapore, said Lee, was in the hands of 'you, the admin. machinery; [and] my colleagues and I, the political leadership'.[88] In short, the political and the administrative elites would be in charge. Lee's renewed emphasis on the elite in 1966 was a direct response to his perception of the consequences of having second-rate administrators in charge during the Malaysia period. From now on, departments would run properly, and the future of the island would be planned by 'a group of men sitting in little rooms, planning, thinking, analysing, watching figures, watching trends'.[89] Under the guidance of the elite, Singapore would 'be a little beacon – a small beacon, but I hope a bright one for Malaysia'.[90]

While Lee's reaction to Malaysian 'sluggishness', combined with the imperatives of his post-separation desperation is probably sufficient to account for his renewed vigour in elite-building, we must remember also that Lee re-read Arnold Toynbee's *A Study of History* at around the time of separation.[91] Since we know that Toynbee influenced the development of Lee's progressivism,[92] it is reasonable to ask whether there was a corresponding influence on the development of his ideas of the elite. The circumstantial evidence to support such a thesis is impressive. Toynbee argued that a small 'creative minority',[93] which bears a remarkable resemblance to Lee's concept of 'the elite', rules a growing society. Like Lee, Toynbee was completely unapologetic for his elitism, and described the 'uncreative majority', which was roughly equivalent to Lee's 'broad base', as 'the sluggish rear-guard' of society.[94] In Toynbee's scenario, the most one can expect of the majority is that they do their best to keep up with the elite's initiatives by practice and imitation[95] because they are completely bereft of the creative instinct on which society depends for survival and growth.[96] For both Toynbee and Lee, therefore, the dichotomy between the leaders and the led is complete and permanent. Toynbee even supplied a rationale for Lee's role in opposition during the late colonial and the Malaysian phases. If Toynbee's elite ceases to be creative, it becomes a merely 'dominant minority' serving its own interests. Then truly creative individuals will become critics of society, rather than its leaders, and will lead the proletariat in opposing the now-illegitimate regime.[97] The apparent influence of Toynbee's 'creative minority' is so obvious that if it could be established as being a seminal influence on Lee, then it would be possible to explain the development of Lee's thoughts on the role of the elite almost completely in Toynbeean terms. Yet there is nothing more than this circumstantial evidence to support the theory that Toynbee's concept of the 'creative minority' directly influenced Lee, either while he was at Cambridge, or when he re-read Toynbee at the end of the Malaysia period. It is more likely that the idea of the 'creative minority' provided a theoretical rationale for his elitist predisposition, and that his identification with the concept of the 'creative minority' may have stimulated Lee's fascination for *A Study of History*.

While the roots of Lee's renewed post-separation elitism reach back into the Malaysia period, it is nevertheless true that the challenge of independence was the immediate cause of the development of Lee's thinking. The renewed attention on the elite was a direct consequence of the 'politics of survival', manifested in his concern that his administration was 'running on the ability, drive and dedication of about 150 people'.[98] Anyone who wished to destroy Singapore, he said, 'need only identify these 150 people and kill them'.[99] Hence there was a pressing need to enlarge 'quickly but systematically' this 'thin crust of leadership'.[100] But there was another new element in Lee's thinking which indicated a more fundamental development than a mere intensification of his focus on these matters. Lee also breathed new life into his scepticism of the value of democracy. In 1966, he spoke of his recent visit to 'a capital where the Army had taken over' because 'the structure had collapsed [and] the State was no longer able to control the politicians. … Society had collapsed'.[101] The concept of the state being an entity independent of politics and controlling politics and politicians is difficult to reconcile with our perceptions of the real world, including Singapore. Yet if we ignore such metaphysical questions and consider simply that Lee's observations of failed democracies confirmed his conclusion that politics was an impediment to good government, then we can see some of the roots that led him to set about removing politics from the arena of government in Singapore. Chan Heng Chee noted in 1975 that Singapore had become an 'administrative state', meaning that real power and meaningful contention had moved from the political arena to the bureaucracy over the previous ten years.[102] Chan argued that

> [this approach] has its roots in the current widespread social doctrine originating in the West that Technology holds all the answers to the important problems facing human civilisation and that society is better off with a rational application of scientific techniques to production and administration as if administration could be separated from politics.[103]

Lee's efforts to depoliticise government were underpinned also by the refinement of his concept of the elite, whose characteristics may be described as follows: supposed freedom from self-interest; a sense of common purpose which gives the group Cabinet-like homogeneity; a paternalistic concern for the well-being of one's subjects; relative freedom from bonds of loyalty to any local sectional interest; a willingness and capacity to take unpleasant and unpopular measures; relative freedom from the whim of an electorate; technical proficiency in the science of government; and smooth continuity from one leader to the next and one generation of leaders to the next. Chan Heng Chee has already attributed some of these characteristics to the first decade of post-separation Singapore.[104] Chan's discussion paper, however, was necessarily restricted to an examination of the alliance between the political and the administrative elite, because at the time she was writing there was only incidental evidence that Lee was thinking beyond these vocational parameters. In 1977, however, Lee declared that the elite encompassed most aspects of civic life:

> Democratic government requires, *inter alia*, that the government alone should not have to carry the responsibility of influencing public attitudes and opinion. To work with the democratic system, leadership at all levels, in particular non-political functional or professional group leaderships, should play their part in educating the people.[105]

This public expression of Lee's perception of the elite was made in response to developments in the Law Society and the Architects' Society, both of which Lee regarded as having breached public trust.[106] While this factor may be considered as evidence that Lee was changing his ideas in response to political developments, there is evidence to suggest that political developments prompted merely the articulation, and probably the refinement, of ideas that he had held for some time. A decade earlier, for instance, Lee was prompted by a dispute with the Vice-Chancellor of the University of Singapore to confirm that members of the elite do not need to stay within politics, nor within the civil service, in order to continue to be part of the governing caste of society. On this occasion, Lee noted that in contrast to the purely academic background of the current Vice-Chancellor of the University of Singapore, the then Master of Cambridge's Trinity College had already served as Deputy Prime Minister, Home Secretary, Foreign Secretary and Chancellor of the Exchequer, 'so he knows what Trinity College, Cambridge, is supposed to do for his country'.[107] Not only did this observation obliquely anticipate the later expansion of Lee's elite beyond the political and administrative vocations, but it indicated also a conception of a hitherto unspoken sense of homogeneity among the elite, which was to prove a crucial element of his thinking in the 1980s. By 1984, Lee's articulation of a cohesive, pan-vocational elite was explicit, as was his perception that his elitism was primarily descriptive rather than prescriptive:

> A well ordered society with an unbroken history, like Britain or Japan has its national solidarity and its establishment based on the king and the royal family, a religion and the elders of the church, the elite in the ruling parties who alternate in power, the elite in the public service and the armed forces, the elite in commerce, industry, and in the professions.[108]

Lee's public expansion of his concept of the elite in 1977 marked roughly the beginning of his use of a new technique of social control, whereby members of the elite were appointed to leadership positions in bodies representing the base of the social 'pyramid'. This development represented a significant change of policy which manifested itself first in the trade unions, and then later in a more diverse range of organisations. Throughout the 1960s and the first half of the 1970s, Lee had recognised that there existed in Singapore a generation of men[109] who had never had the opportunity to receive an education commensurate with their ability. Many of these people had risen nevertheless through civic organisations such as the trade unions and clan associations, and therefore held positions of responsibility. They were on the periphery of the elite without having been 'groomed to govern'. Lee's interim solution was to provide training for these men who, to develop Lee's military analogy, were the non-commissioned officers of society. Thus very early in the life of his government, he established the Labour Research Unit to mould and produce trade union leaders who were 'well-educated, well-trained, well-organised', and who would 'act cohesively and effectively in pursuance of our collective interests'.[110] Yet, these grassroots leaders could never become truly part of the elite without having passed through the traditional halls of learning, just as his friend and colleague, Devan Nair, was never truly accepted into the inner circle of PAP leaders for the same reason. It is difficult to be certain whether Lee's attempts to educate and indoctrinate the existing leadership of society's 'broad mass' was merely the best interim solution Lee could find in the 1950s and 1960s, or whether he believed that it was a viable long-term solution to the perceived dilemma of leadership in civic life. Given Lee's emphasis on the elite since the 1950s, it is likely that he regarded this technique as a mere expedient, and that he had always believed that the ultimate solution was for the elite to appoint its own representatives to provide leadership in each walk of life. Regardless of which scenario is the more accurate, in the 1970s Lee began appointing university graduates, and PAP MPs and ministers to work in and lead trade unions because 'the unions must have their quota of talent'.[111] Moreover in 1980 he took steps to ensure that each housing block had a number of well-educated, successful people as residents, so that the ordinary people would have competent leadership.[112] The ethnic communities were not neglected, and in 1981 the government created a Malay self-help group called the Council for the Development of Muslim Children (MENDAKI), composed of Malays and Muslim Indians who were both well-educated and sympathetic to the government.[113]

Lee took a close personal interest in promotions and appointments in a wide range of government and quasi-government institutions such as statutory boards, government and semi-government commercial ventures and trade unions.[114] In the process of building this elite, therefore, Lee created a society that was permeated at nearly every level by a ruling class whose rise was at least as closely linked to government patronage as it was to intelligence and ability – a situation that enabled Lee to exercise a high level of social and political control beyond the normal scope of a government leader. The story of Francis Seow's 1967 interview with Lee indicates the Prime Minister's technique. Lee summoned Seow specifically to tell him that he had personally overridden objections from the Legal Service Commission to ensure that Seow would be appointed Solicitor-General, and indicated that the position of Chief Justice was within his scope. Seow concluded his account: 'Although the word *beholden* did not once cross [Lee's] lips that fateful day, I was left in no doubt whatsoever as to the underlying purpose of that august summons'.[115]

From Lee's earliest days as Prime Minister, he began replacing civic leaders with people acceptable to the government, which was an effective means of stripping civic life of its independent political content, and bringing most social organisations under the wing of the government. This technique was employed in the trade unions, and in a wide range of social bodies that were often created by the government specifically to facilitate this control. Over the next thirty years, Lee created a ruling class whose legitimacy depended upon borrowing from the government's store of what Francis Fukuyama calls 'social capital',[116] and who could therefore never act or speak with the freedom implied by being at or near the peak of a meritocracy. 'Social capital' is the ability of people to work together for common purposes in groups or organisations, and Fukuyama argues that this 'ability to associate depends ... on the degree to which communities share norms and values and are able to subordinate individual interests to those of larger groups'.[117] In contradiction of Lee Kuan Yew's stated assumption of the naturally communitarian nature of Confucianism, Fukuyama argues that Chinese society, whether found in the People's Republic of China, Taiwan, Hong Kong, or Singapore, has a low level of social capital because the basis of trust is restricted substantially to family and clan members.[118] The consequence of this lack of social capital in all of these societies is the near-absence of successful enterprises other than those owned or dominated by the state, or owned and run by a family.[119] Chinese family companies, argues Fukuyama, have difficulty transforming themselves into modern medium-size or large enterprises precisely because the familial basis of the trust in their societies, which is a boon while such a company is small but growing, inhibits the introduction of professional managers from outside the family when the company needs to expand past the point where the family can keep control.[120] Fukuyama's concern was the economic consequences of this lack of social capital, but there are social and political consequences as well. Singapore was not only numerically, politically and economically dominated by 'low-trust' ethnic Chinese who were themselves divided into a myriad of language and clan groups, but it was further fragmented by significant Malay and Indian components in the population. Despite their communitarian rhetoric of the 1980s and 1990s, Lee Kuan Yew and Goh Keng Swee recognised implicitly the low-trust nature of Singapore society in the 1950s and 1960s. They set about compensating in the economic sphere by using the state and multi-national corporations as the primary mechanisms to industrialise Singapore's hitherto entrepôt economy.[121] The social and long-term political problems were met through the gradual imposition of the government's de facto control over all aspects of civic life, as has been described above. The foundation of this control was the 'social capital' that the PAP created by being seen to be working in the interests of the whole of society. The government was thus able to build, in the words of Leonard Sebastian, 'a social coalition consistent with the goals of the state' that carried sufficient legitimacy in the eyes of the people to enable

the government to quell populist, communist and communalist tendencies.[122]

Lee must have been satisfied with the social and political control which
he acquired by having the elite dependent upon government patronage,
and the conventional wisdom is that Lee's theories of elitism have been
substantially a cover for achieving this control. Yet there is a problem
with this scenario, which lends weight to the thesis that his belief in the
elite as a transpolitical, homogenous ruling entity transcended mere
political technique. This was most evident when, contrary to expectations,
Lee expressed delight when successful Muslim Indians and Malays
snubbed the government-sponsored MENDAKI in 1990 and established
the Association of Muslim Professionals (AMP) to improve the educational
and economic status of the relatively poor Malay community.[123] The
establishment of the AMP was a 'positive development', said Lee, because
it meant that the Malays were 'throwing up their own leaders'.[124] Once
the AMP agreed to prohibit members of any political party, including
the PAP, from becoming members, the government allowed it to operate
without a government representative on its governing body, and also gave
it liberal access to government funds.[125] Although the official response
to the AMP is the most dramatic instance of an apparent change in Lee
and the PAP's attitude towards rival civic organisations, this was not a
totally isolated example. From the mid-1980s Lee had begun taking a
superficially liberal attitude to a small number of other middle-class
special interest groups, which began to provide unsolicited advice to
the government on matters related to their areas of interest.[126] As David
Brown has observed, Lee's enthusiasm for the AMP does not seem to
have been either the result or the beginning of a nascent adoption of
liberalism by Lee, or even by the emerged middle class of Singapore.[127]
Yet Brown noted the following statement made by Lee in June 1991:

> Once you reach a certain level of industrial progress, you've got an
> educated workforce, an urban population, you have managers and
> engineers. Then you must have participation because these are educated,
> rational people. If you carry on with an authoritarian system, you will
> run into all kinds of logjams. You must devise some sort of representative
> system. Then you may get the beginnings of a civic society, with people
> forming their own groups ... Almost spontaneously these will form,
> because being educated, knowing the wider world, will bring like-minded
> people together. Then only do you have the beginnings of what I would
> call an active grassroots democracy.[128]

Garry Rodan believes that on this occasion Lee was avoiding confrontation with the already discontented Malays, and was ensuring that
the rival body would not become politicised.[129] While not taking issue

with Rodan's analysis, it may be argued also that Lee was completely genuine in his public response to the AMP, and that he believed in the emergence of a self-sustaining educated elite, which would not need to be tied by patronage to the government in order to work in society's interests. By this stage of his career, Lee had adapted his theory of the elite to the new world order ushered in by the process of globalisation. He foreshadowed the development of a worldwide, educated elite operating and flourishing in the globalised economy.[130] Such an elite, he argued, could not function in 'a closed social system' because the demands of modern technology and the modern global economy required that 'good managers and engineers' have free access to information.[131] Unlike the population at large, this elite, comprising 'the top 3 to 5 per cent of a society', will benefit from the 'intellectual stimulation' of 'a free-for-all' of ideas, since they 'provide the cutting edge for society'.[132] Regardless of whether a country's political system is democratic or not, this elite must be the dominant political force in a successful modern society. 'Can you imagine such a society governed without participation of the people who are in charge of the economy? It is not possible', Lee argued.[133]

Lee does not appear to have believed that this non-political elite would or could be centrally controlled by the government, but rather the government would be drawn from the cream of the broader elite. The government would then rule in the interests of the whole of society, transcending sectional interests and politics without necessarily making any concessions to Western liberalism. Such a scenario has a distinct fairy-tale quality, but it is consistent with Lee's statements on the Singapore elite throughout his career. If this account of Lee's perception is given credence, then Lee appears to have been genuinely pleased with the development of the AMP, because it showed that sections of the elite were beginning to take initiatives that would put them in their rightful place in society. Providing they did not disturb the plans of the political leadership, which was the crème de la crème of elites, then only good could come from such initiatives. A critical precondition for sustaining this view was Lee's perception of the elite as intrinsically homogenous. Using this definition, of course, any apparent members of the elite who oppose a political leadership which is proving itself to be both united and effective, are not truly members of the elite, but are opportunists, or worse.

Regardless of the importance of the non-political elite in Lee's world, it has always been the political leadership which must take the cream of society's talent and which must occupy the full force of his attention, because 'they settle the major rules of the game'.[134] In 1972, Lee and his senior colleagues began 'a search for talent' by scouring the country's managers, academics and civil servants for a second generation of political leaders who were both willing to conform to the strictures of the PAP ideology, and at the same time measured up to their exacting standards of talent, imagination, leadership and commitment.[135] Lee's concern with the succession is one of the many characteristics of his rule which is atypical of either Western or Asian practice, but which is intrinsic to his view of the nature of the elite. One of the characteristics he expected of the elite was the capacity to provide uncontentious continuity from one leader to the next, and from one generation to the next. The alternative scenario would allow the system he created to be replaced by a political contest, where the elite would be divided, and the result would be determined by the political skills of the contestants, rather than by logic and 'talent'. Further, the political leadership of the country might pass out of the hands of the elite completely, as 'mediocrities and opportunists' took advantage of the disarray.[136] To paraphrase the thoughts Lee expressed in 1966, the state would lose control of the politicians.[137]

An examination of Lee's 'search for talent' reveals another major strand of Lee's thought which has been present since the late 1960s, but which has not been canvassed in this study thus far: Lee's ideas on the relationship between genes and talent. Lee first revealed his geneticism in the 1968. 'What will happen in the next generation? What quality of men or women will they be?' asked Lee.

> First, it depends on what genetic qualities we have in our present generation. ... Unless the better-educated and better-equipped stake out a bigger part of the future for their progeny, then the future will be that much poorer for all....

> Let us for purposes of argument, accept that educational and social performance, more or less, are equal to intelligence and the other qualities which make for better performance. If you look at the population I.Q. pyramid of Singapore, then as a community we want that pyramid to get steeper and higher. At the moment that pyramid is getting broader and lower.[138]

A year later, in his speech on the Abortion Bill, Lee announced:

> Free education and subsidised housing lead to a situation where less economically productive people in the community are reproducing themselves at rates higher than the rest. This will increase the total proportion of less productive people.

> Our problem is how to devise a system of disincentives, so that the irresponsible, the social delinquents, do not believe that all they have to do

is to produce their children and the government then owes them and their children sufficient food, medicine, housing, education and jobs.[139]

Lee granted that every person, 'genius or moron', had the right to 'reproduce himself', and even allowed each couple a third child 'for good measure'. However,

> [b]eyond the three children the costs of subsidised medicine and free education would be transferred to the parent. We have changed the priorities in public housing, by not awarding more points for more children. One day we may have to put disincentives or penalties on the other social services. ...

> One of the crucial yardsticks by which we shall have to judge the results of the new abortion law combined with the voluntary sterilisation legislation law, will be whether it tends to raise or lower the total quality of our population. We must encourage those who earn less than $200 per month and cannot afford to nurture and educate children never to have more than two. ...

> We will regret the time lost if we do not take the first tentative steps towards correcting a trend which can leave our society with a large number of the physically, intellectually and culturally anaemic.[140]

On this occasion Lee justified his views on inherited intelligence by referring to research published in the *New Scientist* in March 1969,[141] but since he already held these views in October 1968, this was obviously a justification for his beliefs, rather than their source.

After the Abortion Bill debate, Lee's views on genetics receded into the background of Singaporean politics until the 1980s, probably because he found little support in Cabinet. Since their retirement, S. Rajaratnam, and E.W. Barker have stated that they never agreed with Lee's views on genetics, and Lee has also identified Toh Chin Chye and Ong Pang Boon as early Cabinet opponents of his elitist policies.[142] Yet even though Lee toned down the public expression of his eugenicist views for the next few years, he continued to pursue eugenicist policies, under the thin disguise of his government's family planning programme. In 1970 a Eugenics Board was constituted to license doctors to perform sterilisations on medical, social, and eugenics grounds.[143] Confinement and antenatal charges in hospitals, access to good schools and housing, and public servants' access to paid maternity leave came to be determined by formulas which took into account the number of children in the family, and whether the mother or father had been sterilised.[144] In 1973 the government reduced from five to three the number of children for whom tax relief was available. The maximum level of tax relief a couple could claim for their children was thus restricted to just over $1,000. This applied to all Singaporeans, except for women in a select group of professions.

In a revealing eugenic twist, women doctors and lawyers could claim child-related tax relief of several thousand dollars.[145]

Lee returned eugenics to the forefront of his agenda in 1982. In his National Day rally speech of that year Lee said:

> What was the most important single factor for Singapore's rapid development since 1959? Without hesitation, my answer is the quality of the people. For not only are our people hard-working, quick to learn and practical, Singapore also had an extra thick layer of high calibre and trained talent.[146]

In 1959, the reason for the 'extra thick' crust of trained talent was that Singapore had an unnaturally large catchment area, which encompassed the Malayan Peninsula, southern India, Sri Lanka and southern China.[147] By the 1970s the catchment area was restricted substantially to Singapore, and 'the Singapore pool of talent is finite and limited'.[148] Lee believed that talent was an inherited characteristic, just like hair colour. Since the 'talent profile' of the population is determined genetically, it should come as no surprise that once equality of educational opportunity had been achieved, Lee expected one's place on the social 'pyramid' to be inherited from generation to generation. Lee argued that Singapore's pool of talent was shrinking because well-educated people were having fewer children than poorly educated people,[149] and that only a small proportion of the population, the potential elite, has talent in abundance:

> We must be grateful that the talent profile, or IQ spread, of our population enables us to produce, from a yearly birth rate, in the 1950s and 1960s, of 60,000 to 50,000, about 60–50 first class minds, an average rate of 1 in 1,000. Alas, not all of these bright minds have strong characters, sound temperament, and high motivation to match their high intelligence. I have found, from studying PSC scholarship awards for the last 15 years, and reading confidential reports on their work in the public service and the SAF, that the scholars who also have the right character and personality, effectively works out to 1 in 3,000 persons. In the 1970s, our annual births went down to 40,000. The number of talented and balanced Singaporeans will be between 12–14 persons per annum at one per 3,000.[150]

Lee made his views on inherited talent the premise of his 1983 National Day speech.[151] This occasion marked the serious beginning of Lee's eugenics programme, by which he hoped to create a pool of talented Singaporeans through selective breeding. Despite the efforts of S. Rajaratnam to water down Lee's statement,[152] Lee himself was forthright about the role he believed genetics played in determining intelligence. 'A person's performance depends on nature and nurture. There is increasing evidence that nature, or what is inherited, is the greater determinant of a person's performance than nurture (or education and environment)', he said.[153] The precise focus of Lee's concern was the results of the 1980 Census, which showed, unsurprisingly, that better-educated women were having fewer children than poorly educated women.[154] Lee foresaw national disaster if the pool of talent continued to be diminished in this way:

> If we continue to reproduce ourselves in this lop-sided way, we will be unable to maintain our present standards. Levels of competence will decline. Our economy will falter; administration will suffer; and society will decline. For how can we avoid lowering performance when for every two graduates (with some exaggeration to make the point), in twenty-five years' time there will be one graduate, and for every two uneducated workers, there will be three?

> ... In all societies, the trend is for the better-educated people to have less children than the less-educated. But no other society has ever compressed this process into just one generation, from the 1950s to the 1970s, and have the first statistical evidence in the 1980 Census. ... In some way or other, we must ensure that the next generation will not be too depleted of the talented.[155]

Lee's National Day speech was followed by what became known as the 'Great Marriage Debate', in which Lee canvassed the possibility of making single parenthood and polygamy socially acceptable for graduates,[156] and actually introduced a graduates' match-making service, called the Social Development Unit.[157] He also initiated a series of incentives for well-educated people to have more children and a series of disincentives to encourage low-educated people to have fewer children and be sterilised.[158]

Lee's views on the genetic nature of talent have led him to approach his self-appointed task of elite-building from an extremely blinkered and idiosyncratic perspective.[159] Once it is accepted that talent is inherited from one's parents, and that no amount of education or nurture will lift the proletariat into the ranks of the elite, then it makes no sense to expect the sons and daughters of the 'broad base' to do more than master the technical skills needed to be productive, work hard and learn not to 'spit all over the place'.[160] The sons and daughters of the well-educated, however, are the candidates for the top echelon of society, and are a precious resource. Operating on the assumption that wealth and education are closely related to intelligence,[161] Lee gave flesh to this idea in 1988, when, with his encouragement, the top schools on the island began converting themselves into fee-charging independent schools. The most significant of these conversions was that of Raffles Institution, the island's most prestigious government school and Lee's

Alma Mater.[162] Despite the provision of some scholarships, this move for the first time effectively linked entry to Raffles Institution primarily to parents' income rather than the child's academic ability.

A further consequence of Lee's views on genetics is that he lays enormous emphasis on the need to test candidates for the elite, which is only to be expected from one who believes that talent is innate rather than acquired. The testing begins early in the school life, especially since 'streaming' was intensified at the beginning of the 1980s.[163] For the potential elite, the testing continues beyond school and university. The academic cream of each year were and are selected for the armed forces, the civil service and government enterprises, not only so that they could be imbued with the conformist culture of these institutions, but also so that Lee Kuan Yew could study them through confidential reports written by their superiors.[164] 'It is a difficult business identifying talent', said Lee in 1976. 'And that is what we are looking for – people who can last the pace, not just one test but having passed it he will have three or four more quickly passed on to him'.[165] In an interview with *The Business Times* in 1978, Lee was prompted to state explicitly that testing rather than training was the essence of the system he had instituted:

BT: How adequate is the present population to produce the necessary number of leaders required?

Lee: It depends on the qualities of the population, the genetic pool we have inherited. We got the leaders that we are capable of throwing up. There is a finite group of people, between the ages of 35 to 45, from which such a leadership must be drawn. ... I do not think you learn leadership ... This attribute called leadership is either in you or it is not.

BT: If the leadership is there, what is the training period supposed to give the man?

Lee: Really to show that he has got it, not that he is hiding the lack thereof behind a show of aplomb and erudition.

BT: It is basically a testing period not a training period? Establishing that the qualities that are apparent are also real and that they can be used in decision-making?

Lee: If you want to put it in an unkind way – yes.[166]

Lee and the PAP, therefore, devote themselves to combing society for talent to be drafted into the higher echelons of the government machine, or perhaps as a Nominated Member of Parliament if the person has a streak of independence which makes him or her unsuitable for being part of the government team. The PAP recruits from lists of scholars and registers of professionals, and the exercise has more in common with commercial head-hunting than with political activism. Lee claims to have modelled his techniques consciously on those of the Shell oil company.[167] Lee boasted in 1984:

> Our methods of absorbing the ablest and the best means that there will be few, if any, outstanding men for the opposition. Anybody with a good brain, even if he disagrees with us on policies, can join us and argue out and amend our policies and do right for the people.
>
> ... When the PAP ceases to co-opt the talented, it will become vulnerable. If we exclude able men of integrity and commitment, they will, when they see things going awry, have one of two choices – get out before the country collapses, or challenge the PAP's right to govern.[168]

Lee's belief in the government's monopoly of talent was important to him, not only because of his theoretically based views on the need to maintain a homogenous elite, but also because he believed that small countries have insufficient genetic and educational resources to supply both a government and an opposition with talent. 'The price of keeping up the myth of an alternative government can be crippling when there is a shortage of trained talent', he told an audience in 1982.[169]

Lee's elitist logic has a circumlocutious quality that gives the ideology a plausible, but ultimately false legitimacy. He has created a political system designed to produce outcomes that accord with his elitism, and then used the system he has created as evidence that his elitism is correct. Yet even then, he needs to resort to syllogistic sleights of hand to cover the weaknesses of his case. PAP dissidents, such as Toh Chin Chye and Ong Pang Boon, used to complain that Lee's system produced only 'careerists, people who have not gone through battle',[170] to which Lee responded that there was no alternative to his method because there had been no battles since the 1960s.[171] Lee, however, has ignored the fact that the only reason there are no 'battles' is that he has imposed conformity. Applying the logic of his elitism, he has emasculated all potential opposition. Lee argues also that the absence of talent in the opposition parties is evidence that he has successfully harnessed Singapore's store of talent. There is, however, little evidence that his assessment of the opposition is valid. As part of his effort to demonstrate the absence of administrative skills among opposition candidates, Lee has devolved much of the administrative responsibility for housing blocks to Town Councils run by local MPs. Lee warned that constituencies that reject PAP candidates cannot be expected to be insulated from the incompetence of their choices. As Lee forecast, the standard of housing and services in opposition-controlled constituencies did, indeed, fall behind the rest of Singapore, but only because of systematic and open political discrimination by the Housing and Development Board in the allocation of funds and services.[172] By creating this discriminatory system of housing funding, Lee purported to demonstrate the lack of talent in the opposition, but he actually deprived himself of a chance to achieve this result. Perhaps the greatest achievement of his ideological campaign is that he has succeeded in defining his own ideology as reality, while labelling those who disagree as 'ideologues'.

Despite the idiosyncrasies and ruthlessness of Lee Kuan Yew's approach to politics, it must be conceded that it has the virtue of having achieved a miraculous transformation of Singapore's economy, society and physical environment. Lee has fathered a system that has delivered stability, economic prosperity and machinery of government virtually free of corruption. Yet in retrospect, there is a case to say that Lee may have erred by failing to review the fundamentals of his elitism in the early 1980s. Lee's insistence on homogeneity led him to pass up an ideal opportunity to allow the development of a more mature civil society in the early 1980s when he responded to the election of J.B. Jeyaretnam to Parliament by launching a vindictive campaign to destroy him through both political and civil actions.[173] He succeeded in his aim of maintaining a society with virtually no politics, but in pursuing homogeneity, he created a culture of timid circumspection. This culture has had its advantages, since it has allowed the PAP a free hand in engineering prosperity, but it has left virtually everyone except a tiny portion of the top echelon of society as passive and compliant citizens who contribute little to decision-making. Singaporean author Philip Jeyaretnam expressed the mentality of compliance eloquently in his novel, *Abraham's Promise*, when he wrote of a particularly insipid character:

> He abjures politics, saying one can be perfectly comfortable keeping within the bounds set by our present rulers, and that there's no reason why anyone should risk his career, or worse, for the sake of more free-dom than he would know what to do with.[174]

Russell Heng captured this mentality in seven words: 'Give me liberty or give me wealth'.[175]

Lee himself sees few problems with the passivity of the Singapore electorate, since he regards society as naturally and inevitably hierarchical. The role of Singapore's quasi-democratic processes is to provide merely a periodical plebiscite on the performance of the government to ensure that the elite remains creative and provides 'good government' for its subjects. There is no serious pretence that the electorate is choosing its government in a free and open contest. Lee's logic, however, demands that members of the elite involve themselves in the political process, and since the elite has shown itself reluctant to involve itself in the PAP, other mechanisms have been created to try to involve the talented in the process of government. These devices include the introduction of Nominated MPs and Non-Constituency MPs in the early 1980s and the creation of a Ministry of Community Development 'Feedback Unit' in 1985, which was designed to enable people to register their concerns and reservations about the government's initiatives and performance. The system has worked to date because Lee and his first-generation colleagues had the experience gained in winning their victories in the face of overwhelming odds, when there was a virile contest between rival ideological and social forces. The second generation of leaders, however, has gained its experience in an environment of conformity, which has had little competition between political, let alone ideological forces. Even since Lee's semi-retirement in 1990, he has retained sufficient authority to ensure that his system has continued to operate with minimal disruption to either efficiency or conformity. Yet as an ideologically driven progressivist, Lee does not think in terms merely of his own generation. Since as early as 1966, he has demonstrated a preoccupation with the future beyond his own lifetime. He told an audience not long after separation from Malaysia:

> The final test of success is that when we are going we know that those who are following after us will take one step forward. It will not go down, it will go forward from where we left it. That is the final test of success. That we have assured for our progeny a better future than us. Better than the one we had. Then really we have succeeded.[176]

As Lee himself knows full well, it is impossible to 'assure' anything about the future, yet since the late 1970s this preoccupation has become an obsession.[177] He has, however, allowed very limited opportunities for Singaporean society to develop the depth needed to ensure that his system continues to work after it is deprived of his leadership. By Lee's own standards of pessimism, it seems imprudent to create a system that maintains the forms of democracy, and depends as much on consensus as it does on coercion, yet gives its new generation of leaders no opportunity to test their limits in one of those two critical fields.

Building upon the work of other researchers, we now have a substantial understanding of the nature of Lee's elitism. This is important in its own right, since without such an understanding, it is difficult to grasp the subtleties of post-independence and current Singaporean politics and society. It is unusual to find a country's history so closely identified with one man. Yet Singapore's history since 1965 is substantially the product of the mind, the prejudices and the energy of Lee Kuan Yew.

By improving our understanding of Lee's 'social pyramid', his identification of the transpolitical, homogenous elite with the state, and the hereditary nature of that elite, we improve our understanding of the tense and brittle political, economic and social entity that is Singapore. In its early years of independence, Singapore's vulnerability derived from its precarious economic position, and its uncertain place in the region. Lee successfully responded to these crises and put Singapore on the road to stability and success. Since the 1980s, however, the brittleness and tensions have been largely the product of Lee's attempts to extend his elitist ideology to its logical conclusion. Despite his avowed pragmatism, he does not appear to have been able to accept that people may not necessarily act according to his ideological precepts. The 'elite' has not only refused to be a homogenous entity, it has also substantially turned its back upon politics. The inherent contradiction in Lee's position is not difficult to discern. He expects his elite to be 'adventurous', 'risk-taking' entrepreneurs with the imagination to 'see the chances' and who have 'the drive and the dare' to succeed,[178] but he also expects them to be compliant towards the political leadership and to act as a homogenous unit. James Minchin expressed the dilemma of Lee's Singapore succinctly in a 1997 radio interview:

> If you deny people a participation in the shaping of their future through political process but say you've got to be inventive in every other area of your life, you are imposing a fundamental contradiction. You can't compartmentalise life in that way.[179]

This contradiction may yet undo Lee's vision for Singapore.

NOTES

1.   Toh Chin Chye in Melanie Chew (ed.), *Leaders of Singapore*, Singapore: Resource Press, 1996, p. 88.

2.   According to James Cotton, 'The party has ... become a shell, a convenient electoral machine for maintaining in office an elite which is ultimately self-selected, self-promoted and self-defined'. James Cotton, 'Political innovation in Singapore: the presidency, the leadership and the party', in Garry Rodan (ed.), *Singapore Changes Guard: Social, Political and Economic Directions in the 1990s*, Melbourne: Longman Cheshire; New York: St Martin's Press, 1993, p. 10.

3.   Lee Kuan Yew's interview with Trevor Kennedy in Kennedy, *Top Guns: Seventeen World Leaders in Politics, Media and Business Tell How They Made It to the Top – and Stayed There*, Melbourne and Sydney: Macmillan, 1988, p. 269.

4.   Lee Kuan Yew, *The Singapore Story: Memoirs of Lee Kuan Yew*, Singapore; New York; London; Toronto; Sydney; Mexico City: Prentice Hall, 1998, p. 34.

5.   *Ibid.*, p. 93.

6.   Letter from Hilton Scharenguivel to the author, 3 December 1996.

7.   *The Straits Times*, 27 April 1995.

8.   Letter from Lee Kuan Yew to Teo Kah Leong, 29 April 1995.

9.   Interview with E.W. Barker, 16 October 1996. Barker describes himself as one of Lee's 'few friends' at school.

10.   James Minchin, *No Man Is an Island: A Portrait of Singapore's Lee Kuan Yew*, Sydney: Allen & Unwin, 1990, p. 310.

11.   Han Fook Kwang, Warren Fernandez and Sumiko Tan, *Lee Kuan Yew: The Man and His Ideas*, Singapore: Times Editions and Singapore Press Holdings, 1998, p. 157.

12.   Lee's address to the University of Singapore Democratic Socialist Club, 15 June 1966, in Lee Kuan Yew, *Prime Minister's Speeches, Press Conferences, Interviews, Statements, etc.*, Singapore: Prime Minister's Office, 1959–90.

13.   Interview with Kiang Ai Kim, 14 October 1996. Kiang was three years ahead of Lee at RI.

14.   Minchin, *No Man Is an Island*, p. 309. Also see Lee, *The Singapore Story*, p. 34.

15.   Minchin, *No Man Is an Island*, p. 309.

16.   Lee in Singapore Legislative Assembly, *Debates Official Report*, 7 March, 1956, column 1919.

17.   Lee's address at the Convent of the Holy Infant Jesus, Serangoon Gardens, 11 December 1965, in Lee, *Prime Minister's Speeches, etc.*

18.   Interview with Teo Kah Leong, 29 October 1996.

19.   Jim Neo planned to send Harry to an English university directly after school, hence her need to save money. See Lee, *The Singapore Story*, p. 38.

20.   Minchin, *No Man Is an Island*, p. 309.

21.   *Ibid.*, p. 311.

22.   *Ibid.*, p. 301.

23.   *Ibid.*, p. 309.

24.   See Chapter 2.

25.   Interview with Teo Kah Leong, 29 October 1996.

26.   *Ibid.*

27.   *Ibid.*

28.   *Ibid.*

29.   Richard Nixon's toast at the exchange of toasts between the President and Prime Minister Lee Kuan Yew of Singapore, 10 April 1973, in Lee, *Prime Minister's Speeches, etc.*

30.   Lee Kuan Yew, *New Bearings in Our Education System*, Singapore: Ministry of Culture, [n.d., c.1966–67], p. 7.

31.   *Ibid.*, p. 15.

32.   Lee Kuan Yew's foreword to the first edition of *The Rafflesian Directory*. Old Rafflesians' Association, *The Rafflesian Directory, 1995 Edition*, Singapore: Old Rafflesians' Association, 1995, p. i.

33.   Lee at the opening of the Third Asian Teachers' Seminar, 20 November 1966, in Lee, *Prime Minister's Speeches, etc.*

34. Press release from the Prime Minister's Office, 26 March 1980, in *ibid.*

35. Eugene Wijeysingha, *The Eagle Breeds a Gryphon: The Story of Raffles Institution 1823–1985*, Singapore: Pioneer Book Centre, 1989, p. 157.

36. *Ibid.*

37. Lee at the opening of the Third Asian Teachers' Seminar, 20 November 1966, in Lee, *Prime Minister's Speeches, etc.*

38. Interview with Velauthar Ambiavagar, 15 October 1996.

39. *Ibid.*

40. Lee at the opening of the Third Asian Teachers' Seminar, 20 November 1966, in Lee, *Prime Minister's Speeches, etc.*; Interviews with Velauthar Ambiavagar, 15 October 1996, Teo Kah Leong, 29 October 1996, and Kiang Ai Kim, 14 October 1996. See also Wijeysingha, *The Eagle Breeds a Gryphon*, p. 157.

41. Interview with Kiang Ai Kim, 14 October 1996.

42. Interviews with Kiang Ai Kim, 14 October 1996; Teo Kah Leong, 29 October 1996; Lim Chin Aik, 21 October 1996; and Velauthar Ambiavagar, 15 October 1996. Letters to the author from Erik Goonetilleke, 4 December 1996 and Hilton Scharenguivel, 3 December 1996.

43. See, for instance, Lee's speech at the Tanjong Pagar Community Centre, 30 October 1965, in Lee, *Prime Minister's Speeches, etc.* This phase of Lee's rhetoric is considered at length in Chapter 5.

44. Lee to the Old Rafflesians' Association, 29 June 1960, in *ibid.*

45. Interview with Teo Kah Leong, 29 October 1996.

46. Interview with Lim Chin Aik, 21 October 1996.

47. *Ibid.*

48. See Linda Low and Toh Mun Heng, *The Elected Presidency as a Safeguard for Official Reserves: What Is at Stake?*, Singapore: Times Academic Press for The Institute of Policy Studies, 1989, for a detailed and sympathetic study of the proposal.

49. See Lee's speech at the inauguration ceremony of the new Tanjong Pager Town Council, 28 March 1992, for his forthright account of the purpose of town councils. Lee Kuan Yew, *Senior Minister's Speeches, Press Conferences, Interviews, Statements, etc.* Singapore: Prime Minister's Office, 1991–95.

50. Wijeysingha, *The Eagle Breeds a Gryphon*, p. 160.

51. *The Straits Times*, 27 April 1995.

52. Interview with Alan Ashbolt in ABC Studios in Canberra, 24 March 1965, in Lee, *Prime Minister's Speeches, etc.*

53. Interview with George Dixon, 11 July 1996.

54. Lee, *The Singapore Story*, p. 110.

55. Interview with Boris Christa, 27 May 1996.

56. Lee's address to the dinner of the Law Society of the University of Singapore, 7 October 1966, in Lee, *Prime Minister's Speeches, etc.*

57. Lee, *New Bearings in Our Education System*, p. 10.

58. *Ibid.*, p. 12.

59. Lee's address to the Rotary Club, 24 February 1960, in Lee, *Prime Minister's Speeches, etc.*

60. Lee in Han, Fernandez, Tan, *Lee Kuan Yew: The Man and His Ideas*, p. 261.

61. See the précis of 'The Returned Student' in Chapter 2.

62. *Legislative Assembly*, 24 November 1955, column 1239.

63. *Ibid.*, 4 October 1956, column 406.

64. *Ibid.*, 27 April 1957, column 1756.

65. *Ibid.*, column 1757.

66. Lee's answer to a question at the University of Singapore, 9 October 1966, in Lee, *Prime Minister's Speeches, etc.*

67. Lee's address at the opening of the Civil Service Study Centre, 15 August 1959, in *ibid.*

68. *Legislative Assembly*, 5 December 1956, column 1088.

69. Lee's address to the Civil Service Study Centre, 15 August 1959, in Lee, *Prime Minister's Speeches, etc.*

70. *Ibid.*

71. *Ibid.*

72. *Legislative Assembly*, 5 December 1956, columns 1086–1088.

73. *Ibid.*, column 1091.

74. Lee, *New Bearings in Our Education System*, p. 13.

75. *Ibid.*, p. 9.

76. *Ibid.*, p. 12.

77. *Ibid.*

78. *Ibid.*

79. *Ibid.*, p. 13.

80. Lee Kuan Yew, *Extrapolating from the Singapore Experience: Special lecture by Lee Kuan Yew, Prime Minister of Singapore, at 26th World Congress of the International Chamber of Commerce, Orlando, Florida, USA on October 5, 1978*, Singapore: Publicity Division, Ministry of Culture, 1978, p. 11.

81. Lee's interview with Neville Peterson of the ABC, 12 August 1965, in Lee, *Prime Minister's Speeches, etc.*

82. Lee's address to civil servants, 30 September 1965, cited in Lee Kuan Yew, 'The Prime Minister Mr Lee Kuan Yew speaks to civil servants', in *Bakti*, vol. 3, no. 2, December 1965, pp. 4–7.

83. *Ibid.*, p. 4.

84. *Ibid.*

85. *Ibid.*, p. 5.

86. *Ibid.*, pp. 6–7.

87. *Ibid.*, p. 7.

88. *Ibid.*, p. 8.

89. Lee's address at Queenstown Community Centre, 10 August 1966, in Lee, *Prime Minister's Speeches, etc.*

90. Lee at a press conference of PAP leaders at Cabinet Office City Hall, 12 August 1965, in *ibid.*

91. Lee's speech at the dinner given by President Julius Nyerere of Tanzania in Dar-Es-Salaam, 5 September 1970, in *ibid.*

92. See Chapter 3.

93. Arnold Toynbee, *A Study of History, Abridgement of Volumes I–VI* by D.C. Somervell, London: Oxford University Press, 1948, p. 214.

94. Arnold Toynbee, *A Study of History, Volume I*, London; New York; Toronto: Oxford University Press, 1935, p. 242.

95. *Ibid.*, p. 373.

96. Toynbee, *Study, Abridgement, Volumes I–VI*, p. 215.

97. *Ibid.*, pp. 533–534.

98. Lee, *New Bearings in Our Education System*, p. 12.

99. *Ibid.*

100. *Ibid.*

101. *Ibid.*, p. 13. He was referring to Burma, as becomes obvious from reading Lee in Han, Fernandez, Tan, *Lee Kuan Yew: The Man and His Ideas*, p. 137.

102. Chan Heng Chee, *Politics in an Administrative State: Where Has the Politics Gone?*, Singapore: Department of Political Science, University of Singapore, 1975, pp. 1–2.

103. *Ibid.*, p. 2.

104. See Chan Heng Chee, *Politics in an Administrative State.*

105. Lee's address to a dinner of the Law Society, 26 March 1977, in Lee, *Prime Minister's Speeches, etc.*

106. See *The Sunday Times*, 3 April 1977; Stella R. Quah, *Balancing Autonomy and Control: The Case of Professionals in Singapore*, Cambridge, Mass.: Center for International Studies, Massachusetts Institute of Technology, 1984, pp. 118–119.

107. *The Sunday Times*, 8 January 1967.

108. Lee's address at a 'dinner for the Establishment', 25 September 1984, in Lee, *Prime Minister's Speeches, etc.*

109. Lee's concept of the elite was almost exclusively male in the 1960s and 1970s.

110. Lee's address to the 4th Delegates' Conference, National Trades Union Congress, 26 April 1967, in *The Mirror*, vol. 3, no. 19, 8 May 1967, p. 6.

111. Lee's address to the National Trades Union Congress May Day campfire at the National Youth Leadership Training Institute, 30 April 1980, in *Singapore Investment News*, August 1980, p. 3.

112. *The Sunday Times*, 30 November 1980.

113. Garry Rodan (ed.), *Singapore Changes Guard: Social, Political and Economic Directions in the 1990s*, Melbourne: Longman Cheshire; New York: St Martin's Press, 1993, p. 29.

114. The knowledge of Lee's involvement in such matters is widespread but difficult to document. Lee's admission in 1982 that he had been studying civil service and SAF reports on promising personnel for fifteen years provides evidence of such involvement. See Lee Kuan Yew, 'The search for talent', in S. Jayakumar (ed.), *Our Heritage and Beyond: A Collection of Essays on Singapore, Its Past, Present and Future*, Singapore: Singapore National Trades Union Congress, 1982, p. 21.

115. Francis T. Seow, *To Catch a Tartar: A Dissident in Lee Kuan Yew's Prison*, New Haven: Yale Southeast Asia Studies, 1994, pp. 43–44. Italics are in the original text.

116. Fukuyama borrowed the term 'social capital' from James Coleman. See Francis Fukuyama, *Trust: The Social Virtues and the Creation of Prosperity*, London; New York; Melbourne; Toronto; Auckland: Penguin, 1995, p. 10.

117. *Ibid.*

118. *Ibid.*, p. 56.

119. It should be acknowledged that Singapore does not fit perfectly into Fukuyama's model of a 'low-trust' society. The historical existence of *kongsi* and other trans-family business entities shows that Singapore's Chinese community had greater stores of 'social capital' than was credited by Fukuyama.

120. Fukuyama, *Trust*, pp. 70–80.

121. See Garry Rodan, *The Political Economy of Singapore's Industrialization: National State and International Capital*, Kuala Lumpur: Forum, 1991, pp. 62–77, for an account of the industrialisation of Singapore in the 1960s.

122. Leonard C. Sebastian, 'The logic of the guardian state: governance in Singapore's development experience', *Southeast Asian Affairs 1997*, Singapore: Institute of Southeast Asian Studies, 1997, p. 288.

123. Rodan, *Singapore Changes Guard*, p. 66.

124. *The Straits Times*, 16 July 1990.

125. Rodan, *Singapore Changes Guard*, p. 66.

126. This new generation of middle-class interest groups includes the Association of Women for Action and Research, which was founded in 1985, and the Malayan Nature Society, known since 1992 as the Nature Society of Singapore. See *ibid.*, pp. 65–66.

127. David Brown, 'The corporatist management of ethnicity in contemporary Singapore', in Rodan, *Singapore Changes Guard*, p. 19.

128. *Ibid.* Lee's original statement is found in *The Economist*, 29 June 1991.

129. Garry Rodan, 'Preserving the one-party state in contemporary Singapore', in Kevin Hewison, Richard Robison and Garry Rodan (eds), *Southeast Asia in the 1990s: Authoritarianism, Democracy and Capitalism*, Sydney: Allen & Unwin, 1993, p. 94.

130. Lee Kuan Yew, 'News from a time-capsule', *The Economist*, 11–17 September 1993, pp. 13–18.

131. Lee's interview with *Yazhou Zhoukan*, 5 March 1990, in Lee Kuan Yew (Lianhe Zaobao [ed.]), *Lee Kuan Yew on China and Hong Kong after Tiananmen*, Singapore: Shing Lee Publishers, 1990, p. 94.

132. Lee's interview with Nathan Gardels of *Global Viewpoint*, 26 September 1995, in Lee, *Senior Minister's Speeches, etc.*

133. Lee's interview by Huang Chao-sung and Hsu Chung-mau of *China Times* (Taiwan), 13 January 1993, in *ibid.*

134. Lee's interview with Roy Mackie and Quek Peck Lim of *The Business Times*, 16 September 1978, in *Lee, Prime Minister's Speeches, etc.*

135. Lee, 'The search for talent', p. 13.

136. *Ibid.*, p. 20.

137. Lee, *New Bearings in Our Education System*, p. 13.

138. Lee's speech at the tenth anniversary celebrations of Eusoff College, 5 October 1968, in Lee, *Prime Minister's Speeches, etc.*

139. Lee's speech to Parliament on the Abortion Bill, 29 December 1969, in *ibid.*

140. *Ibid.*

141. *Ibid.*

142. S. Rajaratnam in Chew, *Leaders of Singapore*, pp. 104, 155; interview with E.W. Barker, 16 October 1996; and, Han, Fernandez, Tan, *Lee Kuan Yew: The Man and His Ideas*, p. 157. In the 1980s, Toh also emerged as an opponent of Lee's revived eugenics programme. See *Far Eastern Economic Review*, 4 October 1984.

143. C.T. Ernest Chew and Edwin Lee (eds), *A History of Singapore*, Singapore; New York: Oxford University Press, 1991, p. 235.

144. *Far Eastern Economic Review*, 12 August 1977.

145. *Ibid.*, 23 July 1973.

146. Lee, 'The search for talent', p. 13.

147. *Ibid.*, pp. 13–14. Although Lee claimed in this speech to have realised only in 1972 the significance of the 'drift of talent' into Singapore during the colonial period, he actually made precisely the same point in a speech in 1964. See Lee's address to a mass rally at Suleiman Court, Kuala Lumpur, 22 March 1964, in Lee, *Prime Minister's Speeches, etc.*

148. Lee, 'The search for talent', p. 21.

149. *Ibid.*

150. *Ibid.*

151. Lee Kuan Yew, 'The education of women and patterns of procreation', *RIHED bulletin*, vol. 10, no. 3, July–September 1983, pp. 1, 4–7.

152. *The Straits Times*, 18 August 1983. Toh Chin Chye, exercising his new-found freedom as a back-bencher, was the only senior PAP figure to disagree publicly with Lee. See *Far Eastern Economic Review*, 8 September 1983, p. 24.

153. Lee, 'The education of women and patterns of procreation', p. 4.

154. *Ibid.*

155. *Ibid.*, pp. 6–7.

156. See *The Straits Times*, 3 January 1987. Lee opined also that giving women equality may have been a mistake. See *New Straits Times*, 6 January 1987.

157. Saw Swee-hock, *Changes in the Fertility Policy of Singapore*, Singapore: Times Academic Press for the Institute of Policy Studies, 1990, p. 13.

158. The government, for instance, introduced a scheme whereby the children of university-educated mothers with three or more children received priority in gaining admission to the best schools, while the children of non-university-educated parents who had been sterilised received a higher priority than the children of still-fertile uneducated parents. As well as these incentives and dis-incentives, the taxation, housing and welfare systems were used for eugenic purposes. Tax breaks were offered to university-educated couples who had children,

while poorly educated people were offered a S$10,000 incentive to be sterilised. The latter inducement took the form of a deposit into the woman's Central Provident Fund (CPF) account that could then be used as a deposit for a Housing and Development Board flat. See *Far Eastern Economic Review*, 2 February 1984, 21 June 1984. In 1985 Tony Tan successfully overturned the policy of linking access to education to the fertility and education of one's parents. See *Far Eastern Economic Review*, 4 April 1985 and Kernial Singh Sandhu and Paul Wheatley (eds), *Management of Success: The Moulding of Modern Singapore*, Singapore: Institute of Southeast Asian Studies, 1989, p. 69. Many other aspects of Lee's eugenicist initiatives have been amended or abandoned as Singapore moved from a generally anti-natal to a pro-natal policy, and as the 'second generation' of leaders exercised their influence. See *ibid.*, p. 181.

159. The origins of Lee's geneticism appear to be connected with his views on race and are considered in Chapter 6.

160. Lee, *New Bearings in Our Education System*, p. 13.

161. Lee's linkage of worldly success and intelligence appears to stem from his childhood. Lee believes that as a child in primary school, he was able to excel so easily because his fellow students 'were poor and they were not very bright and advantaged'. See Lee in Han, Fernandez, Tan, *Lee Kuan Yew: The Man and His Ideas*, p. 26.

162. Lee's speech to the Raffles Institution Foundation, 17 July 1990, in Raffles Institution Foundation, *Raffles Institution: A Tradition of Excellence*, Singapore: Raffles Institution, 1990, pp. 60–61. Lee indicated also that he would have taken this initiative decades earlier except for the need to deal with more pressing educational problems associated with language and community.

163. Streaming from early primary school onwards was one of the measures recommended in Goh Keng Swee and the Education Study Team, *Report on the Ministry of Education 1978*, Singapore: Ministry of Education, 1979, Chapter 6, pp. 1–5.

164. Lee, 'The search for talent', p. 21, and; Tim Huxley, *The Political Role of the Singapore Armed Forces' Officer Corps: Towards a Military-Administrative State?*, Canberra: Strategic and Defence Studies Centre, Australian National University, 1993.

165. Lee in Parliament, 16 March 1976, in Lee, *Prime Minister's Speeches, etc.*

166. Lee's interview with Roy Mackie and Quek Peck Lim, of *The Business Times*, 16 September 1978, in *ibid.* It seems likely that Lee had always held these views on testing, in which case his earlier statements on elite-building must be regarded substantially as a cover for his ideas of elite-testing.

167. Lee in Han, Fernandez, Tan, *Lee Kuan Yew: The Man and His Ideas*, p. 101, 103.

168. Lee's address to the PAP Ordinary Party Conference, *Petir*, November 1984, p. 2.

169. *The Straits Times*, 29 October 1982.

170. Lee in Han, Fernandez, Tan, *Lee Kuan Yew: The Man and His Ideas*, p. 98.

171. *Ibid.*

172. Hewison, Robison and Rodan, *Southeast Asia in the 1990s*, pp. 87–88, 100.

173. Lee made it clear in September 1986 that he was intent on destroying Jeyaretnam politically. See Lee Lai To, 'Consolidation and reorientation in a recession', *Asian Survey*, vol. 27, no. 2, 1987, p. 244.

174. Philip Jeyaretnam, *Abraham's Promise*, Singapore; Kuala Lumpur: Times Books International, 1995, p. 54.

175. Russell Heng, 'Give me liberty or give me wealth', in Derek da Cunha (ed.), *Debating Singapore: Reflective Essays*, Singapore: Institute of Southeast Asian Studies, 1994, pp. 9–14.

176. Lee's speech at Commonwealth Drive Car Park, 1 January 1996, in Lee, *Prime Minister's Speeches, etc.*

177. See, for instance, Lee's speech at PAP's 25th Anniversary Rally, 20 January 1980, *Mirror*, vol. 16, no. 3, p. 1; Lee, 'History is not made the way it is written', *Petir*, March 1980, pp. 8, 10; Lee, 'Our younger team has ability, integrity, commitment', *Petir*, February 1981, p. 8; Lee, 'Full steam ahead – each citizen its [*sic*] own home', *Petir*, December 1981, p. 5, Lee, 'The search for talent'.

178. Lee Kuan Yew, 'Singapore must invest overseas and sprout a second wing', *Petir*, January–February 1993, pp. 22, 27–29.

179. James Minchin on 'Asia Focus', 13 June 1997, ABC Radio Australia, International Service.

· 5 ·

Cultural Revolutions: From Malayanisation to 'Sinicisation'

[Lee Kuan Yew] is not a Confucian. He can't be a Confucian gentleman. But he did say that societies that were under a Confucian theory have certain attributes – Japan, Korea, China, and overseas Chinese – and these attributes were useful. Like saving money, working hard and education. And that's all it amounts to.

Interview with Goh Keng Swee, 1 October 1996.

Despite the amendments that Lee Kuan Yew has made over the decades to his theories of elitism and progressivism, there are clear lines of continuity in these aspects of his ideological development which suggest that the fundamentals of his beliefs have remained constant. The same cannot be said of his views on culture. Lee entered government in 1959 as a clinically detached social engineer advocating a communally neutral multiracialism. If his ideas had any ethnic bias at this stage, it was a superficial orientation towards Malay culture. After separation from Malaysia in 1965, however, he began building a strongly Western-oriented culture balanced, at least in his mind, by ethnically based 'cultural ballast'. In the late 1970s he began moving towards a Sinocentric version of multiracialism which bordered on the 'Chinese chauvinism' that he decried forcefully in other people.[1] There is no simple, let alone definitive explanation for this transformation, yet each phase of this metamorphosis had a profound effect on the lives of Singaporeans. Under Lee's hegemonic rule, Singapore has undergone three 'cultural revolutions' in less than forty years, leaving people, in the words of one senior government minister, feeling as though they live in a hotel, rather than a home.[2] Yet even in this area of great change, there are reasons to believe that Lee's fundamental beliefs may not have changed as drastically as is suggested by a superficial survey of the evidence.

Chapter 3 has already considered many of the personal, political and academic background factors that helped to form Lee's views of the malleability of culture. It considered his need to find a rationale for a world full of constant change, the influence of Jawaharlal Nehru and Arnold Toynbee, and the political and intellectual climate during his time in the Cambridge University Law School. It now remains to consider Lee's use of the concept of social evolution as the premise for a series of highly intrusive and contradictory social engineering programmes. This chapter argues that the premises of cultural evolutionism are the constant factor in the shifting sands of Lee's social and language policies, and provide the key to understanding each of Singapore's cultural revolutions.[3]

From the time Lee entered politics in 1954, he displayed an unusual interest in questions concerning culture. This interest derived partly from the nature of communal and language politics in Malaya at the time, but subsequent events suggest that his interest was intrinsic, rather than merely a function of the political environment. He began his career trying to promote a Malayan cultural identity for Singaporeans, rather than a uniquely Singaporean culture. In his mind, there were sound practical reasons for this move. From the time of his address to the Malayan Forum in London[4] until the height of his troubles with Kuala Lumpur in 1965, he avoided countenancing the possibility that Singapore could be considered a political or a cultural entity in its own right, insisting that the island was historically, economically and culturally part of Malaya. Apart from seeing an independent Singapore as a non-viable economic entity, his great fear was that 'a separate Singapore would lead to a Chinese Singapore making it vulnerable to Chinese influence from China'.[5] The solution was to focus Singaporeans' loyalty upon the prospect of a greater Malaya, most obviously through promotion of a communally neutral ideology of multiracialism, and through the promotion of the Malay language [*Bahasa Melayu*]. When the PAP came to power in 1959, Malay was given special status as the national language, while Mandarin, Tamil and English were other 'official languages'. The national anthem was and is in Malay, Malays were encouraged to send their children to Malay medium schools, and all school students were required to study Malay.[6] In contrast, Chinese medium education was permitted but given no encouragement. Parents could have their children educated in any of the four official languages,[7] but in practice this meant that most Chinese parents chose to have their children educated in English because it provided the best opportunity for economic advancement in adulthood.[8] Besides the promotion of the Malay language, the

PAP government concentrated considerable effort on muting communal differences and loyalties in the first instance, and ultimately aimed to discard communal identity completely.[9] In the place of Chinese, Malay, Eurasian and Indian cultures, the government intended to inculcate 'a sense of solidarity with the bigger group – the nation',[10] being at this stage a hypothetical greater Malaya. Although the Malayanisation campaign was Lee Kuan Yew's first foray into the politics of culture, it must be acknowledged that his role was relatively passive. S. Rajaratnam, the Ceylon-born Minister for Culture, was the great enthusiast for Malayanisation, and he was the master of the campaign at all times. There is, nevertheless, sufficient evidence to confirm that Lee had given the Malayanisation campaign serious thought, and that he concurred with the thrust of Rajaratnam's work.[11]

Lee and the PAP had strong pragmatic reasons to wish to build a Malayan culture, but there is ample evidence to support the argument that Lee was driven at a deeper level by his conviction that culture is a malleable, transitory feature of a society, and that it must be almost infinitely adaptable to the demands of progress. In March and April 1956, Lee delivered two speeches in the Legislative Assembly that explored his ideas of culture in considerable depth. They demonstrated that, apart from his government's programme of Malayanisation, his ideas on the nature and the development of culture *per se* were highly sophisticated, and reflected the worldview of a cultural evolutionist. In March 1956, Lee warned the Legislative Assembly that attempts to protect the cultural and religious practices of the various Singaporean communities could lead to 'the most wonderful crystallisation and mummification of all the various cultures, customs and prejudices of the peoples that ever settled here', while time had 'marched on' in the mother cultures in India and China.[12] Lee suggested that instead of indiscriminately preserving Hindu, Daoist and Buddhist religious practices, many of which had already disappeared in India and China, it would be better to make 'a serious attempt to reconcile religious practices with modern-day needs in a modern-day world'.[13] A month later, Lee emphasised the malleability of culture, and spoke of culture as being 'a dynamic and organic process'.[14] On this occasion he spelt out in some detail his reflections on the evolution of culture:

> The Chinese culture as it will be in the Malaya of 200 years from now is not likely to be what Chinese culture will be 200 years from now in China. That is inevitable.

> Nobody denies that it was the British who first colonised America, and that they speak the English language. But he would be a bold man indeed

to say that in America they have the same identical language and the same culture.

> Indeed this one culture and one language spread over five continents … has gone through permutations. Basically it is the same language and the same Anglo-Saxon culture. But the number of not so pleasant things that I have heard Englishmen in Singapore say, after a trip to Australia, about things other than Australian beer, gives me some appreciation of the differences which language and culture undergo after separation in space and time.[15]

Eight years later, Lee delivered essentially the same message to an audience at Nanyang University, showing that his views on culture were a deeply held conviction, rather than merely convenient public postures:

> Life is a continuous process of adaptation to changing environment … All ancient cultures have a remarkable capacity for adapting and enduring. We should not be too timorous in adapting and adjusting ourselves to the new mood and temper in Malaysia.[16]

Far from being 'timorous' about making adjustments, Lee spent the whole of his public life unapologetically forcing the pace of fundamental changes in the fabric of Singaporean society in the name of progress and survival.

Lee began his public life as a Western-educated social engineer, with little attachment to, or understanding of, the local cultures of Malaya. He learnt at Cambridge to regard culture and tradition as something to be discarded, changed or used according to need. Consequently, while he understood that other people felt more strongly about these matters than he did, his early years in government could be regarded as a crusade for, among other goals, the blending of Singapore's Malay, Chinese and Indian cultures into one amorphous 'Malayan culture'. In Lee's mind, a hypothetical 'Malayan culture' would be most suitable for a modern society, built upon the tenets of egalitarianism that he learnt while he was in England, and incorporating the principles of racial equality, economic growth and rationality. This culture was to be distinctively multiracial, multilingual, and multicultural in character, and he intended that it would focus the loyalty of the people upon Malaya, rather than on ancestral or cultural 'homelands' in India, China, Indonesia or Britain. From the beginning, however, the terms, 'multiracialism' and 'racial equality' did not imply an aspiration towards 'race-blindness' which has become a liberal ideal in the Western world since the 1960s. Rather, Lee's multiracialism accepted the colonial practice of classifying people as Chinese, Malays, Indians and 'Others', a practice that had become an ordinary, unconscious part of the fabric of Singaporean and Malayan society.[17] While Lee sought to have each communal group treated equally, the nature of his multiracialism at this early stage is best appreciated, in the words of Michael Hill and Lian Kwen Fee, as a policy of containment and appeasement:

> Multiracialism sent a clear signal to both Malays and Chinese that ethnic chauvinism would not be tolerated. On the other hand, it could be viewed as a reassurance for the Chinese and the other ethnic communities, who feared Malay domination after merger [with Malaya], that their interests would be safeguarded.[18]

Beyond these short-term objectives, however, Lee's multiracial Malaya was to be a natural step in the progress of the region, taking it, in Toynbeean terms, to a 'higher level of civilisation'.[19] He believed that he was engaged in a 'social revolution' in which the 'rights and privileges ... wrested from the British' would be passed on to the whole of society.[20] Both Malays on the Peninsula and the Chinese in Singapore would have to forgo their self-perception as the dominant community in the new Malaya, because 'no single race should arrogate to itself a superior status'.[21] Malaya in the 1950s was, according to Lee, a 'transitional society ... where the old maps and the old compass is no longer valid and the people are on the march and on the move' because the region is undergoing a 'change from the old order to the new'.[22] Lee had no time for tradition beyond the needs of political expediency, because tradition, in his mind, held back progress: 'Old cultural patterns and family values, designed to meet conditions which prevailed hundreds and thousands of years ago still persist with grave consequences to the problems of economic and industrial growth'.[23] Lee and Rajaratnam made much of the fact that the Malayan culture was not to be a mere carbon copy of American or British culture, but the features which were to distinguish Malayan from Western culture were substantially restricted to those areas of life that had a bearing upon race relations: language, education, and inter-communal respect for traditions and religion.

Perhaps the most salient criticism of Lee's approach to Malayanisation is that it was substantially the product of Lee's personal and academic background and displayed extraordinary ignorance of the force of Malay culture on the Peninsula. Lee's concept of Malayanisation was fundamentally at odds with the tenets of Malay nationalism, which was centred upon Malay 'special rights', the political supremacy of the Malays, Islam and the kampong lifestyle.[24] Lee mistakenly thought that since he intended to build his 'Malayan consciousness' around the Malay language, the Malays would welcome the development. Former Deputy Prime Minister Toh Chin Chye has argued that Lee Kuan Yew had no understanding of Malay culture because he grew up in Singapore, away from the Malay-centred culture of the Peninsula:

> People born and bred in Singapore were inward-looking under colonial rule. They never truly understood the fabric of Malay society which extended from the sultanate, the aristocracy, the Malay bureaucracy down to the village elders or *kepalas* in the kampongs. Malay society was very strong, very traditional. It was bonded by Islam, not by modern political ideas like socialism.

> The Singaporean people never understood Malay society. I was different because I was really a Malayan. I was born in Taiping. Brought up there, studied there. I knew how the Chinese and Indians fitted in and adapted themselves. It was a political ecosystem where different races adapted like different species of fish as you see in a coral reef. The Chinese in Singapore never had to adapt in the same way as the Chinese in Taiping or Kuala Lumpur. They didn't know how to.[25]

Surprisingly for a leader who saw his country's future as being part of Malaya, Lee appears to have discounted the importance of developments on the Peninsula. The idea of artificially constructing a 'Malayan' identity had already been rejected by every significant force on the Peninsula, including the Malays, and both the Chinese-educated and the English-educated Chinese.[26] The United Malays' National Organisation (UMNO) was the dominant party on the Peninsula, and had been created by Malay nationalists in 1946 specifically to block the development of a communally neutral Malayan Union, a task which was accomplished with relative ease the same year.[27] Then in 1951, an official report to the Malayan government on education, written by two English-educated Chinese academics, rejected totally the concept of 'Malayanisation' with these prophetic words:

> No element of the population can be 'Malayanized' for the simple reason that there is no 'Malayan' pattern to which to mould it and because such moulding is not produced by fiat. A new culture can come only from the natural mingling of diverse cultural elements for generations. In the process, elements which do not command appreciation disappear, while those which do need no political or external support.[28]

Blissfully unaware of the limitations of his ideas, Lee engaged upon a programme of enforced cultural evolution. Lee's Minister for Culture, S. Rajaratnam, defended this course of action, saying that 'there is nothing foolish in a people wanting to plan their cultural evolution', and even boasted that the government was trying to create a new culture 'by pressure-cooking'.[29] While the prospect of merger with Malaya was merely hypothetical, the limitations of Lee's perspective were of no great significance, since he was dealing primarily with Singaporean Malays who had long since accommodated themselves to life as an ethnic minority. The practical implications of Lee's lack of understanding of Peninsular Malays assumed immediate importance in 1963 when Singapore joined Malaysia. Lee then had to deal directly with the Malay nationalist leadership of UMNO, with the disastrous results described in Chapters 2 and 3. The shortcomings in Lee's approach to multiracialism should not be surprising, since the seeds of Lee's ideas of 'Malayan culture' germinated, not from his experiences in Singapore, but from his contact with English-educated Chinese Malayans in London. In 1959 he spoke of his visits as a student to London's China Institute. To Lee's surprise, he found that

> [t]he Malayan student could unerringly pick out another Malayan by the way he dressed and talked and his mannerisms. The Malayan English-educated was a definite type. And another strange thing was that the English-educated Chinese from Malaya found that he had more in common with the English-educated non-Chinese from Malaya than with the English-speaking Chinese from Mauritius, West Indies or China.[30]

This incident must have made a lasting impression upon Lee, since he referred to it on two other occasions over the next twenty years.[31]

While Lee's experiences at the China Institute may explain some of the origins of Lee's concept of a Malayan culture, they fail completely to explain his fervour for Malayanisation in the first half of the 1960s. As is the case with much of Lee's career, his passion is explained not by positive convictions or arguments, but by his response to negative factors, which in this case was the supposedly effete English-educated elite being produced by Singapore's education system. Lee told the Legislative Assembly in December 1957:

> It is a sad thing to notice that every time you come across people in the English-educated field, whether in boys' clubs, or other recreational clubs, they need crutches to survive.

> Both in London and in the other big cities where university students from Malaya are studying, there is a prevailing sense of calculated importance, partly because visiting Ministers tell them that they are the future leaders of Malaya. To my mind, nothing is further from the truth. From what I see of them, in free and open competition with other groups vying for leadership in Malaya, they would perish, most of them. ...

> I do not think that they are the future leaders of Malaya. They may be the future technicians of some government in Malaya. What worries me is that many of them will, in fact, be not very efficient technicians at that.[32]

Twenty-one years later, Lee still remembered his disappointment with the English-educated students of the 1950s and 1960s:

> Every time there used to be a riot in Singapore, there was hilarious laughter and fun and games at the University of Singapore. I was amazed. There was light-headedness because they did not understand that this was real revolution – 1950s, 1960s. I watched it in total and utter amazement.[33]

By 1959, Lee had completed his revised assessment of the British culture of his youth as it manifested itself in Malaya. Referring to the 'English-educated' in Malaya, he told the Singapore Union of Journalists in one of his first speeches as Prime Minister that

> [t]heir weak points are, in the case of the Chinese and Indians, that they are devitalised, almost emasculated, as a result of deculturalisation. The syllabus in the English schools in pre-war Malaya had pumped in a completely English set of values and ideals.

By this stage, Lee's disappointment with the English-educated had heightened to pity: 'The English-educated is somewhat uncertain and hesitant, speaking and thinking in a language he has learnt all his waiting [*sic*] life but which is not part of his own being'.[34] Lee was desperate to create a substitute for the devitalising culture, which was emasculating the group that should have been Singapore's 'creative minority'. Since Lee insisted in thinking in terms of a greater Malaya, rather then just Singapore, a multiracial Malayan culture was, in Lee's mind, the only feasible answer.

The Malayanisation campaign came to an abrupt end in August 1965 when Singapore separated from Malaysia. Communally neutral multi-racialism remained a central feature of state ideology, but economic success and national survival replaced Malayanisation as the key elements of nation-building.[35] The consequences of making economic success the centre-piece of the new Singaporean culture were far-reaching, and saw Lee gradually extend the reach of his cultural evolutionism beyond the superficial manifestations which have been observed to date. Driven by the need to entice and accommodate multinational investors,[36] English replaced Malay as the preferred lingua franca, and discipline in the workplace and in society in general became the highest virtues.[37] The most dramatic development was the drafting of the trade union movement into a partnership with the government and business to ensure a profitable environment for overseas capital.[38] After the first frugal years of independence, conspicuous consumption became widespread, accompanied among both the poor and the wealthy by constant com-petitiveness in upgrading one's home, possessions and educational qualifications.[39] In contrast to his relative passiveness during the Malayan-isation campaign, Lee was at the forefront of the post-separation culture-building exercise. He set out to build a 'rugged' and 'tightly knit' society capable of ensuring the country's survival.[40] As we have observed already, the survival motif was used as the vehicle for implementing a profound set of changes in Singapore's culture.[41] Lee's most paradoxical contribution to the campaign was to crush systematically any signs of communal solidarity in the country, especially among the Chinese-educated majority, while simultaneously promoting the idea that communally based 'cultural ballast'[42] was required to insulate Singaporeans from Western influences, which were themselves the direct consequence of the government's developmental and cultural strategies.

The Malayanisation campaign had been based on the assumption that Singapore's future lay with a greater Malaya. This premise was now redundant, and in the new situation, national survival through economic development was the *raison d'être* of government. In the immediate post-separation period, even as the government struggled to ensure Singapore's survival, Lee was able to use the freedom offered by independence to begin a new cultural campaign. Chapter 3 has already considered the process by which Lee, almost certainly inspired by Toynbee's concept of 'Challenge and Response', manipulated the circumstances of separation to exaggerate the climate of crisis and forge a new consensus. To understand the rationale behind this exercise, however, we must divert our study from the post-separation cultural revolution, and survey very briefly the economic development strategy adopted by Singapore in the immediate aftermath of separation. Despite the fact that Lee Kuan Yew is commonly regarded as the architect of Singapore's 'economic miracle', Lee was not generally the driving force on economic policy. Lee was, however, wise enough to accept the lead given by his talented ministers, particularly the first three Finance Ministers, Goh Keng Swee, Lim Kim San and Hon Sui Sen. Goh, Lim and Hon were advised in turn by the Dutch economist, Albert Winsemius, who first came to Singapore in 1960 as an economic advisor attached to the World Bank, and who continued to visit and advise the government for decades thereafter.[43] The advice Lee received and followed was to abandon the traditional development strategy of import substitution, which it had pursued during and before the Malaysia period, and instead to adopt an export-oriented strategy utilising the capital and expertise of multinational companies.[44] The government's strategy was unconventional at a time when multinational companies were demonised as exploiters of the Third World, and developing countries were persisting with the rhetoric of Afro-Asian solidarity. Lee, however, was scornfully dismissive of the effectiveness of economic solidarity among developing nations, saying that 'co-operation between developing nations which, with a few exceptions, have low or no technology is unlikely to bring about a rapid transformation of our backward role as producers of raw materials, oil, minerals, timber or agricultural commodities'.[45] 'We have never suffered from any inhibitions in borrowing capital, know-how, managers, engineers, and marketing abilities', he said in 1978. 'Far from limiting the entry of foreign managers, engineers, and bankers, we encouraged them to come'.[46] As a result of the government's policy, Singapore became, in the words of Philippe Regnier,

> a safe haven for international investment and, within a short time, [it] notch[ed] up one of the highest growth rates in the world. It became host to the regional headquarters of an impressive number of foreign enterprises, and transformed itself into a secondary workshop with both a world vocation and a regional one.[47]

The social implications of these new directions in development policy were profound. With Singapore's future prospects in Malaysia in tatters, there was now no reason to develop Malay as the lingua franca of Singapore, but every reason to adopt English, since this was the principal language of global commerce, and either the primary or the secondary language of most multinational companies. English was already the language of Singapore's government, administration and the ruling elite, and was familiar to some degree to most Indians, many Malays and, of course, to the English-educated Chinese. English was, however, totally foreign to most of the Chinese-educated, who formed the electoral, financial and organisational base of the communist-backed opposition party, Barisan Sosialis [Socialist Front].[48]

The ascension of the English language in Singapore was not, however, the most striking result of the new development policies, since almost 60 per cent of children were already studying in English medium schools, with more studying English as a second language.[49] A much more dramatic shift was instituted in the field of industrial relations. In late 1965, the National Trades Union Congress (NTUC), the Singapore Manufacturers' Association (SMA) and the Singapore Employers' Federation (SEF) jointly ratified a 'Charter for Industrial Progress' that declared 'all partners in the industrialisation programme, worker, employer, government, must pool their efforts and strive for a continuing increase in productivity and output in all enterprises'.[50] Through this exercise, the government recruited, at least in principle, the trade unions and local capitalists into a partnership with the government to pursue economic development ahead of other goals. The practical import of this 'partnership' became clear over the next two years, when the Trade Union (Amendment) Bill of 1966, and the Employment and Industrial Relations (Amendment) Acts of 1968 seriously curtailed trade union activity, and enshrined a regime of low wages, not principally for the benefit of local capital, but to make Singapore attractive to overseas capital.[51] The partnership between the trade unions and the government was cemented at an NTUC seminar held late in 1969, at which the NTUC formally accepted the strictures of the new industrial relations regime.[52] At this seminar, Goh Keng Swee initiated also a programme of establishing union-owned retail and service co-operatives, thus turning the unions into commercial employers. This initiative gave the workers a larger stake in the Singaporean economy, and made the partnership with the government seem more tangible.[53]

The PAP's programme successfully subjugated labour to the will of the government and international capital, but the rhetoric by which it was justified ushered in a new cultural revolution, and foreshadowed changes well beyond industrial relations. Lee Kuan Yew set out to build 'a rugged society',[54] composed of a 'proud' people who regarded themselves as 'co-owners of the new society', and who not only did not disrupt government efforts to industrialise, but who possessed 'a positive urge to work and achieve'.[55] It was in this period also that Lee introduced the concept of the social 'pyramid', consisting of 'top leaders' at the apex, 'good executives' in the middle, and a 'highly civic-conscious broad mass' at the base.[56] As has been described in Chapter 4, Lee emphasised the need to develop 'qualities of leadership at the top, and qualities of cohesion on the ground'.[57]

There is a school of thought, represented most recently by Christopher Tremewan,[58] which dismisses Lee's rhetoric in this period as a cynical attempt to cover a deeper, class-based agenda, and deconstructs Singaporean politics in neo-Marxist terms. It must be admitted that much of the rhetoric of this period can be interpreted, with a little imagination, as a means exploiting and manipulating the working class. The 'Use Your Hands' campaign is a case in point. Education and vocational training had become national priorities to enable Singaporeans to work productively in the new industrial environment,[59] but Singaporeans showed a reluctance to engage in manual labour. Government rhetoric began to focus on the virtues of relatively low-paid and low-status manual labour. Lim Kim San explained the problem to Melanie Chew:

I remember we were trying to convince the public that 'blue collar' work is as worthwhile as 'white collar' work. We had a few vocational schools. They were empty! No one enlisted in the vocational schools. So part of the industrialization scheme was to try to convert the mind set of the Singaporean people. That you should be doing work with your hands [r]ather than being a clerk. The public had to be brought to understand that the future lay in industrialization.[60]

Considering that under Lee Kuan Yew's elitist policies, university-trained professionals and technocrats were to become the dominant class in Singapore, Lee displayed a certain amount of cynicism by promoting the virtues of manual labour over white-collar work.

Yet an examination of the broader social, ethnic and educational policies of the government over this period reveals that behind the rhetoric, Lee and the PAP leadership were being basically honest, and their actions can be understood without recourse to class-based conspiracy theories. A few simple examples demonstrate some of the ways in which the PAP rhetoric had real meaning to Lee and other ministers. While it is true, for instance, that the initial impact of the new industrial relations regime and the policy of enticing multinationals to Singapore was to purge the workforce of its militancy and to increase the amount of relatively menial, low-paid work, Tremewan's assertion that 'in its own class interest, the PAP ... exposed the workers of Singapore to massive exploitation'[61] is a gross caricature of these developments. Later events show that the policies of the time were, as the government maintained, a means of bringing economic growth and creating employment, rather than a surreptitious device for exploiting the workers. At the end of the 1970s, when the government judged that Singapore was no longer competitive as a source of cheap labour, it upgraded its adult training schemes, increased wages by up to 20 per cent, and attempted, initially with indifferent results, to turn Singapore into a high-technology centre employing a skilled, well-paid workforce.[62] Of course the most obvious answer to the charge that the PAP set out to exploit the workers on a class basis is that so many sons and daughters of the working class have risen to enjoy prosperity as wealthy members of Singapore's new middle class.

It should be recognised also that, despite the elements of truth in Tremewan's characterisation of the government's high-density, high-rise housing developments as 'the working-class barracks',[63] this programme did give people, even poor people, a sense of being 'co-owners of the new society'. By 1965, the PAP government had been engaged in a massive exercise in slum clearance and housing development for five years, the need for which Tremewan does not dispute. This programme was spectacularly successful, as is indicated by the fact that the worst of the slums had been cleared by the time of Singapore's separation from

Malaysia. From 1960–65, the proportion of the population living in public housing had increased from 9.1 to 23.2 per cent,[64] and as Thomas Bellows observed of the situation at the time of the 1963 elections, 'no government could have been more effective and responsive [in the field of housing] than had been the PAP'.[65] In 1968 Lee took this programme a step further. He initiated the Central Provident Fund Home Ownership Scheme which, together with government subsidies and government-controlled sale prices, enabled half a million families to become home-owners over the following two decades.[66] The occasion that prompted this initiative was the impending increase in unemployment due to Britain's announcement that it intended to accelerate the closure of its naval base in Singapore.[67] By the early 1970s the housing programme had been so spectacularly successful that, under instructions from London, the colonial administration in Hong Kong had copied the Singapore model in an effort to solve its own housing crisis.[68] Lee's home owner-ship scheme was designed partially to inject new capital into the con-struction industry and so create employment. Behind this immediate concern, however, Lee was consciously fostering the sense of having a stake in the country. 'I decided as a national objective, that each family must be given the opportunity to own his home. Their sons will defend Singapore because the family owns a part of Singapore', he told Parlia-ment in 1994.[69] More pertinent than Lee's retrospective account was Rajaratnam's contemporary justification of the home ownership scheme as 'an attempt to create as large a proportion of the property-owning population as possible so that they would have a deep and abiding stake in the country'.[70] The home ownership programme, combined with other factors such as steadily diminishing unemployment[71] and the building of trade union co-operatives, did indeed create a sense that Singaporeans were 'co-owners of the new society'.

There are grounds also for believing that Lee Kuan Yew took seriously his description of the self-sacrificing nature of the elite. In Lee's mind, this characteristic was demonstrated by the original members of the PAP team who gave up secure and sometimes prosperous careers to fight for a cause which had little chance of success. Lim Kim San, the first Chairman of the Housing and Development Board (HDB) personified this virtue. Lim was a successful businessman who was recruited by Goh Keng Swee in 1959 to take charge of housing development, which became a central pillar of the PAP's programme. He applied himself to the task with enthusiasm. He abolished every committee left over from the previous administration and took each important decision himself. He displayed remarkable energy and initiative and even inspected each building personally. Lim quickly made his mark when he ordered that a partially completed building, commissioned by the previous housing authority, be demolished and rebuilt at the contractor's expense because it was sub-standard. When he discovered that contractors were slowing down and profiteering from the earthworks involved in housing construction, he took this aspect of construction away from the contractors and gave it to the HDB. Lim Kim San performed all of these duties for four years and made the HDB a brilliantly successful enterprise *without drawing a salary*. He was an unpaid volunteer until he reluctantly bowed to Lee Kuan Yew's request to run for Parliament in 1963.[72] With that sort of dedication and ability among Lee Kuan Yew's peers, there is no reason to dismiss his talk of a self-sacrificing elite as a cynical rationale to disguise self-interest.

It is in Lee's ideas of a 'rugged society', however, that the character of his political thought is revealed most clearly. The premises behind the 'rugged society' rhetoric affected the government's programme in unpredictable ways that reflect the uniqueness of Lee Kuan Yew's contribution to Singapore, the region and the art of government. Lee's conception of a 'rugged society' bore little relationship to American or Australian perceptions of a 'rugged society', which, partly because of the former presence of a geographical frontier, built cultures based upon myths of 'rugged individualism' and even rebelliousness. When Lee spoke of a 'rugged society' he meant that the society as an organic whole was to be 'rugged' and resilient. Lee envisioned the 'ruggedness' of the individual members of society as being akin to members of a 'herd'[73] who, due to their cultural 'instincts', are effective 'digits'[74] in the collective. Lee Kuan Yew's idea of a 'rugged society' was fundamentally communitarian in character. That the profit motive and personal wealth accumulation were the driving forces of the cultural instinct on which Lee's 'herd' depended does not diminish the veracity of this argument.

The logic of the 'rugged society' took Lee in a surprising direction in 1966. Singaporeans had become used to Lee Kuan Yew, the English-educated Anglophile who, like Nehru, despaired of the 'antiquated ideas' embodied in ancient traditions.[75] Lee had a reputation for belittling the supposed glory of past cultures.[76] As he told the nation in 1966,

> We are a forward looking, not a backward looking society, not looking to the past for examples of patterns of behaviour and conduct completely irrelevant in the modern society that we now find ourselves. ... Man reaching out for the stars. ... It is to show we do not find our solutions by turning over dusty pages of some chronicle of some ancient time telling us about some ancient customs more relevant to his days, but that we have the forward, the inquiring outlook, and are keen to learn, keen to make a success of the future.[77]

Then, without obvious warning, Lee began bemoaning the lack of tradition in a young country like Singapore, and started placing an uncharacteristic emphasis on the virtues of social traditions. He developed this theme quickly, giving it public expression on two consecutive days at the end of August 1966. On the first occasion Lee told the Singapore Regiment of the Boys' Brigade:

> It is one of the great difficulties of new communities such as ours that almost nobody can trace his ancestors with the history of this island for more than 150 years. ... This means a society that has no built-in reflexes for community survival.
>
> An old and established community develops these reflexes. They are those who look after the survival of a nation; they are those who are born warriors, who have always fought for their country. They are those who were the administrators.
>
> The instinct of a young migrant community often is one of survival. Those who made themselves submissive and meek and self-effacing survived after a fashion when the British were Master, or during the Japanese occupation when the Japanese pushed out and replaced the British; but they survived without the every [*sic*] important quality of self-respect.[78]

The following day, Lee gave his 'social pyramid' speech to school principals, referred to at length in Chapter 4, in which he spoke of the examples of Britain, Australia and other established societies which produce leaders 'with great qualities of discipline and heart' in the traditional elite schools such as Eton, Harrow and Geelong Grammar.[79]

Two months later, in November 1966, the new direction of Lee's thinking emerged as a dominant theme at a meeting at the University of Singapore.[80] In this address, he spoke at length of the positive roles that the local communal cultures of Singapore could play in the development of a 'rugged society'. In contrast to the token respect he showed for communally based cultures during the Malayanisation campaign, on this occasion he expressed deep concern at the weakness of communally based tradition in Singapore, and announced that he was seeking to build a new social consensus based upon the retention of traditional cultures insofar as they were compatible with multiracialism and modernisation. He indicated that he had given up his ideas of creating a new culture in a single generation, and had resigned himself to allowing a Singaporean culture to develop over hundreds of years. In the meantime, he hoped that the members of each community would use their cultural heritage as an anchor, so that each person would be a strong, robust member of society. The cost of losing one's cultural roots without developing an adequate replacement, he said, was becoming 'a soulless creature' and 'a very weak digit'.[81] Addressing his university audience, Lee said:

> You have to have each digit sufficiently self-sufficient, self-composed in itself. And then, give it the maximum amount of common ground with the others. But if you, in giving it the common ground, take away everything – the ballast that they have – then you are left with an enervated population. And this is our problem.
>
> I don't say I have the answer to this but I would have believed that eventually, over a hundred, two hundred, three hundred years … you will have a purely Singaporean multi-racial kind of values …
>
> You might have a particular cultural manifestation of pattern which will form a common basis and then, each will keep a part of his. I mean, if he is a Thaver [an Indian surname], then he is a Thaver. And he has got that little bit of him. And if you destroy that little bit and give him nothing in return, you have a soulless creature. And that is a very weak digit.
>
> And really, this is the problem that faces the English-educated.[82]

While this emphasis on encouraging communal tradition was a novelty, the basis of Lee's logic was not new. We have seen already that Lee's contempt for the effete English-educated spurred his Malayanisation campaign. Furthermore, as early as 1963 he expressed concern that Singapore, as a young society, had 'no deep-rooted traditions'.[83] The new dimension revealed in this statement was the abandonment of the attempt to build a new culture 'in a pressure-cooker', to use Rajaratnam's expression, and the elevation of communally based culture to a positive, even central role in his thinking.

Lee's address foreshadowed major changes in his attitude to the question of nation-building and cultural development. In February 1967 he told a Tamil festival:

> You and I instinctively want to keep something of the past because man does not live by bread alone. He needs that little extra: the lifeline that gives him some sustenance, some succour and comfort in moments of adversity. It is with that sustenance which springs from a knowledge that for thousands of years people like him, acquiring certain techniques of social organism [*sic*], were able to survive all kinds of natural and man-made calamities. And we want to give that positive aid to everybody to keep.[84]

Lee did not reserve his rhetoric on 'cultural ballast' for his domestic audience. In 1971, in his closing address as Chairman of the Commonwealth Conference, he informed the Queen and the assembled heads of government that 'the cultural ballast, the value patterns, the social discipline, the organizational framework of effective government … are crucial ingredients' of national success.[85]

With many of the permutations in Lee's thinking over the decades, researchers have been left to surmise the reason for the change. In this case, however, Lee has spelled out at least some of the immediate causes of his about-face. A little later in his answer at the November 1966 meeting at the University of Singapore, Lee related an incident which affected his thinking profoundly, and in his answer, he also spelled out the task ahead as he saw it. Lee referred to an incident that occurred at the presentation of television sets to the People's Defence Forces (PDF) at Jurong. Two representatives of the PDF, one English-educated and one Chinese-educated, gave their votes of thanks. The contrast between the two young men struck Lee with the force of a blow:

> And the English-educated said, 'Now our evenings won't be so dull'. This is true. This is the absolute truth. 'We have got entertainment. Before it was so dull and listless, and we thank you very much. We will have lots of good fun and games' and so on. Then the Chinese-educated chap stood up and expressed his thanks in Chinese.
>
> You know, as long as I live, I will never forget those two responses. Because one was frivolous and irrelevant and the other was what would make this society endure.
>
> The other chap stood up. He never went beyond primary school. Yet he said he wanted to thank the community and the elders for taking an interest in them. That, in ancient China, soldiers were considered the lowest of the low and he is glad in Singapore they are not considered so. And that this is a demonstration of the growing rapport between the citizenry and the armed forces of our young Republic.[86]

Lee then made clear that despite the problems that Chinese chauvinism posed for Singapore, the Chinese-educated were his model of the ideal citizens, and that he was desperate to find a formula that would give the rest of the population the virtues he saw in the Chinese-educated:

> I went home asking myself, 'How can I give the same responses to the other chap?' He was not thinking, you know ... He never went beyond primary school but there were cultural values which make up a civilization. They were the toughness of a people. And if you come to grips with a people like that, you will find that they have backbone which you cannot break. If you get an emasculated, de-culturalised group you can put them through the mincing machine and they will come out regular sausage-length. This is what I fear is happening to two-thirds of my population.[87]

Lee's shift towards the politics of 'cultural ballast' appears to have begun in 1966, or perhaps even earlier, with a very personal event. In January 1967 Lee told a Sikh audience of a Sikh friend of his who went 'Western':

> I will never forget the lesson which a Sikh friend of mine impressed upon me. He was my friend. I thought I understood him but he was breaking

away from his past too fast and too quickly. He was betwixt and between. And part of the external manifestation of that transition he was making was the abandonment of the turban and the beard – very small things. But it affected his psychic. [*sic*] He threw off his turban, and threw off his beard – but not quite, not quite … He never really had a haircut like I have. And, in the end, under emotional pressures, he cracked. Because he got himself caught between two worlds – a world he was leaving behind and a world, a modern world, with modern moralistic values he was trying to achieve but too quickly. Which leaves me with the abiding belief that perhaps in matters of culture, values and moral standards, it is best to make haste slowly.[88]

A month later, he recounted the story again at a Tamil festival:

You know, every time I think of people whom I have met and known as friends in school or in college, I think of those who became de-culturalised too quickly. I had a friend who was a Sikh. He threw his past away: he shaved his beard: he threw away his turban: he had a hair-cut. No harm at all. But something happened to him and in next to no time, he was doing foolish things. He lost his anchorage. You know, it gets very difficult for a ship without an anchor in a harbour when it gets stormy.[89]

As has been noted already, it is in Lee's reactions to negative stimuli such as these that one usually finds the key to his thinking.

It was a month after his November 1966 address at the University of Singapore that Lee coined the term 'cultural ballast' and began giving flesh to his new ideas about culture. At the heart of his embryonic programme was the study of one's 'mother tongue', based apparently on the assumption that culture was encoded in a language.[90] Bilingualism, of course, had been a feature of Lee's vision of multiracialism since the mid-1950s,[91] but his primary motivation to date had been to use bilingualism to dull communal loyalties and tensions. Now bilingualism was to become the vehicle for delivering 'cultural ballast':

I have had, on many occasions, reason to discuss the sterilizing effects of a completely English-type education which deprives the child of that spiritual line with his past – a failure to identify his formal education – what he learns in school, in an English-language school – with his own social and cultural background.

Therefore, there is the necessity for preserving for each child that cultural ballast and appreciation of his origin and his background in order to give him that confidence to face the problems of his society.[92]

He focused on language, because 'with the language goes the literature, proverbs, folklore, beliefs, value patterns'.[93] Lee saw a nexus between culture and language, and hoped that teaching schoolchildren their 'mother tongue', even as a second language to English, would provide them with the 'cultural ballast' they needed to be strong 'digits' in society.

Lee immediately translated his new-found enthusiasm for bilingualism into policy. Studying a second language had been compulsory in primary school since 1960, but now the languages studied were to be determined by race. Everyone was to study English and their 'mother tongue', being Mandarin for Chinese, Tamil for Indians and Malay for Malays.[94] Studying the second language became compulsory for secondary as well as primary schools, and in 1969 the second language became a compulsory examination subject. In some English medium schools civics and history began being taught in the mother tongue.[95]

Lee's intention to give 'cultural ballast' to the English-educated was, however, not the only purpose of bilingualism. Despite the apparent contradiction, the complementary emphasis on English was intended to weaken the emotional hold of the People's Republic of China over the Chinese-educated. Lee saw bilingualism as a necessary part of the cultural evolution of the Chinese-educated, whereby their minds would be opened to new possibilities and to the world outside the PRC. Lee's passion for the '3-D vision' supplied by bilingualism was expressed in the mid-1970s, and there is no reason to doubt that it was present just as strongly in the late 1960s. Lee said in December 1977:

> I must admit the Government had some moments of concern when it watched some feverish fervour amongst the Chinese Language Society activists in the University of Singapore. But no revolutionary fire has burnt the campus. The bilingual capacity, 3-D vision has been a wholesome corrective. …
>
> I believe that the bilingual capacity of our Chinese-educated has given them binocular vision and a 3-D view of the world. As long as he was monolingual, he saw only a 2-D picture of the world. He could compare only the China of the Communist Party with the China of the past. There was no other comparisons he could make. Now, access to stacks of English language publications, TV, cinema and most important, travel, has widened his horizons.[96]

As well as revealing the role that Lee expected bilingualism to play in the cultural evolution of Singapore, this statement gives some indication of the cultural revolution which had been taking place in himself since 1955, when he began using Chinese proverbs, sayings and fables as part of his own efforts to learn Mandarin. Lee told Raj Vasil in February 1969 that although he had been learning Mandarin since the early 1950s, in 1955 he 'started learning in zest not just the [Chinese] language, but the diction, the slang, the style, the idiom, the proverbs and with it went the mythology of Chinese civilisation and culture and its traditional values' so that he could 'strike a responsive chord' with the Chinese electorate.[97] Lee's own language studies opened his mind to the richness of Chinese culture and literature, and he developed a fascination with the new world he had discovered. Thus, when Lee led Singaporeans in general, and the Chinese-educated and English-educated Chinese in particular, down the path of bilingualism, he was using his own experience as a model. During the 1970s, his perceptions were reinforced in his mind by the example of his own Chinese-educated sons, Hsien Loong and Hsien Yang, when they went overseas to study. Lee told the story in his National Day Rally speech in 1978:

> It requires great strength to keep a crew-cut in a university where every-body has got long hair shoulder length. So when my son went in 1971, I waited to see what would happen. I never discussed it with him. I waited six months, one year, he sent pictures – still short hair. Quite remarkable! Probably the only one in the whole university of some 10,000 people. Five years later, his brother went. Also short hair. After a year, picture came home, still short hair. You see, he has a total value system.[98]

Lee learnt a very simple lesson from Hsien Loong and Hsien Yang's example: they had 'a total value system' because they had been educated in their mother tongue.[99]

Both the Malayanisation and the 'rugged society' phases of Lee Kuan Yew's cultural policies reflect an extraordinarily holistic approach to the role of government in society. As Lee gradually extended his reach further and further into the private sphere of people's lives, he became increasingly confident that he could and should regard every aspect of life as being within the legitimate reach of government. 'I am often accused of interfering in the private lives of citizens', he said in 1986. 'Yes, if I did not, had I not done that, we wouldn't be here today'.[100] By the end of the 1970s, no matter was too small to attract the attention of this Prime Minister. An incident that occurred in 1979 is indicative. As part of his continuing efforts to cultivate an educated elite, Lee wanted the prestigious Christian mission schools to accept the best students from the government schools. The mission schools had acquiesced, but Lee was not satisfied with the numbers of new students they had taken. He met the school principals, explained the purpose and nature of his programme, and sought out the basis of their reluctance. He probed their logic, suggested practical means of overcoming their objections, and even considered the role of school sport in building a school's *esprit de corps*.[101] The exchange concentrated on minutiae that would be regarded normally as being outside the purview of a Prime Minister. In Lee's mind, however, society was an organic whole. Nothing was so private that it did not concern the rest of society, and nothing was so trivial that it was irrevocably beyond his attention. Most people would have been satisfied to leave a clear distinction between the private and the public spheres of life. Lee, however, was supremely confident that he could see beyond the immediate consequences of any development to the long-term effects on the broader community. He applied his 'dazzling and electric intelligence'[102] to the task of social engineering. He found, however, that logic and foresight have severe limitations. In 1966 he discovered that culture and tradition were not toys to be discarded at whim, and responded by intensifying his social engineering agenda, and building 'cultural ballast' through a manipulative language and education policy. Yet Lee, the irredeemable pessimist, was and is, never satisfied. There is always another shortcoming to be overcome and another consequence to be considered. Devan Nair told James Minchin in 1976, two years before Lee began his sinicisation campaign: 'The new elite troubles [Lee]. He is striving to create a new Jerusalem and it turns out to be a new Babylon! What is intended is very different from the result!'[103] Possibly some of Lee's foibles stem from the fact that he took office at such a young age. Hence, he was able to stay in power long enough to be disappointed with the fruits of his own work, and then set about 'fixing' it.

Multiracialism has been one of Lee Kuan Yew's articles of faith since he first emerged as a political leader in the 1950s. When the People's Action Party (PAP) won power in 1959, this tenet became part of Singapore's de facto national ideology. Multiracialism is still part of the national ideology, now formalised as a creed of 'Shared Values'[104] and was the basis of Lee's attacks upon opposition candidate Tang Liang Hong's supposed 'Chinese chauvinism' in the 1996/97 General Election campaign.[105] Yet Lee's multiracialism has changed drastically over the last forty years. Whereas Lee used to advocate a communally neutral multiracialism for Singapore, since the end of the 1970s he has been transforming himself into the champion of a form of Sinocentric multiracialism which is suspiciously close to Chinese chauvinism. This transformation of Lee manifested itself rather abruptly in 1978 and 1979 when, after years of systematically emptying Singapore of its Chinese education and language as an antidote to the dangers of Chinese chauvinism, he launched an unofficial campaign to promote Mandarin, and called for the teaching of Chinese proverbs, common sayings, fables and folk tales in English medium schools.[106] A year later, Lee announced the first annual Speak Mandarin Campaign, which has since become a regular feature of Singaporean life.[107] This was followed by the creation of special schools for gifted Chinese-educated students and a raft of other initiatives which seemed to be transforming Singapore into a Chinese city, making Singapore's minority Malays and Indians feel increasingly un-comfortable.[108] These measures included a high-profile public education campaign on Confucianism, which appeared to breach the precepts of multiracialism. The impression that Chinese culture was moving to centre-stage was confirmed when Lee Kuan Yew criticised J.B. Jeyaretnam, an Indian opposition leader, for possessing qualities that are 'very un-Chinese'. Lee contrasted Jeyaretnam to Chinese opposition politicians who are at least 'on the same side of the river' as himself.[109] The sinicisation of Singapore was matched by an equally dramatic meta-morphosis of Lee himself, as he discarded his identity as a thoroughly Westernised political leader, and reconstructed himself as a Confucian gentleman. Not only have Confucian precepts, as interpreted by the PAP, become part of Singapore's ideological framework, but Lee is now honoured in the People's Republic of China as a great Confucian leader.[110] The remainder of this chapter aims to develop an understanding of the transformation of Lee from the social engineer of the 1950s to the Chinese cultural supremacist of the 1990s, and argues that, regardless of the emotional forces which may be discerned in Lee's attachment to Chinese culture, he is still motivated primarily by the same precepts of cultural evolutionism which drove him in the 1950s and 1960s.[111]

Lee's campaign to sinicise Singapore began on 10 February 1978. On this date he addressed the Historical Society at Nanyang University on three themes that were to dominate educational and cultural discourse in Singapore over the next decade: that the English-educated Chinese should learn and speak Mandarin alongside English; that the Chinese-educated should speak Mandarin instead of a 'dialect'; and that the Chinese-educated should learn and speak English alongside Mandarin.[112] Although most speeches by the Prime Minister were routinely reported in the press, the special significance of this speech was underlined when *The Straits Times* reported Lee's words in full over four consecutive days, with headlines such as 'Lee's Ideal Singaporean' and 'Lee: Why it's difficult to evolve a new culture'.[113] The reason for emphasising the 'mother tongue' was merely an extension of the logic of 'cultural ballast'. English was necessary for Singapore's prosperity as the language of science, technology and commerce, he said, but 'by teaching English in schools, Singapore had deprived itself of the ability to close out foreign influences. This was the biggest price it had to pay'.[114] With knowledge of the 'mother tongue', however, Singapore could 'inoculate' itself against Western influences.[115] Lee's reasons for insisting on Mandarin ahead of dialects were more complex. Hokkien, which was and is the main Chinese dialect spoken in Singapore, was not acceptable to Lee simply because it is a dialect and therefore inferior. He argued that 'if Hokkien prevails, then the standard of written Chinese will go down' because it 'is not congruent with the written Chinese script'.[116] Lee's logic on this point is correct in the details, but the force of the argument dissipates when one considers the fact that Hong Kong has successfully used Cantonese as its lingua franca and has never been accused of having low standards of written Chinese. A more likely basis for Lee's obsession with Mandarin is that he was feeling an emotional attraction to Chinese culture and its homeland, where Mandarin was the official language. He had recently visited the People's Republic of China,[117] and had since described himself as 'an uprooted Chinaman'.[118] There is strong evidence to suggest that he already looked forward to the day when there could be closer cultural links with the PRC. He reflected this aspiration in April 1978 when he declared on television, 'Why Mandarin? Because if we stick to dialect, is it worth the effort? Do we want to cut ourselves off, after spending all this time, from a whole mass of humanity speaking this language?'[119] If this assessment of Lee's motivation is correct, then it suggests that there was a personal, emotional aspect in Lee's sinicisation, which operated beyond any utilitarian considerations.

While his speech at Nanyang can be regarded superficially as the continuation of bilingual policies that had been in place since 1966, it in fact marked the beginning of a fundamental policy shift. Up to this point the PAP's bilingualism policy had been designed primarily to encourage parents to have their children educated in English,[120] while dialects had been regarded as a mere nuisance, rather than the cause of a national crisis. Mandarin, on the other hand, had been taught in schools as a second language in much the same way that Latin or French might be taught in English or Australian schools. Despite the imperatives of 'cultural ballast', it was regarded as merely another subject on the curriculum, rather than as a tool for living. This was to change forthwith. On 6 April 1978, two months after his address at Nanyang, Lee conducted a televised discussion on bilingualism.[121] The messages of 10 February were reinforced and expanded. Dialect-speaking communities would be broken up as part of the housing programme, dialect television programmes would be dubbed in Mandarin, and civil servants would avoid speaking in dialect to the public.[122] Furthermore, no Chinese youth would be admitted to university without a high pass in both English and Mandarin.[123] 'Mandarin', said Lee, 'must be the language in workshops, in hotels, in restaurants, in buses and on television at prime viewing time when the young are watching'.[124] Lee's sinicisation campaign had now begun in earnest. The audacity of Lee's back-flip on Chinese culture was not lost upon observers. For instance, Mary Lee, a Singapore-educated journalist, wrote in the *Far Eastern Economic Review* at the time: 'It is curious that Lee should now be propagating Mandarinisation for Singapore's Chinese when in the early 1970s the murmurings in the Chinese press about "loss of heritage" were slammed as chauvinistic'.[125] In an enviable display of prescience, Mary Lee closed her article expressing the hope that the 1980 Census would not prompt yet another change of language policy. Language policy proved to be safe for the time being, but the 1980 Census did prompt Lee to initiate his eugenics policies!

The development of the sinicisation campaign has been described in great detail and analysed at length by Raj Vasil in his *Asianising Singapore: The PAP's Management of Ethnicity*,[126] and so a brief sketch of the stages of the campaign will suffice to provide the background for this chapter. Lee's February and April forays into language politics were followed by the first annual 'Speak Mandarin Campaign' in 1979.[127] 'Confucian ethics' was introduced as an option in the Ministry of Education's religious knowledge curriculum in 1982,[128] and Special Assistance Plan (SAP) schools for gifted Chinese-speaking students were created in 1980.[129] These initiatives were followed by Lee's efforts, beginning in 1983, to encourage better-educated parents, most of whom were Chinese, to have more children.[130] In 1986 Lee announced his government's intention to maintain the Chinese numerical dominance of the population in the face of declining Chinese fertility rates.[131] Lee's 1989 programme to encourage Chinese immigration from Hong Kong, specifically to maintain the Chinese proportion of the population, completes the chronology of the transformation of Singapore's communally neutral multiracialism into a Sinocentric programme of social engineering.[132] Beyond these specific initiatives, however, Lee succeeded in creating a near-tangible sense of Chinese cultural hegemony over Singapore.

Confucianism was held up as the standard by which all Singaporeans, and the political leaders in particular, were to be judged,[133] and in 1991 Lee even declared that, ostensibly for political reasons, the views of Chinese-educated Cabinet ministers would be given greater weight than the views of other members of Cabinet.[134] When government efforts to make Confucianism the de facto state ideology failed, Lee and his team moved to retain the essence of the campaign through a more generic 'national ideology' which was transfigured into 'Asian values' and then formally adopted as Singapore's 'Shared Values'.[135] The Confucianism and 'Asian values' campaigns have provided the PAP with its theoretical justification of the PAP's 'non-liberal communitarian democracy', whereby the forms of democratic elections are scrupulously maintained, but opposition parties and leaders are emasculated by administrative and legal actions between elections so that they are unable to recruit effectively, build a serious electoral organisation, or challenge freely the dominant ideology in open debate.[136] In 1992 Lee argued that Chinese culture was suitable not only for ethnic Chinese, but in his view it set a good example for Singapore's non-Chinese population:

> In looking back over the last 30 years, I believe we were fortunate that 77 per cent of our people had strong Chinese traditional values which put emphasis on the strength of the family, the bringing up of children to be modest, hardworking, thrifty, filial, loyal and law abiding. Their behaviour had an influence on the non-Chinese Singaporeans.[137]

A year later, speaking in Beijing as the Honorary Chairman of the International Confucian Association, Lee confirmed his belief that Singapore would not have prospered if most of its people had not been imbued with Confucian values.[138] He was even more forthright when he spoke to Greg Sheridan of *The Australian* in the 1990s. Sheridan asked Lee how important Chinese values had been to Singapore's success. 'Without them', answered Lee, 'we could not have done it. No amount of exhortation, laws or coercion could have done it. There has to be those underpinnings in the people: a desire to be educated, to acquire knowledge, to be useful'.[139] This was not a new stance, but mere confirmation of a view that Lee expressed in the early 1970s when he said that Chinese culture 'is the driving force of our economy, the drive and industry of our workforce'.[140] In 1994, Lee even justified political 'rough-house' tactics as being intrinsically Chinese:

> nobody doubts that if you take me on, I will put on knuckle-dusters and catch you in a cul-de-sac. ... Anybody who decides to take me on needs to put on knuckle-dusters. If you think you can hurt me more than I can hurt you, try. There is no other way you can govern a Chinese society.[141]

One wonders how the Malay and Indian minorities felt about this description of Singapore as a 'Chinese society'.

The sinicisation of Singapore was matched by a parallel transformation in Lee Kuan Yew himself. Since the late 1970s, he has littered Singapore, Hong Kong, Taiwan and Beijing with sermons on Confucian virtues and Chinese culture. He has positioned himself as an expert on the tension between Taiwan and Beijing, the place of democracy in Chinese culture, the role of Chinese culture in bringing about the Tiananmen Square massacre, and the return of Hong Kong to the PRC.[142] Today, Lee attributes his own virtue to his Confucian upbringing.[143]

Although there is little doubt that his commitment to sinicisation springs directly from his adult experiences rather than from childhood, there is reason to believe that Lee's early family life imbued in him a generic Chinese Confucian worldview. As a young child, Lee was certainly exposed to Chinese culture through the ordinary family environment. Lee has told us that Chinese New Year and other Chinese festivals were always a time of 'much commotion' as aunts, uncles and cousins gathered for the festivities.[144] His father prayed when the sun was about to 'eat the moon' or vice versa,[145] and the family left food at the family altar and burnt joss-sticks for its ancestors and household gods, all of which has led Lee to claim that he had 'a typical Daoist-Buddhist-Confucianist' upbringing.[146] Kuan Yew's privileged position as the eldest son and grandson is also typically Chinese and Confucian. Perhaps in these experiences lie the roots of his typically Chinese respect for the teacher, for authority, for the perception of an established social hierarchy and for the male bloodline. Such a traditional Chinese worldview could provide the ultimate basis for his conviction that people must be driven to achieve something, otherwise they are little better than animals.[147] Yet his *baba* upbringing was, in fact, more English than Chinese. The family did not address him as 'Kuan Yew', but called him by his English name, Harry, and the family spoke English and pidgin Malay at home, with the only exposure to Chinese language coming from some play-mates who spoke Hokkien.[148] Even before he went to school, Lee had forcefully rejected his Chinese culture in favour of that of his colonial masters. Although his maternal grandmother insisted that young Harry attend a Chinese kindergarten before he began school, her efforts were undermined by Harry's mother, Chua Jim Neo, who told him, 'Well, no, that is very silly because in a Chinese school you are just repeating all this by memory, reciting in class. You must learn how to think independently'.[149] With his mother's prompting, Lee rebelled against his Chinese heritage and at the time 'scrubbed it out' of his mind.[150]

Despite his rejection of Chinese culture as a pre-schooler, Lee believes that in his early childhood he was inculcated in a generic moral code of right and wrong which has stayed with him throughout his adult life. He told a Chinese audience in 1987:

> I think basic values of right and wrong, whether you call it religion or Confucianism or Chinese culture, is a certain norm which is inculcated into the young child. This is done and that's not done. My morality is not all that different between the ideal Confucianist gentleman and a Christian gentleman. They are about the same: you just don't do evil things or dishonourable things to yourself or your friends.[151]

Lee has since reminisced that thanks to his family environment and the influence of friends, he did not lose these values which, by the 1990s, he characterised simply as 'Chinese'.[152] While many observers may dispute that Lee's morality bears much resemblance to Confucianism or Christianity, most will concede that beneath his Machiavellian ruthlessness he does harbour a strict code of conduct which guides his personal life and his public conduct. Lee is no doubt correct when he asserts that his pre-school family life and the family environment in which he grew up were seminal in moulding his character.[153] But rather than learning about good and evil, being respectful to elders and being well-behaved, as Lee maintains,[154] his family life seems to have been responsible mainly for fostering his traits of ruthlessness, self-assurance and arrogance. The picture painted in Chapter 4 is that of a self-centred boy, fawned upon by a doting mother and grandparents, and favoured at the expense of his siblings. It seems likely that the code of conduct of which Lee speaks so fondly was the result of the civilising, perhaps Victorian influence of Telok Kurau English School and Raffles Institution, where Lee finally found role models who lived up to his expectations, and where he realised that he needed to conduct himself by a stricter set of rules if he was to succeed in life. Lee now prefers to be seen as the product of Chinese values and a Confucian upbringing, but this seems to be more a matter of wishful thinking than an accurate representation of the past.

At Raffles Institution (RI) Lee continued to disregard his Chinese culture, and developed a persona as a 'King's Chinese'. Hilton Scharenguivel was in Lee's year at RI, and recounts the following story:

> Because [Lee] could not speak Chinese, the bigger boys at the back of the class would pass derogatory remarks loudly until one day he stood up, faced them, and challenged them to a fight. Something you only heard that English boys in England's public schools would do when they were bullied. After that the others in the class took care not to get on his wrong side.[155]

It is clear from Scharenguivel's account that this 'English' behaviour had not been learnt from the other boys. It was an acquired characteristic. According to Scharenguivel,

> When we wrote our English compositions it was about the honest Civil Service and the fair judiciary and our rule of law and how the neighbouring countries compared unfavourably with us in the British colony: there was lawlessness in Siam, and a lack of freedom in French Indo-China and the Dutch East Indies. Ninety-eight per cent of the English-speaking Chinese, Eurasians, Ceylonese and Malays were pro-British or at least aped the West.[156]

Apart from the formal school curriculum, there were other influences that reinforced the enculturation of the boys at RI. Scharenguivel and another classmate, Erik Goonetilleke, have written independently of the great celebrations in the colony to mark the Coronation of King George VI.[157] Scharenguivel wrote that 'the school joined in the celebrations waving Union Jacks, wearing trinkets and badges with photos of the Royal family, singing *God Save the King* and *Land of Hope and Glory*'.[158]

Although Lee continued to reject his Chinese heritage while he was at RI, it is unclear whether he felt self-consciousness or discomfort as a result. If he did, it could be argued that his later sinicisation might have had its roots in Lee's experiences at RI. There are sound reasons for considering the possibility that some cultural consciousness was stirred during this period. Lee must, for instance, have been surprised and possibly perplexed when his Scottish mentor, D.W. McLeod, urged the Chinese boys to study Mandarin, just as he urged the boys from the other communities to study their mother tongues.[159] McLeod's broad-minded approach to the various cultures of Singapore was not Education Department policy, but reflected his personal disposition towards fostering the boys' links with their past, even as they prepared themselves for success in English-speaking society.[160] Although many Chinese boys consequently enrolled at the Singapore Mandarin School, Lee did not act upon McLeod's suggestion. It was probably impractical for Lee to have studied Mandarin at this stage of his life because, unlike many of his Chinese classmates, he did not have any knowledge of a Chinese dialect, and so would have been starting his studies from scratch. Yet his maternal grandmother's words must have come back to haunt him when he heard McLeod's words and subsequently saw some of his classmates attending the Mandarin School after class. Another consideration is the possible impact of the rise of Chinese nationalism among Singapore's Chinese community which, thanks to the Japanese invasion of China, reached new heights just as Lee entered RI. Kiang Ai Kim was a first-generation, dialect-speaking *peranakan*, and was very conscious of the upsurge of Chinese nationalism.[161] This evidence suggests a superficially plausible case for believing that Lee was probably conscious of these forces, but this argument is undermined by further enquiry. Lim Chin Aik and Teo Kah Leong were both *baba*s like Lee, whose family had lived in Singapore for several generations, and who spoke no Chinese. For these reasons, they are more reliable guides to Lee's level of consciousness of Chinese culture and nationalism. Since neither man had any awareness of this resurgence while they were at school,[162] we are forced to conclude that Lee may well have been equally unconscious of these forces at this stage of his life. Yet it is still possible that McLeod's example was a background factor which prompted Lee in later years to encourage, and eventually to make compulsory, the study of one's 'mother tongue' in order to gain 'cultural ballast'.

This survey of the influences on Lee's childhood leaves little room to doubt that he entered adulthood without a conscious knowledge or appreciation of Chinese culture, regardless of what subliminal influence it may have exercised. This conclusion raises the question of how he came to acquire his purported love of Chinese culture in adulthood. The answer to this enquiry is of critical importance in assessing the underlying motivations of his later sinicisation. Fortunately, once possible childhood influences are discounted, there is a fairly clear trail indicating the main cause of Lee's sinicisation: his growing admiration for the products of Chinese education. While there is no firm evidence to confirm it, the Occupation may have marked the beginning of this trend in his thinking. Lim Chin Aik, Lee's classmate from Raffles Institution, recalled:

> When the Japanese came in, we suddenly realised the difference between the Chinese-educated and the English-educated. Whereas we surrendered ourselves to be protected by the Australians, the Indian forces and the local volunteer forces, we never suspected that the Chinese[-educated] would be the ones who would rally forward, and they were the ones who gave the Japanese opposition.[163]

Lim's respect for the Chinese-educated increased immensely during the Occupation, and it is possible that Lee's attitude underwent a similar revision. In 1993 Lee told the Chinese-language newspaper, *Lianhe Zaobao*: 'Many people were prepared to sacrifice their lives to hit out and bring the Japanese invaders down. They were the real heroes. Many died under torture in the hands of the *Kempeitai*'.[164] Lee was almost certainly thinking of the Chinese-educated on this occasion, since they provided the only significant opposition to the Japanese throughout the Occupation.[165] Regardless of whether this assessment is accurate, the substantial seeds of his sinicisation were planted firmly in 1954 when he came into personal contact with communist Chinese students and trade union leaders. He told of his impressions of this period in a political radio broadcast in 1961:

> Then one day in 1954 we came into contact with the Chinese-educated world. The Chinese middle school students were in revolt against national service and they were beaten down. Riots took place, charges were preferred in court. Through devious ways they came into contact with us.
>
> We bridged the gap into the Chinese-educated world – a world teeming with vitality, dynamism and revolution, a world in which the Commun-

ists had been working for over the last thirty years with considerable success.[166]

Lee's first contact with communist Chinese-educated students impressed him greatly, but he was even more admiring of the communist Chinese trade union officials with whom he came into contact soon after:

> I came to know dozens of them. They are not crooks or opportunists. These are men with great resolve, dedicated to the Communist revolution and to the establishment of the Communist state believing that it is the best thing in the world for mankind. Many of them are prepared to pay the price for the Communist cause in terms of personal freedom and sacrifice.[167]

Not only was Lee impressed by the strength of resolution and discipline displayed by the Chinese-educated, but also he felt inadequate in dealing with these people because he could not communicate with them. Robert Elegant was a Mandarin-speaking journalist at the founding meeting of the PAP in November 1954 and again six months later at its first Annual Conference. In 1990 he wrote:

> At that inaugural meeting, no more than 60% of the assembly was Chinese – and most of those Chinese spoke English.

> The passage of half a year worked a radical change. When the People's Action Party convened its first annual conference in June 1955, Secretary-General Lee Kuan Yew appeared isolated, almost pitiable. It was a Chinese-speaking meeting – and he could not yet speak Mandarin. ...

> Lee Kuan Yew stood alone. Physically and psychologically, he was distanced from both the ordinary members of the PAP in the hall and the officers on the stage. Lim Chin Siong, the labour activist, student leader, and secret member of the Malayan Communist Party, dominated the meeting. He dispensed the revolutionary rhetoric the crowd wanted – in Mandarin. ... The man who then rose was not Lee Kuan Yew; it was Harry Lee. Speaking in English, he spoke across an abyss.[168]

Such experiences spurred Lee to intensify his study of Mandarin. He had begun his post-war Mandarin studies soon after he returned from London, having quickly realised that he had underestimated the significance of the Chinese-educated electorate.[169] Now he threw himself into learning, not just the language, but the proverbs, mythology, culture and values:

> It was only when I started campaigning for electoral support, when I had to mount a platform and suddenly, in 1955, in my first election, face a crowd of about fifty thousand, then I felt painfully how I must communicate with them. To create the rapport between you and the audience you speak the same language, which means the same idiom and slang.

> You must present your ideas in a style, a form, which your audience finds attractive and can strike a responsive chord. If you present it in a Western style, Western ideas dressed up in Western metaphors, it cannot pull at their heart strings. From that moment I started learning in zest not just the language, but the diction, the slang, the style, the idiom, the proverbs and with it went the mythology of Chinese civilisation and culture and its traditional values.[170]

This newly zealous attempt to learn Mandarin gave Lee his first adult exposure to the riches of Chinese culture, and he was greatly impressed by the new world he discovered. In fact, there can be little doubt that his later conviction that culture and language are intimately related stems largely from his personal experience in this period. 'I have had to study Chinese since the 1950s and I am still doing so', he said years later:

> And it is not just learning the language. With the language goes the fables, and proverbs. It is the learning of a whole value system, a whole philosophy of life, that can maintain the fabric of society intact, in spite of exposure to all the current madness around the world.[171]

By the mid-1950s he had already become disillusioned with the English-educated students. As early as 1954, Lee was reported in the Chinese press praising the Chinese middle school students for their 'discipline', which in Lee Kuan Yew's vocabulary is one of the highest accolades.[172] In stark contrast to his assessment of the frivolous character of the English-educated, Lee has observed of the Chinese-educated in the 1950s and 1960s:

> In Nanyang, they were making the revolution. There was no fun and games. When I went there, they barracked me and they put the heat on me. I watched a revolution in the making in the hands of a few student manipulators.[173]

While he pitied the English-educated as being 'somewhat uncertain and hesitant', he observed that the Chinese-educated is 'supremely confident, speaking and thinking in a language which is part of his being and his cultural world'.[174] In this period, Lee seemed to develop a passion for all things Chinese. Lee's interest in Chinese communism was forced upon him by his involvement with the Chinese middle school students in 1954,[175] but it quickly developed beyond necessity. In the mid-1950s, one of the topics of conversation among Lee's Malayan Forum friends in London was the devotion with which he was studying the first English translation of *The Collected Works of Mao Zedong*. Lee's friends were unsure of whether he was reading it simply to know his enemy, or whether he found the ideas attractive.[176] In fact, he was doing both. By 1956, Lee was quoting Mao approvingly in the Legislative Assembly, and described him as 'one of the rare brains in this world'.[177]

167

The attraction to Lee was not Mao's economics nor his Marxist theory, but his thoughts on the nature of power, leadership and action. In the Legislative Assembly, Lee lectured the honourable members on Mao's teaching that 'a new society comes out of the rifle barrel' and quoted Mao at considerable length.[178] Lee repeated this lesson on power five months later, once again quoting the 'great Chinese theoretician'.[179]

Lee's perception of the dynamic quality of Chinese culture was demonstrated also in other statements. In an address to foreign journalists in 1959, for instance, Lee explained that the Malays were the main obstacles to progress in Malaya, while the Chinese were the prime engine of progress:

> The urban Chinese population may chafe at what they consider the slow pace determined by a Malay weighted government. And there are bound to be groups who are prepared to exploit the dissatisfaction of the urban Chinese by making communal appeals, [but] ... the pace of the social revolution in Malaya is as fast or slow as the Malays in the kampongs want it, not as the Chinese in the towns desire it. The towns can act as a catalyst on the kampongs, but it is the kampongs that decide the pace.[180]

Granted that the prime objective of society was, in Lee's view, to deliver progress, beginning with economic progress, these comments confirm an underlying attitude in Lee's mind, whereby the Chinese were the 'catalyst' of progress, and the Malays were, to use Toynbee's terminology, the 'sluggish rear-guard' of society.[181] Although this statement was made in 1959, his perception, which was commonly held in the region at the time, helps to explain his frustration in the period of Singapore's membership of Malaysia. In March 1965, when Lee's problems with Kuala Lumpur were approaching their height, he spoke of the peninsula's Malay-dominated society and Singapore's Chinese-dominated society as being two societies moving 'at two different speeds' and likened them to 'a high-revolution engine and a low-revolution engine'.[182] Even in the 1990s, when Lee was speaking of a Singapore Malay who had gone into business and had done well for himself, Lee retained not only the essence of his racial stereotyping, but even the metaphor of the engine. He said, without any intention of being condescending: 'He is acting just like a Chinese. ... Here is one [Malay] who has moved, shifted gears and has made his life a success'.[183] Chapter 4 has already documented Lee's perception that the Malay administrators who ran the Singapore civil service during the Malaysia period were mediocrities who allowed standards to slip to unacceptable levels. When it is realised that Lee regarded the Chinese as the catalyst of economic progress as well as superior managers, one can appreciate how the Malaysia period must have heightened the racial prejudices that Lee had brought with him from childhood. His speech to civil servants in October 1965 speaks volumes for the racial stereotyping present in his thinking at this stage, even though race was not mentioned explicitly. He argued in this speech that Singapore was expelled from Malaysia 'because we had will, we had vigour, we had vitality', while in Malaysia, they 'still go about crawling on four legs, bowing and scraping'.[184] Further, it can be stated with certainty that despite his non-communalist rhetoric, he had seen his role in Malaysia in communal terms. Several days after Singapore's 'expulsion' from Malaysia, Lee confirmed that 'we represented a spark of hope to 5 and a half million, nearly 6 million, non-Malays in the rest of Malaysia. And with us out, the thrust, the impetus ... is gone'.[185] To be fair to Lee, in the political environment of this period it would have been difficult to avoid thinking in racial stereotypes. If he intended to break into Malaysian politics, he had little choice but to base his strategy on the realities of communal politics on the Peninsula. The significance of underlining his perception of the Malays, Chinese and himself at this time is not to criticise his de facto communalism, but to establish that he held these views, and that his experience in the Malaysia period seems to have heightened his prejudices.

Lee Kuan Yew's changing approach to culture can be described fairly as reactionary in the sense that the development of his ideas was dictated by his reactions to changes and challenges. These external stimuli were not restricted to Malays. As was the case in the 1950s, the English-educated Chinese also stood condemned by Lee, and he contrasted their perceived weaknesses with the strength of character displayed by the Chinese-educated. This chapter has already detailed some of his experiences in late 1965 and 1966 that contributed to Lee's perception of the virtues of the Chinese-educated.[186] Later in the decade a new challenge arose which reinforced the lessons of the 1950s and mid-1960s: the response of young Singaporeans to the rise of the student protest movement and the 'hippie culture' in the West. Lee spelt out his concerns in several speeches delivered throughout 1971:

> At a time when new nations require their peoples to work hard and be disciplined to make progress, their peoples are confused by watching and reading of the happenings in the West. They read in newspapers and see on TV violent demonstrations in support of peace, urban guerrillas, free love and hippieism. ...

> If they are to develop, people in new countries cannot afford to imitate the fads and fetishes of the contemporary West. The strange behaviour of demonstration and violence-prone young men and women in wealthy America, seen on TV and the newspapers, are [*sic*] not relevant to the social and economic circumstances of new underdeveloped countries. The importance of education, the need for stability and work discipline,

the acquisition of skills and expertise, sufficient men trained in the sciences and technology and the their ability to adapt this knowledge and techniques to fit the conditions of their country: these are vital factors for progress.

... Those who have been brought up in their own traditional lifestyles and cultural values have greater resistance to Western ills. By all means the pill to keep the birth rate down. But must it lead to promiscuity, venereal diseases, exhibitionism and a breakdown of the family unit? I do not have all the answers. I can only hope the pill plus the traditional importance of the Asian family unit, where paternity is seldom in doubt, can prevent the excesses from imitating contemporary Western sexual mores. [187]

In November 1971, he told an English audience that he was confident that Singapore could to some extent 'inoculate and immunise the people [from Western vices], through their cultural and social values', but that his real concern was whether this could be maintained once Singapore became prosperous.[188] A year later, Lee began paying frequent and favourable attention to the virtues and the importance of Chinese culture in Singapore.[189] Goh Keng Swee has also testified to the importance of the example of the Chinese-educated in Lee's thinking at that time:

[Lee Kuan Yew] and I and many among the old guard have an immense respect for the product of the Chinese language schools, although we fought them, hammer and tongs, when they were manipulated by the underground Communist Party of Malaya. They were men with their own views of life, men who had a feeling towards their fellow men.

When the counter culture of the West developed, it was the Chinese educated who held it in contempt. But the less educated among the English educated, fell for it. The more educated, on the other hand, found themselves taken in by the liberal philosophy of the West, believing that that is the way life in Singapore should be arranged.[190]

From the above accounts, together with his earlier speeches of the mid-1950s and mid-1960s, there can be little doubt that Lee looked to the Chinese-educated as his model of the strong, self-confident Singaporean. Lee tried to use his strategy of promoting 'cultural ballast' through bilingualism and communally neutral multiracialism during this period, but the conscious aim of the strategy was to reproduce the perceived strength and resilience of the Chinese-educated in all of the communities of Singapore, without fostering either ethnic chauvinism or communism. By 1976, Lee seems to have been having doubts about the success of his programme. It was at this time that Devan Nair told James Minchin that Lee was deeply troubled by the quality of the new elite.[191] By 1978, these doubts had flourished, and although it was not obvious at the time, he took the first steps on his campaign to move Chinese culture to the centre-stage of Singaporean life.

There is no strong reason to disbelieve Lee's contention that he harbours a genuine emotional attachment to the Chinese homeland and to Chinese culture, however defined, but Lee's programme of sinicisation owes more to his cultural evolutionism and social engineering impulses than to his emotions. From 1965 to 1978, Lee had approached nation-building from the same cultural evolutionary premises that he had applied up to the time of separation from Malaysia, but had merely adjusted his programme to meet the needs of an independent Singa-pore, and to take into account his new assessment of the role of traditional communal cultures in building a nation of strong 'digits'. As one would expect of a progressivist, he had no intention of fostering traditional cultures in their pure forms, but wanted to expunge them of their regressive and anachronistic characteristics, and make them suitable for use in 'modern society'.[192] Even as he was advocating 'cultural ballast', he was warning that the China and India of even two generations ago 'has no relation to the Singapore of today'.[193] 'Change is the essence of life', he declared in April 1967. 'The moment we cease to change, to be able to adapt, to respond effectively to new situations, then we have begun to die'.[194] As late as 1970, more than three years after he coined the term, 'cultural ballast', Lee was still able to speak of the need to 'shake off the debris of past beliefs, habits and inhibitions' and 'adopt attitudes and values which enable speedier acquisition of industrial-technological knowledge, skill and techniques'.[195] On this occasion he showed unambiguously that his admiration for Chinese culture and tradition was highly qualified. His admiration certainly did not extend to the traditional Confucian culture of Imperial China, which he regarded as an impediment to progress. Significantly, he regarded the introduction of the English language and imposition of British colonialism as positive steps in Chinese cultural evolution:

> The Chinese script, with ideographs in place of phonetic alphabets, is one of the most difficult in the world. It was developed for a scholarly elite, designed to leave ordinary people illiterate and in awe of mandarins. ... However, over a century ago, through the introduction of the English language, the Chinese in Hongkong and Singapore have had their ideo-graphic blinkers removed.

> Next, learning by rote, for about 2,000 years, was a system calculated to maintain stability and discourage innovation. ... However, the price for stability was the exclusion of Imperial China from the great scientific and technological discoveries of the West, and the industrial revolution. On the other hand, when you have left the ancestral home and are no

longer governed by mandarins trained in the *Analects,* but by British administrators trained on general orders which enjoin them to hold the ring fairly and honestly for all who live under their dispensation, it is that much easier to break out of the barren confines of the past.[196]

Yet only a year later, Lee felt no embarrassment in saying that Chinese culture 'is the driving force of our economy, the drive and industry of our workers'.[197]

The contradiction between these two statements is explained if we presume that Lee was speaking from a cultural evolutionary perspective, and that he regarded the Chinese cultures of British-ruled Singapore and Hong Kong as being legitimate heirs of traditional Chinese culture. This reading of Lee's words not only has the virtue of allowing two apparently contradictory statements to be read as being consistent, but it accords loosely with the precepts of 1978 National Day Rally speech in which he spelt out precisely which phase of Chinese culture he found admirable. The object of Lee's admiration was the nationalist phase of China's history:

> I'll summarise in five minutes what I have observed over 30, 40 years – the difference between a Chinese-educated and an English-educated student. They are different now ... but I am now talking of 20, 30, 40 years ago. ...
>
> [The Chinese-educated] has a sense of purpose – a total value system, total cultural system. The textbooks, the teachers were the product of 200 to 300 years of revulsion, disgust at the ineptitude of successive Chinese Emperors and Empress Dowagers and foreign domination. And it threw up the 1911 Revolution – long before the communists – and the textbooks and the teachers that came down with it had a sense of social purpose. And society takes first precedence over everything else. The result was a very dynamic student. He is able to organise his own picnics. He can organise strikes. He can fix bombs, he can bump people off. The communists got them to do this.
>
> But the revolution really started in 1911 against foreign domination. That was the good part of it – the desire for social unity and cohesion without which nothing is achieved. And I say without that, Singapore would not have made it. If there wasn't this thrust, we couldn't have made it in the last 13 years. It was this willingness to sacrifice.[198]

In this passage, Lee was arguing that the nationalist period was the high point of Chinese culture, and that the communists took the strengths, which this culture offered and diverted it into violence and revolutionary activity. Later in the speech, Lee argued that to bring about progress, the nationalist phase should have been followed by a period which retained the strengths of that culture while adopting the Western 'scientific approach, the search for universal truth and its application'.[199] This was the logical next step in the progress of Chinese cultural evolution, and this was what he had been trying to achieve over the previous thirteen years. Significantly, Lee implied that he held these views in the 1950s, and provided as evidence the type of education he gave his own children:

> What do we want? Ideally, I want to do what I have done in the schools, what I have done, succeeded in doing for three of my children. I don't ask people to do things which I don't do myself. I know how it works. I sent them to Chinese schools where they learnt a philosophy, a complete culture system. I made sure they had enough English so that they would master science, technology and understand the scientific approach, the search for universal scientific truth and its application – which is the reason why the West, first Europe, then America, then Japan is way out in front. There is none of this obscurantism, mysticism, superstitions. It's the search for truth, hard truth: the scientific approach.[200]

In 1956, Lee referred to his decision to send his eldest son to a Chinese medium school in basically the same terms as those used in 1978, though without specific reference to the nationalist and communist phases of Chinese cultural evolution.[201] From this account, it is clear that regardless of his emotional attachment to China and Chinese culture, Lee's decision to move Chinese culture to the centre-stage of Singaporean life was based upon the premises of social engineering, cultural evolutionism and progressivism, rather than on any conscious sentimentality. As Lee confided in the 1990s:

> Genes cannot be created, right? Unless you start tinkering with it as they may be able to do one day. But the culture you can tinker with. It's slow to change, but it can be changed – by experience – otherwise human beings will not survive. If a certain habit does not help survival, well, you must quickly unlearn that habit.[202]

Significantly, he made a similar declaration in 1979, right at the beginning of his sinicisation campaign:

> I have travelled, read, and asked wise men and scholars what makes some societies outstanding successes and others dismal failures. I have ceaselessly compared and contrasted, trying to identify the essential elements present in the successful and absent in others. I have argued with my colleagues who have done their own observations and come to their sometimes different conclusions. I have adapted and incorporated those features, those principles, which I believe made for a successful society, those which are not inherited from the genetic make-up of another people; for it is not possible to change the genetic make-up of Singaporeans except over many generations of selective procreation.[203]

So, was Lee a genuine chrysalid as he transformed himself from a Western gentleman into a Confucian gentleman? Or was his move a cynical strategy, as Goh Keng Swee claims, to promote virtues like deference to authority, and 'saving money, working hard and education'?[204]

Yes, Lee was genuine in his passion for Confucianism and Chinese culture and yes, Lee was engaged in a manipulative political exercise. He was enthralled by Confucianism, and so he appropriated it. Since Confucianism is not a religion with firm dogma, but a loose body of thought which had evolved over millennia, he had no need to be squeamish about emphasising the parts that were useful to him and discarding the elements that would hinder progress. This was a familiar pattern for Lee. By this stage of his career, he had applied the same principle to socialism, democracy, capitalism, and the theories of Arnold Toynbee. He had believed in all of them at different stages of his life, and they had all served useful purposes. And since Lee was not interested in ideas 'as ideas themselves', but only 'insofar as they can galvanise ... society',[205] there was no need to ask deep and inconvenient questions about consistency, truth or the meaning of life. Goh Keng Swee has known and worked alongside Lee Kuan Yew for forty years and has no doubt that he does not worry about deeper questions.[206] Such challenges simply do not appear on Lee's horizon, and therefore never need to be answered.

Lee Kuan Yew's personal and political cultural revolutions are among the most enigmatic aspects of his public career. Yet within the context of his ideological progressivism and cultural evolutionism, the various stages of Lee's treatment of culture make sense. Once the premises of his arguments are granted, an internal coherency in his logic becomes apparent. Yet there is something unsatisfactory in the explanation of the last, most dramatic shift in Lee's thinking. While Lee did approach sinicisation from the unremarkable premises of the social engineer, there was something more personal about this phase which went beyond ideology and touched upon Lee's perception of himself as a Chinese. Such questions, of course, revolve around race, and are explored in the following chapter.

NOTES

1.   See *The Straits Times Weekly Edition*, 4 and 11 January 1997, for Lee's attacks on Tang Liang Hong for his 'Chinese chauvinism'.

2.   George Yeo, 'Civic society – between the family and the state', *Ministerial Speeches*, vol. 15, no. 3, p. 79.

3.   A concise and informative account of Singapore's cultural revolutions is given in David Brown, *The State and Ethnic Politics in Southeast Asia*, London and New York: Routledge, 1994, pp. 66–111.

4.   Han Fook Kwang, Warren Fernandez and Sumiko Tan, *Lee Kuan Yew: The Man and His Ideas*, Singapore: Times Editions and Singapore Press Holdings, 1998, pp. 256–262.

5.   Letter from Lee Kuan Yew to Robert Menzies, Prime Minister of Australia, 20 April 1965.

6.   Lily Zubaidah Rahim, 'The Singapore dilemma: The political and educational marginality of the Malay community', PhD thesis, Department of Government and Public Administration, University of Sydney, 1994. This thesis has since been published as a book.

7.   Michael Hill and Lian Kwen Fee, *The Politics of Nation Building and Citizenship in Singapore*, London and New York: Routledge, 1995, p. 77.

8.   S. Gopinathan, 'Education', in C.T. Ernest Chew and Edwin Lee (eds), *A History of Singapore*, Singapore; New York: Oxford University Press, 1991, p. 275.

9.   S. Rajaratnam, in *The Sunday Mail*, 27 September 1959, cited in Chan Heng Chee and Obaid ul Haq (eds), *The Prophetic and the Political: Selected Speeches and Writings of S. Rajaratnam*, Singapore: Graham Brash; New York: St Martin's Press, 1987, pp. 111–115. Rajaratnam backed away from his call for discarding communal cultures a week later, claiming that only the 'anachronistic elements' in communal cultures would be discarded. See Rajaratnam in *The Sunday Mail*, 4 October 1959, cited in *ibid.*, p. 117. His earlier article was nevertheless unambiguous and is more likely to indicate his true intent.

10.   Rajaratnam in *The Sunday Mail*, 4 October 1959, in *ibid.*, p. 118.

11.   See especially: Singapore Legislative Assembly, *Debates: Official Report*, 25 May 1955, columns 261–268, where Lee demonstrated that he had given considerable thought to the question of Singapore's lingua franca and Singapore's future in Malaya. See also *ibid.*, 25 November 1955, column 1539, where Lee demonstrated concern that both education and television be harnessed for the purposes of building 'a Malayan nation'; *ibid.*, 7 March 1956, columns 1717–1719, in which Lee delivered an extensive discourse upon the nature and the significance of cultural evolution and on the character of the communal cultures of Singapore; and *ibid.*, 12 April 1956, columns 1913–1920, in which Lee spoke with passion on matters pertaining to culture and cultural evolution.

12.   *Ibid.*, 7 March 1956, columns 1718–1719.

13.   *Ibid.*, column 1719.

14.   *Ibid.*, 12 April 1956, column 1914.

15.   *Ibid.*, columns 1913–1914.

16.   Lee's address to the Nanyang University Fellowship Union, 9 November 1964, in Lee Kuan Yew, *Prime Minister's Speeches, Press Conferences, Interviews, Statements, etc.*, Singapore: Prime Minister's Office, 1959–90.

17.   See Nirmala Purushotam, *Disciplining Differences: 'Race in Singapore'*, Singapore: Department of Sociology, National University of Singapore, 1995.

18.   Hill and Lian, *The Politics of Nation Building and Citizenship in Singapore*, p. 98.

19.   Lee's address to a multi-party symposium sponsored by the Historical Society of the University of Malaya, Kuala Lumpur, 28 August 1964, in Lee Kuan Yew, *Some Problems in Malaysia*, Singapore: Ministry of Culture, 1965, p. 6.

20.   Lee's address to the Singapore Union of Journalists, 16 August 1959, in Lee, *Prime Minister's Speeches, etc.*

21.   Lee's address to Chinese Union of Journalists, 1 September 1959, in *ibid.*

22. Lee's address to the Political Society of Singapore Polytechnic, 6 April 1961, in *ibid.*

23. Lee's address to the International Conference on Planned Parenthood, 10 February 1963, in *ibid.*

24. The mentality of the Malay nationalists has been studied in several books, including James P. Ongkilli, *Nation-Building in Malaysia, 1946–1974*, Singapore; Oxford; New York: Oxford University Press, 1985.

25. Toh Chin Chye's interview in Melanie Chew (ed.), *Leaders of Singapore*, Singapore: Resource Press, 1996, p. 96.

26. *Ibid.*, pp. 107–109.

27. Ongkilli, *National-Building in Malaysia 1946–1974*, pp. 40–52.

28. *Ibid.*, p. 108, quoting Dr William P. Fenn and Dr Wu Teh-yau, authors of *Chinese Schools and the Education of Chinese Malayans. The Report of a Mission Invited by the Federation Government to Study the Problem of Education of Chinese in Malaya.*

29. S. Rajaratnam, *Malayan Culture in the Making*, Singapore: Ministry of Culture, 1960, pp. 4–5.

30. Lee Kuan Yew's address to the Singapore Union of Journalists, 16 August 1959, in Lee, *Prime Minister's Speeches, etc.*

31. Lee Kuan Yew's speech at the University of Singapore, 9 October 1966, cited in Lee Kuan Yew, *We Want to Be Ourselves: Speech by Mr Lee Kuan Yew, Prime Minister of Singapore, at Seminar on 'International Relations' on October 9 1966 at the University of Singapore*, Singapore: Ministry of Culture, 1967, p. 1; Lee's address to National Day Rally, 13 August 1978, in Lee, *Prime Minister's Speeches, etc.*

32. Lee in *Legislative Assembly*, 18 December 1957, columns 3176–3177.

33. Lee's speech to the National Day Rally, 13 August 1978, cited in Lee, *Prime Minister's Speeches, etc.*

34. Lee's address to the Singapore Union of Journalists, 16 August 1959, in *ibid.*

35. See Chua Beng Huat, *Communitarian Ideology and Democracy in Singapore*, London and New York: Routledge, 1995, pp. 104–105.

36. See Philippe Regnier, *Singapore: City-State in South-East Asia*, Honolulu: University of Hawaii Press, 1991, for a more comprehensive account of the economic strategies employed by the PAP. See especially pp. 50–55 for an overview of the post-separation period.

37. Garry Rodan, *The Political Economy of Singapore's Industrialization: National State and International Capital*, Kuala Lumpur: Forum, 1991, pp. 88–93.

38. *Ibid.*, p. 91.

39. Chua, *Communitarian Ideology and Democracy in Singapore*, p. 105.

40. There are many examples of Lee speaking of a 'tightly knit' or 'rugged' society or using similar terms. One of the earliest is Lee's speech at the Tanjong Pagar Community Centre, 30 October 1965, in Lee, *Prime Minister's Speeches, etc.*

41. See Chapter 3.

42. Lee in Questions and answers after Prime Minister's address on 'University Autonomy and Social Responsibility' at the Historical Society Meeting at the University of Singapore, 24 November 1966, in Lee, *Prime Minister's Speeches, etc.*, p. 6.

43. Kees Tamboer, 'Albert Winsemius: "founding father" of Singapore', *IIAS (International Institute of Asian Studies) Newsletter*, vol. 9, 1996, p. 29.

44. *Ibid.*; Regnier, *City-State in South-East Asia*, p. 54, and; Lee Kuan Yew, *Extrapolating from the Singapore Experience: A Special Lecture by Lee Kuan Yew, Prime Minister of Singapore, at the 26th World Congress of the International Chamber of Commerce, Orlando, Florida, USA, on October 5, 1978*, Singapore: Publicity Division, Ministry of Culture, 1978, p. 13.

45. Lee's address at the Third Summit Conference of Non-Aligned Countries, Lusaka, 9 September 1990, *Singapore Newsletter*, 1 October 1970, p. 5.

46. Lee, *Extrapolating from the Singapore Experience*, p. 13.

47. Regnier, *City-State in South-East Asia*, p. 54.

48. See Raj Vasil, *Asianising Singapore: The PAP's Management of Ethnicity*, Singapore: Heinemann Asia, 1995, pp. 38–43.

49. S. Gopinathan, 'Education', in Chew and Lee, *A History of Singapore*, p. 275. Lee has stated plainly that although there was no compulsion to study English in the immediate post-separation years, it was the government's intention for English to become the dominant stream. See Lee Kuan Yew, 'Mass politics and parliamentary politics', *Petir*, July 1977, p. 4.

50. Rodan, *The Political Economy of Singapore's Industrialization*, p. 91.

51. *Ibid.*, pp. 91–93.

52. *Ibid.*

53. *Ibid.*; and Goh Keng Swee, 'The basic strategy for rapid co-operative development', in National Trades Union Congress, *Why Labour Must Go Modern*, Singapore: NTUC, 1970, pp. 35–46.

54. Lee's speech at Tanjong Pagar Community Centre, 30 October 1965, in Lee, *Prime Minister's Speeches, etc.*

55. Lee Kuan Yew, 'The harsh realities of today', in NTUC, *Why Labour Must Go Modern*, pp. 19, 21.

56. Lee Kuan Yew, *New Bearings in Our Education System*, Singapore: Ministry of Culture [n.d., c.1966–67], p. 13.

57. *Ibid.*, p. 9.

58. Christopher Tremewan, *The Political Economy of Social Control in Singapore*, London: Macmillan Press; New York: St. Martin's Press, 1994.

59. Goh Keng Swee, *The Practice of Economic Growth*, Singapore; Kuala Lumpur; Hong Kong: Federal Publications, 1977, pp. 121–128.

60. Lim Kim San in Chew, *Leaders of Singapore*, p. 167. Also see Jon S.T. Quah, 'Singapore: towards a national identity', *Southeast Asian Affairs 1977*, p. 215.

61. Tremewan, *The Political Economy of Social Control in Singapore*, p. 34.

62. Regnier, *City-State in South-East Asia*, pp. 55–57.

63. Tremewan, *The Political Economy of Social Control in Singapore*, p. 45.

64. Hill and Lian, *The Politics of Nation Building and Citizenship in Singapore*, p. 119.

65. Thomas Bellows, *The People's Action Party of Singapore: Emergence of a Dominant Party System*, Monograph Series No. 14, New Haven: Yale University Southeast Asian Studies, 1970, p. 51.

66. The Central Provident Fund (CPF) is a centralised accumulation retirement fund that was created before the PAP took office. The CPF Home Ownership Scheme enabled participants to use some of their CPF money as a deposit for a mortgage. The CPF then provided the member with a low-interest mortgage. Between 1968 and 1984, 529,000 CPF members used their CPF facilities to purchase flats. See Lim Chong Yah *et al.*, *Report of the Central Provident Fund Study Group*, Singapore: Department of Economics and Statistics, National University of Singapore, 1985, pp. 4, 81–83, 94.

67. *Parliamentary Debates: Official Record*, 1 August 1968, column 787.

68. Chris Patten, *East and West*, London: Macmillan, 1998, pp. 196–197.

69. Lee's speech to Parliament on 1 November 1994, cited in Lee Kuan Yew, *Senior Minister's Speeches, Press Conferences, Interviews, Statements, etc.*, Singapore: Prime Minister's Office, 1991–95.

70. *Parliamentary Debates*, 1 August 1968, column 797.

71. Full employment was achieved in 1975. See Goh Keng Swee (Linda Low [ed.]), *Wealth of East Asian Nations*, Singapore; Kuala Lumpur; Hong Kong: Federal Publication, 1995, p. 28.

72. Lim Kim San in Chew, *Leaders of Singapore*, pp. 163–166.

73. Lee's address to the Political Study Centre, 15 April 1965, in Lee, *Prime Minister's Speeches, etc.*

74. Lee, *New Bearings in Our Education System*, p. 19.

75. Lee's interview with Fred Emery, *The Times* (London), 13 August 1965, in Lee, *Prime Minister's Speeches, etc.*

76. Lee's address to Singapore and Malaysian students in London, 22 April 1966, in *ibid.*

77. Lee's speech on eve of National Day Rally, 8 August 1966, in *ibid.*

78. Lee's address at the Annual Review and Display of the Boys' Brigade, Singapore Battalion, 28 August 1966, in *The Mirror*, vol. 2, no. 36, 5 September 1966, p. 1.

79. Lee, *New Bearings in Our Education System*, especially p. 10.

80. Lee in Questions and answers after Prime Minister's address on 'University Autonomy and Social Responsibility' at the Historical Society Meeting at the University of Singapore, 24 November 1966, in Lee, *Prime Minister's Speeches, etc.*

81. *Ibid.*

82. *Ibid.*

83. Lee's address to the Buddhist Union, 8 May 1963, in *ibid.*

84. Lee's speech at Tamil Festival, 5 February 1967, in *ibid.*

85. Lee's closing address as Chairman of the Commonwealth Conference, 22 January 1971, in *Singapore Newsletter*, 1 February 1971, p. 11.

86. Lee at the Historical Society Meeting at the University of Singapore', 24 November 1966, in Lee, *Prime Minister's Speeches, etc.*

87. *Ibid.*

88. Lee's speech to the third anniversary celebrations of Sri Guru Govind Singh, 14 January 1967, in *ibid.*

89. Lee's speech at the Tamil festival, 5 February 1967, in *ibid.*

90. S. Gopinathan, 'Educational development in Singapore: connecting the national, regional and the global', *Australian Educational Researcher*, vol. 24, no. 1, 1997, p. 4.

91. Bilingualism was, for instance, the basis of his position on the All-Party Committee on Chinese Education in 1955. See Hill and Lian, *The Politics of Nation Building and Citizenship in Singapore*, pp. 74–76.

92. Lee's address at the opening of the seminar on 'Education and Nation-building', 27 December 1966, in Lee Kuan Yew (Loy Teck Juan, Seng Han Tong, Pang Cheng Lian [eds]), *Lee Kuan Yew and the Chinese Community in Singapore*, Singapore: Singapore Chinese Chamber of Commerce and Industry and Singapore Federation of Chinese Clan Associations, 1991, p. 29.

93. Raj Vasil, *Governing Singapore*, Singapore: Eastern Universities, 1984, p. 175.

94. Lai Ah Eng, *Meanings of Multiethnicity: A Case-study of Ethnicity and Ethnic Relations in Singapore*, Kuala Lumpur; Oxford; Singapore; New York: Oxford University Press, 1995, p. 145.

95. Chew and Lee, *A History of Singapore*, p. 278.

96. Lee's question and answer session after his address to the Political Association of the University of Singapore, 23 December 1977, reported in *The Business Times* (Singapore), 31 December 1977.

97. Vasil, *Governing Singapore*, p. 173.

98. Lee's speech at the National Day Rally, 13 August 1978, in Lee, *Prime Minister's Speeches, etc.*

99. *Ibid.*

100. Lee in *The Straits Times*, 18 August 1986.

101. Transcript of questions and answers during 'Seminar on Education', 24 January 1979, in Lee, *Prime Minister's Speeches, etc.* It should be noted that the 'reasonable' side of Lee presented in this description was balanced by a background of threats to have people dismissed if they persisted in resisting change. An excerpt of this exchange is reproduced in Chapter 8.

102. Michael Lever's description of the Lee he knew at Cambridge, in his undated letter to the author, received 5 June 1996.

103. Devan Nair in James Minchin, *No Man Is an Island: A Portrait of Singapore's Lee Kuan Yew*, Sydney: Allen & Unwin, 1990, p. 24.

104. Government of Singapore, *Shared Values, White Paper 1991*, Singapore: Singapore National Printers, 1991.

105. *The Straits Times Weekly Edition*, 4 and 11 January 1997.

106. See, for example, *The Straits Times*, 12 February, 14 February, 21 April 1978; and *New Nation*, 21 April and 1 June 1978.

107. *Far Eastern Economic Review*, 26 October 1979 and 21 March 1980.

108. Vasil, *Asianising Singapore*, pp. 64–77. Also see Eddie C.Y. Kuo, *Confucianism as Political Discourse in Singapore: The Case of an Incomplete Revitalization Movement*, Singapore: Department of Sociology, National University of Singapore, 1992.

109. *Far Eastern Economic Review*, 19 July 1990.

110. In 1993, for instance, Lee was appointed the founding Honorary Chairman of the Beijing-based International Confucian Association. See *The Business Times* (Singapore), 6 October 1993.

111. The author has chosen to characterise Lee as a 'Chinese cultural supremacist' rather than a 'Chinese chauvinist' for two reasons. First, the term 'Chinese chauvinist' carries a pejorative connotation that can be seen as being derisive of any ethnic Chinese who loves and defends his or her culture. Second, Lee's advocacy of Chinese culture is heavily qualified and displays too many signs of utilitarianism to be considered in the same breath as the attitude of one who loves Chinese culture for its own sake. The term 'Chinese cultural supremacist' describes simply Lee's belief that Chinese culture, however defined, has qualities that make it superior to its rivals. Lee's racial views, which are described in Chapter 6, are best characterised separately as 'Chinese racial supremacist' views.

112. Lee Kuan Yew, *Bilingualism in Our Society*, Singapore: Ministry of Culture, 1978, pp. 36–46. The exhortation to learn English was hardly needed, since in 1977 only 10 per cent of new students enrolled in Chinese-medium schools. See Chew and Lee, *A History of Singapore*, p. 174.

113. *The Straits Times*, 11, 12, 13, 14 February 1978.

114. *Ibid.*, 14 February 1978.

115. *Ibid.*

116. Lee, *Bilingualism in Our Society*, p. 46.

117. Lee made his first visit to China in 1976. There can be little doubt that Lee had been waiting for Prime Minister Zhou Enlai to die before undertaking such a visit or fostering closer connections with the PRC because Zhou once called Lee a 'banana', meaning he was yellow on the outside and white on the inside. See Lynn Pan, *Sons of the Yellow Emperor: The Story of Overseas Chinese*, London: Secker & Warburg, 1990, p. 274. Zhou died in January 1976. Four months later, Lee was visiting Beijing as an official guest of the PRC. See Lee's speech at the banquet given by Hua Guofeng, Premier of the PRC, in Beijing, 11 May 1976 in Lee, *Prime Minister's Speeches, etc.*

118. Lee's speech to Parliament, 23 February 1977, in 'Mass politics and parliamentary politics', *Petir*, July 1978, p. 15.

119. Lee, *Bilingualism in Our Society*, p. 24. It is possible that Lee was already considering the possible economic advantages of ties with the PRC, but there is no evidence to support this thesis.

120. Lee in Han, Fernandez, Tan, *Lee Kuan Yew: The Man and His Ideas*, pp. 81, 134.

121. Lee, *Bilingualism in Our Society*, pp. 1–35.

122. *Ibid.*, pp. 12, 27.

123. *Ibid.*, p. 8.

124. *Ibid.*, p. 46.

125. *Far Eastern Economic Review*, 16 June 1978.

126. See Vasil, *Asianising Singapore*, especially from pp. 64 ff. Also see Lai, *Meanings of Multiethnicity*, pp. 141–153.

127. Vasil, *Asianising Singapore*, pp. 65–73.

128. *Ibid.*, p. 73.

129. *Ibid.*, pp. 75–77.

130. Lee Kuan Yew, 'The search for talent', in S. Jayakumar (ed.), *Our Heritage and Beyond: A Collection of Essays on Singapore, Its Past, Present and Future*, Singapore: Singapore National Trades Union Congress, 1982, pp. 21–22.

131. *The Straits Times*, 15 December 1986, cited in Rahim, 'The Singapore dilemma', p. 76.

132. *The Straits Times*, 21 August 1989.

133. Chua, *Communitarian Ideology and Democracy in Singapore*, pp. 151–167, 193–194.

134. Vasil, *Asianising Singapore*, pp. 123–124.

135. Government of Singapore, *Shared Values, White Paper* 1991.

136. Chua, *Communitarian Ideology and Democracy in Singapore*, pp. 194–202.

137. Lee Kuan Yew's interview with Cai Xi Mei of Xinhua News Agency, 25 August 1992, in Lee, *Senior Minister's Speeches, etc.*

138. *The Business Times* (Singapore), 6 October 1993.

139. Lee in Greg Sheridan, *Tigers: Leaders of the New Asia-Pacific*, Sydney: Allen & Unwin, 1997, p. 68.

140. Lee at the Kampong Sungei Tengah Community Centre, 8th Anniversary Celebrations, 22 May 1971, Lee, *Prime Minister's Speeches, etc.*

141. Lee in Han, Fernandez, Tan, *Lee Kuan Yew: The Man and His Ideas*, p. 126.

142. See collections of Lee's speeches and interviews in Lee Kuan Yew, *Lee Kuan Yew on the Chinese Community in Singapore*, and Lee Kuan Yew (Lianhe Zaobao [ed.]), *Lee Kuan Yew on China and Hongkong after Tiananmen*, Singapore: Lianhe Zaobao, 1991.

143. See, for example, Lee's interview in Trevor Kennedy, *Top Guns: Seventeen World Leaders in Politics, Media and Business Tell How They Made It to the Top – and Stayed There*, Melbourne and Sydney: Macmillan, 1988, p. 272; Lee's address at the National Day Rally, 26 August 1990, in Lee, *Lee Kuan Yew on the Chinese Community in Singapore*, p. 41.

144. Lee's speech to the Chinese New Year's Party at Tanjong Pagar Constituency, 1 February 1987, in *ibid.*, p. 85.

145. Lee Kuan Yew's address to civil servants 15 October 1965, in Lee, 'The Prime Minister Mr Lee Kuan Yew speaks to civil servants', in *Bakti*, vol. 3, no. 2, December 1965, p. 10.

146. Lee's interview with *Lianhe Zaobao*, cited in *The Straits Times Weekly Edition*, 25 September 1993.

147. Lee's press conference at TV Singapura studios, 5 March 1965, in Lee, *Prime Minister's Speeches, etc.* Also see Chapter 3.

148. Lee Kuan Yew, *The Singapore Story: Memoirs of Lee Kuan Yew*, Singapore; New York; London; Toronto; Sydney; Mexico City: Prentice Hall, 1998, p. 35.

149. Lee, *Bilingualism in Our Society*, p. 32.

150. Lee's speech at Singapore Teachers Union's 26th Anniversary Dinner, 5 November 1972, in Lee, *Lee Kuan Yew on the Chinese Community in Singapore*, p. 31.

151. Lee's interview in Kennedy, *Top Guns*, p. 272.

152. Lee's address at the National Day Rally, 26 August 1990, in Lee, *Lee Kuan Yew on the Chinese Community in Singapore*, p. 41.

153. Lee in *The Straits Times Weekly Edition*, 25 September 1993.

154. *Ibid.*

155. Letter from Hilton Scharenguivel to the author, 3 December 1996.

156. *Ibid.*

157. *Ibid.*, and letter from Erik Goonetilleke, 4 December 1996.

158. Letter from Hilton Scharenguivel to the author, 3 December 1996.

159. Interviews with Teo Kah Leong, 29 October 1996, and Kiang Ai Kim, 14 October 1996. Teo was Lee's classmate and Kiang was a student at RI three years ahead of Lee.

160. Interview with Teo Kah Leong, 29 October 1996.

161. Interview with Kiang Ai Kim, 14 October 1996.

162. Interviews with Teo Kah Leong, 29 October 1996 and Lim Chin Aik, 21 October 1996.

163. Interview with Lim Chin Aik, 21 October 1996.

164. *The Straits Times Weekly Edition*, 25 September 1993.

165. Cheah Boon Kheng, *Red Star over Malaya: Resistance and Social Conflict during and after the Japanese Occupation, 1941–1946*, (2nd edn), Singapore: Singapore University Press, 1987, pp. 57–100.

166. Lee Kuan Yew, *The Battle for Merger*, Singapore: Ministry of Culture, [n.d., c.1961], p. 16.

167. *Ibid.*, p. 17. A dramatic account of these events is contained in Dennis Bloodworth, *The Tiger and the Trojan Horse*, Singapore: Times Books International, 1986, pp. 66–77, and in Lee, *The Singapore Story*.

168. Robert Elegant, 'The Singapore of Mr Lee: "Confucian" ethics, Asian values', *Encounter*, vol. 74, no. 5, June 1990, p. 24.

169. Lee's address at PUB Auditorium, 24 January 1979, in Lee, *Prime Minister's Speeches, etc.*

170. Lee in Vasil, *Governing Singapore*, p. 173.

171. Lee's speech to the Singapore Teachers Union's 26th Anniversary Dinner, 5 November 1972, in Lee, *Lee Kuan Yew on the Chinese Community in Singapore*, p. 31.

172. Lee reported in *Nanyang Siang Pau*, 15 October 1954, cited in Colony of Singapore, *Weekly Digest of Non-English Press, 1954–59*, Singapore: Colony of Singapore, 1954–59.

173. Lee Kuan Yew's speech to the National Day Rally, 13 August 1978, cited in Lee, *Prime Minister's Speeches, etc.*

174. Lee Kuan Yew's address to the Singapore Union of Journalists, 16 August 1959, in *ibid.*

175. Lee, *The Battle for Merger*, p. 16.

176. Author's interview with Wang Gungwu, who was visiting London at the time.

177. *Legislative Assembly*, 6 November 1956, column 581.

178. *Ibid.*, columns 506, 581–583.

179. *Ibid.*, 27 April 1957, column 1757.

180. Lee's address to the Foreign Correspondents' Association, 16 September 1959, in Lee, *Prime Minister's Speeches, etc.*

181. Arnold Toynbee, *A Study of History, Volume I,* London; New York; Toronto: Oxford University Press: 1935, p. 242.

182. Lee's interview with Alan Ashbolt of the ABC, 24 March 1965, in Lee, *Prime Minister's Speeches, etc.*

183. Lee in Han, Fernandez, Tan, *Lee Kuan Yew: The Man and His Ideas*, p. 184.

184. Lee Kuan Yew's address to civil servants, 15 October 1965, in *Bakti,* vol. 3, no. 2, December 1965, pp. 9–10.

185. Lee's interview with Neville Peterson of the ABC, 12 August 1965, in Lee, *Prime Minister's Speeches, etc.* Goh Keng Swee has also confirmed in his interview with the author (1 October 1996) that Lee saw himself as leading the Chinese in Malaysia.

186. See Lee in Questions and answers after Prime Minister's address on 'University Autonomy and Social Responsibility' at the Historical Society Meeting at the University of Singapore', 24 November 1966, in Lee, *Prime Minister's Speeches, etc.*

187. Lee's address to the General Assembly of the International Press Institute at Helsinki, 9 June 1971, in Devan Nair (ed.), *Socialism That Works ... the Singapore Way,* Singapore; Kuala Lumpur; Hong Kong: Federal Publications, 1976, pp. 174–175.

188. Lee's speech on reception of an Honorary Doctor of Law, University of Liverpool, *The Straits Times,* 5 November 1971.

189. Excerpts of many of these speeches have been collected in Lee, *Lee Kuan Yew on the Chinese Community in Singapore.*

190. Interview with Goh Keng Swee in *The Straits Times,* 4 February 1982.

191. Minchin, *No Man Is an Island,* p. 24.

192. Lee's speech on the eve of National Day Rally, National Theatre, 8 August 1966, in Lee, *Prime Minister's Speeches, etc.*

193. Lee's address to the Tamil Festival, 5 February 1967, in *ibid.*

194. Lee's address to the 4th Delegates' Conference, National Trades Union Congress, 26 April 1967, *The Mirror,* vol. 3, no. 19, 8 May 1967, p. 1.

195. Lee's address at his Reception of an Honorary Degree of Doctor of Law from Hong Kong University, 5 March 1970, in *Far Eastern Economic Review,* 8 March 1970.

196. *Ibid.*

197. Lee's address at the Kampong Sungei Tengah Community Centre, 8th Anniversary Celebrations, 22 May 1971, in Lee, *Prime Minister's Speeches, etc.*

198. Lee's speech at the National Day Rally, 13 August 1978, in *ibid.*

199. *Ibid.*

200. *Ibid.*

201. *Legislative Assembly,* 12 April 1956, column 1920.

202. Lee in Han, Fernandez, Tan, *Lee Kuan Yew: The Man and His Ideas*, p. 179.

203. Lee Kuan Yew, 'The past is relevant to the future?', People's Action Party, *People's Action Party 1954–1979. Petir*, 25th anniversary issue, Singapore: Central Executive Committee, People's Action Party, 1979, pp. 39–40.

204. Interview with Goh Keng Swee, 1 October 1996. See the full quote at the front of this chapter.

205. Lee's address to a dinner of the Law Society of the University of Singapore, 7 October 1966, in Lee, *Prime Minister's Speeches, etc.*

206. Interview with Goh Keng Swee, 1 October 1996.

· 6 ·

Culture, Race and Genes

Three women were brought to the Singapore General Hospital, each in the same condition and each needing a blood transfusion. The first, a Southeast Asian was given the transfusion but died a few hours later. The second, a South Asian was also given a transfusion but died a few days later. The third, an East Asian, was given a transfusion and survived. That is the X factor in development.

Lee Kuan Yew at the University of Singapore, 27 December 1967, as reported by Chandra Muzaffar in his letter to the author, 14 August 1996.

Understanding any aspect of Lee Kuan Yew's career requires a syncretic approach, but fully understanding his racial views stretches holistic analysis to new limits. Lee's views on race have been a matter of much private, but little published comment. This now changes with the recent publication of his authorised biography, *Lee Kuan Yew: The Man and His Ideas*,[1] in which Lee speaks about race with unprecedented candour. Upon close inspection, Lee's racial beliefs prove not to be an aberration or idiosyncrasy in his thinking, but the consummation of other elements of his worldview and his political thought: progressivism, elitism, geneticism and cultural evolutionism.

Until the late 1990s, Lee rarely allowed his public record to be sullied by any explicit statement that could be construed as racist, though on occasions he has come close to doing so. He has, for instance, argued that there are links between economic performance and race. In 1993 Lee wrote an article for *The Economist* in which he speculated on the state of the world in the twenty-first century, with special emphasis on Asia.[2] Lee put his own views into the mouth of a fictional Chinese Singaporean, Wang Chang, who then discussed his views with his friend, Ali Alkaff. Lee painted a picture of a prosperous twenty-first-century East Asian industrial belt consisting of Japan, Korea, Taiwan, Hong Kong and coastal China, while South and Southeast Asia (except for Singapore) languished by comparison. Singapore, although geographically part of Southeast Asia, was economically on a par with the more prosperous

East Asian region.[3] In the subsequent 'discussion' of these predictions, 'Wang Chang' made it clear that race was a factor in his assessment, since he based his forecasting 'on a people's culture, heredity and organisational strengths'.[4] A few years earlier, Lee used his 1989 National Day Rally address to defend the government's programme of encouraging Chinese immigration from Hong Kong on the basis that the birth rate of Singapore's Chinese is lower than that of the Indians and Malays. The numerical preponderance of the Chinese must be maintained, said Lee, 'or there will be a shift in the economy, both the economic performance and the political backdrop that makes that economic performance possible'.[5] Lee enumerated several reasons why maintaining the Chinese proportion of the population at current levels was necessary for economic prosperity – including the 'culture' and 'nature' of the Chinese. Without a hint of irony, Lee also took the opportunity to assure Malays that they need not fear Hong Kong immigrants taking their jobs because the immigrants will all be high-income earners.

In 1977 Lee treated Parliament to a four-hour post-election victory speech which could best be described as 'uninhibited'. In this speech, Lee told the multiracial chamber: 'I understand the Englishman. He knows deep in his heart that he is superior to the Welshman and the Scotsman. … Deep here, I am a Chinaman'.[6] In recent times, Lee has not only been more forthright about his racial views, but he has also confirmed that he held them at least as early as the beginning of the 1970s. In October 1989, in an interview with Malaysia's *New Straits Times*, Lee revealed that after he read Mahathir Mohamad's *The Malay Dilemma*[7] in 1971 or 1972, he found himself 'in agreement with three-quarters of his analysis of the problem' of the economic and educational under-performance of the Malays.[8] According to Lee and Mahathir, the problem was both cultural and genetic.[9] Lee noted with approval that Mahathir's views were the 'result of his medical training, and … he was not likely to change them'.[10] His racial stereotyping extended also to the Thais, of whom he said in 1967: 'If you give them a sophisticated surface-to-air missile, you will have to have the instructor there till the end of time'.[11]

Despite the impression created by this litany, Lee has been circumspect on racial matters throughout most of his public life. The occasions of his indiscretions have been relatively few, even if they have sometimes been spectacular in their audacity. The earliest such documented occasion was on 27 December 1967, when Lee addressed a meeting at the University of Singapore.[12] After his speech there was a question-and-answer session, in which a question was asked about 'the most important factor, the X-factor, in development'.[13] Chandra Muzaffar and Herman

Paul were both members of the audience and they have given the author independent and almost identical accounts of Lee's answer.[14] Muzzafar's account of Lee's answer is given in the quotation that opens this chapter. Lee revealed in this speech, as reported by Muzaffar, a perception of a racial hierarchy of Asians, in which the Chinese and other East Asians are at the top, Malays and other Southeast Asians are at the bottom, and Indians and other South Asians are in between. On this occasion Lee made no attempt to disguise his views on race with discussion of related factors, such as culture. He was talking about the inherent, genetic strength and weakness of the different races. The emphasis that Lee has placed on culture and race in economic development has varied over the years. Only twenty-seven months after Lee argued that race is the 'X-factor' in development, Lee credited 'ethnic factors' with being one of the variables in economic development, though on this occasion he contradicted his December 1967 statement by arguing that these 'ethnic factors' were a minor consideration compared to 'cultural factors'.[15] Regardless of the balance between the two factors in Lee's thinking, there is no room to doubt that both race and culture play related if different roles in Lee's political thought.

The hierarchy of races revealed in Lee's December 1967 parable helps to explain a similar hierarchy of humiliation to which Lee referred four years earlier, when he said: 'Humiliation and degradation by foreign European powers is bad enough. It was worse at the hands of a conquering Asian nation like Japan – and it will be even worse if it should be by a neighbouring power in South East Asia'.[16] In fact, Lee's racial hierarchy is much more complex than he indicated on either of these occasions. In 1982 he revealed his belief that Jews share with East Asians a place at the top of the racial pyramid, and that both occupy a higher place than Americans:

> Let us not deceive ourselves: our talent profile is nowhere near that of, say, the Jews or the Japanese in America. The exceptional number of Nobel Prize winners who are Jews is no accident. It is also no accident that a high percentage, sometimes 50 per cent, of faculty members in the top American universities on both the east and west coasts are Jews. And the number of high calibre Japanese academics, professionals, and business executives is out of all proportion to the percentage of Japanese in the total American population.[17]

More recently, commenting upon Richard Herrnstein and Charles Murray's *The Bell Curve: Intelligence and Class Structure in American Life*,[18] Lee told his authorised biographers:

> The Bell curve is a fact of life. The blacks on average score 85 per cent on IQ and it is accurate, nothing to do with culture. The whites score on

average 100. Asians score more … the Bell curve authors put it at least 10 points higher. These are realities that, if you do not accept, will lead to frustration because you will be spending money on wrong assumptions and the results cannot follow.[19]

A reading of the evidence cited above suggests that Lee has always had an agenda based on the racial and cultural superiority of Singapore's Chinese population. If this analysis is accurate, however, it requires a complementary argument that accounts adequately for the fact that Lee did not begin acting on these beliefs until the late 1970s. On the surface, such a line of argument appears plausible, since there is no shortage of external factors that could have restrained Lee's Sinocentric bias until the early 1980s. His early hostility to Chinese education, culture and language, for instance, can be explained by the fact that Lee regarded Chinese culture as a threat to Singapore's stability because it was so closely associated with Chinese chauvinism, Chinese communism and loyalty to the People's Republic of China.[20] As well as these internal communal factors, Lee believed that allowing even the appearance of creating a Sinocentric culture in the 1960s or 1970s would have heightened tensions between Singapore and its Malay neighbours.[21] These were sufficient reasons for Lee to continue his campaign of gutting Chinese education and building a communally neutral multiracialism. By 1979, however, Singapore's political and regional landscape had been transformed totally. Chinese culture was succumbing to the constant incursion of English-language education and Western influence through the media. Nanyang University, almost the last institutional bastion of Chinese culture and Chinese communism, was demoralised,[22] and the Chinese-educated were on the verge of becoming a minority in the electorate.[23] This meant that Chinese culture was no longer seen as a major threat to Singapore's internal stability. Furthermore, Singapore's relations with both Malaysia and Indonesia had reached a new high thanks to the spirit of regional solidarity within ASEAN, prompted by the fall of Vietnam in 1975.[24] The post-separation siege mentality towards the Malay world was now redundant, if it had ever been valid. This development coincided roughly with the retirement, enforced or otherwise, of most of the 'old guard' of PAP leaders. By the mid-1980s Lee had surrounded himself with younger second-generation leaders substantially dependent upon his patronage, thus relieving him of another constraint. The sinicisation of Singapore was now a political possibility for Lee, and according to the logic of this argument, he then took the opportunity to act on his racial beliefs.

While this thesis goes some way towards explaining Lee's actions, it faces serious problems. It is important, for instance, to acknowledge that not only did Lee show no signs of acting on Chinese racial or cultural supremacist beliefs until the very end of the 1970s, but for many of those years he was widely demonised as an enemy of Chinese culture. Alex Josey wrote in 1974 that 'within ten or fifteen years, Lee Kuan Yew expects the Chinese language to be unimportant',[25] and this seemed a fair assessment. The majority of Chinese parents were choosing English as the first language for their children's education since English was the language that led to good jobs and upward social mobility.[26] Nanyang University was struggling to survive and was under a continuing cloud of suspicion that it was fostering Chinese chauvinism and communism. This suspicion had led the government to 'disperse' former communist Chinese-educated students to universities in Australia, Canada and New Zealand, rather than allow them to study at Nanyang.[27] In 1971 two Chinese-language newspapers, *Sin Chew Jit Poh* and *Nanyang Siang Pau* were brought to heel for allegedly promoting Chinese chauvinism, and accusing the government of killing Chinese education and the Chinese language.[28] These factors by themselves undermine the thesis that Lee was always a closet Chinese supremacist.

Consideration must be given also to the testimony of Lee's close associates from those early decades, who flatly contradict the picture of Lee Kuan Yew as a Chinese cultural or racial supremacist. Goh Keng Swee was Lee's right-hand man for twenty years in government, at one stage rising to the position of First Deputy Prime Minister. When Goh was shown Chandra Muzaffar's account of Lee's December 1967 parable, he was genuinely shocked and lost for words. Finally he stammered: 'I can't imagine he spoke in such crude terms'.[29] E.W. Barker, a minister in Lee's Cabinet for more than twenty years and his friend for more than two decades before that, was equally adamant in interview that 'there was nothing of this race business in Cabinet. I wouldn't have served if it was a pro-Chinese government, but it was not'.[30] While Lee believed in his heart that the Chinese were genetically and culturally superior, he made an effort to separate his beliefs from his public policy. Only in the late 1970s did his racial beliefs begin to exert an overt influence upon public policy. The discrepancy between the picture of the Chinese racial and cultural supremacist which we are able to paint from a collage of Lee's words is barely reconcilable with Lee's public record up to the late 1970s and with the accounts given by his close associates of forty and fifty years. It is obvious that the thesis that Lee was restrained from acting on his beliefs by external forces is insufficient. As is the case with most aspects of Lee's career, the story is much more complicated, and requires a detailed study of the gradual development of his political thought.

At this stage it is important to consider the origins of Lee's racial views. It is natural to assume that Lee's beliefs stem directly from prejudices that he learnt as a child. While there is a certain likelihood in this line of approach, Lee's own accounts suggest that he arrived at his racial views as a result of observation, empirical enquiry and study as an adult:

> I started off believing all men were equal. I now know that's the most unlikely thing ever to have been, because millions of years have passed over evolution, people have scattered across the face of this earth, been isolated from each other, developed independently, had different intermixtures between races, peoples, climates, soils.
>
> … I didn't start off with that knowledge. But by observation, reading, watching, arguing, asking, that is the conclusion I've come to.[31]

Lee maintains that at some stage before the late 1960s he had acted under the assumption that all races were equal, but bitter disappointment convinced him that reality was otherwise:

> When we were faced with the reality that, in fact, equal opportunities did not bring about more equal results, we were faced with [an] ideological dilemma. … In other words, this Bell curve, which Murray and Herrnstein wrote about, became obvious to us by the late 60s.[32]

The evolution of Lee's racial views was a long process. According to Lee himself, he began to form his views on race while he was a student in London.[33] He has described how his ideas firmed in 1956 on a visit to Europe and London,[34] and then reached their full force in the Malaysia period.[35]

Lee's account of the development of his racial views is considered later in this chapter, but one must be sceptical that his adult mind was ever a tabula rasa on the question of race. Lee likes to consider himself a pure empiricist who can rise above preconceptions and prejudices, but it seems reasonable to assume that the very questions he asked as an adult, and his early fascination with questions of race, sprang from an existing, possibly unconscious worldview in which race was an all-pervasive feature. In pre-war Singapore, with its limited opportunities for intercommunal liaison, racial stereotyping must have acted as necessary adjunct, if not a substitute for personal knowledge of other races, and the dominant stereotypes were generally uncomplimentary to the Indians and Malays and bear a striking resemblance to Lee's own prejudices.

In recent times Lee has spoken of some of the stereotypes with which he grew up, although he does not seem to recognise the significance of his own words. In the mid-1990s, Lee spoke to Australian journalist and author Paul Sheehan in terms strongly reminiscent of his December 1967 parable: 'Any doctor will tell you in our hospitals, that even if you just touch an Indian with an injection he is howling. The Chinaman isn't. He has got a very high tolerance for pain'.[36] Such homespun 'truths' are unspectacular insofar as they are the very fabric of stereotyping in every society. The fact that Lee still accepts such perceptions unquestioningly, however, shows how deeply he learnt the lessons of childhood. In his interview with Sheehan, Lee also hinted at the critical contribution of British colonial stereotyping in the development of Lee's thinking:

> When doing a project [the British] would put the Chinese in the middle and put the Indians at the side, and the Indians were expected to keep the pace of the Chinese. And there was a hell of a problem, because one Chinese would carry one pole with two wicker baskets of earth, whereas two Indians would carry one pole with one wicker basket between them. So it's one quarter. Now that's culture. Maybe it has to do with genetic characteristics, I'm not sure.[37]

This passage bears a remarkable similarity to many first-hand colonial accounts of the races of Singapore and Malaya. From the earliest days of colonial rule, British authorities viewed Malays as being even more slow and lazy than Indians, largely because they were reluctant to exchange their agrarian, kampong lifestyle for the arduous work of the rubber plantation or the tin mine.[38] British stereotyping was aptly summed up by Frank Swettenham, a colonial administrator from the turn of the century:

> [The Malay] is ... lazy to a degree, is without method or order of any kind, knows no regularity or order of any kind, knows no regularity in the hours of his meals, and considers time of no importance. His house is untidy, even dirty, but he bathes twice a day, and is very fond of personal adornment in the shape of smart clothes.[39]

Despite the disparaging tone of this and many such British assessments of Malays, by the time Lee became aware of it the predominant attitude had mellowed into dispiriting condescension. Lee himself identified this attitude in his memoirs, apparently without recognising how deeply he had imbibed the colonial prejudices: 'The British put it out that they were needed in Malaya to protect the Malays, who would otherwise be eclipsed by the more hardworking immigrants'.[40] It is hardly surprising that Lee accepted Malay inferiority so unquestioningly because it was accepted by Malays as part of their rationalisation for accepting favouritism in matters such as access to education, government jobs and government licences, first in colonial and then in independent Malaya. While he was still at Raffles Institution, more than two decades before Mahathir Mohamad wrote *The Malay Dilemma*, Lee sensed that

> there was a strong sense of solidarity among the Malays, which I was to learn grew from a feeling of being threatened, a fear of being over-

whelmed by the more energetic and hardworking Chinese and Indian immigrants. ...

One student from Kedah told me in my second year, after we had become friends, 'You Chinese are too energetic and too clever for us. In Kedah, we have too many of you. We cannot stand the pressure'. He meant the pressure of competition for jobs, for business, for places in schools and universities. The Malays were the owners of the land, yet seemed to be in danger of being displaced from top positions by recent arrivals, who were smarter, more competitive and more determined.[41]

We might believe Lee when he maintains that he had, at some stage in his early adult life, come to the intellectual conviction that all races are equal. His childhood, however, was steeped in racial stereotyping that meant that questions of race were never far from the surface of his dynamically inquisitive mind, and deep-seated stereotypes were always ready to challenge race-blind explanations of the world. Hence, when he visited other countries, even as a student, he took his racial consciousness with him, just as he unquestioningly took his progressivist worldview. He has told his biographers: 'I visited Europe during my vacation (as a student) and then saw India, Pakistan, Ceylon, Indonesia, Japan, Germany ... You look for societies which had been more successful and you ask yourself why'.[42] Note Lee's assumption that a society's 'success' can be judged by a universal standard of progress and development. Lee's ideological progressivism was so firmly entrenched in his psyche that it was the unquestioned premise for his enquiries. For Lee it was natural to judge peoples according to how high up the ladder of progress they had climbed, and his background made him prone to place people in racial and cultural categories when making such judgements.

Lee may have brought the kernel of his racial prejudices intact from childhood, but as an adult he has woven an intricate argument to rationalise and develop his views. The entire edifice of his logic is underpinned by progressivism and elitism, threaded into an argument that is at the same time highly sophisticated, and extraordinarily primitive – demonstrating that a Western education and a brilliant mind are no defence against the unconscious demands of prejudices learnt in childhood. Lee's rationalisation of his racial views began with his interpretation of Arnold Toynbee. Chapter 3 has established already that Toynbee had been a powerful influence upon Lee since his days at Cambridge University, and that Toynbee's ideas were instrumental in developing and refining Lee's progressivist worldview. The connection between Toynbee's thesis and Lee Kuan Yew's racial beliefs is more convoluted and less logical, but it is the lynchpin of Lee's rationalisation of his Chinese racial suprematism.

Central to the thesis propounded by Toynbee in *A Study of History* was the notion that societies and civilisations develop in response to certain challenges. Toynbee argued that 'civilizations come to birth in environments that are unusually difficult and not unusually easy'.[43] The Sinic civilisation, wrote Toynbee, was nurtured in the north of China, where the climate was severe, and swamps and regular floods made agriculture difficult, and so it became a 'hard' society.[44] Conversely, societies that were nurtured in easy environments, without challenges from people or nature, are inherently weak. In Volume I of *Study,* Toynbee repeated a parable originally told by Ellsworth Huntington in his *Civilisation and Climate.* It was the story of a group of savages from the tropics who travelled north into the colder climate. Upon the onset of the first winter, some returned to the tropics, 'resumed the old life and their descendants are untutored savages to this day'.[45] All of the others perished except for one group which invented clothes, constructed shelter, learned to dry meat and store it, and discovered how to make fire. 'And in the process of adjusting themselves to a hard environment they advanced by enormous strides, leaving the tropical part of Mankind in the rear'.[46] No one should suggest that Lee, Toynbee or Huntington believed that this parable was literally true. The story does demonstrate, however, Toynbee's lesson of the importance of the challenge of climate and more generally, of the environment, whereby those people whose civilisations grew in the 'soft' life of the tropics were left behind by their hardier cousins in harsher climates. Lee has taken Toynbee's arguments and used them to justify a dismissive attitude towards the Malay and Indian cultures. This logic explains the hierarchy of hardiness of the three women in Lee's parable. The Southeast Asian died first because she came from an easy tropical climate. The South Asian lived a little longer because the climate of the subcontinent is less amenable than that of tropical Southeast Asia. The East Asian lived because she – or at least her ancestors – came from a very harsh climate, which brought out tougher qualities in her people.

With a harsh climate come many challenges that develop a plethora of cultural and racial characteristics in a people. In 1965, in an interview on Australian television, Lee discussed the differences between the Malays and the Chinese in Malaysia:

> One is the product of a civilisation which has gone through all its ups and downs, of floods and famine and pestilence, breeding a people with very intense culture, with a belief in high performance, in sustained effort, in thrift and industry. And the other people, more fortunately endowed by nature, with warm sunshine and bananas and coconuts, and

therefore not with the same need to strive so hard. Now, these two societies really move at two different speeds. It's like the difference between a high-revolution engine and a low-revolution engine. I'm not saying that one is better or less good than the other. But I'm just stating a fact that one was the product of another environment, another history, another civilisation, and the other is a product of another different climate, different history.[47]

Lee found an unwitting ally for his views on cultural suprematism in the Swedish social scientist, Gunnar Myrdal. The connection was made by Lee himself in his 1971 commemorative lecture at his old college at Cambridge University, in which he argued this case at length:

> It is in part the difference between the more intense and exacting Sinic cultures of East Asia and the less demanding values of Hindu culture of South and South-East Asia, that accounts for the difference in industrial progress between Eastern and Southern Asia. The softer and more benign Hindu civilisation spread through Burma, Thailand, Laos and Cambodia, meeting the Sinic civilisation on the borders of Vietnam. ...

> Gunnar Myrdal, in his 'Asian Drama',[48] voluminously sets out the reasons for lower achievements amongst these peoples [of South and Southeast Asia]. He terms them 'soft societies'. Their expectations and desire for achievement are lower. Had he studied the Sinic civilisations of East Asia – Korea, Japan, China and Vietnam – he would have come to the opposite conclusions, that these were hard societies.[49]

While references to Gunnar Myrdal began only after the publication of Myrdal's *Asian Drama* in 1968, Lee had expressed similar views long before this. In 1965, at the height of both Indonesia's confrontation with Malaysia, and Singapore's difficulties with Kuala Lumpur, Lee made a revealing speech in which he dismissed the threat from Indonesia because of the soft and indulgent nature of its culture, though at this stage the term 'soft culture' was not part of Lee's vocabulary:

> [T]hese were not cultures which created societies capable of intense discipline, concentrated effort, over sustained periods. Climate, the effects of relatively abundant society and the tropical conditions produced a people largely extrovert, easy-going and leisurely. They've got their wars, they have their periods of greatness when the Hindus came in the 7th and again in the 12th centuries, in the Majapahit and the Srivijaya empires. But in between the ruins of Borobudur and what you have of Indonesia today, you see a people primarily self-indulgent.[50]

These are merely two examples of Lee's many Myrdalian statements which express a condescending attitude towards the indigenous cultures of South and Southeast Asia. Early in 1967, Lee expounded his views on the stultifying effects of living in the tropics, and explained why Singapore is the exception to the rule:

> There is only one other civilization near the Equator that ever produced anything worthy of its name. That was the Yucatan peninsula of South America – the Mayan civilization. There is no other place where human beings were able to surmount the problems of a soporific equatorial climate. You can go along the Equator or 2 degrees north of it, and they all sleep after half past two – if they have had a good meal. They do! Otherwise they must die earlier. It is only in Singapore that they don't.
>
> And there were good reasons for this. First, good glands, and second, good purpose.[51]

There are three noteworthy points in this excerpt, apart from the confirmation of Lee's environmental determinism. First, the reference to the Mayan civilisation is almost certainly derived directly from Arnold Toynbee's *Study*.[52] Second, Lee has either overlooked or dismissed the former greatness of the Javanese culture, since acknowledging it would have qualified his theory of environmental determinism. Third, this quotation introduces Lee's idiosyncratic ideas about the role of glands, and allows Lee to take a deft step from justification by culture to justification by physiology and thus genetics.

According to Lee, ductless glands, especially the adrenal gland, play a crucial role in determining the drive of people, both as individuals and as races. In 1966, Lee told the Socialist International:

> There are believed to be two influences on the efficacy of human resources. First, biological, and second cultural factors. Anthropologists all emphasize the cultural influence as the factor which causes variations in capacity between men, tribes and nations but they do not discount altogether the possibility of biological differences between man and man because of differences in their ductless glands. I would have certain reservations about attributing all differences completely to cultural factors for I remember the Australian aborigines, who, in spite of considerable exposure to a new society they were suddenly confronted with, have yet been unable to adjust and to emerge as an equal in his new environment. As against that, we have the negroes in Africa transported into slavery in America who have emerged as scientists, doctors. lawyers, boxers, high jumpers, runners and so on.[53]

Leaving aside the question of Lee's ignorance of Australian Aborigines and African-Americans, this speech demonstrated that Lee perceived that there was a direct link between ductless glands, the drive to achieve, and race. In 1971, Lee explicitly linked his views on ductless glands to Toynbee's 'Challenge and Response' thesis, and erroneously attributed his own ideas to Toynbee. Describing the challenge of planning a reserve army after Singapore's separation from Malaysia, Lee said: 'Toynbee's "Challenge and Response" summed up our position. If we did not have it in us, enough output from the adrenal and other ductless glands, we would have fallen flat on our faces'.[54] The author's research has failed to uncover any reference in *Study* which could justify Lee's attribution of his views on glands to Toynbee, which is not surprising since, despite the impression created by Lee, Toynbee devoted sixty-four pages of *Study* to arguing that race is *not* a factor in determining a civilisation's rate of development.[55] Lee, however, has taken Toynbee's views on the role of the environment, and developed a view of race based on a much stricter theory of environmental determinism than was ever advocated by Toynbee.

The connection in Lee's mind between race and the development of the ductless glands is based upon his adherence to his personal Lamarckian theory of evolution, according to which acquired characteristics can be inherited. Hence, 'hard' and 'soft' countries not only produce 'hard' and 'soft' cultures, but their people acquire 'hard' and 'soft' physiological characteristics. This explains why in Lee's parable of December 1967, the woman from the 'hard' East Asian society survived her operation, while the women from the 'soft' South Asian and Southeast Asian societies died. The evidence for believing that Lee holds a Lamarckian view of evolution is found most overtly in a series of speeches in the 1960s. These speeches express his admiration for the energy and drive displayed by those of 'migrant stock', who have inherited their 'good glands' from their parents, and his peculiar notion of acclimatisation as genetically passed down through generations. The speeches also reveal a fear that he and the ethnic Chinese of Singapore will lose the drive which has made them successful, not only because they are have left the 'hard environment' of their forebears and are now living in the tropics, but because they are also living in a more prosperous, but 'softer' and thus inferior, culture.[56]

Lee developed, or at least rationalised his Lamarckian theories during his two-month tour of Australia and New Zealand in 1965, though his thoughts had been turned in this direction for some time. Soon after his return from the tour, Lee gave a lecture to public servants at the Political Study Centre. There he told his audience that he began his tour grappling with the problems of large-scale migration. He was fascinated by the similarities between Australia, New Zealand and Singapore, insofar as they are all new communities built by migrants from nothing.[57] Throughout the tour, Lee's preconceived but unclear ideas were confirmed and he became increasingly convinced that the similarities between Australia, New Zealand and Singapore were of major significance in that each of them were migrant communities that were evolving further away from their 'original stock'.[58] Lee opined that the tough migrant cultures of Australia, New Zealand and Singapore had produced societies with 'a tremendous amount of enterprise' which he characterised as a 'frontier spirit'.[59] The problem in Lee's mind, however, was that as prosperity comes to a migrant people, life becomes easier, the culture becomes softer, and the genes 'go down':

> We are not unlike the other migrant groups in the South Pacific. We share a lot of their characteristics. We share a lot of their problems. And one of these problems is to secure what we have created for prosperity. Which means, you and me, the genes going down.
>
> ... You have come with certain equipment. Your cultural values, your habit patterns, your techniques, the drive, the push, the thrust, to conquer nature and make a life. But in the process you become a different people.[60]

Migrants and their descendants, it appears, have tremendous reserves of stamina and determination, but they are constantly faced with the challenge of maintaining their genetic inheritance because they are now living in a culture and an environment different from the one in which their ancestors developed their good genes. Less than a week later, Lee resumed his theme with a slightly different twist at an Institute of Engineers' dinner after his hostess unwisely told him that she was thinking of migrating to Australia or New Zealand:

> I was spending the whole evening advising my hostess what a ghastly error it is for people to migrate ... I told her of my experience. Three generations here, and I haven't got a climate I am used to yet.[61]

Lee believes that he is acclimatised to northern China because that was the ancestral home of the paternal line of his ancestors. For some reason, possibly related to the patrilineal nature of Chinese culture, Lee chooses to ignore the ancestors of his mother, who is generally thought to have been part Malay.[62] He seems also to have forgotten the difficulty he had in coping with the cold of England while he was a student at Cambridge University.[63]

It is tempting to discount Lee's words as an aberration, especially when taken in the context of the rest of this undisciplined speech, some of which is quoted later in this chapter. It is now known that earlier in the day, Lee sent a secret letter to the Australian Prime Minister, Robert Menzies, in which he expressed deep pessimism for the future of Malaysia, and pleaded with Menzies to speak to Tunku Abdul Rahman on Singapore's behalf.[64] There can be little doubt that the mood of despair expressed in the letter continued into the evening, and was deepened when his hostess rather insensitively sought his advice about emigrating. It may have been Lee's black mood that prompted him to speak wildly on this occasion, but there can be little doubt that he was nevertheless conveying his true thoughts, since he presented the same argument in an interview with Gerald Stone seven years later:

Lee: I'm extremely sensitive to changes in temperature, humidity, mainly because I think after four generations here I'm still not acclimatised.

Stone: You came from Northern China?

Lee: Mid-China, but the climate doesn't suit me.[65]

Although Lee regularly complains about Singapore's stifling humidity, he wears his discomfort like a badge of honour. He believes that he does not belong in the tropics, but was 'stranded' there by his great-grandfather nearly one hundred years before he was born.[66] 'My great grandfather came here with nothing', Lee told an audience in 1967. 'He made something and decided to get out while the going was good! My tragedy started when he left his son behind … and here I am'.[67] In Lee's mind, finding the humidity uncomfortable is a sign that he still has the 'good genes' and the 'good glands' of his ancestors. The Chinese of Southeast Asia have yet another reason to be proud of their genes, because not only are they mostly Chinese, but they are of 'migrant stock' which by its nature is more hardy and enterprising than the genes of those who accepted the world as it was and stayed at home:

> We came here into the mud flats and built this out of the marshes. And I felt what they felt that if anybody feels they can come over in a canoe and take it over, then I say, over my dead body. … That, I think, is at least one of the qualities of the migrant. He carries with him some of the qualities of the desperate circumstances which impelled his fore-fathers to leave their more comfortable societies and pit their luck and skill against unknown odds.[68]

Two years later, Lee proudly proclaimed that 'very few such cities on the Equator – the climate and the stupor, the heat and the humidity notwithstanding – have the cultural verve and dynamism of a migrant community which have made this place throb with life and vitality'.[69] One cannot help wondering how much of Lee's admiration of migrants derives from his self-perception as a Hakka, since the Hakkas regard them-selves as the great pioneering migrant community – the 'frontiersmen' – of China. Regardless of his logic's psychological origins, however, it is just as well for Lee that migrants' genes are hardier than average, because in other ways they are of a lower standard than those of their racial confrères, since they are descended from 'peasant stock'.[70] If he and other Chinese Singaporeans can maintain their genetic and glandular standards, it is good news for Singapore, but it is a constant battle against the climate and the environment. As Lee explained to a group of trade unionists in Adelaide:

> The Chinaman who came out to Southeast Asia was a very hard working, thrifty person. I mean he faced a tremendous stride [*sic*] because he faced floods, pestilence, famine ... [but] we are getting soft. You know, all sunshine and bananas growing on trees and coconuts falling down by themselves – this affects people. To a certain extent, you can try and counter it ... Up to a point we can strive to lessen the burden. ... This is a problem all migrants face. You are part of one culture, one civilization and culture. But it is a different climate.[71]

In fact, climate is only one of the factors against which the Chinese had to battle in coming to Southeast Asia. They were also coping with the debilitating effect of moving from a superior to an inferior civilisation. At the Institute of Engineers' dinner in April 1965, Lee continued his dissertation on the problems of migrating to Australia or New Zealand:

> I told my hostess that where I think it is a ghastly error all this large movements of human beings seeking a better life is that one has got to be quite sure that in the end [one] is going to offer a higher civilization. Otherwise, you end up just eating more beef steak and pork chops and mutton chops and what happens when people cease to want to buy your dairy produce and leave you stranded in the South Pacific as I am stranded in Southeast Asia.
>
> ... I advised her against settling in Australia and New Zealand because I am quite sure that her progeny will regret all this because they were unlikely to create a civilization vaster and greater than the one they left behind. I say, before you leave behind all these things just make sure you are going to create something better. And if you are not going to, then perhaps it shouldn't be done because this is the way I thought about my great grandfather leaving me here.[72]

Lee argued that the debilitating effects of climate and moving to an inferior civilisation were too great to resist in the long term,[73] although measures could be taken to slow down their effects.

The last plank of Lee's racial logic is his view of cultural eugenics and dysgenics. Lee believes that some cultures have social customs that are naturally eugenic while others are burdened with dysgenic sexual mores. During the eugenics debate of the 1980s it emerged that Lee admired indiscriminate fecundity among intelligent and successful men. He admired particularly former Japanese Prime Minister Kakuei Tanaka 'as a man who had a wife and a mistress and children by both', suggesting that 'the more Tanakas there were in Japan, the more dynamic its society would be'.[74] The Catholic Church, on the other hand, suffers from a dysgenic culture: 'All the bright young men became Catholic priests and did not marry. Bright priests, celibate, produce no children. And the result of several generations of bright Fathers producing no children? Less bright children in the Catholic world'.[75]

Of more practical relevance to the development of Lee's political thought is his view that the genetic quality of the Malays is low because of their dysgenic culture. As we saw earlier in this chapter, in 1989 Lee confirmed his general agreement with Mahathir Mohamad's *The Malay Dilemma*, which argued in part:

> Malays abhor the state of celibacy. To remain unmarried was and is considered shameful. Everyone must be married at some time or other. The result is that whether a person is fit or unfit for marriage, he or she still marries and reproduces. An idiot or a simpleton is often married off to an old widower, ostensibly to take care of him in his old age. If this is not possible, backward relatives are paired off in marriage. These people survive, reproduce and propagate their species. The cumulative effect of this can be left to the imagination.[76]

Of these and other arguments that purportedly account for the supposed backwardness of Malays, Lee said:

> From that book I realised that [Dr Mahathir] believed in it as a medical man – that these were problems of the development of the Malay race, anthropological problems, and these were strongly-held views.

> Indeed, I found myself in agreement with three-quarters of his analysis of the problem – that the Malays had always withdrawn from competition and never really entered into the mainstream of economic activity; that the Malays would always get their children or relatives married off, regardless of whether it was good or bad.[77]

The Ashkenazi Jews, on the other hand, are among an elite of races and have a thoroughly eugenic culture:

> From the 10th to 11th century in Europe, in Ashkenazim, the practice developed of the rabbi becoming the most desirable son-in-law because he is usually the brightest of the flock. ... So he becomes the richest and wealthiest. He marries young, is successful, probably bright. He has large numbers of children and the brightest of the children will become the rabbi and so it goes on.[78]

The Chinese also have benefited from centuries of practising cultural eugenics, though his logic works only if you assume that a person's economic status directly reflects his or her intelligence and energy:

> In the older generations, economics and culture settled it. The pattern of procreation was settled by economics and culture. The richer you are, the more successful you are, the more wives you have, the more children you have. That's the way it was settled. I am the son of a successful chap. I myself am successful, so I marry young and I marry more wives and I have more children. You read Hong Lou Meng, *A Dream of the Red Chamber*, or you read Jin Ping Mei, and you'll find Chinese society in the

16th, 17th century described. So the successful merchant or the mandarin, he gets the pick of all the rich men's daughters and the prettiest village girls and has probably five, six, seven, eight, nine, ten different wives and concubines and many children. And the poor labourer who's dumb and slow, he's neutered. It's like the lion or the stag that's outside the flock. He has no harems, so he does not pass his genes down. So, in that way, a smarter population emerges.[79]

If Lee believes that this is the natural order of affairs for Chinese, it is no wonder that he raised the possibility of reintroducing polygamy as part of his eugenics programme.[80] Lee's propensity to identify intelligence with economic status seems to have been a deep-seated trait dating back to his childhood. In his old age he told his authorised biographers: 'In primary school, I had no trouble doing well. Probably because my fellow students were poor and they were not very bright and advantaged ... I had no trouble staying ahead of the class'.[81] It must be acknowledged that Lee was speaking retrospectively, and that his words stop just short of explicitly drawing a direct, let alone a causal link between the economic status of parents and the intelligence of children. His words are not, therefore, unequivocal proof that Lee formed these ideas in childhood. They do, however, suggest that many of his ideas of the elite are built upon the prejudices associated with economic class. For all of Lee's supposed empirical reasoning and his theorising, his elitism and geneticism look suspiciously like the conceit born of a pampered and privileged childhood.

Lee's racial hierarchy appears to have been based initially on his interpretation of Toynbee, but Lee needed to confirm his theories by observation. Speaking of his racial views in the 1990s, he told his biographers:

> This is something which I have read and I tested against my observations. We read many things. The fact that it's in print and repeated by three, four authors does not make it true. They may all be wrong. But through my own experience, meeting people, talking to them, watching them, I conclude: yes, there is this difference. Then it becomes part of the accepted facts of life, for me.[82]

We will probably never know all of the experiential factors which fostered Lee's perception of racial differences, but he has intimated that his travels in Europe during the 1940s and 1950s contributed to a perception of a European racial hierarchy similar to that which he revealed for Asia in the 1960s. His reminiscence also indicates how little it took to convince Lee that he was correct once he had already made up his mind:

> On my first visit to Germany in 1956, we had to stop in Frankfurt on our way to London. We had [earlier] stopped in Rome. This languid Italian voice over the loudspeaker said something. ... And there were Italian workers trundling trolleys at the airport. It was so relaxed, the atmosphere and the pace of work.

Then the next stop was Frankfurt. And immediately, the climate was a bit cooler and chillier. And a voice came across the loudspeaker: '*Achtung! Achtung!*' The chaps were the same, porters, but bigger-sized and trundling away. These were people who were defeated and completely destroyed and they were rebuilding. I could sense the goal, the dynamism.

... I also visited Switzerland when I was a student in '47, '48, on holiday. I came down by train from Paris to Geneva. Paris was black bread, dirty, after the war. I arrived at Geneva that morning, sleeping overnight. It was marvellous. Clean, beautiful, swept streets, nice buildings, marvellous white pillowcases and sheets, white bread after dark dirty bread and abundant food and so on. But hardworking, punctilious, the way they did your bed and cleaned up your rooms. It told me something about why some people succeed and some people don't. Switzerland has a small population. If they didn't have those qualities, they would have been overrun.[83]

Lee did not spell out explicitly the logic of environmental determinism, but this passage reveals an emerging pattern in Lee's thinking. First, he is apparently blessed with the ability to determine a culture's character from an airport stopover or from a short holiday. Second, cultures that evolved in cooler, harsher climates were more worthy of his admiration than those which developed in warmer and more sultry climes. Although he did not highlight the climatic difference between Geneva and Paris, as he did between Frankfurt and Rome, it is unlikely to be a coincidence that in both instances Lee perceived the harsher, cooler climate as having produced the 'people who succeed'.

The logic by which Lee synthesised his first principles is now evident. We know that Lee took Toynbee's 'Challenge and Response' thesis and turned it into a theory of environmental determinism whereby the characteristics of a people, both cultural and physiological, are largely the result of environmental influences. In his own mind, Lee has obscured the division between culture and genetics. As he told his authorised biographers, the 'drive to protect your own offspring is ... in the genes. And built into that is a certain cultural pattern, which varies from society to society'.[84] He considers those peoples who evolved in a harsh climate, such as the Chinese, to be tougher, more resolute and more innovative than those who evolved in tropical climes. The effect of the environment on people was thus comprehensive. It affected both the character of the civilisation that they created, and their physiology, because inherited characteristics can, in Lee's Lamarckian view of evolution, be inherited. This means that people who lived in an environment that required more stamina to survive and flourish passed on to their offspring some of the improvements that they inadvertently made in themselves: better genes and better ductless glands. Those of 'migrant stock' have particularly good genes because their forefathers must have had exceptionally good glands, otherwise they could not have braved the unknown and made a new life for themselves. Lee's great fear, however, is that the good genes which developed through living in a harsh environment can be lost through living an easier life in a softer climate.

Lee's perception of the migrant's good glands is actually critical to his racial hierarchy as it applies in Singapore, since most Singaporean Chinese are descended from illiterate peasants who, in China's culturally eugenic society, would normally be 'neutered'. Lee's emphasis on the migrant's good glands flatly contradicts his elitism, the logic of cultural eugenicism, and his usual practice of blindly equating economic status with talent and intelligence. It is difficult to avoid the conclusion that it is a rationalisation developed specifically for the 'benefit' of Southeast Asia's Chinese population who, on the basis of his usual logic, should be dumb and slow. The fact that Lee resorts to such a deft piece of sophistry supports the argument that his racial worldview, as explained and defended in adulthood, is an attempt to justify his preconceived notions of the racial hierarchy, rather than the result of dispassionate logic applied to empirical evidence. While his adult experiences probably did influence the development of his worldview and his political thought, the essence of his conclusions regarding the hierarchy of Asian races owes more to the prejudices that he learnt as a child than it does to his observations of the porters at Rome and Frankfurt airports, or to his reading of Arnold Toynbee and Gunnar Myrdal.[85]

Near the beginning of this chapter, E.W. Barker was quoted expressing disbelief at the suggestion that Lee ran a pro-Chinese government.[86] While we can accept Barker's disclaimer that 'there was nothing of this race business in Cabinet', Lee's racial assumptions nevertheless affected policy unconsciously. This is seen most clearly in the treatment of the Malay community. For two decades after separation, for instance, the Singapore government had an unofficial policy of excluding Malays from the Singapore Armed Forces and the police force because of concerns about their loyalty. Not only did this practice deny Malays a traditional source of employment, but it made other employers reluctant to hire them because they were, technically, still eligible to be called up.[87] At the same time, the government exaggerated, possibly unintentionally, the structural impediments to Malays' educational advancement. At the time of separation from Malaysia, Malay students in Singapore had already been disadvantaged inadvertently because they were streamed through Malay-language schools which were staffed by under-qualified teachers, and which used substandard Malay-language textbooks.[88] These schools had very high attrition and failure rates from the beginning, but after separation even the successful students faced unique linguistic and academic hurdles in their pursuit of higher education. After separation, not only did the Malays find that their language had little economic value, but they discovered that their schools had not prepared them for tertiary education in the new Singapore. The first problem was that unlike Chinese-educated Chinese attending Nanyang University, and English-speaking Chinese, Indians and Eurasians attending the University of Singapore, the Malays had no tertiary institutions in which they did not face a language barrier. In fact Malay students' command of English was so poor that they alone were required to take an oral test as part of their entry requirements to university. Further, as part of the 'politics of survival' in newly independent Singapore, university scholarships were restricted to those students pursuing technical and science disciplines, and the inadequately staffed and poorly resourced Malay-stream schools had left their students singularly ill-equipped to qualify or compete for these scholarships.[89] The Malays' problem was compounded by their continuing socio-economic marginalisation,[90] and by the near-universal presumption – fostered initially by Lee Kuan Yew – that their under-achievement reflected their racial and cultural deficits: they had grown up in the 'soft', lethargic Malay culture which did not encourage studiousness, enterprise, or hard work. In a backhanded tribute to Lee's ideological hegemony, even Singapore's Malay teachers came to accept this 'cultural deficit' explanation of Malay underachievement.[91] By 1992, Lee was so confident that Malay under-achievement and Chinese academic excellence were innate and ethnically based that he proposed that teaching practices be modified according to race to allow for the different aptitudes of the various communities.[92] Between their educational and employment disadvantages, and the psychological impact of being told continually that their problems were the result of their ethnic culture, it is not surprising that Malays are still at an economic and educational disadvantage a generation later. Perhaps the most revealing aspect of the saga of Singapore's Malays is to be found not in the actual practice of discrimination, but in the fact that these preconceptions are so deep-seated, not least of all in Lee himself, that there is little consciousness that these discriminatory structures and practices are even in operation.

This chapter has described in detail the character of Lee Kuan Yew's racial views, substantially using his own words as evidence. After a lifetime of being circumspect on the question of race, Lee has finally spoken openly. Yet it would be a mistake to condemn Lee as a hard-line racist. Such a characterisation of his views would be a distortion of both his logic and his natural disposition. There can be no doubt that Lee believes that some races and some ethnically based cultures are inherently superior to others. His own words leave no doubt about this assertion, though it should be recognised that this in itself hardly makes him remarkable in Asia. He has also integrated his racial views into his political agenda and has created a regime that accentuates racial categorisation. This assertion, too, is beyond dispute, yet it should be acknowledged that affirmative action programmes in the United States and Australia are based upon racial classifications and are widely accepted as part of modern liberal orthodoxy.

Of equal significance to our study of his political thought are the aspects of political and personal racial views that Lee has avoided by his eclectic approach. Lee's idiosyncratic rationalisation of his racial views, for instance, has undermined the tendency to dismiss any race as being irredeemably inferior, or unchangeably superior. He has not conceived of any race as being supreme, even though some are more intelligent and hardy than others. Unlike Social Darwinian racists, he does not base his views on the assumption that any race is a lower or higher evolutionary form of humanity. He sees no unbridgeable divide between races. Although his environmental determinism, Lamarckian view of evolution and cultural eugenicism may explain the higher intelligence and better glands of those who hail from a 'hard' society, they also create a firm line of continuity between the different races, and give each race the capacity to change for the better or the worse: hence Lee's efforts to 'improve' racial communities by 'tinkering' with their cultures.[93] The result has been that despite some instances of overt racial discrimination by Lee's government, and more common occasions of discrimination in Singaporean society, Lee has created a society that has a relatively low level of racial tension, despite having a high level of racial consciousness. Considering his own racial views and the nature of the society he inherited, this is a remarkable achievement which, despite its shortcomings, should be acknowledged.

Our understanding of the nature of Lee's views on cultural and racial evolution now enables us to perceive a new depth in Lee's public policies and in the development of his political thought in the areas of culture, education, eugenics, progressivism, elitism, immigration and his attitude to the Malays. More significantly, it gives us a fresh insight into the deep fears that have driven Lee throughout his public life, and especially since his sinicisation in the late 1970s. Lee has married pessimism, progressivism and geneticism to produce a vision of a horrible world where every step on the road to progress creates new problems which will drag civilisation down to the depths again – unless the elite takes charge and applies itself creatively and scientifically to overcoming these challenges. Such an attitude is, of course, the height of hubris, but this does not concern Lee. By the late 1970s Lee was very comfortable with hubris. He had been almost single-handedly transforming and re-transforming the physical, political, linguistic and cultural landscape of Singapore for nearly two decades. He had been making and breaking careers and industries, politicians and ideologies, and setting patterns of work, procreation and education for about two million people. He had assumed more control of his countrymen's lives than the Pope claims over the lives of Catholics. Furthermore, by the early 1980s ill health and old age amongst his colleagues meant that he could now foresee the day when he would be the last of the 'old guard' left in Cabinet: a paramount leader without rivals, rather than a *primus inter pares*.

Lee himself spoke of the difference that this set of retirements has made to Cabinet. The old guard leaders were never compliant and were forthright in their opposition to many of Lee's policies.[94] After their retirement, however, he did not 'waste time taking opinions all around' the Cabinet, but simply told his colleagues what he wanted and it was up to them to disagree.[95] One does not have to be a Western liberal to see that this near-omnipotence and unrivalled pre-eminence is not healthy for either the nation or the leader. Lee's new freedom, combined with his perception that cultural and dysgenic disasters were imminent, seems to have been at the heart of Lee's quixotic approach to politics in the 1980s. His eugenics policies and the sinicisation programme converged as the complementary answers to the challenge of the West, degenerating genes and the search for talent.

NOTES

1.   Han Fook Kwang, Warren Fernandez and Sumiko Tan, *Lee Kuan Yew: The Man and His Ideas*, Singapore: Times Editions and Singapore Press Holdings, 1998.

2.   Lee Kuan Yew, 'News from a time-capsule', *The Economist*, 17 September 1993, pp. 13–18.

3.   *Ibid.*, pp. 13–14.

4.   *Ibid.*, p. 18.

5.   *The Straits Times*, 21 August 1989.

6.   Lee Kuan Yew, 'Mass politics and parliamentary politics', speech to Parliament, 23 February 1977, *Petir*, July 1978, p. 15.

7.   Mahathir bin Mohamad, *The Malay Dilemma*, Singapore; Kuala Lumpur: Times Books International, 1970.

8.   Lee's interview with *New Straits Times*, 14 October 1989 in Lee Kuan Yew, *Prime Minister's Speeches, Press Conferences, Interviews, Statements, etc.*, Singapore: Prime Minister's Office, 1959–90. Also see *The Straits Times*, 18 October 1989.

9. Lee's representation of Mahathir's views is accurate. See Mahathir, *The Malay Dilemma*, pp. 1–3, 16–31.

10. Lee's interview with *New Straits Times*, 14 October 1989 in Lee, *Prime Minister's Speeches, etc.* Contrary to Lee's assessment, Mahathir has since recanted the views he expressed in *The Malay Dilemma*. See *New Straits Times*, 12 May 1997.

11. Lee's television interview with Scandinavian journalists, 8 November 1967, in Lee, *Prime Minister's Speeches, etc.*

12. Letter from Chandra Muzaffar (14 August 1996) and Herman Paul (8 December 1996) to the author. Muzaffar and Paul were members of the audience that Lee addressed. The meeting, which was held under the auspices of the University of Singapore Students' Union, was not reported in the English-speaking press and the speech is not included in the official collection of Lee's speeches issued by the Prime Minister's Office. See Lee, *Prime Minister's Speeches, etc.* Herman Paul recalls a report of Lee's speech being carried in the student union newsletter but the student union records covering this period are unavailable so this cannot be confirmed. Neither the National University of Singapore Students' Union, the University Registrar's Office, the Student Liaison Office, nor the Archives and Reference sections of the NUS Library were able to find any student union records from this period. The open shelves and microfilm sections of the NUS Library did contain some student union publications from the 1960s, but the missing volumes included the period in question.

13. Letter from Chandra Muzaffar to the author, 14 August 1996.

14. *Ibid.*, and letter from Herman Paul to the author, 8 December 1996.

15. Lee Kuan Yew, 'A tale of two cities', speech at reception of an Honorary Degree of Doctor of Law from Hong Kong University, *Far Eastern Economic Review*, 8 March 1970, p. 49.

16. Lee's address to a mass rally, 25 August 1963, in Lee, *Prime Minister's Speeches, etc.*

17. Lee Kuan Yew, 'The search for talent', in S. Jayakumar (ed.), *Our Heritage and Beyond: A Collection of Essays on Singapore, Its Past, Present and Future*, Singapore: Singapore National Trades Union Congress, 1982, pp. 21–22.

18. Richard J. Herrnstein and Charles Murray, *The Bell Curve: Intelligence and Class Structure in American Life*, New York; London; Toronto; Sydney; Tokyo; Singapore: The Free Press, 1994.

19. Lee in Han, Fernandez, Tan, *Lee Kuan Yew: The Man and His Ideas*, p. 153.

20. See Lee Kuan Yew's letter to Australian Prime Minister Robert Menzies, 20 April 1965.

21. Lee Kuan Yew began expressing his fear of being surrounded by Malay/ Muslim neighbours in 1966. See Lee Kuan Yew, *New Bearings in Our Education System*, Singapore: Ministry of Culture, [n.d., c.1966–67], p. 4.

22. Lai Ah Eng, *Meanings of Multiethnicity: A Case-study of Ethnicity and Ethnic Relations in Singapore*, Kuala Lumpur; Oxford; Singapore; New York: Oxford University Press, 1995, p. 145.

23. Lee has said that the English-educated became the majority in the electorate in 1981. See Lee Kuan Yew, 'Why Singapore disallows foreign press to interfere in domestic politics', *Ministerial Speeches*, vol. 12, no. 2, March–April 1988, p. 13.

24. Lee's address to the Commonwealth Heads of Government Meeting, London, 8 June 1977, in *The Contemporary Asia Review*, vol. 1, no. 1, 1977, p. 2.

25. Alex Josey, *Lee Kuan Yew: The Struggle for Singapore*, Sydney: Angus & Robertson, 1974, p. 115.

26. James Minchin, *No Man Is an Island: A Portrait of Singapore's Lee Kuan Yew*, Sydney: Allen & Unwin, 1990, p. 256.

27. *The Straits Times*, 8 July 1972.

28. C.T. Ernest Chew and Edwin Lee (eds), *A History of Singapore*, Singapore; New York: Oxford University Press, 1991, pp. 172, 307.

29. Interview with Goh Keng Swee, 1 October 1996. At the time of the interview I had no corroboration of Muzaffar's account.

30. Interview with E.W. Barker, 16 October 1996.

31. Lee in Han, Fernandez, Tan, *Lee Kuan Yew: The Man and His Ideas*, p. 175.

32. *Ibid.*, p. 157.

33. *Ibid.*, p. 173.

34. *Ibid.*

35. *Ibid.*, pp. 181, 183.

36. Paul Sheehan, *Among the Barbarians: The Dividing of Australia*, Sydney: Random House Australia, 1998, p. 77.

37. *Ibid.*

38. See Sumit Ganguly, 'Ethnic policies and political quiescence in Malaysia and Singapore', in Michael E. Brown and Sumit Ganguly (eds), *Government Policies and Ethnic Relations in Asia and the Pacific*, Cambridge, Mass.; London: The MIT Press, 1997, pp. 233–272.

39. *Ibid.*, p. 238.

40. Lee Kuan Yew, *The Singapore Story: Memoirs of Lee Kuan Yew*, Singapore; New York; London; Toronto, Sydney; Mexico City: Prentice Hall, 1998, p. 51.

41. *Ibid.*, pp. 41–42.

42. *Ibid.*, p. 42.

43. Arnold Toynbee, *A Study of History, Volume II*, London; New York; Toronto: Oxford University Press, 1935, p. 259.

44. Toynbee, *A Study of History, Volume I*, London; New York; Toronto: Oxford University Press, 1935, pp. 318–321.

45. *Ibid.*, p. 192.

46. *Ibid.*

47. Lee's interview with Alan Ashbolt in ABC studios, Canberra, 24 March 1965, in Lee, *Prime Minister's Speeches, etc.*

48. Gunnar Myrdal, *Asian Drama: An Inquiry into the Poverty of Nations, Volumes I, II and III*, London: Allen Lane; The Penguin Press, 1968.

49. *The Straits Times*, 9 November 1971.

50. Lee Kuan Yew's address to the students of Canterbury University, Christchurch, New Zealand, 15 March 1965, in Lee, *Prime Minister's Speeches, etc.*

51. Lee's speech to a dinner given by the United Kingdom Manufacturers' Association and the Confederation of British Industry Representatives, Raffles Hotel, 7 February 1967, in *ibid.*

52. Toynbee, *A Study of History, II*, pp. 321–322.

53. Lee's speech to the Special Conference of the Socialist International Congress, at Uppsala, 27 April 1967, in Lee, *Prime Minister's Speeches, etc.*

54. Lee's interview in *New Nation*, 30 March 1971.

55. Toynbee, *A Study of History, I*, pp. 207–271.

56. See, for example, Lee's address to the Political Study Centre, 15 April 1965, in *University of Singapore Students' Union*, [n.d., c.1965], pp. 22–27, especially p. 25.

57. *Ibid.*, p. 22.

58. *Ibid.*, p. 23.

59. *Ibid.*, p. 25.

60. *Ibid.*

61. Lee's address to the Institute of Engineers' Dinner, 20 April 1965, in Lee, *Prime Minister's Speeches, etc.*

62. Lynn Pan, *Sons of the Yellow Emperor: The Story of Overseas Chinese*, London: Secker & Warburg, 1990, p. 268.

63. According to Alex Josey, Lee took up golf in England because it was the only sport he could play all year round 'whilst clad in sweater and gloves – essential clothing most of the time in England for a man born in the tropics'. Alex Josey, *Lee Kuan Yew: The Crucial Years*, Singapore; Kuala Lumpur: Times Books International, 1980, pp. 5–6. He had tried his hand at rowing but quit when he realised that he was expected to participate even if it was snowing. Lee, *The Singapore Story*, p. 108.

64. Letter from Lee Kuan Yew to Robert Menzies, 20 April 1965.

65. Lee's interview with Gerald Stone of the ABC, 7 July 1972, in Lee, *Prime Minister's Speeches, etc.* In fact Lee's Hakka ancestors moved from the cold climate of northern China to the sultry climate of southern China over 1,000 years ago.

66. Lee to the Institute of Engineers' Dinner, 20 April 1965 in *ibid.*

67. Lee to the UK Manufacturers' Association and the Confederation of British Industry Representatives, 7 February 1967 in *ibid.*

68. Lee's address to the Institute of Engineers' Dinner, 20 April 1965 in *ibid.*

69. Lee's address at the inauguration ceremony of the Citizens' Consultative Committee of the River Valley Constituency and the Management Committee of the River Valley Community Centre, 19 January 1967, in *ibid.*

70. Lee at the opening of the Singapore Polytechnic New Campus, 7 July 1979, in *ibid.*

71. Lee's speech to representatives of South Australian trade unions, Adelaide, 30 March 1965, in *ibid.*

72. Lee to Institute of Engineers dinner, 20 April 1965 in *ibid.* It is difficult to believe that Lee was referring to Malaysia or Singapore as the 'vast' and 'great' civilisation which the lady would be leaving if she went to Australia. This was probably a reference to Singapore's tenuous links with Chinese civilisation.

73. Lee's address to South Australian trade unionists, 30 March 1965 in *ibid.*

74. Geraldine Heng and Janadas Devan, 'State fatherhood: the politics of nationalism, sexuality, and race in Singapore', in Andrew Parker, Mary Russo, Doris Sommer

and Patricia Yaeger (eds), *Nationalisms and Sexualities*, New York and London: Routledge, 1992, p. 362, note 17.

75. Lee in Han, Fernandez, Tan, *Lee Kuan Yew: The Man and His Ideas*, p. 172.

76. Mahathir, *The Malay Dilemma*, p. 29.

77. Lee's interview with *New Straits Times*, 14 October 1989 in Lee, *Prime Minister's Speeches, etc.*

78. *Ibid.* Lee told his biographers that he read this account in *The Jewish Mystique*, which was recommended to him by an American Jewish banker. Lee makes clear in this account, however, that his belief in the superior intelligence of the Ashkenazi Jews, and his interest in the question predated his reading of this book.

79. Lee in Han, Fernandez, Tan, *Lee Kuan Yew: The Man and His Ideas*, p. 169.

80. *The Straits Times*, 3 January 1987.

81. Lee in Han, Fernandez, Tan, *Lee Kuan Yew: The Man and His Ideas*, p. 26.

82. *Ibid.*, p. 175.

83. *Ibid.*, p. 173.

84. *Ibid.*, p. 163.

85. In fact Toynbee and Myrdal are just two of many academic sources by which Lee has rationalised his racial and eugenic views. A full consideration of the academic sources he has cited over the decades has not been attempted in this book, because it would occupy considerable space without adding appreciably to our understanding of Lee.

86. Interview with E.W. Barker, 16 October 1996

87. Tania Li, *Malays in Singapore: Culture, Economy and Ideology*, Singapore; Oxford; New York: Oxford University Press, 1989, pp. 108–109.

88. Lily Zubaidah Rahim, 'The Singapore dilemma: the political and educational marginality of the Malay community'. PhD thesis, Department of Government and Public Administration, University of Sydney, 1994, p. 205.

89. *Ibid.*, pp. 205–206.

90. The structural, economic and social disadvantages faced by Malay students are much more extensive than are indicated above. Rahim provides a good study of these factors in *ibid.*, Chapter 8, pp. 198–227. Tania Li has also described various mechanisms of discrimination used by employers in Li, *Malays in Singapore: Culture, Economy and Ideology*, pp. 109–111.

91. Rahim, 'The Singapore dilemma', p. 203. Rahim supports her claim that Malay teachers accept the 'cultural deficit thesis' by citing her own interviews with Malay teachers, as well as those reported in *The Straits Times*, 23 June 1986, and in Li, *Malays in Singapore*, p. 176.

92. Rahim, 'The Singapore dilemma', p. 202.

93. Lee in Han, Fernandez, Tan, *Lee Kuan Yew: The Man and His Ideas*, p. 179.

94. *Ibid.*, p. 157.

95. *The New Paper*, 7 June 1989

· 7 ·

Beneath Ideology: The 'Essential' Lee Kuan Yew

Nobody doubts that if you take me on, I will put on the knuckle-dusters and catch you in a cul-de-sac. … Anybody who decides to take me on needs to put on the knuckle-dusters. If you think you can hurt me more than I can hurt you, try. There is no other way you can govern a Chinese society.

Lee Kuan Yew, speaking in 1994, quoted in Han Fook Kwang, Warren Fernandez, Sumiko Tan, *Lee Kuan Yew: The Man and His Ideas*, Singapore: Singapore Press Holdings and Times Editions, 1998, p. 126.

This book has devoted four chapters to exploring the origins and the nature of Lee Kuan Yew's ideology. The current chapter will look at Lee's career from a different perspective. It will argue that despite his outwardly Western upbringing and the obvious influence of Western ideas upon his thinking, Lee's approach to politics and society instinctively reflects the main tenets of a 'traditional Chinese' worldview. Chapters 2, 4 and 5 have already given enough background on Lee's childhood to show that despite his Anglo-centric schooldays, he was raised, in many respects, in a typical Chinese household. It is therefore not unreasonable to accept as a working hypothesis the premise that Lee absorbed many aspects of the traditional Chinese approach to social relations and hierarchies during his early childhood. Granting this assumption, this chapter sets out to show that in his approach to government, politics and society, Lee accepts many of the major premises of mainstream Chinese political culture as it has been practised for two millennia. Further, the chapter argues that whether or not Lee was deriving his ideas consciously from Chinese culture, these elements have always been part of his political thought, and can therefore be regarded as being part of the 'essential Lee'. Although this argument pivots on the early part of his career, when the 'Chinese' elements were most obscure, it is convenient to begin our study in the latest phase of his life, when he was parading his Chinese cultural heritage like a badge of honour.

211

Lee has finished his ideological journey as an architect of twentieth-century Confucianism. He has played a critical role in restoring the respectability of Confucianism in the Chinese world after it was viciously attacked during the May Fourth Era (1915 to the early 1920s)[1] and subsequently denounced and superseded with the establishment of the People's Republic of China in 1949. Tu Wei-Ming has identified three kinds of Confucianism: Confucianism as a system of personal ethics, as a mode of scholarship and as a political ideology.[2] Lee has attempted to resurrect 'modernised' versions of each of these elements, but the factor that is of primary concern to our study of the 'essential Lee' is Confucianism as a political ideology. Perhaps the most revealing aspects of the nature of Lee's Confucianism concerns the most basic of the questions with which Confucius concerned himself: what is the key to good government? There was no doubt in Confucius's mind that the critical factor in determining the quality of government was the quality of the ruler and his advisers. Put simply, government is of people, not of laws.[3] In Confucianism's humanistic ideal, the *junzi* [gentleman] is the key to good government. The *junzi* is a 'gentleman' in the sense of being a person of 'virtue, culture, talent, competence, and merit'.[4] He has attained *ren* [humanity, humaneness].[5] Confucius held up his culture and high-minded detachment from the world as an ideal, and so for Confucians the *junzi* is 'the highest attainment of Man'.[6] At many important levels, Lee Kuan Yew's approach to the personnel of government is unambiguously Confucian, and has been so since the beginning of his career. 'Let us face facts', he told the Legislative Assembly in 1957:

> If a people have lost faith completely in their democratic institutions, because they cannot find men of calibre to run them, however good that system, it perishes. Ultimately, it is the men who run the system who make it come to life.[7]

Lee's whole notion of an educated elite which is 'groomed to govern'[8] fits comfortably into the Confucian model of the mandarinate. Lee's 'search for talent', with its emphasis on finding people with 'strong characters, sound temperament, and high motivation to match their high intelligence'[9] confirms the impression that Lee shares the Confucian humanistic approach to government. Lee has projected a Confucian ideal of leaders who are morally upright, well-educated and cultured. Chua Beng Huat has identified Lee's projection of this ideal as one area of his Confucian revival that has enjoyed limited success:

> [The PAP leadership] may be said to have 'Confucianised' itself by prescribing for itself a code of ethics, that of the *junzi* or honourable individual. They have set themselves up as the model of a moral leader-

212

ship which governs in the interest of the people rather than through self-interest. ... This 'self-Confucianisation' does not mean that the PAP leadership will not behave like other politicians in their desire to win votes and stay in power. This desire is, however, rationalised in terms of the public interest which provides the warrant for their actions. Indeed, having claimed the moral high ground and regarding themselves as having fulfilled their mission creditably, they are often puzzled by the level of anti-PAP votes in general elections.[10]

As Chua suggests in this extract, the complementary aspect of the teaching of the *junzi* was the expectation that virtue in a ruler would be rewarded by unquestioning quasi-filial loyalty from subjects. 'The moral power of the gentleman is wind, the moral power of the common man is grass. Under the wind the grass must bend', wrote Confucius in a passage which became a favourite teaching of Chinese emperors.[11]

Many commentators regard the justification of authoritarianism as a prime motivation of Lee's enthusiasm for Confucianism, and it must be admitted that submission to authority featured prominently in Singapore's Confucian school textbooks of the 1980s.[12] It would be a mistake, however, to regard Lee's Confucian revival in such narrow terms. His emphasis on education, rational argument and exhortation also accord with the spirit of Confucianism, which has always placed great emphasis on education in general and moral education in particular. The Confucian emphasis on education, combined with the implied benevolence of patriarchal government, spilled over into a didactic approach to government. In the ideal Confucian world, wrote Pao Chao Hsieh

> the mandates of the emperor, instead of being issued in a commanding tone, reasoned with the people, and expected to win by reasoning rather than by exacting the people's obedience to laws; the written regulations were to be upheld because of their reasonableness rather than that they were backed by governmental authority.[13]

The resonance between this description of the ideal Confucian ruler and Lee's approach to public campaigns is very strong. Not only has education played a crucial part in Lee's own life; he has also regarded it as an important element of his political technique since the 1950s.[14] If the people of Singapore were in error, whether in their political views or in their social habits, then Lee set out to correct their opinions and improve their social habits by argument and exhortation, as well as by various means more coercive. Thus we witness not only Lee's extraordinary emphasis on education *per se*, but his use of stage-managed public debates and Maoist-style national campaigns to win over the populace on everything from merging with Malaya and speaking Mandarin,[15] to flushing public toilets and being courteous. Indeed, we saw in Chapter

4 that Lee consciously adopted the teacher–pupil relationship as his model of politics.[16]

Yet despite the clear elements of Confucian influence in Lee's approach to government, there is a considerable amount of scepticism about Lee's Confucian revival. Simon Leys in his Notes on the *Analects*, has made one such criticism:

> [According to Confucius,] rites [or civility] play in civilized society the role that is devolved to *laws* in a social environment where morality has broken down. In this respect, the inflation of legal codification and the multiplication of judicial activity are really a paradoxical measure of the brutalization and moral *lawlessness* of a society. (This paradox seems to have escaped a more activist school of modern Confucianism; the government of Singapore, in its naïve but somewhat misguided enthusiasm, recently enacted *laws* to enforce Confucian morality: if they feel neglected by their adult children, parents can now take their unfilial offspring to court!) Hence, the Confucian hostility toward the very concept of law: laws make people cunning, they foster amorality and cynicism, ruthlessness and a perverse spirit of strife and contention.[17]

The *junzi* is meant to bring his country peace and prosperity by the example of his virtue, not by the enforcement of laws. When Confucius said, 'Raise the straight and put them above the crooked, so that they may straighten the crooked',[18] he was not telling his disciple to enforce virtue by enacting laws: 'A gentleman brings out the good that is in people, he does not bring out the bad. A vulgar man does the opposite.[19] … If you steer straight, who would dare not go straight?'[20] Leys' criticism of Lee may, nevertheless, be a trifle unfair. First, it should be noted that although Confucius was a humanist who did not like to rely upon laws, at no time did he say that laws or legal proceedings should play no part in society. At one point he told his disciples: 'I could adjudicate lawsuits as well as anyone. But I would prefer to make lawsuits unnecessary'.[21] Confucius preferred to make lawsuits unnecessary, but he made no suggestion that laws themselves were redundant. Indeed, if people generally followed the law so that there were few lawsuits, then that was a sign of the high quality of the administration and the virtue of the administrators.[22] Unlike Leys, when Pao Chao Hsieh looked at the historical context in which Confucius taught, he identified the core of his political philosophy simply as a belief in 'the fallibility of political institutions' for which he tried to compensate by creating a new standard of virtue and competence among rulers and their ministers.[23] If Pao's assessment is given credence, then Lee Kuan Yew fits comfortably within the full Confucian tradition. Second, it should be acknowledged that even if Lee's record of government fails to meet Confucius's standards, it does accord broadly with

Confucianism as it has been applied by emperors ever since it was cynically proclaimed the Chinese state ideology by the Emperor Han Wudi in 136 BC. Han Wudi was not even a convinced Confucian. He was an autocrat who governed according to the principles of Legalism, but who decided that Confucianism could provide ideological reinforcement of his power.[24] Legalism became an officially despised but practically intrinsic part of Chinese dynastic governance and culture. Like Confucianism it has deep roots in Chinese tradition and became recognised as a distinct school of thought soon after Confucius's lifetime.[25] According to Frederick Mote, Legalism was not so much a philosophy as

> a system for manipulating human behaviour, for making people forgo their natural individual interests in the service of the state. Legalism had no speculative interest in the inapplicable, like cosmology and meta-physics, and it could abandon logic, since it was based on stronger forces than reason. Ethics was irrelevant, yet the Legalistic state was happy to see that people's lives could be normalized and made predictable by adherence to codes of behaviour, as long as these did not interfere with state interests or diminish the sovereign's range of action.[26]

The Han and successive dynasties retained the essence of Legalism, but justified their regimes by reference to a tamed 'imperial Confucianism', which emphasised a subject's duties to the ruler.[27] Yet even as it served to support dynastic rule, Confucianism retained the essence of its original humanism and eventually created among the people and the mandarinate an expectation that the Emperor and his ministers would be *junzi*, and would bring the country peace, stability and prosperity.[28] These expectations have served to ameliorate the harshest aspects of Chinese autocracy, and led dynastic rule to operate fairly humanely, despite the theoretically boundless power of the Emperor.[29] Whether by design or by instinct, Lee Kuan Yew has followed in the great dynastic tradition of marrying the theoretically incompatible, but practically, pragmatically and essentially linked movements of Confucian humanism and the Legalist approach to power. Legalist principles provided Lee with the basis of the practical art of statecraft, while Confucian ideology served the twin political purposes of justifying the rule of the elite, and imposing an ethical standard on the government.

Lee's masterful use of power – whether one labels it Legalist or not – is an essential element in his political praxis which calls for further consideration. Not only did his upbringing make him comfortable with hierarchies of power, but he has learnt how to use power prudently: to achieve a result without unnecessarily fanning flames of dissent or discontent. From the Japanese Occupation he learnt the role of raw power in government, even as he was repelled by the brutality of the regime.[30]

Even before he came to office – during the Malayan Emergency, which was surely another object lesson in the exercise of power – he had studied Mao's essays on power[31] and had developed a close working relationship with Special Branch's Richard Corridon, whereby they would exchange information and assessments of people.[32] After he came to power Lee retained Corridon's services and, under Corridon's tuition, took a deep and personal interest in the operations of Special Branch. At one of his press conferences in the aftermath of separation from Malaysia, Lee was able to give this account of a typical Special Branch operation:

> I'll give you an example of how Lim Chin Siong used to do it when we were in the government. He knows he's followed. He comes to a traffic stop in a taxi. Car stops. He gets off the taxi, pays him, hops across the road, gets into the bus. The chap in the taxi is left behind. So, chaps are chasing all around, you see, who did he meet and what for? And, for one chap, one key man, you may have as much as 20 people involved.[33]

Seven years later, in 1972, he explained to Gerald Stone of the ABC the need to use repressive security measures sparingly:

> The more indiscriminately you use [detention and security measures], the blunter the instrument becomes. I mean, people know that we do not just lock a man up, just because we disagree with him, or because he's a nuisance to us, because then you are going to breed a reaction in the people. They'd go against you, just like what's happened in Malagasy, where Syranana says, 'Tat, tat, tat, that's what I'll do to you students if you keep on protesting'. And within five days he's out, he's had to hand over power.[34]

Lee's expertise in the prudent use of security measures has, by now, been honed to the point where an unofficial, 'friendly' visit from Singapore's Internal Security Department (ISD) personnel is usually enough to deter potential dissidents without exposing the government to any backlash. Perhaps it is not a coincidence that Lee's preference for avoiding the formal use of security measures accords roughly with Confucian disdain for lawsuits.

The ISD is, however, merely the bluntest of Lee's control mechanisms. His full armoury of coercive tools includes the selective use of taxation investigations,[35] selective scrutiny of the work practices of troublemakers who also happen to be in government-related employment,[36] the ruthless pursuit of libel and other actions in the courts,[37] and at times an almost arbitrary use of the law.[38] By the 1980s, Lee had every arm of government and most arms of society at his disposal in the exercise of power. One of the strongest, most all-pervasive, yet subtlest of these weapons was the government's almost unfettered control of land usage. Singapore's small size was one of the great challenges facing the PAP as the government charted the island's future over the early decades, but it has also provided Lee's single greatest tool for creating social and economic vassalage. Control of housing and land featured regularly in Lee's social engineering campaigns. In his effort to promote Mandarin, he announced that dialect-speaking communities would be broken up as part of the housing programme and dispersed throughout the community.[39] Access to housing was also a tool in Lee's 1980s eugenics campaign.[40] Housing policy is now used routinely by the government to discourage social behaviour of which it does not approve (such as single motherhood) and to reward and facilitate socially desirable behaviour (such as living near one's aged parents in traditional Confucian style).[41]

The techniques that Lee used in the exercise of power have been considered in the light of Chinese tradition, but it is in his approach to the *nature* of power that Lee's worldview is most closely attuned to the mainstream of traditional Chinese political thought. The Confucian conception of power is bound up in its concept of legitimacy of government, and the nature of the quasi-familial relationship that traditionally existed between the ruler and the people. Confucius conceived of the relationship between the ruler and the ruled as being akin to the strongly authoritarian and hierarchical relationship which binds a father and his children in the traditional Chinese family. 'A man who respects his parents and his elders would hardly be inclined to defy his superiors', he said.[42] There were, however, significant differences between Confucius's perception of these two relationships. Whereas a son owed his father unequivocal obedience by virtue of the generational relationship between them, a subject's loyalty to his ruler could be questioned or even broken if the ruler was unworthy.[43]

There came to be a mystical aspect to the Confucian notion of legitimacy. Famine, flood, storm, earthquake, or any natural disasters were all considered to be signs that there was lack of harmony in society, which could only be due to the ruler's lack of virtue[44] – though a more commonplace basis of disaffection was a failure to deliver peace and prosperity. In Confucius's mind, the proper way for an ordinary subject to disengage himself from an unworthy ruler was to emigrate.[45] A scholar, on the other hand, was obliged to withdraw from public life rather than continue to serve an unworthy ruler who refused to heed his advice.[46] A ruler was deemed to be worthy of loyalty if he was virtuous and the kingdom enjoyed peace and prosperity.[47] Although the emphasis on stability and prosperity is reminiscent of Lee Kuan Yew's approach to political justification, it is, perhaps, more significant to note the passivity of the people in this compact. Although the ruler had obligations towards his subjects, and, in a limited but very real sense, required their consent to rule, there was no provision for people other than official advisers to make popular desires, wishes or needs known to the ruler. If ordinary people were unhappy they had two choices: they could leave or they could stay. Several generations later, Mencius took Confucius's thinking considerably further. Even more so than Confucius, Mencius emphasised the duties of the ruler towards his subjects, saying, 'the people first, territory next, the king last'.[48] In Mencius's world, the people's happiness and economic welfare were the yardsticks by which the virtue (and therefore the legitimacy) of the ruler was measured.[49] Mencius's signs of a well-governed state were, according to Pao Chao Hsieh, 'lack of complaints, general economic sufficiency, ready and unconditional obedience to laws, and willingness of the able and the wise to serve the state',[50] as well as an absence of natural disasters. Once again, the passivity of the populace is noteworthy. For while Mencius was emphasising the duties of the ruler towards his subjects, he took the compliance of the people for granted unless they had powerful reasons to complain or defy the authorities. Mencius introduced a cosmic dimension in his idea of the 'Mandate of Heaven' to explain why the people should give passive consent to be governed by those in power. According to Mencius, rulers needed heavenly consent to govern legitimately, and heaven gave its blessing only to rulers who were both virtuous and competent, and presided over a prosperous, peaceful society.[51] The notion of the Mandate of Heaven took deep root in Chinese thinking, which has lasted through to the twentieth century. As Pao wrote:

> Even in the days of the Republican regime we still find in many state papers, the mystical term 'heaven' constantly employed instead of the plain and simple word 'public opinion'. No doubt, the traditional and classical value of that still mystical word has a firm grip upon the 'subtle' minds of 400,000,000 Orientals.[52]

The Mandate of Heaven was not only a basis for measuring the legitimacy of a government, but it also provided the theoretical justification for overthrowing an unvirtuous ruler – a possibility that Confucius did not consider. Thus Mencius added violent revolution to Confucius's list of possible responses to an unworthy ruler. He judged that if conditions for the people were so bad that they were determined to revolt, and the condition of the state was so poor that the government was unable to respond adequately, then the ruler had obviously lost the Mandate of Heaven and deserved to be overthrown.[53] Although the right of rebellion subsequently became an intrinsic part of Chinese political thought, it was always regarded as a last resort. The risks to the rebel and the slim chances of success meant that few were keen to invoke this particular right.[54] Yet short of actual rebellion, there was little opportunity for the people to make known their complaints or express their dissent. As we have already seen, the people's role in the Confucian world was intrinsically passive. The obverse to popular passivity in Confucian politics was that rulers had to ensure that the people were looked after and governed well.

The similarities between the passivity implied in the notion of the Mandate of Heaven and that demanded of Singaporeans by Lee Kuan Yew since 1965 are striking. Lee's constant demands for 'social discipline', and the quashing of public politics in the development of the 'administrative state' throughout the 1960s and 1970s were two obvious manifestations of the demand for passivity from the electorate.[55] His insistence that no organisation can comment on politics unless it is a registered political society[56] is also based on an assumption that the electorate should play a fundamentally passive role. Lee's obsessive concerns over emigration rates among the elite,[57] and the leakage of any government support to opposition candidates[58] accord perfectly with this Confucian perspective of the role of the populace. His insistence on co-opting the cream of the educated elite into the machinery of government and thus ensuring the homogeneity of the elite[59] is a near-perfect reflection of Confucian precepts of the mandarinate's endorsement of the worthy ruler. Lee's conception of democracy has always reflected the expectation that all political initiatives stemmed from the government, which should try, in turn, to judge and respond to the wishes of the passive electorate.[60] As early as the 1960s he defined democracy in these terms:

> that there is some measure of popular will, of popular support; that, from time to time, as accurately as is possible with trying to find out what human beings in a large group want or feel or think, one tries to act in accordance with the wishes of the majority.[61]

During the same period, he said:

> I have enumerated in several of my talks what I consider to be the three basic essentials for successful transformation of any society. First, a determined leadership, an effective, determined leadership; two, an administration which is efficient; and three, social discipline.[62]

'Social discipline' here should obviously be read as willing acquiescence on the part of Singaporeans to the wishes of the government. Clearly, Lee's precepts for good government owe very little to democratic traditions, but they sit squarely in the Confucian/Legalist tradition.

Although many observers, including this writer, may be tempted to question the depth of Lee's personal commitment to a revived Confucianism, it is almost meaningless to ask to what extent it is genuine. Confucianism is not a religious faith. It is a set of ideas and principles designed to foster humane, stable and effective government. The distinction between one who sees Confucianism as a high ideal and one who sees it as a tool in statecraft is slight, since for both it is ultimately a means to an end. Scepticism, however, can be directed much more reasonably towards Lee's 'Asian values' campaign, which became a facade for the sinicisation of Singaporean society and politics. The 'Asian values' campaign was launched officially in 1977 at a conference on 'Asian values and modernization'.[63] 'Asian values' has never been easy to define. As S. Rajaratnam said at the outset of the Asian values campaign in 1977:

> I have very serious doubts as to whether such a thing as 'Asian values' really exists – or for that matter 'Asian' anything – Asian unity, Asian socialism, Asian way of life and so on. It may exist as an image but it has no reality. If it has any meaning at all it is merely a convenient way of describing the heterogeneous, conflicting and complex network of beliefs, prejudices and values developed in the countries which for geographical purposes have been grouped as being in Asia. Only as a geographical expression does the term 'Asia' have any reality.[64]

The 'Asian values' conference marked a false start for the campaign. Apart from Rajaratnam's unhelpful contribution, the only Asian values Ho Wing Men identified were those that held back the process of modernisation,[65] while Peter Chen found such diversity among Asian cultures that he announced that he was limiting his discussion to the values of 'East Asian culture' and intended to ignore the rest.[66] It should come as no surprise that Lee, too, took Sinic culture as the prime reference point of his approach to Asian values, since he regarded these instinctively as being at the core of his social vision and he had long regarded 'Chinese values' as being the key to Singapore's success.[67] The Chinese character of Lee's 'Asian values' shone forth in the 'core values' identified by the government in 1989: 'placing society above self, upholding the family as the basic building block of society, resolving major issues through consensus instead of contention, and stressing religious tolerance and harmony'.[68] Perhaps even more significant than the heavily Confucianist character of these core values were the alternative influences that were missing. Where were the values derived from India's ancient democratic traditions, or her Buddhist and Hindu-inspired tradition of non-violence, and acceptance of one's lot in life? Where was the Malay emphasis on the paramount importance of bonds of loyalty based upon friendships? These, and a myriad of other South and Southeast Asian values, are completely absent from the government's proclamation, and from Lee's speeches.[69] This absence is neither surprising nor malicious, since we know from Chapter 6 that Lee considered South and Southeast Asian cultures to be 'soft' and therefore inherently inferior to the 'hard' East Asian cultures. These absences are nevertheless real and perhaps hold the key to the government's diffidence about making any practical use of Singapore's 'Asian', or 'Shared' values even after Parliament adopted them formally in 1991.[70]

There can only be tentative answers to the question of Lee's 'Chineseness', however he might wish to define it. Yet there can be little doubt that there are real and clearly identifiable elements of traditional mainstream Chinese political and social thought at the heart of Lee's view of society and government. Confucianism, whether latent or explicit, is easily discernible in his didactic approach to politics, his assumption of the passivity of the electorate, his emphasis on building an effective and ethical governing elite, and his notions of legitimacy and 'good government'. His clever and pragmatic approach to the exercise of power seems to be very much in the spirit of the 'Great Tradition' of Chinese dynastic politics. Lee's identification with Chinese culture has, of course, been very obvious since the early 1980s when he publicly and perhaps cynically became the champion of a revived Confucianism. Yet his almost unconscious adoption of a Confucian/Legalist approach to politics as early as the 1950s – when his interest in Chinese political culture was only just being sparked – suggests that there is more to his 'conversion' than mere political expediency. He appears to have approached politics and society from Confucian/Legalist premises even before he discovered the glories of Chinese culture. When he began studying the great Chinese traditions as part of his language and political studies in the 1950s,[71] he discovered a new and wondrous world with which he was already familiar and in which he felt completely at home. It was a world where his every instinct and belief was confirmed and placed in the context of a tradition that stretched back two millennia.

This chapter has not attempted to establish a causal connection between Lee's self-proclaimed 'Chineseness' and his ideology. Its main recourse has been to inference, supported by evidence that is, for the most part, circumstantial. It is, nevertheless, a reasonable inference to believe that at a deep level of his psyche, Harry Kuan Yew Lee is and always has been 'Chinese': that at a very early age he internalised the basic precepts of Chinese culture and its view of the world. Wu Teh Yao tells the story of two figures from the May Fourth Movement who devoted themselves to denouncing Confucianism, but whose lives nevertheless were governed unconsciously by Confucian precepts.[72] In a similar vein Harry Lee as a schoolboy and a young adult consciously rejected Chinese culture and set out to become, in his grandfather's words, the 'equal of any Englishman'.[73] Yet deep within his worldview lay a Chinese cultural element which, when he entered politics, led him instinctively to act upon traditional Chinese precepts, perhaps without even realising that he was doing so.

NOTES

1.   James E. Sheridan, *China in Disintegration: The Republican Era in Chinese History 1912–1949*, New York: The Free Press; London: Collier Macmillan, 1975, pp. 107–122.

2.   Tu Wei-Ming, *Confucian Ethics Today: The Singapore Challenge*, Singapore: Curriculum Development Centre of Singapore and Federal Publications, 1984, p. 204.

3.   Frederick W. Mote, *Intellectual Foundations of China*, New York: Alfred A. Knopf, 1971, p. 49.

4.   Simon Leys, *The Analects of Confucius*, New York; London: W.W. Norton and Company, 1997, Notes, p. 105.

5.   *Ibid.*, Notes, pp. 108, 130–131.

6.   Wu Teh Yao, *The Confucian Way*, Singapore: The Institute of East Asian Philosophies, 1987, pp. 18–19.

7.   Singapore Legislative Assembly, *Debates: Official Report*, 27 April 1957, column 1757.

8.   *Ibid.*, 5 December 1956, column 1088.

9.   Lee Kuan Yew, 'The search for talent', in S. Jayakumar (ed.), *Our Heritage and Beyond: A Collection of Essays on Singapore, Its Past, Present and Future*, Singapore: Singapore National Trades Union Congress, 1982, p. 21.

10.   Chua Beng Huat, *Communitarian Ideology and Democracy in Singapore*, London and New York: Routledge, 1995, pp. 193–194.

11.   Leys, *The Analects of Confucius* (12.19), p. 58, and notes, pp. 179–180.

12.   See Joseph B. Tamney, *The Struggle over Singapore's Soul: Western Modernization and Asian Culture*, Berlin and New York: Walter de Gruyter, 1996, pp. 37–40, 46–47, 65.

13.   Pao Chao Hsieh, *The Government of China (1644–1911)*, New York: Octagon Books, 1966, p. 3.

14.   See, for instance, Lee's address to the Malayan Forum in 1950 in Han Fook Kwang, Warren Fernandez and Sumiko Tan, *Lee Kuan Yew: The Man and His Ideas*, Singapore: Times Editions and Singapore Press Holdings, 1998, pp. 256–262.

15.   See Chapter 5.

16.   Lee Kuan Yew, *New Bearings in Our Education System*, Singapore: Ministry of Culture, [n.d., c.1966–67], p. 7.

17.   Leys, *The Analects of Confucius*, notes, pp. 175–176. The italics are in the original.

18. *Ibid.* (12.22), p. 59.

19. *Ibid.* (12.16), p. 58.

20. *Ibid.* (12.17), p. 58.

21. *Ibid.* (12.13), p. 57.

22. *Ibid*, notes, p. 179.

23. Pao Chao Hsieh, *The Government of China (1644–1911)*, pp. 2–3.

24. Zhengyuan Fu, *Autocratic Tradition and Chinese Politics*, Cambridge; New York; Melbourne: Cambridge University Press, 1993, pp. 50–51.

25. Mote, *Intellectual Foundations of China*, pp. 116–117, 134. Also see H.G. Creel, *Chinese Thought from Confucius to Mao Zedong*, Chicago: The University of Chicago Press, 1953, pp. 135–158.

26. Mote, *Intellectual Foundations of China*, p. 122. The practice of Legalism as a method of government is described in Edwin O. Reischauer and John K. Fairbank, *East Asia: The Great Tradition*, London: George Allen & Unwin, 1960, pp. 82–90.

27. Mote, *Intellectual Foundations of China*, p. 115.

28. Charles O. Hucker, *The Traditional Chinese State in Ming Times (1368–1644)*, Tucson: The University of Arizona Press, 1961, pp. 60–73.

29. Pao Chao Hsieh, *The Government of China (1644–1911)*, p. 3.

30. Lee Kuan Yew, *The Singapore Story: Memoirs of Lee Kuan Yew*, Singapore; New York; London; Toronto; Sydney; Mexico City: Prentice Hall, 1998, pp. 74, 53–58.

31. *Legislative Assembly*, 6 November 1956, columns 506, 581–583, and 27 April 1957, column 1757.

32. Lee Kuan Yew, *The Singapore Story*, pp. 157–159, 195, 290.

33. Lee at a press conference at Broadcasting House, 9 August 1965 in Lee Kuan Yew, *Prime Minister's Speeches, Press Conferences, Interviews, Statements, etc.*, Singapore: Prime Minister's Office, 1959–90.

34. *New Nation*, 7 July 1972.

35. This technique was used against Tang Liang Hong in 1997. See *The Straits Times Weekly Edition*, 24 May 1997.

36. This technique was used against Chee Soon Juan in 1992 when he was dismissed from his lecturing position at the National University of Singapore. See Chua Beng Huat, 'Beyond formal strictures: democratisation in Singapore', *Asian Studies Review*, vol. 17, no. 1, July 1993, p. 105, note 17, and *The Straits Times Weekly Edition*, 10 May 1997.

37. See Chapter 2 for details of the treatment of J.B. Jeyaretnam in the courts during the 1970s, 1980s and 1990s.

38. For a commentary upon the Singapore government's use of law, see Chapter 8.

39. Lee Kuan Yew, *Bilingualism in Our Society*, Singapore: Ministry of Culture, 1978, pp. 12, 27.

40. See Chapter 4.

41. Goh Chok Tong's address to the 1994 National Day Rally, in Goh Chok Tong, 'Social values, Singapore style', *Current History*, December 1994, p. 421.

42. Leys, *Analects of Confucius*, (1.2), p. 3.

43. Pao Chao Hsieh, *The Government of China (1644–1911)*, pp. 2–3.

44. *Ibid.*, p. 4.

45. Leys, *Analects of Confucius*, notes, pp. 182–183.

46. *Ibid.* (15.7), p. 75; notes, p. 193.

47. Fu, *Autocratic Tradition and Chinese Politics*, pp. 31–32.

48. Pao Chao Hsieh, *The Government of China (1644–1911)*, p. 6.

49. *Ibid.*

50. *Ibid.*

51. *Ibid.*, pp. 8–9.

52. *Ibid.*, p. 9.

53. Mote, *Intellectual Foundations of China*, p. 58.

54. Pao Chao Hsieh, *The Government of China (1644–1911)*, p. 25.

55. See Chapter 4.

56. Chua Beng Huat, *Communitarian Ideology and Democracy in Singapore*, p. 196. Also see Douglas Sikorski, 'Effective government in Singapore: perspective of a concerned American', *Asian Survey*, vol. 36, no. 8, 1996, pp. 825–829.

57. See, for instance, Lee's address at the Institute of Engineers' Dinner, 20 April 1965, in Lee, *Prime Minister's Speeches, etc.*; Lee's address at the International Alumni Dinner, *Sunday Times*, 7 September 1969; and Lee's National Day Rally Speech, *The Straits Times*, 21 August 1989.

58. See, for instance, Lee's discussion with PAP MPs, 17 November 1981, *Petir*, December 1981, pp. 4–15; Lee's address to PAP helpers in Anson by-election, 31 October 1981, *Petir*, December 1981, pp. 16–19; and report in *The Straits Times*, 24 December 1984. Also see Chapter 2 for a fuller treatment of Lee's response to the emergence of a small opposition in the 1980s.

59. See, for instance, Lee's address to the PAP Ordinary Party Conference, *Petir*, November 1984, p. 2; and *The Straits Times*, 29 October 1982. See Chapter 4 for a comprehensive treatment of Lee's attitude towards the homogeneity of the elite and its relationship with the government.

60. It is of passing interest to note that Lee's introduction of revitalised feedback mechanisms in the 1980s fits comfortably in the Confucian tradition, at least as it has been practised for long periods of dynastic history. The Sung and Ming dynasties, for instance, each had their own 'feedback mechanisms' for transmitting complaints about government policy and bureaucratic practice to the central government. See Reischauer and Fairbank, *East Asia: The Great Tradition*, pp. 200–201, 297–298; and Hucker, *The Traditional Chinese State in Ming Times*, pp. 50–51.

61. Alex Josey, *Lee Kuan Yew: The Crucial Years*, Singapore; Kuala Lumpur: Times Books International, 1980, p. 68.

62. Lee's speech at the Political Study Centre, 14 June 1962 in Lee, *Prime Minister's Speeches, etc.*

63. Seah Chee Meow (ed.), *Asian Values and Modernization*, Singapore: Singapore University Press, 1977, pp. vii–viii.

64. S. Rajaratnam, 'Asian values and modernization', in *ibid.*, p. 95.

65. Ho Wing Meng, 'Asian values and modernization', in *ibid.*, pp. 1–20.

66. Peter S.J. Chen, 'Asian values and modernization: a sociological perspective', in *ibid.*, p. 29.

67. See Lee at the Kampong Sungei Tengah Community Centre, 8th Anniversary Celebrations, 22 May 1971, in Lee, *Prime Minister's Speeches, etc.*; and Lee Kuan Yew's interview with Cai Xi Mei of Xinhua News Agency, 25 August 1992, in Lee, Lee Kuan Yew, *Senior Minister's Speeches, Press Conferences, Interviews, Statements, etc.*, Singapore: Prime Minister's Office, 1991–95. Lee reported in *Business Times*, 6 October 1993; and Lee in Greg Sheridan, *Tigers: Leaders of the New Asia-Pacific*, Sydney: Allen & Unwin, 1997, p. 68.

68. The President's speech to Parliament, January 1989, cited in Government of Singapore, *Shared Values: White Paper 1991*, Singapore: Singapore National Printers, 1991, p. 1. Under Singapore's variation of the Westminster system, the President was speaking on behalf of the government.

69. David Martin Jones has written a useful overview of the various social and political traditions which operate in the Malay world, including the Confucian-Legalist, Hindu-Buddhist and enculturated Islamic traditions. See David Martin Jones, 'Democracy and identity: the paradoxical character of political development', in Daniel A. Bell, David Brown, Kanishka Jayasuriya and David Martin Jones, *Towards Illiberal Democracy in Pacific Asia*, London: St Martin's Press, 1995, pp. 44–56.

70. Chua Beng Huat, *Communitarian Ideology and Democracy in Singapore*, pp. 32–33. It should be noted that the 'Shared Values' White Paper went to great lengths to explain that it was not just Confucian in inspiration. The force of the disclaimer was undermined, however, by the fact that it took up nearly 10 per cent of the entire document. See Government of Singapore, *Shared Values: White Paper 1991*, pp. 7–8.

71. See Chapter 5.

72. Wu Teh Yao, *The Confucian Way*, p. 66, note 1.

73. Lee in *Legislative Assembly*, 7 March 1956, column 1919.

· 8 ·

Fear and Fortune: Singapore under the Later Lee

If [Singapore] breaks up, it will never come back. It's man-made, it's very contrived to fit the needs of the modern world and it has to be amended all the time as the needs change. The moment it no longer fulfils that role, it will begin to decline. I would put it at one chance in five.

Lee Kuan Yew, 3 August 1995 in Lee Kuan Yew, *Senior Minister's Speeches, Press Conferences, Interviews, Statements, etc.*, Singapore: Prime Minister's Office, 1991–95.

There is a permanent sense of crisis [in Singapore]. … Change, construction, urgency are the keywords. But why? What is the ultimate purpose of all this activity…? Nobody quite knows, for the system seems to require that today's solution is tomorrow's problem.

John Clammer, *Singapore: Ideology, Society and Culture*, Singapore: Chopmen Publishers, 1985, p. 27

Lee Kuan Yew is a fascinating subject for study in his own right, but most of the interest in the man stems from his role as the architect of modern Singapore. Throughout this book, there has always been the implicit question: 'How have Lee's ideas influenced the development of Singaporean politics and society?' In this chapter we shall take our analysis a step further and draw upon the various strands of Lee's syncretic ideas to illuminate his legacy, and ask explicitly what sort of Singapore Lee has created.

Lee's system of government, like the man himself, is not easy to label. The Singapore of the 1980s and 1990s has been described variously as 'semidemocracy',[1] 'restricted Asian Democracy',[2] 'non-liberal communit-arian democracy',[3] 'soft authoritarian',[4] 'technocratic authoritarian',[5] and 'inclusionary corporatist'.[6] Of all of these attempts at categorisation, Eric Paul's 'technocratic authoritarian' label is probably the most informative at a glance, but it fails to convey the genuine, though limited elements of social and political inclusion which are implied in the 'semidemocracy', 'Asian democracy', and 'communitarian democracy' descriptions. On the other hand, labels that treat the Singapore system as a variant of democracy disregard the intrinsically authoritarian nature of Lee's elitist system.[7] David Brown's term, 'inclusionary corporatist state' is a much more accurate description of Singaporean society, since it captures the elements of both authoritarianism and participation. At the risk of oversimplifying Brown's argument, 'inclusionary corporatism' might be described as a system of social and political organisation which is at once authoritarian and inclusionary, and which organises society through vertically integrated interest groups led by officially recognised elites. Under this definition, the Singapore regime is characterised as a benign version of authoritarianism, as befits a system based on elitism, rather than as a variant of democracy. The regime's authoritarianism is tempered, not so much by a smattering of democratic forms which are regarded by Lee Kuan Yew as an inconvenient legacy of Singapore's colonial history,[8] as by the inclusionary aspects of Lee's post-1970s elitism. William Case made a centrally important point in his article on 'semidemocracy':

> Because elites are elites only in the context of constituents – their status depends on wider acknowledgement – limits exist even on their conceptual separability. In short, despite some autonomy and distinctness, elites are grounded finally in what are variously conceptualized as mass attitudes, social bases, and structural forces.[9]

Though Case was writing about 'semidemocratic' elites in general, Lee's conception of elitism has taken the intrinsic relationship between the elite and its constituency – or, to use Lee's terminology, between the apex and the lower levels of the social pyramid[10] – and made it the basis of an inclusionary approach to authoritarian government. The level of inclusion is admittedly limited, and the role of most of the population is deemed to be basically passive in the Confucian/Legalist tradition, but the contribution, participation and support of all levels of society is sought, primarily through their own elites, using vehicles such as trade unions,[11] Residents' Committees, and an extraordinary number of ethnically based interest associations.[12] Both Brown and Case emphasise the vertical integration of fractions of society through their respective elites, with Brown emphasising the degree of control that this gives the government,[13] and Case focusing on the role that the 'subordinate elites' play in representing their members' interests to the government.[14] This 'corporatist' structure facilitates a two-way traffic of initiatives and the expression of grievances between the ruling elite and the grassroots, as well as circumventing the creation of broadly based and truly independent interest groups at either the grassroots or the elite level. This, in essence, is what Brown means by 'inclusionary corporatism'.

Yet if there is so much 'inclusion' in Singapore, it raises the question of who or what is excluded. What are the parameters of acceptable dissent or even self-expression, and what are the consequences of straying beyond the pale? The answers to these questions have varied over the years, and they have never been entirely clear. It appears to be an integral part of the Singapore system that beyond the near-sacrosanct realm of private conversation, no one knows exactly where the limits of acceptable activities and dissent lie because the line is drawn only retrospectively. The Law Society seems to have had no idea that it was crossing a line when it criticised the Newspapers and Printing Presses Act in 1986, but the government responded by passing legislation to reconstruct the organisation totally, and it appears to have singled out the Society's President, Francis Seow, for individual attention.[15] Left-wing Catholic activists were probably aware that they were stretching the limits of dissent in 1987 when they agitated over social justice issues, but their spectacular detention without trial under the Internal Security Act and the government's extraordinary accusations of a Marxist conspiracy caught everyone by surprise.[16] Chee Soon Juan almost certainly did not realise that he was crossing the line when he stood for Parliament on an opposition ticket in 1992, and it has never been stated clearly why he was singled out for victimisation. Yet victimised he was and he has lost his house, and both his academic and political careers as a result of the inexorable escalation of civil and other actions against him.[17] And considering the government's new openness towards the celebration of communal cultures, Tang Liang Hong could not have realised the storm he was unleashing when he decided to campaign in the 1996/97 general elections on a platform promoting Chinese culture, but he is now a de facto exile from his native country.[18] The problem for those operating under such vague parameters was expressed by Derek Davies of the *Far Eastern Economic Review* when reporting the de facto expulsion of the magazine's Singapore bureau chief in 1987: 'We have done our best to play the game. It would be nice to know the rules'.[19]

The above are several of many examples of people overstepping the line in ignorance, but there are rarer examples of the inverse. For instance, the leaders of the Association of Muslim Professionals (AMP) and the Association of Women for Action and Research (AWARE) courted danger in the 1980s and 1990s only to find that their activities were given de facto official endorsement: the AMP was given financial and institutional support, and an early President of AWARE was later invited to join Parliament as a Nominated MP.[20]

The dilemma of the undrawn line is the direct result of Lee's 'Confucian' approach to power, as described in the previous chapter. In Singapore, power resides in people rather than in institutions or the law, and the main restraint on the exercise of that power is the ideological restrictions of the regime. There are certainly no effective constitutional, institutional or judicial constraints. The Parliament is unicameral and is totally subservient to the Executive. Opposition parties and other interest, religious and professional groups are not allowed to pose a serious challenge to the government, and most have been co-opted into Singapore's corporatist state. The press is compliant, and the trade unions are controlled by and dependent upon the PAP. Even the law is a tool in the exercise of power. Kanishka Jayasuriya made this point in 1996:

> Law [in Singapore] is not understood as a restraint on bureaucratic and state power but as a means of extending and consolidating this power. Singapore provides the clearest example of the state consciously deploying legal techniques for state-building objectives. ... The key point here is that legalism, in the European context, provided the ideological basis for the autonomy of the legal profession from intrusive state power. On the other hand, in Singapore, legalism has been employed to shackle the independence of the legal profession. ...
>
> A further paradox of this legalism is that while liberal accounts of the 'rule of law' emphasize the constitutional foundations of law, in Singapore, legalism does not rely on such a constitutional foundation. In this sense, Singapore could be said to have law without constitutionalism. The fundamental norms that [are] essential to the functioning of legal systems ... are absent in Singapore. This can be explained by the fact that ultimately, the operation of law depends on its usefulness – or otherwise – to the PAP and its dominant leader, Lee Kuan Yew.[21]

The uncertainty emanating from the arbitrary use of power has created an atmosphere of circumspection in Singapore, which permeates the whole of society. Everyone with a public opinion on anything remotely connected with politics engages in self-censorship: opposition figures, Nominated MPs, government ministers, PAP parliamentarians, journalists, academics, post-graduate researchers, professionals and student, religious, ethnic and trade union leaders. Most people avoid trouble successfully by refraining from expressing opinions in public, but the widespread pervasion of the culture of insecurity has ensured that ordinary Singaporeans have earned a reputation for risk-aversion, circumspection and indecision. Foreign business people, professionals and even tradesmen regularly complain in private that the locals are almost universally unwilling to take the responsibility of making an important decision. Lee Tsao Yuan and Linda Low have identified this characteristic as the *kia su,* or 'afraid to lose' attitude:[22]

> It is a mentality where failure is perceived to be a disgrace and to bring shame to the individual and to the family. It therefore follows that failure is to be avoided at all costs. As a result, there is a strong streak of risk aversity in the society. ...
>
> How did this *kia su* attitude become embedded in the Singapore culture? We suspect that it is a by-product of the very strong achievement-oriented society that Singapore has become. In the drive for growth and economic success, the system has become the epitome of meritocracy. There is no room for failure in such a meritocratic and elitist state.[23]

Lee and Low believe that this 'intolerance of failure has filtered down to every fibre of local society' and that the very culture of Singapore breeds 'risk aversity and cautiousness from the very start',[24] an attitude which is, ironically, the exact opposite of that which Lee set out to build.

The general climate is one of low-level fear, but it would be unfair to say simply that the people fear their government. Rather, every aspect of life seems to be permeated with insecurities. The 1964 racial riots are still within living memory, as is Sukarno's *Konfrontasi* and the trauma of separation from Malaysia. Thanks largely to Lee's Jeremiah-like pessimism, Singaporeans have never been allowed to take either economic prosperity or regional stability for granted. The government cannot be blamed for all the crises that have fostered Singapore's climate of fear, but it does seem to have encouraged them and treated them cynically as nation-building and political assets. A central component of Singapore's culture of fear is what Donald Emmerson has called the 'third person' or 'gullible-other' effect.[25] By this Emmerson referred to the tendency of Singaporeans to be confident in their own stability and prudence, but to 'exaggerate the susceptibility of others to excitement'.[26] He posed the question:

> Why did the government of Singapore go to such lengths to punish the *International Herald Tribune* for carrying articles suggesting that the city-state's judiciary might be 'compliant' and its politics 'dynastic' if not to prevent the putatively credulous populace from being swayed by negative messages in the mass media?[27]

Emmerson suggested that the 'gullible-other' effect had conditioned people's responses to the government's communitarian demands. He told an anecdote that is barely admissible as evidence, and yet it rings so true that it is worth reporting, despite its length:

> In the middle of a long night some years ago I found myself in Singapore, tired after a trans-Pacific flight, riding a taxi down the multilane straightaway from Changi Airport into town. The highway at that hour was nearly empty and the police were nowhere in sight. Whenever the driver exceeded the speed limit, a mellifluous chime sounded from underneath his dashboard, ceasing only when he slowed down. The chime was then and still is required on all cabs in Singapore. As the chime went on and off, I asked my driver jokingly whether, at traffic-free times like this, he had ever thought of disconnecting it. He was not amused. If he unhooked his chime, he told me, other cabs would follow suit. Soon everyone would speed. Accidents would break out all over the city, paralyzing traffic. He pictured Singapore sinking into lawless anarchy. ...
>
> Was it realistic of him to think that his own negative behaviour – disabling the speed governor under his dashboard – would be contagious enough to cause mayhem and gridlock? Surely not. But if enough of the other cab drivers on the roads also overestimate the susceptibility of their colleagues, a shared misperception could have acquired its own behavioural truth, as drivers acted on their individually false but collectively effective assumptions.[28]

The condition described by Emmerson accords neatly with Francis Fukuyama's concept of the 'low-trust' society, which was examined briefly in Chapter 4.[29] According to the logic of the Fukuyama and Emmerson theses, strong, high-trust societies like that of white, middle-class America can afford to cherish and maximise personal autonomy. A low-trust society, on the other hand, needs a strong, interventionist government in order to create prosperity, because the low levels of 'social capital' make it difficult to find more natural bases of trust and co-operation.

If we accept the low-trust character of Singaporean society as fact, we may ask how it is related to the country's climate of insecurity and circumspection and to what extent the government has contributed to this state of affairs. The origins of Singapore's low-trust society and its national culture of insecurity appear to have been substantially beyond the influence of Lee or his government. If Fukuyama is correct, then the strongly familial character of Chinese culture is intrinsically low-trust.[30] Further, it must be acknowledged that the British originated the ethnic and linguistic compartmentalisation and stereotyping of Singaporeans, which is surely the basis of communal mistrust.[31] There is also good reason to suppose that Singaporeans' perception of their economic insecurity is basically accurate. Peter Katzenstein has, in fact, argued that small, economically open countries are faced with the 'inescapable fact' of vulnerability to the international economy.[32] Katzenstein, in his case study of Austria and Switzerland, extended this thesis to argue that this fear of economic vulnerability, combined with a traumatic recent history, is responsible for both countries' highly co-operative national cultures, each of which demands the sacrifice of sectional interests to the national good.[33] Katzenstein's line of reasoning is suggestive, but it is a moot point whether it was primarily the countries' small size, their vulnerability, or their traumatic past which had the greatest impact on their development. The existence of similarly co-operative – even communitarian – national cultures in large, strong countries such as Germany and Japan suggests that size may be less important than cultural and historical factors. Fukuyama, for one, argues that culture is the prime determining factor. This book is not the place to resolve such questions, but these reflections give a reasonable indication of the sorts of natural pressures that foster low-trust, insecure, communitarian societies: culture, fear of national economic vulnerability, and a traumatic recent history – to which we might also add ethnic mistrust.

In Singapore's case, however, one of these factors – culture – is not unquestionably natural. Lee Kuan Yew has set out to build and rebuild Singapore's culture, and although his cultural ideals and models have varied over the decades, he has consistently emphasised Singapore's vulnerability. The economic element of this vulnerability may be taken at face value, but many others seem to have been exaggerations, if not concoctions. In 1966, for instance, Lee likened Singapore's security position to that of Israel:

> There are countries in the world which because of the tight nature of their social organisation, are able to withstand much larger neighbours. ... There are only 2.7 million Jews in Israel, surrounded by 200 million Arabs, who are divided into many Arab states, but they are all bent on destroying Israel.
>
> It is regrettable for a country to be found in such a position. But this is the position in which we have found ourselves. ... If we have not [begun preparing ourselves like Israel], at the end of ten years Singapore will find itself a dependency of some other country.[34]

Yet in 1972, Defence Minister Goh Keng Swee dismissed Lee's image of Singapore as 'an Israel in a Malay-Muslim sea' as 'a far-fetched analogy'.[35] Granted what we know of Lee's pessimism, his racial stereotyping, and the fact that his friend and confidante, Alex Josey, had been feeding him anti-Muslim talk of 'Mad Mullahs',[36] Lee's fears were probably genuine, but they bore little re-semblance to reality until his government invited Israel to supply military advisers to assist with the creation of the Singapore Armed Forces (SAF).[37] Thus Lee created a reality based upon his own fears.

The fear of neighbours did not, however, begin at Singapore's borders. Not only did (and does) Singapore have an indigenous Malay-Muslim population whom Lee and his government regarded with suspicion and patronising concern,[38] but the Chinese-educated Chinese could not be trusted because of their chauvinistic and communist tendencies while the English-educated Chinese were unduly influenced by the 'counter-culture' movement in the West.[39] It is difficult to know how seriously Lee's cultural fears were taken by the community at large, but even if there was a degree of scepticism, the electorate responded enthusiastically to Lee's leadership in order to achieve social stability and economic and national survival. The goal of Lee's racial and cultural policies was not, however, to achieve race blindness, nor even to foster some natural dissipation of communal mistrust. He aimed to reinforce communal identity, while using racial quotas in housing estates, along with other artificial mechanisms to force ethnic communities to interact with studied and elaborate tolerance. So it was that even as Rajaratnam was expressing concern that he was witnessing a dangerous new form of Chinese self-assertion in the late 1980s,[40] Malays, Indians and Eurasians were being given official and financial encouragement to identify, organise and express themselves, each through their own ethnic elites.[41] This heightened consciousness of ethnicity has also been forced upon Singapore's political parties such as they are, through the creation of Group Representative Constituencies which demand that teams of candidates include candidates from minority communities. This aspect of Lee's multiracialism has been exaggerated since the beginning of the 1980s, but has been present since 1965. His government has ensured that communal identification, differences and mistrust have remained central to Singaporeans' identity, with social harmony being maintained only by multifarious devices of corporatism. Hence, as Ien Ang and Jon Stratton have observed, the Singapore discourse on race and culture continually mobilises 'crisis' and 'struggle' as its prime rhetorical terms.[42]

We can see Lee's ideological success in the Singaporean perception of race and culture and in the electorate's broad, though qualified, acceptance of communitarian principles. This seems to be based upon a culture of subliminal fear much more subtle than that attributed to him by his ideological enemies of the left and liberal camps. Yet the area where the influence of this culture and Lee's ideological success is seen most glaringly is the apparently universal acceptance of his concept of the meritocratic elite. The most compelling tributes to Lee's elitist conceptual framework have been made by the opposition parties, who have embraced completely the spirit and the letter of Lee's elitism. All three of the main opposition parties – the Workers' Party (WP) of J.B. Jeyaretnam, the Singapore Democratic Party (SDP) of Chee Soon

Juan, and the Singapore People's Party (SPP) of Chiam See Tong – have imitated the PAP's elitist party structure by introducing from the outset secret 'cadre' members whose power cannot be challenged, except from within its own elite.[43] Further, the opposition parties consciously seek parliamentary candidates from within the meritocratic elite: hence the SDP's delight when it was able to nominate an academic with a PhD – the ill-fated Chee Soon Juan – to run against Prime Minister Goh Chok Tong in 1992. As Garry Rodan has observed, 'The bulk of the population has internalised the PAP's ideology of meritocracy, and measures the suitability of candidates almost exclusively in these terms. Opposition parties cannot ignore this reality'.[44] Rodan continued:

> Neither major opposition party [at that stage the WP and SDP] directly contests the ruling party's central ideological concepts. This does not necessarily indicate a conscious endorsement of PAP ideology, but it does at least reflect an inability to formulate alternatives: surely an important measure of the PAP's ideological hegemony.[45]

Such is the dominance of the PAP ideology that even J.B. Jeyaretnam, the most courageous and most left-wing opposition parliamentarian that Singapore has seen since the 1960s, challenged only the periphery of the PAP's meritocratic elitism during his several partial terms in Parliament.[46] Singaporeans give every appearance of having embraced elitism as unquestioningly as the West has embraced democracy. Looking from the outside, one can label Singapore's elitism an ideology, but to people who have grown up and been educated on that island, it is part of their accommodation with their society and consequently an intrinsic part of their worldview. Lee has successfully linked his elitism to the latent insecurities that permeate Singaporean society. Many Singaporeans wish for a stronger opposition in Parliament, and much of their acceptance of elitism may even be a pragmatic accommodation to the realities of Singaporean society, but there is, nevertheless, a real fear of the consequences should the elite be displaced. Like Donald Emmerson's taxi driver who envisioned the country sinking into lawlessness and gridlock if he disconnected his speeding chime, there appears to be a widespread subliminal assumption that the country would sink into incompetent mediocrity, if not anarchy and poverty, should the elite not be allowed to assume its 'rightful' leadership role.

On the surface, it does appear as if Lee has taken a series of natural and to some extent logical fears and made a conscious decision to control and use them rather than assuage them. Yet rather than focus upon Lee's cynical manipulation of people's fears, it is of more significance to note the extent to which he has projected his own fears and his own cognitive processes on to an entire society. How has Lee succeeded so thoroughly in moulding Singapore in his own image? There is no simple answer to this question, but it is surely not unrelated to a number of features that are, in combination, particular to Lee Kuan Yew and to the Singapore he inherited. First, we must acknowledge Lee's uniqueness. In the words of Ezra Vogel, he combines 'the articulate English-debating style with the confidence of the Chinese mandarin and the raw energy and wit of the street-smart, local Chinese trader'.[47] His willingness to storm heaven itself – or even the US Congress – to argue his case, combined with his capacity to make the most outrageous arguments seem plausible, enabled him to establish intellectual hegemony over virtually anyone with whom he came in regular contact. It was not for nought that UMNO's Dr Ismail warned Malaysia's Prime Minister Razak: 'Don't talk to that fellow too long – he'll persuade you of anything'.[48] The kudos attached to being Singapore's first and most pre-eminent nationalist leader, and the results of his policies augmented Lee's powers of persuasion. By the 1970s Lee was Singapore's saviour several times over, as well as the nation's founding father. By the late 1970s, he had put in place a regime of strict social control that enabled him to intervene in the minutiae of everyday life. When, for instance, he decided to instigate his Speak Mandarin Campaign in 1979, he was able, seemingly with as little effort as it takes to make a telephone call, to institute official discrimination against dialect speakers. For example, Lee made the following promulgation in 1978:

> In government departments, slowly over the years, where a counter officer has to meet the public, for those below 40, he will address them in Mandarin and not in dialect: those below 40, who speak dialect will be last in the queue, and attended to at the end of the queue. Or those below 30, if we want to be kind to those who have missed it. So in this way you can change their language habits by altering the ground rules.[49]

Lee's command of the details of geopolitics and grand schemes of social engineering is legendary, but his mastery of the minutiae involved in the implementation of policy has been taken largely for granted. The following exchange exemplifies this feature. It has been selected from a meeting in which Lee was trying to convince school principals to accept more 'immersion students':

> Brother Kevin Byrne of St Joseph's Institution: Mr Prime Minister, our
>   school is very old and the classrooms are rather small. We have
>   raised the number to forty in each class now in Secondary 1. We
>   have taken in forty-four immersion students in the Secondary 1
>   and we have increased our number …

Lee: Forty-four out of? What's your total?

Byrne: Four hundred students.

Lee: Four hundred Secondary 1?

Byrne: Yes. We have increased our number of classes by one in order to take these in. In Secondary 1 we have taken seventy immersion students. So we are very contained where space is concerned.

Lee: You have moved out your pre-university classes, haven't you?

Byrne: Yes.

Lee: You've got the Catholic Junior College now?

Byrne: Yes.

Lee: Have you filled up the space vacated by the pre-university students?

Byrne: Yes, the number of classes – there are fifteen Secondary 4 classes.

Lee: Suppose we found space for your Secondary 4 elsewhere, do you feel that your Secondary 4 students would suffer a loss? I am thinking of next year.[50]

And so the extraordinary exchange continued with Lee always one step ahead of his interlocutor. Lee's attention to detail is a tribute to his intelligence, memory and legal training, but it is also a reflection of the small size of his realm. In the previous chapter we considered how Lee used the restrictions of Singapore's size to enable him to apply land use as a tool for exercising power, but the reality goes far beyond this simple observation. It is inconceivable that Lee could have exercised power as effectively as he has in any polity other than a city-state.

The exercise of power was, nevertheless, merely a means to an end. If Lee had been an ordinary politician, or even an ordinary nationalist hero, rather than a visionary, then Singapore would be very different today. It would probably be less prosperous, clean and efficient, but there might also have been less tension, control and fear in the national culture. Lee's driving ambition and his innate pessimism have become determining factors in Singapore's life. Lee approaches life like an addicted gambler, risking all to win all. From the moment the Japanese Occupation ended and he took over Tan Chong Chew's Harbour Board contract rather than return to Raffles College, he appeared determined to approach life through taking the riskiest paths in the hope that they would lead to the highest peaks. Lee became the master of brinkmanship, with his skills letting him down only during the Malaysia period. As the dominant personality and the leading strategist in the government over a forty-year period, it was almost inevitable that he would lead Singapore along similarly risky and rewarding paths. By opting consistently for high-risk solutions, whether to security, economic or social questions, he created the situations of tension that he had always expected to find, and imposed his own view of the world on the national psyche. With his ideologically driven focus, his innate competitiveness, high risk-orientation and his deeply embedded Toynbeean rationale of 'Challenge and Response', it was natural for him to narrow the parameters of Singapore's options so that it became increasingly difficult even to conceive of problems in terms other than his own. Thus Lee transferred his own sense of ambition on to a nation. Just as he had set out to be the 'equal of any Englishman',[51] Lee's Singapore set out to be the equal of any country. He has thus made Singapore very much in his own image: highly ambitious and successful, but rigidly controlled, and always living in fear of catastrophe.

NOTES

1.   William F. Case, 'Can the "halfway house" stand? Semidemocracy and elite theory in three Southeast Asian countries', *Comparative Politics*, vol. 28, no. 4, pp. 437–464.

2.   Clark D. Neher and Ross Marlay, *Democracy and Development in Southeast Asia: The Winds of Change*, Boulder, Col. and Oxford: Westview Press, 1995, p. 142.

3.   Chua Beng Huat, *Communitarian Ideology and Democracy in Singapore*, London and New York: Routledge, 1995, pp. 184–185. Chua was describing the PAP's vision of the Singapore system, but stopped short of giving his personal endorsement to the 'non-liberal communitarian democracy' label.

4.   Nisha Gopalan, 'Bread versus liberty: the East Asian path to development'. Unpublished PhD thesis, Department of Political Science, University of Waterloo, Canada, 1993, p. 27. Gopalan borrowed the term, 'soft authoritarian' from Chalmers Johnson, who applied it more generally to the 'non-socialist Newly Industrialised Countries' of East Asia.

5.   Eric C. Paul, *Obstacles to Democratization in Singapore*, Melbourne: Centre for South-East Asian Studies, Monash University, 1992, p. 36.

6.   David Brown, *The State and Ethnic Politics in Southeast Asia*, London and New York: Routledge, 1994, p. 89.

7.   Case may have erred in trying to find one label to describe Singapore, Malaysia and Thailand. His 'semidemocracy' label seems to fit the latter two countries at the time of writing much better than the intense, tightly controlled society in Singapore.

8.   In 1962 Lee complained that 'we are all caught in this system [democracy] which the British ... export all over the place hoping that somewhere it will take root'. See Lee's address to the Royal Society of International Affairs (Chatham House), London, May 1962, in Lee Kuan Yew, *Prime Minister's Speeches, Press Conferences, Interviews, Statements, etc.*, Singapore: Prime Minister's Office, 1959–90.

9.   Case, 'Can the "halfway house" stand?', pp. 440–441.

10. Lee Kuan Yew, *New Bearings in Our Education System*, Singapore: Ministry of Culture, [n.d., c.1966–67], p. 13.

11. Singapore's trade unions are often regarded derisively as 'tame' and 'subservient to the government' because they are so obviously part of the PAP's machinery of social control. Although these labels are broadly accurate, it can be argued convincingly that their strategy of working in close co-operation with the government has been successful in increasing their members' standard of living and their working conditions. For one such argument, see Tan Ern Ser and Irene K.H. Chew, 'The new role of trade unionism in the 21st century: lessons from Singapore', *Economic and Labour Relations Review*, vol. 8, no. 1, 1997, pp. 7–21.

12. See Brown, *The State and Ethnic Politics in Southeast Asia*, pp. 89–111. Singapore's ethnically based organisations include the PAP Malay Affairs Bureau, the Islamic Religious Council, the Council for the Development of the Malay-Muslim Community, the Association of Muslim Professionals, the Singapore Malay-Muslim Congress, the Sikh Advisory Board, the Singapore Indian Development Association, the Eurasian Association, the Chinese Chamber of Commerce, the Singapore Federation of Chinese Clan Associations, and the Chinese Development Assistance Council.

13. *Ibid.*

14. Case, 'Can the "halfway house" stand?', p. 442.

15. See *Far Eastern Economic Review*, 26 June and 11 September 1986 and Case, 'Can the 'halfway house' stand?', p. 444. See Francis T. Seow, *To Catch a Tartar: A Dissident in Lee Kuan Yew's Prison*, New Haven: Yale Southeast Asia Studies, 1994 for the story of Francis Seow's rise, fall, detention and de facto exile.

16. Garry Rodan, 'State-society relations and political opposition in Singapore', in Garry Rodan (ed.), *Political Oppositions in Industrialising Asia*, London and New York: Routledge, 1996, pp. 101–102. Also see James Minchin, 'The Singapore detentions: defending S.E. Asia's Israel?', *National Outlook* [Australia], November 1987, pp. 22–24.

17. Chee's story is told in Chapter 2.

18. See *The Straits Times Weekly Edition*, 4 and 11 January 1997, for Lee's attacks on Tang Liang Hong for his 'Chinese chauvinism'. Tang was sued for S\$12.9 million, though the court found against Tang for 'only' S\$8 million. See *The Straits Times Weekly Edition*, 31 May 1997.

19. *Far Eastern Economic Review*, 14 May 1987.

20. Rodan, 'State–society relations and political opposition in Singapore', pp. 102–110.

21. Kanishka Jayasuriya, 'Review of Christopher Tremewan, *The Political Economy of Social Control in Singapore*', *South East Asia Research*, vol. 4, no. 1, 1996, pp. 91–92.

22. Lee Tsao Yuan and Linda Low, *Local Entrepreneurship in Singapore: Private and State*, Singapore: The Institute of Policy Studies and Times Academic Press, 1990, p. 191. '*Kia su*' is a Hokkien term.

23. *Ibid.*

24. *Ibid.*, p. 192.

25. Donald K. Emmerson, 'Singapore and the "Asian values" debate', *Journal of Democracy*, vol. 6, no. 4, 1995, p.103.

26. *Ibid.*

27. *Ibid.*, pp. 103–104.

28. *Ibid.*, pp. 95, 104.

29. See Francis Fukuyama, *Trust: The Social Virtues and the Creation of Prosperity*, London; New York; Melbourne; Toronto; Auckland: Penguin, 1996. Also see Chapter 4 for some details.

30. *Ibid.*, p. 56.

31. C.M. Turnbull, *A History of Singapore: 1819–1975*, Kuala Lumpur; London; New York; Melbourne: Oxford University Press, 1977, p. 22.

32. Peter Katzenstein, 'Small nations in an open international economy: the converging balance of state and society in Switzerland and Austria', in Peter Evans, Dietrich Rueschemeyer, Theda Skocpol (eds), *Bringing the State Back In*, Cambridge; New York; Port Chester; Melbourne; Sydney: Cambridge University Press, 1985, p. 227.

33. *Ibid.*, pp. 235–236.

34. Lee Kuan Yew, *New Bearings in Our Education System*, pp. 4, 6.

35. C.M. Turnbull, *A History of Singapore*, p. 330.

36. Toh Chin Chye in Melanie Chew (ed.), *Leaders of Singapore*, Singapore: Resource Press, 1996, p. 98. Some corroborative evidence of Josey's attitude towards the Malays is found in his article, 'Some musty skeletons: Malaysia's racial war of words', in *The Bulletin* (Australia), 19 June 1965, pp. 37, 39, where he described the second tier of the UMNO leadership as 'the ultras, the zealots, the extremists, the racists, the wild men…'

37. Turnbull, *A History of Singapore*, p. 330.

38. Malays were unofficially barred from the SAF because of fears of their loyalty. See See Tania Li, *Malays in Singapore: Culture, Economy and Ideology*, Singapore; Oxford; New York: Oxford University Press, 1989, pp. 108–109.

39. Interview with Goh Keng Swee in *The Straits Times*, 4 February 1982.

40. S. Rajaratnam's letter to *The Straits Times*, 27 September 1991, cited in Raj Vasil, *Asianising Singapore: The PAP's Management of Ethnicity*, Singapore: Heinemann Asia, 1995, p. 127.

41. See Lai Ah Eng, *Meanings of Multiethnicity: A Case-study of Ethnicity and Ethnic Relations in Singapore*, Kuala Lumpur; Oxford; Singapore; New York: Oxford University Press, 1995, p. 162.

42. Ien Ang and Jon Stratton, 'The Singapore way of multiculturalism: Western concepts/Asian cultures', *Sojourn*, vol. 10, no. 1, 1995, p. 79.

43. Rodan, 'State–society relations and political opposition in Singapore', pp. 116, 119.

44. *Ibid.*, p. 116.

45. *Ibid.*, p. 118.

46. *Ibid.*, p. 117.

47. Ezra F. Vogel, 'A little dragon tamed', in Kernial Singh Sandhu and Paul Wheatley (eds), *Management of Success: The Moulding of Modern Singapore*, Singapore: Institute of Southeast Asian Studies, 1989, p. 1053.

48. James Minchin, *No Man Is an Island: A Portrait of Singapore's Lee Kuan Yew*, Sydney: Allen & Unwin, 1990, p. 169.

49. Lee Kuan Yew, *Bilingualism in Our Society*, Singapore: Ministry of Culture, 1978, pp. 10–11.

50. Lee's question and answer session at a 'Seminar on education', 24 January 1979, in Lee, *Prime Minister's Speeches, etc.*

51. Lee in Singapore Legislative Assembly, *Debates Official Report*, 7 March 1956, column 1919.

$$\cdot\ 9\ \cdot$$

Faith, Conceit and Achievement: An Understanding of Lee Kuan Yew

The idea of progress is, in this modern age, one of the most important ideas by which men live, not least because most hold it unconsciously and therefore unquestioningly. It has been called the modern religion, or the modern substitute for religion, and not unjustly so.

Sidney Pollard, *The Idea of Progress: History and Society,* New York: Basic Books, 1968, pp. ix–x.

Lee Kuan Yew is a man who has evoked extreme reactions in people over the decades. To his admirers, both domestic and international, he is the brilliant leader who overcame tremendous odds and almost single-handedly built modern Singapore. To his critics he is a racist, eugenicist autocrat who has ridden roughshod over democracy and human rights. The truth is that neither of these descriptions is a satisfactory assessment of the man or his career. It is not easy to find a basis for assessing Lee that does not tend to either lionise or demonise him. It seems sensible, however, to conclude this book with a cautious assessment of the reasonableness of his ideas.

The two central elements of Lee's worldview are progressivism and elitism. These are the first principles of his thinking, lodged so deeply in his mind that he would not recognise them as anything other than self-evident truths. Progressivism comes in many forms, from Comte and Spencer's organicism to Marx's dialectical materialism. In searching for a reasonable characterisation of Lee's progressivism, however, we do not turn to explicit theorists of progress, but to the almost atheoretical 'whig' historians who dominated his history lessons at school. The term 'whig' historian was coined by Herbert Butterfield in 1931, when he criticised the dominant school of English historians of his day for their practice of 'dividing the world into the friends and enemies of progress'.[1] As an impressionable and studious schoolboy in the 1930s studying the

British Empire's contribution to the betterment of the world, Lee was exposed to the unspoken assumptions of this genre of historiography: the use of the present as the primary reference point for viewing the past. As Butterfield wrote:

> The whig interpretation of history lies in a trick of organisation, an un-examined habit of mind that any historian may fall into. ... It is the result of the practice of abstracting things from their historical context and judging them apart from their context – estimating them and organising the historical story by a system of direct reference to the present.[2]

The most direct effect of using the present as the reference point for a study of the past is the tendency to make the present appear inevitable – as if the outcome of each battle, each social, religious or constitutional shift, and each imperial conquest were a predetermined and necessary step on the path to the present.[3] Add to this an assumption that the present is intrinsically better than the past, and it becomes natural to view each political and military encounter in the relevant past as an example of 'progress' fighting and defeating 'reaction'.[4] Thus we arrive at the underlying tension in Lee's progressivism: it is an ideology where the sentiments of inevitability and struggle live cheek by jowl in apparent contradiction, each vying for supremacy in his mind. Both of these senti-ments were reflected in Lee's words of 1960: 'We must not go against what is historically inevitable. This does not mean that we passively wait for history to unfold itself. We must actively strive to accelerate the process of history'.[5]

Lee's progressivism is a crusading creed, where the world is, in Butterfield's words, a 'conflict of the future against the past, the fight of what might be called progressive versus reactionary'.[6] Thus during the Malaysia period, Lee saw Singapore as 'an innovating society, prepared to reach for the stars', while Malaysia was 'a conservative, static society wanting to keep what was in the past'.[7] The victory of progress on a global basis might be assured, but in the meantime it is a long, hard struggle in which Singapore was continually at risk of being left behind by its more progressive rivals – becoming a stagnant backwater in a sea of progress.[8] It is hardly surprising that Lee found appeal in Toynbee's 'Challenge and Response' thesis, which also combined a sense of near-inevitability with the notion of a constant struggle for progress. It is also little wonder that his political praxis was dominated by high-risk, crisis-driven brinkmanship.

Chapter 3 has already presented a substantial account of the pro-gressivist nature of the Raffles Institution history course during Lee's time as a student and demonstrated how he has retained and used this perspective throughout his life. Yet it is unlikely that Lee learned his progressivism as a matter of conscious choice. As a schoolboy he was not even interested in history, except as an examination subject,[9] but this did not diminish the power of progressivist concepts over Lee's young mind. The aspect of the 'whig interpretation of history' to which Herbert Butterfield took the strongest exception, was the fact that its most fundamental assumptions were unstated and the result of 'an unexamined habit of mind'.[10] Lee's generation of school-children had little defence against such a subtle and unconscious form of indoctrination. Interviews with Lee's contemporaries and near-contemporaries at school and university have shown that the assumptions of progressivism were deeply ingrained in the modes of thought of his generation,[11] and some of these people appeared to have accepted progressivism so fully that even in their old age, they were surprised that anyone could conceived of the world in another way.[12] When an ideology, a worldview or a religious faith has been adopted or retained by a conscious decision, it can be said to be an act of the intellect. In Lee's case, however, all the indications point to the conclusion that at least until early adulthood, he never made a conscious decision to accept a progressive worldview. Rather he was unquestioningly using the modes of thought that he was given as a child. It seems likely that at some stage in his adult life – possibly during his reflective period of recuperation after the separation of Singapore from Malaysia – he did question his progressivism, and modified some of the more simplistic assumptions of his youth.[13] Yet at heart, Lee's progressivism could never be more than a secular faith. Progressivism cannot be derived from history – certainly not from the history of the twentieth century – but can only be imposed upon it. If one begins from progressivist assumptions, it is not difficult to selectively choose evidence that supports one's premise, without even realising that one has engaged in a subjective process of selection. This is the heart of Butterfield's critique of the 'whig interpretation of history', which is the very mode of historiography through which Lee learned to see his place in the world.

Lee's progressivist faith has played a vital role as the ideological expression of his personal need for achievement and the rationalisation of his quest for power. It is obvious that Lee has enjoyed being a ruler, but even if, at heart, he has found his deepest satisfaction in the exercise of power, he has nevertheless needed to feel that he was achieving something vital while doing so. Lee's life has been dominated consciously by the need for achievement. As he said in March 1965, at the height of the Malaysia crisis: 'You have got to believe in something. You ... have got to have the ideological basis. ... Nations have gone through tremendous privations and hardships in order to achieve specific goals which have inspired and fired their imagination'.[14] Lee was not only expressing his views about nations and peoples: he was also speaking for himself. *He* had to 'believe in something' and to have an 'ideological basis'. *He* needed 'to achieve specific goals' to inspire and fire his imagination. As we saw in Chapter 3, Lee found his 'ideological basis' in a thoroughly Western progressivist culture of continual achievement, whereby both he and his society had to 'advance' continually. The need to achieve seems to have been one of the most powerful forces in Lee's psyche, and his progressivism has been both a manifestation and rationale of this imperative. And lest it be thought that Lee's progressivism died with his faith in socialism, it should be noted that as late as 1986, he could still speak passionately of the 'mentality of progress', which he described as a desire for 'constant improvement' and 'the certainty of being able to do better today than yesterday, and less well than tomorrow'.[15] Lee has never been religious, but in considering his progressivism the word 'faith' does not seem out of place. Its precepts are so firmly embedded in his approach to life and politics that it is difficult to separate them from any aspect of his life or his career. Inspired by his vision of an infinitely improving future, and driven by his personal need to achieve, he had the motivation he required to devote himself to politics without succumbing overtly to the temptations of avarice or vainglory. With this rationalisation he could enjoy his power with a clear conscience, but he could not rest on his laurels. Something had to be happening all the time in his pursuit of constant improvement, and although Lee's restlessness sometimes drove him in peculiar directions, throughout the 1960s and 1970s it provided him with the inspiration to give the dynamic leadership that dragged Singapore out of third world status and made it a post-colonial success story.

Progressivism made yet another simple but critical contribution to Lee's success as a political leader. Since Lee's progressivism was based on an assumption of continual change, it gave him an openness to new ideas which is unusual in an ideologue. He considered ideas to be mere tools in his armoury, and so he has always been open to the possibility that even cherished ideas might be replaced by new ones. The exceptions to this rule were the core elements of his ideology – progressivism itself, and elitism – which were so deeply ingrained in his worldview that he was barely conscious that they might be other than plain matters of fact. Beyond these first principles, however, Lee welcomed challenges to existing orthodoxies, and he actively sought out new ideas and techniques:

> You have to keep an open mind and do not allow ideology or religion or social or cultural prejudice from excluding any explanation of a problem

and the solution to it. Whenever what is previously an accepted truth is contradicted by actual happenings, actual reality, you must be prepared to re-examine your previous assumptions.[16]

There is a fascinating parallel between Lee's self-description and that given by his friend, Michael Lever, writing of the Harry Lee he knew at Cambridge University over four decades earlier. He described Lee as a man who 'travels light' because he wanted to move fast, 'unencumbered by the heavy luggage of doctrine, whether political or religious'.[17] Considering that in the intervening decades, Lee has remade himself from a Fabian socialist into a Confucian capitalist, it is sobering to realise just how little he has changed in other ways. It is, nevertheless, ironic that despite Lee's purported freedom from ideology and the 'heavy luggage of doctrine', he was yet the captive of a worldview, the ultimate validity of which had to remain an article of faith.

The other fundamental principle of Lee's worldview is his elitism. Lee's elitism begins from the premise that regardless of anyone's desire to have it otherwise, the world is run by elites, and there is no other practical way to organise society. From there he moves to a conviction that elites are good: that societies are most successful when elites have the power and freedom to get on with the job of running the world.[18] Lee then assumes that there exists a rough correlation between the existing class structure in any society and the innate intelligence and talent of the members of different classes. Thus he assumes that the upper class of England, the mandarinate of pre-revolutionary China, and the financially successful members of overseas Chinese communities (such as his two grandfathers), represent sinkholes of genetically based talent which should be harnessed and perpetuated into the next generation.[19]

In making a fair assessment of Lee's views on the elite, it must be conceded that his original premise is defensible: the world does seem to be run by small groups of people who could be described reasonably as elites, and this seems to be the practical outcome of all systems of government. It is also not unreasonable to postulate that there exists a genetic component in human intelligence and in what may be described broadly as 'talent'. One may doubt that genes play such a strong role as that attributed to them by Lee, and there are overwhelming reasons to doubt that discernible eugenic results can be achieved by government action, but it should, nevertheless, be conceded that his general proposition of genetically inherited intelligence and talent is not preposterous. It is even conceivable that there are statistically discernible differences between the aptitudes of various racial or ethnic groups. Beyond these unproven, and indeed vigorously contested possibilities, however, Lee's approach to the elite borders on the absurd. The point at which his logic most obviously breaks down is his acceptance of the existing order as being a reflection of innate intelligence and talent. At the beginning of the twenty-first century the suggestion that the English upper class is a genetic sinkhole of talent hardly warrants further comment. Yet even Lee's acceptance that the pre-revolutionary mandarins won their positions purely by their talent, without recourse to social and economic advantages, deserves closer scrutiny. In his old age Lee gave his views forthrightly to his authorised biographers. He described how the successful rich Chinese had lots of wives and children, while the labourer missed out. In this way, Lee argued, 'a smarter population emerges'.[20] Even leaving aside his geneticist assumptions, Lee's argument accepts unquestioningly the premise that mandarins achieved their positions purely by their ability, and the 'poor labourer' is in his proper social position, not because of an accident of birth, but because he is 'dumb and slow'. Yet there is good reason to think that these social outcomes were due as much to inherited wealth and position as to inherited intelligence. Imperial China's public and charitable education systems were piecemeal at best, and all examinations were dominated, though not monopolised, by the sons of families who could support them and pay for their tuition, if not purchase their degrees.[21] These families fell into three categories from which the 'gentry class' was drawn: the families of those already employed in the bureaucracy, landowners (who usually inherited their property), and merchants.[22] Although the sons of peasant families were not actively excluded from becoming scholars and entering the bureaucracy, and there is ample evidence that many succeeded in doing just this,[23] they were certainly not competing on a level playing field with their economic and social superiors. It may be considered surprising that a person as intelligent as Lee could base his thinking on such an obviously shaky premise. It should be realised, however, that his Chinese culture and his English education formed a powerful nexus on the question of elitism and class, since each of them encouraged his blind acceptance of hierarchies of power and wealth. Despite his brilliant analytical mind, Lee was probably incapable of assessing critically these premises of his thinking, and he based the core of his approach to life, politics and society on a demonstrably erroneous proposition.

Yet another basic element of Lee's elitism might be examined fruitfully: his conviction that rule by elites not only is inevitable, but is the basis of a successful society. This premise leads Lee to his conviction that democracy and notions of egalitarianism should not be allowed to constrain the power or the privileges of a ruling elite. This premise cannot be dismissed as easily as his perceived conjunction of class and intelligence because it is, in essence, a subjective value judgement – specifically that of the 'whig' historian. Because he viewed history through the prism of 'whig' progressivism, Lee concluded that rule by elites must be both a result of progressive improvement in the social order and a factor in a society's success. Granted this assumption, it was not unreasonable to conclude that enhancing the power of elites was the logical way for society to continue its advance. This logic has appeal only if one accepts the progressivist assumptions upon which it is based, and we have already seen that the basis of these premises is problematical, to say the least. Yet despite the appeal that a progressivist justification of elitism must have held for Lee, it is doubtful that he needed it as more than a rationalisation for his natural disposition. Lee has always seen himself as being part of the elite, and his elitism seems to spring largely from his own conceited perception of his place in the world. He had little doubt about this from an early age,[24] and the success of his public life has given him no reason to revise his assessment. If his progressivism is a prism through which Lee views the world, his elitism is intrinsic to how he perceives himself. Lee's elitism is built upon three pillars: his conceited self-perception, his unquestioning acceptance of the hierarchies of society, and his faith in progressivism. Although there are aspects of his elitist logic that stand apart from these elements and are easily defensible, the active ingredients of his elitism rest upon these dubious foundations. None of this criticism detracts from Lee's accomplishments. Nor does it alter the fact that he has achieved his successes through his elitist policies. Yet one can acknowledge the wisdom of promoting high standards of education in the population, and of demanding intelligence and ability in government without endorsing the full gamut of Lee Kuan Yew's views of the social 'pyramid'[25] and the elite.

Lee's cultural evolutionary views are in a different category to his elitism and his progressivism. Whereas the latter two precepts are an intrinsic part of his character and his worldview, his cultural evolutionism is an intellectual construction, which has been open to challenge and amendment. The gradual development of Lee's cultural evolutionism should rather be seen as a developing body of policy measures that met a variety of perceived needs. There were, nevertheless, two dominant features of Lee's thinking which remained relatively constant throughout the span of his culture-building endeavours. First, he remained convinced that culture was, in essence, malleable. Second, he saw culture and the world instinctively through the prism of race and ethnicity. Let us consider each of these elements individually.

In its early and most extreme form, Lee's cultural evolutionism led him to view culture dismissively as a transient phenomenon, significant only for its effect – positive or negative – on modernisation and progress. The early Lee believed that culture could be made and moulded at will from above to suit the needs of the ruling elite. These notions derived from the intellectual climate that dominated the Cambridge University Law School, and from Lee's personal history as a deracinated Chinese and a disillusioned Anglophile.[26] Lee retreated from this dismissive view of culture after the separation of Singapore from Malaysia, only to replace it with a more rounded version which still stressed modernisation and progress, but which acknowledged that culture was deeply embedded in most people's lives. He had seen how seriously the Malays and the Chinese-educated embraced their cultural heritage, and he had seen a Sikh friend go through some sort of breakdown after trying to 'break away from his past too fast and too quickly'.[27] Thus he began promoting 'cultural ballast' through the 'mother tongue' to give Singapore's youth the 'anchorage' they needed to be effective 'digits'[28] in Singapore's modern, industrialised economy. Further, he was becoming firmer in his conclusion – which had been simmering in his mind since the mid-1950s – that there was much in Chinese culture that was admirable, and that it appeared to carry values that gave people strength of purpose and character.[29] As the cultural challenge of the West's student revolt began to be felt in Singapore, Lee and some of his colleagues became increasingly struck by the strength of the Chinese-educated in resisting these trends.[30] By the early 1970s he had become convinced of the inherent strength and value of Chinese culture. Yet despite his shift from the clinical view of culture which he held in the 1950s, he still viewed it through the eyes of a social engineer, and he was still operating from an implausible premise: he identified the essence of a culture with knowledge of the language, and yet thought that English could be used as a functional tool without transmitting any cultural values.[31]

Language has continued to play a pivotal role in Lee's approach to culture, but by the late 1970s he had come to the conclusion that a more direct approach was needed. This resulted in his decision to give Chinese culture a more central role in Singaporean life, variously through language, Confucianisation and 'Asian values' campaigns. In retrospect we can date the public opening of Lee's sinicisation campaign to his address to the Historical Society at Nanyang University on 10 February 1978,[32] but the concerns which prompted it appear to have been growing for some time. By the late 1970s and early 1980s, Lee had revised his cultural evolutionism as its limitations became increasingly apparent.

At this point his personal affection and admiration for Chinese culture converged with his need to find a stronger basis for nation-building. Although there was never any official acknowledgement that the basis of multiracialism changed in the early 1980s, it appears that Lee decided to restructure Singapore's multiracialism to emulate the established and successful Malaysian model, whereby a tolerant, multiracial society had been built upon the foundations supplied by a dominant ethnic culture. Lee modelled his cultural ideal on the short nationalist period of China's history,[33] conveniently ignoring nationalist hostility to Confucianism. In doing so, he was deliberately applying the social engineering precepts that he had learnt at Cambridge University.[34]

The second persistent feature of Lee's approach to culture has been his insistence on categorising people according to their race and ethnicity. This practice came to prominence only after separation from Malaysia,[35] and reached exaggerated proportions with the sinicisation campaign of the 1980s and 1990s, but it had always been at least a background factor in Lee's worldview. As far back as his carefree days as a Cambridge undergraduate, he tended to compartmentalise people into ethnic and racial categories and then judge them as a unitary whole.[36] Lee has devoted considerable attention to justifying his racial prejudices, and in doing so he has integrated his racial views with his cultural evolutionism, his elitism, and his progressivist worldview.[37] Perhaps more significantly, he has integrated his racial views into his personal pessimism, his achievement-driven personality, and his conceited view of his own place in the world. Yet, no matter how much he engages in rationalisation, Lee's ideas remain a reworking of the racial prejudices which have been common in both the European and Chinese communities of Malaya since the nineteenth century.

So where does this leave our assessment of the 'reasonableness' of Lee Kuan Yew's approach to culture? First, it confirms the impression already established in our study of his progressivism and elitism, that his long-standing claim of being empirically objective and free of ideology is cant. Second, it establishes the tenuous nature of the logic – if that is the right word – and assumptions upon which Lee has created his cultural evolutionary edifice. Yet even if we were to engage in a willing suspension of disbelief and grant credence to Lee's cultural and racial views, his cultural policies still fail the test of 'reasonableness' in one critical respect. Was it reasonable to believe that a mere human being could successfully manipulate social evolution with the pinpoint precision that his designs required? Should he have been surprised that he was continually disappointed with the results of his efforts and that they were fraught with unintended consequences? Surely the answer to each of these questions is in the negative, and yet his social engineering efforts down the decades continued to be both revolutionary and tightly targeted. Lee was, in the deepest fibre of his being an elitist, and was therefore vulnerable from his earliest days to hubris, and the enjoyment of power for its own sake. Although he seems to have resisted the temptation to use his power for personal or financial gain, power nevertheless corrupted his judgement and his sense of his own importance. It seems that it simply never occurred to him that his grand plans of guided social evolution might be beyond the scope of human endeavour, or inappropriate for a modern nation-state.

How, then, should Lee Kuan Yew be judged? As an ideologue? As a leader? A *junzi* [Confucian gentleman]? Or merely as a politician? We might ask how Lee himself would like to be judged. Surely none of the categories given above would satisfy Lee, though *junzi* and leader might come close. Perhaps at this point we should return to the themes which were developed in Chapter 7, where the 'essential Lee' was identified as the Chinese autocrat, ruling imperiously for the benefit of his subjects, and providing 'good government' – stability, prosperity and good example – in the Confucian/Legalist tradition. Judged in this way, Lee is a success, and his many foibles can be dismissed as just that: inevitable human frailties which do not diminish his outstanding achievements. Such an assessment could be made reasonably, even without stepping into the 'Chinese mind'. Who, other than Lee, could have delivered stability and prosperity out of the mayhem of the 1950s and 1960s? No other candidates combined Lee's intelligence, courage and hard-headed ruthlessness with his ability to win people's trust and loyalty. Goh Keng Swee and Toh Chin Chye were certainly intelligent and courageous, and Goh might have been even more ruthless than Lee if given the chance, but neither of them possessed Lee's capacity to lead and to build a rapport with the public. This was Lee's strongest talent, and it was only because of the fertility of his mind and the strength of his ideological vision that he began to squander his rapport with his people in the 1980s. Ironically, even as his elitism, progressivism and expertise in wielding power in many ways provided the keys to Lee's early success, they also provided the basis for Lee's spectacularly idiosyncratic foibles. Perhaps Robert Gamer was correct when he observed as early as 1965 that 'Lee Kuan Yew's political style, like Sir Winston Churchill's, may be better adapted for consolidating power than for administering it',[38] for when, by the late 1970s, all of the obvious victories had been won and everything was running smoothly, Lee again became restless and sought new quixotic adventures in cultural and eugenic revolutions. In the words of a foreign journalist of the period, Lee was 'basically under-employed in his tiny fiefdom' and 'always "lifting manhole covers", ... restlessly looking for things to improve'.[39] It would be a shame, however, if he were remembered primarily for his restlessness rather than for the achievements that preceded and accompanied it.

NOTES

1. Herbert Butterfield, *The Whig Interpretation of History*, London: G. Bell & Sons, 1931, p. 5.

2. Butterfield, *The Whig Interpretation of History*, pp. 30–31.

3. *Ibid.*, pp. 24–25.

4. *Ibid.*, p. 28.

5. Lee Kuan Yew's speech to the Guild of Nanyang Graduates, 6 November 1960, in Lee Kuan Yew, *Prime Minister's Speeches, Press Conferences, Interviews, Statements, etc.*, Singapore: Prime Minister's Office, 1959–90.

6. Butterfield, *The Whig Interpretation of History*, p. 45.

7. Lee's speech to the Medical Society, Singapore, 26 February 1965, in Lee Kuan Yew, *Are There Enough Malaysians to Save Malaysia?*, Singapore: Ministry of Culture, 1965, p. 2.

8. Lee expressed his fears of being left behind on a number of occasions in the 1960s. See, for instance, Lee's speech to Malayan students in London, 14 September 1962 in Lee, *Prime Minister's Speeches, etc.* and Lee's address to a symposium organised by the Historical Society of the University of Malaya, 28 August 1964 in Lee Kuan Yew, *Some Problems in Malaysia*, Singapore: Ministry of Culture, 1965, pp. 6–7. See Chapter 3 for a more thorough elaboration of this theme.

9. Interview with Teo Kah Leong, 29 October 1996.

10. Butterfield, *The Whig Interpretation of History*, p. 15. Also see pp. 22–23.

11. Interviews with Teo Kah Leong, 29 October 1996; Lim Chin Aik, 21 October 1996; Kiang Ai Kim, 14 October 1996; David Allan, 10 May and 3 June 1996; and Goh Keng Swee, 1 October 1996. See Chapter 3 for more details.

12. Interviews with Kiang Ai Kim, 14 October 1996 and Goh Keng Swee, 1 October 1996.

13. There is no substantial evidence to support this contention, but it is a reasonable inference to draw from the overall picture painted in Chapter 3.

14. Lee's press conference at TV Singapura studios, 5 March 1965, in Lee, *Prime Minister's Speeches, etc.*

15. Lee's speech at the Opening of Productivity Month, 31 October 1986, in *Productivity Digest*, vol. 5, no. 10, December 1986, p. 8. Lee was quoting Kohei Goshi, former Chairman of the Japan Productivity Centre, in this excerpt, but the context makes clear that he was enthusiastically endorsing the sentiments expressed.

16. Lee's interview with Cai Xi Mei of Xinhua News Agency, 25 August 1992, in Lee, *Prime Minister's Speeches, etc.*

17. Letter from Michael Lever to the author, undated, received 5 June 1996.

18. See Chapter 4.

19. See, for instance, Lee Kuan Yew, *New Bearings in Our Education System*, Singapore: Ministry of Culture, [n.d.; 1966–67], p. 10.

20. Lee in Han Fook Kwang, Warren Fernandez, Sumiko Tan, *Lee Kuan Yew: The Man and His Ideas*, Singapore: Times Editions and The Straits Times Press, 1998, p. 169.

21. For an account to the general impediments faced by peasants wishing to take the examinations, see Ping-ti Ho, *The Ladder of Success in Imperial China: Aspects of Social Mobility, 1368–1911*, New York: John Wiley & Sons, 1964, especially pp. 168–221. Also see Wolfram Eberhard, *Social Mobility in Traditional China*, Leiden: E.J. Brill, 1962, especially pp. 264–266. The practice of purchasing degrees was peculiar to particular historical periods and particular regions. See, for instance, Ho, *The Ladder of Success in Imperial China*, pp. 30–34, 46–50, and Barry C. Keenan, *Imperial China's Last Classical Academies: Social Change in the Lower Yangzi, 1864–1911*, Berkeley, Cal.: The Regents of the University of California, 1994, p. 9.

22. Edwin O. Reischauer and John K. Fairbank, *East Asia: The Great Tradition*, London: George Allen & Unwin, 1960, pp. 306–311, especially p. 310.

23. See Ho, *The Ladder of Success in Imperial China*, especially pp. 107–125.

24. See, for instance, Lee's interview with Trevor Kennedy in Kennedy, *Top Guns: Seventeen World Leaders in Politics, Media and Business Tell How They Made It to the Top – and Stayed There*, Melbourne and Sydney: Macmillan, 1988, p. 269. See Chapter 4 for more details.

25. Lee, *New Bearings in Our Education System*, p. 13.

26. See Chapter 5.

27. Lee's speech to the Third Anniversary Celebrations of Sri Guru Govind Singh, 14 January 1967, in Lee, *Prime Minister's Speeches, etc.*

28. Lee's address to a Tamil Festival, 5 February 1967, in *ibid.*

29. Lee at the Historical Society Meeting at the University of Singapore, 24 November 1966, in *ibid.* See Chapter 5 for more details.

30. Interview with Goh Keng Swee in *The Straits Times*, 4 February 1982.

31. Lee's speech to the Singapore Teachers' Union's 26th Anniversary Dinner, 5 November 1972; Lee Kuan Yew, *Lee Kuan Yew on the Chinese Community in Singapore* (Loy Teck Juan, Seng Han Tong, Pang Cheng Lian [eds]), Singapore: Singapore Chinese Chamber of Commerce and Industry and Singapore Federation of Chinese Clan Associations, 1991, p. 31.

32. Lee Kuan Yew, *Bilingualism in Our Society*, Singapore: Ministry of Culture, 1978. See Chapter 5 for details.

33. Lee's speech at the National Day Rally, 13 August 1978, in Lee, *Prime Minister's Speeches, etc.*

34. See Chapter 5.

35. Lai Ah Eng, *Meanings of Multiethnicity: A Case-study of Ethnicity and Ethnic Relations in Singapore*, Kuala Lumpur; Oxford; Singapore; New York: Oxford University Press, 1995, p. 145.

36. See Lee in Han, Fernandez, Tan, *Lee Kuan Yew: The Man and His Ideas*, p. 173.

37. See Chapter 6.

38. Robert E. Gamer, 'Lee Kuan Yew's style', *Demos* [Singapore], vol. 1, no. 3, November 1965–January 1966, p. 3.

39. Michael Malik in *Far Eastern Economic Review*, 3 July 1986.

Selected Bibliography and Other Sources

ARCHIVAL SOURCES

Letter from Lee Kuan Yew to Robert Menzies, 20 April 1965, held in the National Library of Australia.

Letter from Lee Kuan Yew to Teo Kah Leong, 29 April 1995, held by Teo Kah Leong.

The Rafflesian, 1935, 1936 and various special editions thereafter, held in the Raffles Institution Archives.

Raffles Institution, Singapore, *Syllabus of Instruction, 1937*, held in the Raffles Institution Archives.

Supplement to the Handbook of the Cambridge Law School 1946–1947, held by David Allan.

University of Singapore Students' Union [n.d. c. 1965, c. 1970], held in the National University of Singapore Library.

NEWSPAPERS, MAGAZINES, PERIODICALS AND BULLETINS

Singapore publications, various years from 1950 to 1998

Asia Research Bulletin

Bakti (civil service)

The Business Times

The Contemporary Asia Review

Eastern Sun

Malayan Law Journal

The Mirror: A Weekly Almanac of Current Affairs (Ministry of Culture)

New Nation

The New Paper

Petir (People's Action Party)

Productivity Digest

RIHED bulletin (Research in Higher Education and Development)

Singapore Business

Singapore Business Yearbook

Singapore Economic Bulletin

Singapore Herald

Singapore Investment News

The Singapore Monitor

Singapore Newsletter

Speeches: A Monthly Collection of Ministerial Speeches (Information Division, Ministry of Communications and Development)

The Straits Times

The Straits Times Weekly Edition

The Sunday Mail

The Sunday Times

Weekly Digest of Non-English Press (Colonial Office, then the Ministry of Culture)

Malaysian newspapers and periodicals 1987–98

New Business Times

New Straits Times

New Sunday Times

Third World Economics: Trends & Analysis

Other newspapers and magazines, various years from 1950–98

Asiaweek

The Australian

The Bulletin (Australia)

The Economist

Far Eastern Economic Review

National Outlook (Australia)

The Times (London)

LEGISLATIVE AND PARLIAMENTARY RECORDS AND PAPERS

Government of Singapore, *The Merger Plan, Command 33 of 1961*, Singapore: [Government Printing Office, 1961].

—— [and the Government of Malaya], *Malaysia Agreement: Exchange of Letters, Singapore Legislative Assembly Papers, Misc. 5 of 1963*, Singapore: Government Printing Office, 1963.

——, *Separation: Singapore's Independence on 9th August 1965*, Singapore: Ministry of Culture, 1965.

——, C.V. Devan Nair, *Circumstances Relating to Resignation of the President of Singapore, Command 8 of 1988*, Singapore: Singapore National Printers, 1988.

——, *Maintenance of Religious Harmony, White Paper, Command 21 of 1989*, Singapore: Singapore National Printers, 1989.

——, *Shared Values, White Paper 1991*, Singapore: Singapore National Printers, 1991.

Singapore Legislative Assembly, *Debates: Official Report*, 1955–63.

Singapore Parliament, *Parliamentary Debates: Official Record*, 1965–68.

OTHER SOURCES

Ang, Ien and Jon Stratton, 'The Singapore way of multiculturalism: Western concepts/Asian cultures', *Sojourn*, vol. 10, no. 1, April 1995, pp. 65–89.

Baillie, John, *The Belief in Progress*, London: Oxford University Press, 1950.

Baker, Maurice (ed.), *The Heart Is Where It Is: The NUSS Story*, Singapore: National University of Singapore Society, 1994.

——, *A Time of Fireflies and Wild Guavas*, Singapore: Federal Publications, 1995.

Ban Kah Choon and Anne Pakir (eds), *Imagining Singapore*, Singapore: Times Academic Press, 1992.

Barr, Michael D., 'Lee Kuan Yew in Malaysia: a reappraisal of Lee Kuan Yew's role in the separation of Singapore from Malaysia', *Asian Studies Review*, vol. 21, no. 1, 1997, pp. 1–17.

Bell, Daniel A., David Brown, Kanishka Jayasuriya, David Martin Jones, *Towards Illiberal Democracy in Pacific Asia*, London: St Martin's Press, 1995.

Bellows, Thomas J., *The People's Action Party of Singapore: Emergence of a Dominant Party System*, Monograph Series no. 14, New Haven: Yale University Southeast Asian Studies, 1970.

Bloodworth, Dennis, *The Tiger and the Trojan Horse*, Singapore: Times Books International, 1986.

Brecher, Michael, *Nehru: A Political Biography*, London; New York; Bombay; Toronto: Oxford University Press, 1959.

Brown, David, 'The corporatist management of ethnicity in contemporary Singapore', in Garry Rodan (ed.) *Singapore Changes Guard: Social, Political and Economic Directions in the 1990s*, Melbourne: Longman Cheshire; New York: St Martin's Press, 1993, pp. 16–31.

——, *The State and Ethnic Politics in Southeast Asia*, London and New York: Routledge, 1994.

——, 'The politics of reconstructing national identity: a corporatist approach', *Australian Journal of Political Science*, vol. 32, no. 2, 1997, pp. 255–269.

Brown, Michael E. and Sumit Ganguly (eds), *Government Policies and Ethnic Relations in Asia and the Pacific*, Cambridge, Mass.; London: The MIT Press, 1997.

Buchanan, Iain, *Singapore in Southeast Asia: An Economic and Political Appraisal*, London: Bell, 1972.

Bury, J.B., *The Idea of Progress: An Inquiry into Its Origins and Growth*, London: Macmillan, 1920.

Butterfield, Herbert, *The Whig Interpretation of History*, London: G. Bell & Sons, 1931.

Caldwell, Malcolm, *Lee Kuan Yew: The Man, His Mayoralty and His Mafia*, London: FUEMSSO [c. 1979].

Case, William F., 'Can the "halfway house" stand? Semidemocracy and elite theory in three Southeast Asian countries', *Comparative Politics*, vol. 28, July 1996, pp. 437–464.

Chan Heng Chee, *Singapore: The Politics of Survival 1965–1967*, Singapore and Kuala Lumpur: Oxford University Press, 1971.

——, *Politics in an Administrative State: Where Has the Politics Gone?*, Singapore: Department of Political Science, University of Singapore, 1975.

——, *The Dynamics of One Party Dominance: The PAP at the Grass-roots*, Singapore: Singapore University Press, 1976.

—— and Haq Ou (eds), *The Prophetic and the Political: Selected Speeches of S. Rajaratnam*, Singapore: Graham Brash; New York: St Martin's Press, 1987.

Chan, Joseph, 'Hong Kong, Singapore and "Asian values": an alternative view', *Journal of Democracy*, vol. 8, no. 2, 1997, pp. 35–48.

Cheah Boon Kheng, *Red Star over Malaya: Resistance and Social Conflict during and after the Japanese Occupation, 1941–1946*, (2nd edn), Singapore: Singapore University Press, 1987.

Chen, Peter S.J., 'Asian values and modernization', in Seah Chee Meow (ed.), *Asian Values and Modernization*, Singapore: Singapore University Press, 1977, pp. 21–40.

Chew, C.T. Ernest and Edwin Lee (eds), *A History of Singapore*, Singapore and New York: Oxford University Press, 1991.

Chew, Melanie (ed.), *Leaders of Singapore*, Singapore: Resource Press, 1996.

Chia, Felix, *The Babas Revisited*, Singapore: Heinemann Asia, 1994.

Chua Beng Huat, 'Beyond formal strictures: democratisation in Singapore', *Asian Studies Review*, vol. 17, no. 1, 1994, pp. 99–106.

——, *Communitarian Ideology and Democracy in Singapore*, London and New York: Routledge, 1995.

Clammer, John, *Singapore: Ideology, Society and Culture*, Singapore: Chopmen Publishers, 1985.

Cotton, James, 'Political innovation in Singapore: the presidency, the leadership and the party', in Rodan, Garry (ed.), *Singapore Changes Guard: Social, Political and Economic Directions in the 1990s*, Melbourne: Longman Cheshire; New York: St Martin's Press, 1993, pp. 3–15.

Creel, H.G., *Chinese Thought from Confucius to Mao Tsê-tung*, Chicago: The University of Chicago Press, 1953.

da Cunha, Derek, *Debating Singapore: Reflective Essays*, Singapore: Institute of Southeast Asian Studies, 1994.

Dikötter, Frank, *The Discourse of Race in Modern China*, London: Hurst, 1992.

Drysdale, John, *Singapore: Struggle for Success*, Sydney and London: George Allen & Unwin; Singapore: Times Books International, 1984.

Dutt, R.C., *Socialism of Jawaharlal Nehru*, New Delhi: Abhinav Publications, 1981.

Eberhard, Wolfram, *Social Mobility in Traditional China*, Leiden: E.J. Brill, 1962.

Elegant, Robert, 'The Singapore of Mr Lee: "Confucianism", ethics and Asian values', *Encounter* [Great Britain], vol. 74, no. 5, 1990, pp. 21–29.

Emmerson, Donald K., 'Singapore and the "Asian Values" debate', *Journal of Democracy*, vol. 6, no. 4, 1995, pp. 95–105.

Evans, Peter B., Dietrich Rueschemeyer and Theda Skocpol, *Bringing the State Back In*, Cambridge; New York; Port Chester; Melbourne; Sydney: Cambridge University Press, 1985.

Fong Sip Chee, *The PAP Story: The Pioneering Years (November 1954–April 1968) A Diary of Events of the People's Action Party: Reminiscences of an Old Comrade*, [Singapore]: Times Periodicals [1979].

Fraser, Derek, *The Evolution of the British Welfare State: A History of Social Policy since the Industrial Revolution* (2nd edn), London: Macmillan, 1984.

Fu, Zhengyuan, *Autocratic Tradition and Chinese Politics*, Cambridge; New York; Melbourne: Cambridge University Press, 1993.

Fukuyama, Francis, *Trust: The Social Virtues and the Creation of Prosperity*, London; New York; Melbourne; Toronto; Auckland: Penguin, 1996.

Gamer, Robert E., 'Lee Kuan Yew's style', *Demos*, vol. 1, no. 3, November 1965–January 1966, pp. 3, 9.

George, T.J.S., *Lee Kuan Yew's Singapore*, London: André Deutsch, 1973.

Goh Chok Tong, 'Social values, Singapore style', *Current History*, December 1994, pp. 417–422.

Goh Keng Swee, *Urban Incomes and Housing: A Report on the Social Survey of Singapore 1953–54*, Singapore: Government Printing Office, 1958.

——, *Decade of Achievement (1970 Budget Speech)*, Singapore: Ministry of Culture, 1970.

——, 'The basic strategy for rapid co-operative development', in National Trades Union Congress, *Why Labour Must Go Modern*, Singapore: NTUC, 1970, pp. 35–46.

——, *The Economics of Modernization*, Singapore; Kuala Lumpur; Hong Kong: Federal Publications, 1972, 1995.

——, *The Practice of Economic Growth*, Singapore; Kuala Lumpur; Hong Kong: Federal Publications, 1977, 1995.

——, (Linda Low [ed.]) *Wealth of East Asian Nations, Speeches and Writings by Goh Keng Swee*, Singapore; Kuala Lumpur; Hong Kong: Federal Publications, 1995.

—— and the Education Study Team, *Report of the Ministry of Education, 1978*, Singapore: Government of Singapore, 1979.

Gopinathan, Saravanan, 'Education', in C.T. Ernest Chew and Edwin Lee (eds), *A History of Singapore*, Singapore; New York: Oxford University Press, 1991, pp. 272–286.

——, 'Educational development in Singapore: connecting the national, regional and the global', *Australian Educational Researcher*, vol. 24, no. 1, 1997, pp. 1–12.

Gopalan, Nisha, 'Bread versus liberty: the East Asian path to development'. Unpublished MA thesis, Department of Political Science, University of Waterloo, Canada, 1993.

Han Fook Kwang; Warren Fernandez and Sumiko Tan, *Lee Kuan Yew: The Man and His Ideas*, Singapore: Times Editions and The Straits Times Press, 1998.

Hanna, Willard, *Success and Sobriety in Singapore*, New York: American Universities Field Staff, 1968.

Heng, Geraldine and Janadas Devan, 'State fatherhood: the politics of nationalism, sexuality and race in Singapore', in Andrew Parker, Mary Russo, Doris Sommer and Patricia Yaeger (eds), *Nationalisms and Sexualities*, New York and London: Routledge, 1992, pp. 343–364.

Heng Pek Koon, *Chinese Politics in Malaysia: A History of the Malaysian Chinese Association*, Singapore; London; New York: Oxford University Press, 1988.

Heng, Russell, 'Give me liberty or give me wealth', in Derek da Cunha (ed.), *Debating Singapore: Reflective Essays*, Singapore: Institute of Southeast Asian Studies, 1994, pp. 9–14.

Herrnstein, Richard J. and Charles Murray, *The Bell Curve: Intelligence and Class Structure in American Life*, New York; London; Toronto; Sydney; Tokyo; Singapore: The Free Press, 1994.

Hewison, Kevin, Richard Robison and Garry Rodan (eds), *Southeast Asia in the 1990s: Authoritarianism, Democracy and Capitalism*, Sydney: Allen & Unwin, 1993.

Hill, Michael and Lian Kwen Fee, *The Politics of Nation Building and Citizenship in Singapore*, London and New York: Routledge, 1995.

Ho, Ping-ti, *The Ladder of Success in Imperial China, Aspects of Social Mobility, 1368–1911*, New York: John Wiley & Sons, 1964.

Ho Wing Meng, 'Asian values and modernization', in Seah Chee Meow (ed.), *Asian Values and Modernization*, Singapore: Singapore University Press, 1977, pp. 1–20.

Hucker, Charles O., *The Traditional Chinese State of Ming Times (1368–1644)*, Tucson: The University of Arizona Press, 1961.

Huxley, Tim, *The Political Role of the Singapore Armed Forces' Officer Corps: Towards a Military-Administrative State?*, Canberra: Strategic and Defence Studies Centre, Australian National University, 1993.

International Commission of Jurists [Stuart Littlemore], *ICJ Full Report: Report to the International Commission of Jurists, Geneva, Switzerland on a Defamation Trial in the High Court of Singapore, Goh Chok Tong vs J.B. Jeyaretnam, August 18–22 1997*, cited on Young PAP Homepage, http://ypn.youngpap.org.sg, 15 October 1997.

Jackson, R.M., *The Machinery of Justice in England*, Cambridge: Cambridge University Press, 1939, 1953 (revised edn).

Jayakumar, S. (ed.), *Our Heritage and Beyond: A Collection of Essays on Singapore, Its Past, Present and Future*, Singapore: Singapore National Trades Union Congress, 1982.

Jayasuriya, Kanishka, 'Review of Christopher Tremewan, *The Political Economy of Social Control in Singapore*', *South East Asia Research*, vol. 4, no. 1, 1996, pp. 85–94.

Jeyaretnam, Philip, *Abraham's Promise*, Singapore; Kuala Lumpur: Times Books International, 1995.

Jones, David Martin, 'Democracy and identity: the paradoxical character of political development', in Daniel A. Bell, David Brown, Kanishka Jayasuriya, and David Martin Jones, *Towards Illiberal Democracy in Pacific Asia*, London: St Martin's Press, 1995, pp. 41–77.

Josey, Alex, *Lee Kuan Yew: The Struggle for Singapore*, Sydney: Angus & Robertson, 1974.

———, *Lee Kuan Yew: The Crucial Years* (Revised edition of *Lee Kuan Yew*, 1968. First published in revised form in 1971), Singapore; Kuala Lumpur: Times Books International, 1980.

Katzenstein, Peter, 'Small nations in an open international economy: the converging balance of state and society in Switzerland and Austria', in Peter Evans, Dietrich Rueschemeyer and Theda Skocpol (eds), *Bringing the State Back In*, Cambridge; New York; Port Chester; Melbourne; Sydney: Cambridge University Press, 1985, pp. 227–251.

Kaye, Barrington, *Upper Nankin Street, Singapore: A Sociological Study on Chinese Households Living in a Densely Populated Area*, Singapore: University of Malaya Press, 1960.

Keenan, Barry C., *Imperial China's Last Classical Academies: Social Change in the Lower Yangzi, 1864–1911*, Berkeley, Cal.: The Regents of the University of California, 1994.

Kellas, James G., *The Politics of Nationalism and Ethnicity*, New York: St Martin's Press, 1991.

Kennedy, Trevor, *Top Guns: Seventeen World Leaders in Politics, Media and Business Tell How They Made It to the Top – and Stayed There*, Melbourne and Sydney: Macmillan, 1988.

Khoo Boo Teik, *Paradoxes of Mahathirism: An Intellectual Biography of Mahathir Mohamad*, Kuala Lumpur: Oxford University Press, 1995.

Koh, Tommy T.B., 'A world statesman', *Trends*, a publication of the Institute of Southeast Asian Studies, issued in *the Straits Times*, 27 December 1990.

Kuo, Eddie C.Y., *Confucianism as Political Discourse in Singapore: The Case of an Incomplete Revitalization Movement*, Singapore: Department of Sociology, National University of Singapore, 1992.

Lai Ah Eng, *Meanings of Multiethnicity. A Case-Study of Ethnicity and Ethnic Relations in Singapore*, Singapore: Oxford University Press, 1995.

Lee Kuan Yew, *Prime Minister's Speeches, Press Conferences, Interviews, Statements, etc.*, Singapore: Prime Minister's Office, 1959–90.

———, *Senior Minister's Speeches, Press Conferences, Interviews, Statements, etc.*, Singapore: Prime Minister's Office, 1991–95.

——, *Socialism and Reconstruction in Asia*, [Singapore: Ministry of Culture, n.d., c. 1960s].

——, *The Battle for Merger*, Singapore: Government Printing Office [n.d., c. 1961].

——, *Malaysia Comes of Age*, Singapore: Ministry of Culture, 1964.

——, *One Hundred Years of Socialism*, Singapore: Ministry of Culture, 1964.

——, *The Winds of Change*, Singapore: Ministry of Culture, 1964.

——, *The Battle for a Malaysian Malaysia*, Singapore: [Ministry of Culture, n.d.; c.1965].

——, *Towards a Malaysian Malaysia*, Singapore: Ministry of Culture, 1965.

——, *Are There Enough Malaysians to Save Malaysia?*, Singapore: Ministry of Culture, 1965.

——, *Some Problems in Malaysia*, Singapore: Ministry of Culture, 1965.

——, *Turning Point in Malaysia*, [Singapore: Ministry of Culture, 1965].

——, *Socialist Solution for Asia: A Report on the 1965 Asian Socialists' Conference in Bombay*, Singapore: Ministry of Culture, 1965.

——, *We Want to Be Ourselves: Speech by Mr Lee Kuan Yew Prime Minister of Singapore at Seminar on 'International Relations' on October 9 1966 at the University of Singapore*, [Singapore: Ministry of Culture, 1966].

——, *New Bearings in Our Education System*, Singapore: Ministry of Culture, [1966–67].

——, *Social Revolution in Singapore*, Singapore: Government Printing Office, [n.d., c. 1966–67].

——, *Leadership in Asian Countries*, [Singapore: Ministry of Culture, 1967].

——, *Socialism and the Realities of Life*, Singapore: Ministry of Culture, [n.d., c. 1968].

——, *The Commonwealth: A Continuity of Association after Empire*, London: Cambridge University Press, 1969.

——, 'The harsh realities of today', in National Trades Union Congress, *Why Labour Must Go Modern*, Singapore: NTUC, 1970, pp. 19–23.

——, *Social Revolution in Singapore*, Singapore: Asia Pacific Press, 1972.

——, *Bilingualism in Our Society*, Singapore: Ministry of Culture, 1978.

——, *Extrapolating from the Singapore Experience: A Special Lecture by Lee Kuan Yew, Prime Minister of Singapore, at the 26th World Congress of the International Chamber of Commerce, Orlando, Florida, USA, on October 5, 1978*, Singapore: Publicity Division, Ministry of Culture, 1978.

——, 'The search for talent', in S. Jayakumar (ed.), *Our Heritage and Beyond: A Collection of Essays on Singapore, Its Past, Present and Future*, Singapore: Singapore National Trades Union Congress, 1982, pp. 13–23.

——, (Loy Teck Juan, Seng Han Tong, Pang Cheng Lian [eds]), *Lee Kuan Yew on the Chinese Community in Singapore*, Singapore: Singapore Chinese Chamber of Commerce and Industry and the Singapore Federation of Chinese Clan Associations, 1991.

———, (Lianhe Zaobao [ed]), *Lee Kuan Yew on China and Hongkong after Tiananmen*, Singapore: Lianhe Zaobao, 1991.

———, *Lee Kuan Yew* [computer file/CD-ROM], Singapore: Singapore Press Holdings and Sony Systems Design International, 1996.

———, *The Singapore Story: Memoirs of Lee Kuan Yew*, Singapore; New York; London; Toronto; Sydney; Mexico City: Prentice Hall, 1998.

Lee Lai To, 'Singapore in 1986: consolidation and reorientation in a recession', *Asian Survey*, vol. 27, no. 2, 1987, p. 242–253.

Lee Tsao Yuan and Linda Low, *Local Entrepreneurship in Singapore: Private and State*, Singapore: Times Academic Press for the Institute of Policy Studies, 1990.

Leys, Simon (pseudonym of Pierre Ryckmans), (Translation and Notes), *The Analects of Confucius*, New York; London: W.W. Norton & Co., 1997.

Li, Tania, *Malays in Singapore: Culture, Economy and Ideology*, Singapore: Oxford University Press, 1990.

Lim Chong Yah *et al.*, *Report of the Central Provident Fund Study Group*, Singapore: Department of Economics and Statistics, University of Singapore, 1985.

Lim Si Moi, *Lim Tay Boh, Professor of Economics 1960, Vice-Chancellor, University of Singapore 1965–1967*, Singapore: Landmark Books, 1995.

Low, Linda and Toh Mun Heng, *The Elected Presidency as a Safeguard for Official Reserves: What Is at Stake?*, Institute of Policy Studies, Singapore, Occasional Paper no. 1, 1989.

Mahathir bin Mohamad, *The Malay Dilemma*, Singapore: D. Moore for Asia Pacific Press, 1970.

Mauzy, Diane K., 'Singapore's dilemma: coping with the paradoxes of success', *Southeast Asian Affairs 1997*, Singapore: Institute of Southeast Asian Studies, 1997, pp. 163–277.

Means, Gordon P., *Malaysian Politics: The Second Generation*, Singapore; Oxford: Oxford University Press, 1991.

Minchin, James, *No Man Is an Island: A Portrait of Singapore's Lee Kuan Yew*, Sydney: Allen & Unwin, 1986, 1990.

———, interview on 'Asia Focus', 13 June 1997, ABC Radio Australia, International Service.

Ministry of Information and the Arts, Singapore, *Singapore 1996*, Singapore: Ministry of Information and the Arts, 1996.

Montague, M.F. Ashley (ed.), *Toynbee and History: Critical Essays and Reviews*, Boston: Porter Sargent, 1956.

Mote, Frederick W., *Intellectual Foundations of China*, New York: Alfred A. Knopf, 1971.

Myrdal, Gunnar, *Asian Drama: An Inquiry into the Poverty of Nations*, 3 vols, London: Allen Lane and Penguin Press, 1968.

Nair, C.V. Devan (ed.), *Socialism that Works … the Singapore Way*, Singapore; Kuala Lumpur; Hong Kong: Federal Publications, 1976.

National Trades Union Congress, *Why Labour Must Go Modern*, Singapore: Stanford College Press for the NTUC, 1970.

Neher, Clark D. and Ross Marlay, *Democracy and Development in Southeast Asia: The Winds of Change*, Boulder, Col. and Oxford: Westview Press, 1995.

Nehru, Jawaharlal, *India and the World*, London: George Allen & Unwin, 1936.

——, *The Discovery of India*, New York: John Day, 1946.

——, *Glimpses of World History: Being Further Letters to his Daughter, Written in Prison, and Containing a Rambling Account of History for Young People*, London: Lindsay Drummond, 1949.

——, (K.T. Narasimha Char [ed.]), *The Quintessence of Nehru*, London: George Allen & Unwin, 1961.

——, *Jawaharlal Nehru: An Autobiography, with Musings on Recent Events in India*, Bombay; New Delhi; Calcutta; Madras: Allied Publishers, 1962.

Old Rafflesians' Association, *The Rafflesian Directory, 1995 Edition*, Singapore: Old Rafflesians' Association, 1995.

Ong Siow Heng and Nirmala Govindasamy-Ong, *Metaphor and Public Communication: Selected Speeches of Lee Kuan Yew and Goh Chok Tong*, Singapore: Graham Brash, 1996.

Ongkilli, James Peter, *Nation-Building in Malaysia, 1946–1974*, Singapore; Oxford; New York: Oxford University Press, 1985.

Osborne, Milton E., *Singapore and Malaysia*, Ithaca, NY: Cornell University Southeast Asian Program, 1964.

Pan, Lynn, *Sons of the Yellow Emperor: The Story of Overseas Chinese*, London: Secker & Warburg, 1990.

Pao Chao Hsieh, *The Government of China (1644–1911)*, New York: Octagon Books, 1966.

Parker, Andrew, Mary Russo, Doris Sommer and Patricia Yaeger (eds), *Nationalisms and Sexualities*, New York and London: Routledge, 1992.

Patten, Chris, *East and West*, London: Macmillan, 1998.

Paul, Eric C., *Obstacles to Democratization in Singapore*, Melbourne: Monash University, Centre for South-East Asian Studies, 1992.

People's Action Party, *The Tasks Ahead, PAP's Five Year Plan, 1951–1964, Parts 1–2*, Singapore: People's Action Party, 1959.

—— *Petir, 25th Anniversary Issue*, Singapore: Central Executive Committee, People's Action Party, 1979.

Pollard, Sidney, *The Idea of Progress: History and Society*, New York: Basic Books, 1968.

Purushotam, Nirmala, *Disciplining Differences: 'Race in Singapore'*, Singapore: Department of Sociology, National University of Singapore, 1995.

Quah, Jon S.T., 'The political thought of Lee Kuan Yew (1963–1965)', *Journal of the Historical Society, University of Singapore*, July 1970, pp. 48–54.

——, 'Singapore: towards a national identity', *Southeast Asian Affairs 1977*, Singapore: Institute of Southeast Asian Studies, 1977, pp. 207–219.

—— and Quah, Stella R., 'The limits of government intervention', in Sandhu, Kernial Singh and Paul Wheatley (eds), *Management of Success: The Moulding of Modern Singapore*, Singapore: Institute of Southeast Asian Studies, 1989, pp. 102–127.

Quah, Stella R., *Balancing Autonomy and Control: The Case of Professionals in Singapore*, Cambridge, Mass.: Center for International Studies, Massachusetts Institute of Technology, 1984.

Raffles Institution Foundation, *Raffles Institution: A Tradition of Excellence*, Singapore: Raffles Institution, 1990.

Rahim, Lily Zubaidah, 'The Singapore dilemma: the political and economic marginality of the Malay community'. PhD thesis, Department of Government and Public Administration, University of Sydney, 1994.

Rajaratnam, S., *Malayan Culture in the Making*, Singapore: Ministry of Culture, 1960.

——, 'Asian values and modernization', in Seah Chee Meow (ed.), *Asian Values and Modernization*, Singapore: Singapore University Press, 1977, pp. 95–100.

——, (Ang Hwee Suan [ed.]), *Dialogues with S. Rajaratnam, Former Senior Minister in the Prime Minister's Office*, Singapore: Shin Min Daily News, 1991.

Regnier, Philippe, *Singapore: City-State in South-East Asia*, Honolulu: University of Hawaii Press, 1991.

Reid, Anthony (ed.; assisted by Kristine Alilunas Rodgers), *Sojourners and Settlers: Histories of Southeast Asia and the Chinese*, Sydney: Asian Studies Association of Australia and Allen & Unwin, 1996.

Reischauer, Edwin O. and John K. Fairbank, *East Asia: The Great Tradition*, London: George Allen & Unwin, 1960.

Robinson, Howard, *The Development of the British Empire*, Boston: Houghton Mifflin [n.d., c. 1922].

Rodan, Garry, *The Political Economy of Singapore's Industrialization: National State and International Capital*, Kuala Lumpur: Forum, 1989, 1991.

—— (ed.), *Singapore Changes Guard: Social, Political and Economic Directions in the 1990s*, Melbourne: Longman Cheshire; New York: St Martin's Press, 1993.

——, 'Preserving the one-party state in contemporary Singapore', in Kevin Hewison, Richard Robison and Garry Rodan (eds), *Southeast Asia in the 1990s: Authoritarianism, Democracy and Capitalism*, Sydney: Allen & Unwin, 1993, pp. 77–108.

—— (ed.), *Political Oppositions in Industrialising Asia*, London and New York: Routledge, 1996.

——, 'State-society relations and political opposition in Singapore', in (ed.), *Political Oppositions in Industrialising Asia*, London and New York: Routledge, 1996, pp. 95–127.

Rose, J. Holland, A.P. Newton, E.A. Benians (eds), *The Cambridge History of the British Empire, Volume I, The Old Empire from the Beginnings to 1783*, Cambridge: Cambridge University Press, 1929.

Sandhu, Kernial Singh and Paul Wheatley (eds), *Management of Success: The Moulding of Modern Singapore*, Singapore: Institute of Southeast Asian Studies, 1989.

Saw Swee-Hock, *Changes in the Fertility Policy of Singapore*, Singapore: Times Academic Press for the Institute of Policy Studies, 1990.

Seah Chee Meow, *Community Centres in Singapore: Their Political Involvement*, Singapore: Singapore University Press, 1973.

—— (ed.), *Asian Values and Modernization*, [Singapore]: Singapore University Press, 1977.

Sebastian, Leonard C., 'The logic of the guardian state: governance in Singapore's development experience', *Southeast Asian Affairs 1997*, Singapore: Institute of Southeast Asian Studies, 1997, pp. 278–298.

Seow, Francis T., *To Catch a Tartar: A Dissident in Lee Kuan Yew's Prison*, New Haven, Conn.: Yale Center for International and Area Studies, 1994.

Sheehan, Paul, *Among the Barbarians: The Dividing of Australia*, Sydney: Random House Australia, 1998.

Sheridan, Greg, *Tigers: Leaders of the New Asia-Pacific*, Sydney: Allen & Unwin, 1997.

Sheridan, James E., *China in Disintegration: The Republican Era in Chinese History, 1912–1949*, New York: The Free Press; London: Collier Macmillan, 1975.

Sikorski, Douglas, 'Effective government in Singapore – perspective of a concerned American', *Asian Survey*, vol. 36, no. 8, 1996, pp. 818–832.

Silcock, Thomas, *A History of Economics Teaching and Graduates in Singapore* [alternate title: *A History of Economics Teaching and Graduates: Raffles College and the University of Malaya in Singapore 1934–1960*], Singapore: Department of Economics and Statistics, National University of Singapore, 1985.

Skinner, G. William, 'Creolized Chinese societies in Southeast Asia', in Anthony Reid (ed.; assisted by Kristina Alilunas Rodgers), *Sojourners and Settlers: Histories of Southeast Asia and the Chinese*, Sydney: Asian Studies Association of Australia and Allen & Unwin, 1996, pp. 51–93.

Ganguly, Sumit, 'Ethnic policies and political quiescence in Malaysia and Singapore', in Michael E. Brown and Sumit Ganguly (eds), *Government Policies and Ethnic Relations in Asia and the Pacific*, Cambridge, Mass.; London: The MIT Press, 1997, pp. 233–272.

Tamboer, Kees, 'Albert Winsemius, "founding father" of Singapore', *IIAS Newsletter* [International Institute of Asian Studies], no. 9, 1996, p. 29.

Tamney, Joseph B., *The Struggle over Singapore's Soul: Western Modernization and Asian Culture*, New York: Walter de Gruyter, 1996.

Tan Ern Ser and Irene K.H. Chew, 'The new role of trade unionism in the 21st century: lessons from Singapore', *Economic and Labour Relations Review*, vol. 8, no. 1, 1997, pp. 7–21.

Toynbee, Arnold, *A Study of History, Volumes I–III*, London; New York; Toronto: Oxford University Press, 1935.

——, *A Study of History, Volumes IV–VI*, London; New York; Toronto: Oxford University Press, 1939.

——, *A Study of History, Volumes VII–X*, London; New York; Toronto: Oxford University Press, 1954.

——, *A Study of History, Abridgement of Volumes I–VI* by D.C. Somervell, London: Oxford University Press, 1948.

——, *A Study of History, Abridgement of Volumes VII–X* by D.C. Somervell, London: Oxford University Press, 1961.

Tremewan, Christopher, *The Political Economy of Social Control in Singapore*, London: Macmillan Press; New York: St Martin's Press, 1994.

Tu Wei Ming (ed.), *The Triadic Chord: Confucian Ethics, Industrial East Asia and Max Weber: Proceedings of the 1987 Singapore Conference on Confucian Ethics and the Modernization of Industrial East Asia*, Singapore: Institute of East Asian Philosophies, 1991.

Turnbull, C.M., *A History of Singapore: 1819–1975*, Kuala Lumpur; London; New York; Melbourne: Oxford University Press, 1977.

Vasil, Raj K., *Politics in a Plural Society: A Study of Non-Communal Political Parties in Malaysia*, Kuala Lumpur; Singapore; London; New York: Oxford University Press for the Australian Institute of International Affairs, 1971.

——, *Governing Singapore*, Singapore: Eastern Universities Press, 1984.

——, *Asianising Singapore: The PAP's Management of Ethnicity*, Singapore: Heinemann Asia, 1995.

Vogel, Ezra, 'A little dragon tamed', in Kernial Singh Sandhu and Paul Wheatley (eds), *Management of Success: The Moulding of Modern Singapore*, Singapore: Institute of Southeast Asian Studies, 1989, pp. 1049–1066.

Wells, H.G., *The Work, Wealth and Happiness of Mankind*, London: Heinemann [n.d., c. 1932].

Wijeysingha, Eugene, *The Eagle Breeds a Gryphon: The Story of Raffles Institution 1823–1989*, Singapore: Pioneer Book Centre, 1989.

Wilairat, Kawin, *Singapore's Foreign Policy: The First Decade*, Singapore: Institute of Southeast Asian Studies, 1975.

Wingfield-Stratford, Esmi, *The History of British Civilisation*, New York: Hartfield Brace & Company, 1932.

Wu Teh Yao, *The Confucian Way*, Singapore: Institute of East Asian Philosophies, 1987.

Yeo Kim Wah, *Political Development in Singapore: 1945–1955*, Singapore: Singapore University Press, 1973.

Zakaria, Fareed, 'Culture is destiny: conversation with Lee Kuan Yew', *Foreign Affairs*, vol. 73, March/April 1994, pp. 109–126.

INTERVIEWS

Allan, David	3 June 1996, 10 May 1996, 13 February 1997
Ambiavagar, Velauthar	15 October 1996
Baker, Maurice	25 October 1996
Barker, E.W.	16 October 1996
Christa, Boris	27 May 1996
Dixon, George	11 July 1996
Goh Keng Swee	1 October 1996
Kiang Ai Kim	14 October 1996
Lim Chin Aik	21 October 1996
Lim Si Moi	23 September 1996
Teo Kah Leong	29 October 1996
Wang Gungwu	8 October 1996

CORRESPONDENCE (LETTERS TO THE AUTHOR FROM)

Goonetilleke, Eric O.	4 December 1996
Lever, Michael	undated – received 5 June 1996, 6 July 1996, 1 August 1997
Lim Kim San	27 September 1996
Muzaffar, Chandra	14 August 1996
Paul, Herman	8 December 1996
Scharenguivel, Hilton	3 December 1996
Wayper, Leslie	24 May 1996,[1] 13 June 1996

---

1. The first letter from Dr Wayper was actually addressed to Mrs C.M. Knapton of the Cambridge Union, but was intended to be passed on to the author.

Index